American Globalization, 1492–1850

Following a study on the world flows of American products during early globalization, here the authors examine the reverse process. By analyzing the imperial political economy, the introduction, adaptation and rejection of new food products in America, as well as of other European, Asian and African goods, *American Globalization, 1492–1850,* addresses the history of consumerism and material culture in the New World, while also considering the perspective of the history of ecological globalization.

This book shows how these changes triggered the formation of mixed imagined communities as well as of local and regional markets that gradually became part of a global economy. But it also highlights how these forces produced a multifaceted landscape full of contrasts and recognizes the plurality of the actors involved in cultural transfers, in which trade, persuasion and violence were entwined. The result is a model of the rise of consumerism that is very different from the ones normally used to understand the European cases, as well as a more nuanced vision of the effects of ecological imperialism, which was, moreover, the base for the development of unsustainable capitalism still present today in Latin America.

Bartolomé Yun-Casalilla is Full Professor at Universidad Pablo de Olavide, Spain.

Ilaria Berti teaches history of the Americas at Università degli Studi di Firenze, Italy.

Omar Svriz-Wucherer is Postdoctoral Researcher at Project GECEM (ERC-StG.- 679371) and teaches Early Modern History at Universidad Pablo de Olavide, Spain.

Early Modern Iberian History in Global Contexts: Connexions

Jean-Frédéric Schaub
École des Hautes Études en Sciences Social
Mafalda Soares da Cunha
Universidade de Évora
María José Vega
Universidad Autónoma de Barcelona
Bartolomé Yun-Casalilla
Universidad Pablo de Olavide

Early Modern Iberian History in Global Contexts: Connexions features studies that address Iberian societies and cultures from a variety of standpoints and theoretical perspectives. It understands Iberian history as a plural way of approaching an ensemble of individuals and groups made up of similarities, connections, contrasts and colliding trajectories. Its aim is to connect the different national and transnational research traditions in the field of Iberian historical studies, and showcase the multifaceted character of the Iberian past, encompassing its many voices as well as the tensions, the violence and the conflicts that opposed its various components, both across the Iberian Peninsula and across the globe.

Empire, Political Economy, and the Diffusion of Chocolate in the Atlantic World
Irene Fattacciu

Luke Wadding, the Irish Franciscans, and Global Catholicism
Edited by Matteo Binasco

Juan Rena and the Frontiers of Spanish Empire, 1500–1540
Jose M. Escribano-Páez

American Globalization, 1492–1850
Trans-Cultural Consumption in Spanish Latin America
Edited by Bartolomé Yun-Casalilla, Ilaria Berti, and Omar Svriz-Wucherer

For more information about this series, please visit: www.routledge.com/Early-Modern-Iberian-History-in-Global-Contexts/book-series/EMIHIGC

American Globalization, 1492–1850

Trans-Cultural Consumption in Spanish Latin America

Edited by Bartolomé Yun-Casalilla, Ilaria Berti, and Omar Svriz-Wucherer

Routledge
Taylor & Francis Group
NEW YORK AND LONDON

First published 2022
by Routledge
605 Third Avenue, New York, NY 10158

and by Routledge
2 Park Square, Milton Park, Abingdon, Oxon, OX14 4RN

Routledge is an imprint of the Taylor & Francis Group, an informa business

Library of Congress Cataloging-in-Publication Data
A catalog record for this book has been requested

ISBN: 978-0-367-76676-4 (hbk)
ISBN: 978-1-032-02443-1 (pbk)
ISBN: 978-1-003-16805-8 (ebk)

DOI: 10.4324/9781003168058

Typeset in Sabon
by Apex CoVantage, LLC

Contents

Figures

Maps

Tables

Acknowledgments

This book is the result of a collective task that goes beyond the work of its editors. The research has been mainly possible thanks to the HAR2014–53797-P "Globalización Ibérica: Redes entre Asia y Europa y los cambios en las pautas de Consumo en Latinoamérica" [Iberian Globalization: Networks Between Asia and Europe and Changes in Consumption Patterns in Latin America] Project, funded by the Spanish Ministry of Science and Competitiveness, of which Bartolomé Yun-Casalilla has been principal investigator and in which the editors and most of the authors have been integrated. But it is also the result of the activity of the different research groups whose contribution is appreciated, or, in some specific cases, the publication in open access of the corresponding chapters, whose main researchers are professors Bethany Aram, Igor Pérez Tostado and Manuel Pérez García. We must also thank the MSCA Individual Fellowship "Imperial Recipes", post-doctoral program, which financed Ilaria Berti's research in Seville, and the Spanish Ministry of Science and Culture, which sponsored the research of Omar Svriz-Wucherer's PhD at the Area of Early Modern History at the Universidad Pablo de Olavide.

It is also a pleasure to acknowledge Penelope "Penny" Eades's hard work and patience in translating the introduction and chapters 1, 2, 3, 4, 5, 6, 10, 11, 12 and 13, as well as Bethany Aram's always selfless help in editing the English version of these chapters. The first manuscript of this volume received excellent critical comments from an anonymous referee who was not only able to grasp its general meaning but also contributed notably to the improvement of the different works and whose efforts we would like to record here. Likewise, the editors want to thank the members of the PAI group HUM-1000, "Historia de la Globalización: Violencia, negociación e interculturalidad" [History of Globalisation: Violence, Negotiation and Interculturality] for having created the favorable intellectual climate for the exchange of ideas and interests that made this publication possible.

A special thanks also goes to our colleague Harald Braun, from the University of Liverpool, whose patience and good work are already more than known by many colleagues, as well as Pedro Cardim, from the Universidade Nova de Lisboa. Both have always supported its publication in a collection that already owes them so much.

In Florence, Seville and Valladolid (separated by Covid-19), on October 23, 2020.

Ilaria Berti
Omar Svriz-Wucherer
Bartolomé Yun-Casalilla

Introduction[1]

Bartolomé Yun-Casalilla

The history of consumerism and material culture has undergone a radical turnaround in recent decades. Until the end of the past century, it focused mainly on an analysis of the transformations experienced by consumption models in specific and well-defined geographical regions.[2] Since the first decades of the twenty-first century, however, the influence of the so-called spatial turn has been decisive. The result is a series of studies that have taken the process of globalization as a point of reference to focus on the circulation of goods between different regions and the contact between forms of material culture of diverse geographical backgrounds. To a large extent this has been achieved through the analysis of the movement of certain products across the globe and the way in which this movement has been influenced by economic, social and cultural factors.[3]

In this context, America and Latin America in particular, figured prominently and soon became an area whose globalization attracted ongoing and increasing interest.[4] The reasons are obvious. Since 1492 America had been not only a new player on the world stage, flooding the globe with new products, some of which contributed decisively to changing societies in other areas of the planet. It was also the region that most rapidly and dramatically witnessed changes in the consumption patterns and social structures of its original peoples. Both processes constitute what we have chosen to call "American globalization", starting out from the ideas expressed by Andre Gunder Frank (1998), whereby primitive or early globalization – within the period from 1492 to the industrial revolution – had polycentric characteristics.[5] In that context, the changes caused by American products beyond American borders, as well as those experienced within them due to the influence of external agents, were at the epicenter of American globalization from an analytical perspective.

The present volume is the logical follow-up to a previous work that studied how certain products circulated from Latin America to other, distant areas of the planet (Aram and Yun-Casalilla 2014). It should be noted that there is an essential difference in approach in the two investigations. When it comes to the question of how American products affected other areas of the planet, there has been a lack of meaningful and

DOI: 10.4324/9781003168058-1

coherent argument relating to the effects of the phenomenon. In fact, the role of America in globalization – and Latin America in particular – has often been related to the development of capitalism perceived as the driving force of markets and – quite frequently – relationships of economic dependency of the colonial areas to the centres of world economies. In a sense, these investigations have been inscribed in the narrative of the transition to capitalism or have been approached from the perspective of explaining modern economic growth.[6] The fact is that we do not have a coherent and structured monograph that evaluates the impact of America in Europe, Asia and Africa (and Oceania), encompassing the overall influence of phenomena as diverse as the circulation of silver, syphilis, vicuña, yuca, corn, potato, cochineal grana, cocoa, the long list of herbs that Europeans and Asians used for medicinal purposes, and an extensive list of animals, plants, microbes, and the like, which affected diverse and distant areas, societies and ecosystems. We certainly have partial and very fragmentary studies, but not a comprehensive vision.[7] Moreover, it is quite possible that, were we to approach the issue in this way, we could get bound up in a question – or a series of questions – that could prove difficult to answer and for which we can count only on partial studies for the time being.[8]

However, precisely because this is a series of complementary studies to this perspective, the following chapters analyze the opposite process: the way in which contact with other worlds produced profound transformations in the consumption patterns of the continent and especially the lands that stretch from the Rio Grande, on the current border between Mexico and the United States, to the region of Patagonia in Argentina. This process has been the focus of special attention from historians and anthropologists, and we even have monographs that have presented solid and well-informed arguments in this regard. These works have also succeeded in creating a relatively coherent account, highlighting above all the effect of Spanish domination and its capacity to change consumption patterns, which at times involved resorting to violence, and drawing attention to the way in which ecological imperialism changed patterns of food consumption. Within this framework, other aspects have also been studied and variants of the general ideas have been presented.[9] The chapters that follow are intended to offer a solid contribution in this regard and provide greater complexity to the image we already have. To this end, we have selected a series of case studies on products that are either for the most part little known or which focus on their heretofore lesser known or unexplored aspects.

Emphasizing the features and introductory processes of products before the massive circulation of these goods across America, this volume is organized into three complementary analytical levels. It starts out with an analysis of the political economy and some of the institutions that governed the process of selection and introduction of new products across the Atlantic. To that end, we examined a series of key components such as the form of trade organization – in this case, of enslaved persons (García-Montón), the circulation of information in Europe (Díaz Blanco), the role of the state as a formal institution in the introduction of a product of high strategic value such as hemp (Díaz-Ordóñez) and the involvement of informal networks and institutions in the form of family connections and, specifically, of the women who acted within them (Almorza).[10] In some cases, these are subjects and areas of knowledge virtually unexplored by historians of consumerism, for whom the state has seldom been viewed as a major agent or by whom the role of women has seldom been analyzed in the transatlantic perspective adopted here.[11] Similarly, the circulation of news within Europe regarding the products and goods to be taken to America is broached here from a new angle – the translation of essential works on trade – emphasizing the ways in which changes to the political economy of the empire affected the supply of an essential labour force whose scarcity affected that of other basic products in the mid-seventeenth century.

The next section focuses on the sphere of consumerism and in particular food consumption. It goes without saying that this is a crucial sector. On the one hand it is a consumer segment strongly influenced by the conquest. But it is also a sector very clearly marked by the transformations in the original ecosystems, on which it would also have a profound impact. It examines the introduction of products that were crucial for America and yet almost unknown to historians until now, such as chickens (Saldarriaga).[12] It also analyzes the way in which different social sectors were influenced through a variety of methods – ranging from coercion to persuasion – including symbolic consumption in the early encounters with new European products and the unleashing of mechanisms of mistrust and rejection in some pre-Columbian social groups (Córdoba).[13] The case of rice (Aram and García-Falcón) is also particularly interesting in that it introduces players and distribution channels for products that are not of Iberian origin. This section can also be viewed as part of a significant broad discussion, such as the different species that existed of the same products and the possibility that there were American precedents for them. In turn, the case of breadfruit and potato (Earle) expands on a theme defined by a previous work, by highlighting other products that have not come from generally recognized areas, such as the Pacific islands, and underscoring the global character – beyond their specific origins – of these goods.[14] This is followed by an analysis of the social interaction that takes place in areas of encounter between different consumption patterns, such as that of cooking (Berti).[15] In all these chapters, the focus of analysis is on the introduction of products in America based on the study of the exact point of cultural interference. In this way, forgotten or neglected aspects of historiography are revealed. Such is the case of the decisive character of apparently innocuous products, such as chickens, in the formation of markets and in changes within family economies. And the same is true of the study of the problems existing in the relationship between the first conquerors and the American original elites, as well as the way in which consumerism created very complex forms of connections, trust and distrust. The works of Earle, on the one hand, and Aram and García-Falcón, on the other, contrast in showing how introductory processes were adopted at different times by very different protagonists, thus highlighting the complexity of the processes studied. Its complement, without a doubt, is the way in which the food relationship between masters and slaves was dealt with in the Caribbean in the nineteenth century in terms of cooking, and the way in which slaves could transfer food patterns to the former; an area that renders even more multifaceted the image we have of food transfers.

The third and final section includes work on the entry of other nonfood products and the global dimension of these goods over and above relations with Spain. It demonstrates how forms of negotiation and violence, as well as market mechanisms and other processes, intervened in the dissemination of non-food products. Also included here is a chapter on the introduction of Chinese porcelain that provides a transatlantic comparison between Mexico and Seville (Gasch-Tomás),[16] and the analysis of a hitherto virtually unknown product, such as weapons (Svriz-Wucherer).[17] The section closes with a work which has often been considered more specifically in terms of culture but not in terms of trade – the Sevillian art market in Portobelo and its effects in Seville (Quiles).[18] To conclude, we offer a general overview that attempts to address some aspects of the history of consumerism and material culture in Latin America, while broadening the perspective to include questions of a more general nature, such as the process of introducing, adapting and rejecting products in America from the perspective of the history of ecological globalization (Yun-Casalilla). The consequences of the selection of these works are obvious. This perspective permits broadening the field of analysis to place these goods in wider contexts of circulation. In doing so, it is also possible to enter into aspects such as the global character of some of these commodities regardless of their origin, or to link with debates that have so far been seldom dealt with by studies in this area, such as the globalization of the military revolution and its consequences on social structures, while at the same time underlining how artistic influences have not always been derived from cultural relations but also from mechanisms of an economic nature.

From a geographical point of view, areas ranging from Central America to Argentina are studied, including Mexico, the Caribbean, Panama, present-day Colombia, Peru, the Chaco and the border area between Paraguay and Argentina; and all this is considered from the varying perspectives of Seville, Cadiz and London, Africa, the Pacific – from Tahiti to the Philippines – and so forth.[19] In terms of the history of cultural transfers, what emerges is a more complex panorama than the one usually understood by the term. It can refer to societies close to one another or in which violence and coercion were not so prevalent in these transfers.[20] At the same time, it deals with a great variety of primary and secondary products, some of strategic military value, others in daily use, some agricultural and others produced industrially, even, to name one example, luxury goods. At the same time very diverse social agents are identified individually within the transfer process. The result is a multifaceted landscape full of contrasts.

It is up to the reader to discover many of these dimensions. But I wish to concentrate on two in particular – the players involved in introducing products before they became massive commodities and the role of coercion – that have featured prominently throughout this collective research.

As for the first of these, what the microanalysis of the selected cases reveals is a plurality of circumstances which, nevertheless, are linked to considerations and problems of a general nature. In contrast with simplistic visions, what comes to light is the tremendous diversity of actors in the process of adaptation and introduction of new products. This is not a top-down process between colonizers and colonized, which is the most widely studied aspect to date focusing on the role of merchants, *encomenderos* and conquerors. On the contrary, these essays often argued that both social groups, colonized and colonizers, acted almost on an equal footing in the hybridization of their consumption habits.[21] Furthermore, some of these analyses also show that the Crown and the state in its broadest sense played an essential role even in areas such as the spread of hens or hemp, which proved largely unsuccessful, and even rice. And it did so thanks to mechanisms based, not only on coercion involving the pure and simple imposition of habits associated with attempts at civilization, but also on resistance from below and negotiation both in the *repúblicas de indios* and in the Cimarron communities of Panama. The process is all the more complex because it also took place "horizontally", not only between the world of the colonizers and that of the Amerindian population, but also as a result of the increasing cultural diversity of the New World itself. As a matter of fact, it would have been immigrants belonging to a lower class, like the African slaves, for example, who brought their culture with them and – as was the case with the cooks of the Caribbean region – who even became the primary transmitters.[22] The process disseminating new products demonstrates how far the subaltern classes were from the passivity with which they have often been regarded and which was attributed to them in European writings on the subject in the case of Europe. Their capacity for action is very visible in the case of the Guaraní who learned not only how to use firearms but also how to produce them, and – as has already been said – among slaves of African origin. Despite being marginalized in that society in many ways, the prevalence of initiatives undertaken by women is also striking, a fact that confirms what other studies underline in other areas, particularly in Europe. As in the European model, it is the women of the Mexican elite who spearheaded the introduction of Asian porcelain – and of silks too – in Mexico (Gasch Tomás 2018).[23] The same is true of the emigrants from Seville in many other areas of consumerism and family culture, and in particular in dressing habits. However, less well known is the leading role that may have been played by the Guaraní women or those of Nueva Granada who engaged in forms of cultivation which, while still largely centred on corn, increasingly included wheat or chickens, thanks to the family division of labour derived to a large extent from the menfolk's significant involvement in warfare (Svriz-Wucherer 2019). In other respects, it is also evident how, over time, not only the methods but also the protagonists of these transfers gradually changed to such an extent that one could feel tempted to propose a model of general evolution. From the early days of the conquest when conquerors and religious seem to have played an essential role, we have moved on to a situation in which patriotic societies and other formal institutions played a fundamental part. While merchants were influential protagonists in broadcasting news about marketable goods in the Indies through their more or less private letters and communications, the example of the newspaper *Norte de la Contratación* shows how diplomats and non-commercial agents could already exercise this function in the eighteenth century. In a sense, this marked a shift from a mercantile distribution system in which private correspondence was the only form of advertising, as was the case with the sale of art at the Portobelo fairs, to another in which communication was more evident in the public sphere.

While violence and coercion, as stated in some of these works, are prevalent in the relationships between all these social actors, cultural transfers are also based on the ability of some of these actors to gain the trust of others from extremely different cultural universes. Perhaps the clearest example once again is the case of the slave cooks who worked for the Caribbean elite around 1800, as it is true that trust was essential in the food sector where not only the likes and dislikes of the diners were at stake but also their health and safety. And it was trust – and in a sense the lack of it – that determined the provision of weapons to the Guaraní by the Jesuits or that governed relations between the first conquerors and the original chiefs at the first banquets they offered to each other.

All of the above leads to a final reflection. These studies, in recognizing the plurality of the actors involved in cultural transfers, refute what was one of the initial working hypotheses of this research. If it is not, as I have stressed, a bilateral process of action between dominators and dominated, neither is it a bilateral relationship between Spain and America. Africa is very present, and so too is Asia. Furthermore, one must underline the existence of relevant resistances to the convergence and homogenization of American consumption patterns. Despite the tendency to uniformity brought by colonization, a plurality of racial and cultural differences persisted after 1492. Unlike the European model in which scholars tend to see – maybe wrongly – a trend towards the equalization of consumer behaviors, the forces that obstructed a similar process in America must have been very important. Moreover, what we have here is even more ground-breaking – a multipolar process of expansion of American products in America, alongside products from other diverse areas of the planet, such as the Pacific islands.[24] It is also worth noting that, from many points of view America preceded Europe in the globalization of products (Chinese porcelain is a good example) associated in the Old World with refinement and decorum. Likewise, the ability of the Spanish American elites to introduce the Enlightenment's ideas – and not strictly the European Enlightenment – regarding the use of overseas goods is a demonstration of those elites' precocious globalization (Rebecca Earle).

Although this entire volume is based on case analysis, the truth is that these works contribute to a better understanding of the great processes of American history, as we have endeavoured to discuss in the final chapter. It is in this game of scales that the social and cultural history that dominates most of the volume is instrumental in contributing to a greater understanding of the changes that occurred in the economic and ecological sphere. The changes are necessarily enormously varied and complex across different areas, as are the chosen case studies. But the collection as a whole creates a coherence that impinges on the major debates of our time and contributes to a broader understanding of the history of consumerism. For, whereas in Europe the history of consumerism has been linked to industrialization and social modernization, it is quite possible that in the case of Latin America it has to be interpreted in two senses. On the one hand, it is a way of understanding the "modernization" of the American elites and the formation of markets that gradually became part of a global economy. But it is also a way of understanding cultural diversity, the social hybridization between classes not belonging to these elites, and the fractures between social and ethnic groups, as well as the other side of triumphant capitalism since the end of the eighteenth century: the development of ecologically unsustainable economies that began long before industrial capitalism itself and which originated from complex negotiation processes but also high levels of social and cultural violence which remain present today in Latin America.[25]

Notes

1. The chapters included in this volume are the result of research carried out by the group HAR2014–53797-P, "Globalización Ibérica: Redes entre Asia y Europa y los cambios en las pautas de Consumo en Latinoamérica" [Iberian Globalization: Networks Between Asia and Europe and Changes in Consumption Patterns in Latin America], financed by Ministerio de Economia y Competitividad, Spain. This research group is included in the PAI Group

HUM-1000, "Historia de la Globalización: violencia, negociación e interculturalidad" [History of Globalisation: Violence, Negotiation and Interculturality], which is financed by the Regional Government of Andalusia. The open access for this chapter has been financed by the ERC Starting Grant-679371 GECEM, "Global Encounters between China and Europe: Trade Networks, Consumption and Cultural Exchanges in Macau and Marseille, 1680–1840", whose principal investigator is Professor Manuel Pérez García.

2. This has been the tenor of many publications too numerous to enumerate here, but represented by works like those of McKendrick et al. 1982, Shammas 1990 and Brewer 2013. Perhaps the best and most important exception is the work of Braudel (1967), which heralds the current works on the subject.
3. Although this approach had its most important starting point in Braudel 1967, its development has been more marked in recent years. See, above all, the pioneering work of Mintz 1985, as well as that of Nützenadel and Trentmann 2008, 1–21, and Brewer and Trentmann 2006, and a long list to follow since then. Two of the most representative of this last phase are those of Riello 2013, and Beckert 2014. The subject is part of a major trend in European historiography. See Muchembled and Monter 2006–2007.
4. In reality this has been true even in works such as that of Bauer 2001, where the intention was not to study the circulation of products but only the transformations brought about on American soil. This is logical if one considers that they dealt with transformations derived from contact and colonization and for that reason can reflect flows of goods often on a global scale.
5. See also Perez García and De Sousa 2018.
6. There are abundant examples of writings in this vein, but we find that it is best exemplified in the works of Wallerstein 1974. Regarding the second, it is similarly difficult to select examples, but K. Pomeranz's work is one of the most emblematic. See Pomeranz 2000.
7. An example from the early days of this process, but which logically could not account for the process in the longer term, is the book by Russell-Wood 1992.
8. This is precisely what was intended with Aram and Yun-Casalilla 2014.
9. Undoubtedly Bauer 2001, provides the best synthesis.
10. These issues were also the subject of Almorza's doctoral thesis, now published as a book. See Almorza Hidalgo 2019.
11. See an important precedent in Vicente 2006.
12. Saldarriaga devoted an extensive study to products such as corn, yuca and others in Saldarriaga 2011.
13. Córdoba Ochoa's doctoral thesis on the war in the New Kingdom of Granada covers aspects related to the consumption of some products for the period subsequent to the one considered here. See Córdoba Ochoa 2013.
14. By the same author, see also Earle 2012.
15. For a broader perspective see Berti forthcoming.
16. A broader study by the author that includes many more aspects, Gasch Tomás 2018.
17. Also with a broader dimension which this work forms part of Svriz-Wucherer 2019.
18. By the same author Quiles 2009.
19. I wish to express the three editors' frustration with the exclusion of a chapter on Portuguese America, which, despite being planned within the original research project, had to be canceled due to personal reasons. It is very evident that one cannot speak of American globalization leaving out such an

important part of the continent. We hope that the great variety of studies and perspectives presented here will palliate this deficiency.
20. Muchembled and Monter 2006–2007. For a more global perspective, see some of the works already included in Schwartz 1994.
21. Nancy Farriss affirmed that in terms of material culture, it would be difficult to affirm who assimilated whom, that is, if any kind of assimilation actually took place. See Farriss 1984, chapter 3. An interesting case is the introduction and production of coconut wine by the Chinese population in Colima, perhaps a precursor of mezcal. See Machuca 2016. My thanks to Sergio Serrano for his reference to this work.
22. The subject has given rise to considerable and justified interest in recent times. See, for example, Eltis, Morgan and Richardson 2007.
23. Among other works, see also Vicente 2006, and Almorza Hidalgo 2019.
24. An overview of the different ways of introducing a product in Latin America from the perspective of global and multidirectional history may be found in cotton. See Riello 2013.
25. Although the attention paid to Latin America in this period is surprisingly scarce, it is worth rereading the perspective provided by Sven Beckert in a far-reaching work on cotton as a global commodity. See Beckert 2014.

Bibliography

Almorza Hidalgo, Amelia. 2019. *No se hace pueblo sin ellas. Mujeres españolas en el Virreinato de Perú: Emigración y movilidad social (siglos XVI-XVII)*. Sevilla: Diputación de Sevilla.

Aram, Bethany and Bartolomé Yun-Casalilla, eds. 2014. *Global Goods and the Spanish Empire, 1492–1824. Circulation, Resistance and Diversity*. New York: Palgrave Macmillan.

Bauer, Arnold J. 2001. *Goods, Power, History: Latin America's material culture*. Cambridge, New York: Cambridge University Press.

Beckert, Sven. 2014. *Empire of Cotton: A Global History*. New York: Alfred A. Knopf.

Berti, Ilaria. Forthcoming. *Colonial Recipes in the Nineteenth-Century British and Spanish Caribbean. Food Perceptions and Practice*. Amsterdam: Amsterdam University Press.

Braudel, Fernand. 1967. *Civilisation matérielle et capitalisme (XVe- XVIIIe Siècle)*. Paris: Librairie Armand Colin.

Brewer, John. 2013. *The Pleasures of the Imagination. English Culture in the Eighteenth Century*. London: Routledge.

Brewer, John and Frank Trentmann, eds. 2006. *Consuming Cultures, Global Perspectives. Historical Trajectories, Transnational Exchanges*. New York: Berg.

Córdoba Ochoa, Luis Miguel. 2013. "Guerra, Imperio y violencia en la Audiencia de Santa Fe, Nuevo Reino de Granada, 1580–1620." PhD diss., Universidad Pablo de Olavide.

Earle, Rebecca. 2012. *The Body of the Conquistador: Food, Race, and The Colonial Experience in Spanish America, 1492–1700*. Cambridge and New York: Cambridge University Press.

Eltis, David, Philip Morgan, and David Richardson. 2007. "Agency and Diasporas in Atlantic History. Reassessing the African Contribution in the Americas." *The American Historical Review* 112 (5): 1329–58.

Farriss, Nancy. 1984. *The Maya Society under Colonial Rule: The Collective Enterprise of Survival*. Princeton, NJ: Princeton University Press.

Frank, Andre Gunder. 1998. *ReOrient: Global Economy in the Asian Age*. Berkeley: University of California Press.

Gasch Tomás, José Luis. 2018. *The Atlantic World and the Manilla Galleons. Circulation, Market, and Consumption of Asian Goods in the Spanish Empire, 1565–1650*. Leiden: Brill.

Machuca, Paulina. 2016. *El vino de cocos en la Nueva España. Historia de una transculturación en el siglo XVII*. Zamora: El colegio de Michoacán.

McKendrick, Neil et al. 1982. *The Birth of a Consumer Society. The Commercialization of Eigteenth-Century England*. Bloomington, IN: Indiana University Press.

Mintz, Sidney W. 1985. *Sweetness and Power: The Place of Sugar in Modern History*. New York: Viking Penguin.

Muchembled, Robert, and William Monter, eds. 2006–2007. *Cultural Exchange in Early Modern Europe*. Cambridge and New York: Cambridge University Press.

Nützenadel, Alex, and Frank Trentmann, eds. 2008. *Food and Globalization. Consumption, Markets and Politics in the Modern World*. Oxford: Berg.

Pérez García, Manuel and Lucio De Sousa, eds. 2018. *Global History and New Polycentric Approaches: Europe, Asia And the Americas in a World Network System*. New York: Palgrave Macmillan.

Pomeranz, Kenneth. 2000. *The Great Divergence. China, Europe, and the Making of the Modern World Economy*. Princeton, NJ: Princeton University Press.

Quiles, Fernando. 2009. *Sevilla y América en el Barroco. Comercio, ciudad y arte*. Sevilla: Bosque de Palabras.

Riello, Giorgio. 2013. *Cotton: The Fabric that Made the Modern World*. Cambridge and New York: Cambridge University Press.

Russell-Wood, Anthony J. R. 1992. *A World on the Move: The Portuguese in Africa, Asia and America, 1415–1808*. Manchester: Carcanet in association with the Calouste Gulbenkian Foundation.

Saldarriaga, Gregorio. 2011. *Alimentación e identidades en el Nuevo Reino de Granada, siglos XVI y XVII*. Bogotá: Editorial Universidad del Rosario.

Schwartz, Stuart, ed. 1994. *Implicit understandings. Observing, Reporting, and Reflecting on the Encounters between Europeans and other peoples in the Early Modern Era*. Cambridge: Cambridge University Press.

Shammas, Carole. 1990. *The Pre-industrial Consumer in England and America*. Oxford: Clarendon Press; New York: Oxford University Press.

Svriz-Wucherer, Pedro Miguel Omar. 2019. *Resistencia y negociación. Milicias guaraníes, jesuitas y cambios socioeconómicos en la frontera del imperio global hispánico (ss. XVII-XVIII)*. Rosario: Prohistoria.

Vicente, Marta A. 2006. *Clothing the Spanish Empire. Families and the Calico Trade in the Early Modern Atlantic World*. New York: Palgrave Macmillan.

Wallerstein, Immanuel. 1974. *The Modern World-System: Capitalism Agriculture and the Origins of the European World-Economy in the Sixteenth Century*. New York and London: Academic Press.

Part I

The Political Economy of the Spanish Empire and the Introduction of Eurasian Goods in the New World

1 Trans-Imperial, Transnational and Decentralized

The Traffic of African Slaves to Spanish America and Across the Isthmus of Panama, 1508–1651

Alejandro García-Montón[1]

Introduction

Spanish America was the destination of the first and the last ships loaded with slaves that crossed the Atlantic between the early sixteenth century and the mid-nineteenth century. Recent studies estimate that this traffic was responsible for the forced migration of at least two million people from Africa to Spanish America, the Spanish colonies being the second most important American destination after Brazil (Borucki, Eltis, and Wheat 2015). The effects of the slave trade varied widely in Spanish America. They led to the diversification of the population of the American continent and the appearance of new groups of hybrid origin, as well as the emergence of new social identities, cultural forms and consumer behavior. From an economic point of view, we still lack a study that concerns itself with measuring the commercial impact of the African slave trade compared to the trade of other products or goods in the Spanish empire, or estimating the effects of the arrival of forced labor on the colony's economy. It is not our purpose here to resolve such matters; nonetheless, it is important to emphasize that the Spanish colonization of the Americas was viable thanks to the contribution of populations of African origin. In this sense, the colonization of America also turned out to be a process of Africanization of the continent (Wheat 2016).

The trafficking of African slaves to Spanish America remains largely unknown today by comparison with the trade in goods and merchandise that developed between Spain and its American colonies through the Carrera de Indias, or the slave trafficking systems set up by other empires of the Atlantic world. This chapter traces the main lines of the political economy of the African slave trade to Spanish America and its specific characteristics as a commercial endeavor. Three elements characterized the slave trade in comparison to the regular Atlantic trade in goods and merchandise to Spanish America through the Carrera de Indias system. First, the routes that supplied slaves to Spanish America

DOI: 10.4324/9781003168058-2

were of a trans-imperial nature. Second, the merchant networks controlling this infamous trade had a strong transnational component. Third, the shipping of slaves was highly decentralized with respect to Spain. These three key elements underpinned the structure of the slave trade to Spanish America for more than three centuries (Mendes 2008; Borucki 2012; Delgado Ribas 2013). A focus on these three aspects should help us better understand the various distribution mechanisms set up in the "New World" for the introduction of enslaved people, new products and goods, whose conditioning factors tended to vary considerably.

The following pages concentrate on the period that runs from the early sixteenth century to the mid-seventeenth century and represents the golden age of the Iberian empires' slave trade in the Atlantic. During this period, the Portuguese and Spanish empires laid the foundations for the transatlantic slave trade and were its main protagonists, both in terms of the supply of African slave labor and in relation to market demand from America. With the Isthmus of Panama as its main geographic reference, this chapter is divided into three sections. First, we present the irreplaceable role played by the African population in the conquest and colonization of this Isthmus of Panama, which was the main route connecting the Atlantic and the Pacific Ocean in the framework of the Spanish empire during the sixteenth and seventeenth centuries. Next, we explain the commercial structure surrounding the importation of African slaves to this area. The third section analyzes in detail the decade of the 1640s, which registered an unusual fall-off in the volume of African slaves officially arriving in Spanish America and a major restructuring of the trafficking routes. An analysis of the reasons for these changes and the way in which different cities of the colonial sphere, such as Panama, reacted to the diminished supply of slaves sheds light on two issues that often go unnoticed. Firstly, the importance of trans-imperialism, transnationalism and decentralization in fashioning the African slave trade to Spanish America; and secondly, the distinctive characteristics of this traffic within the overall framework of the Spanish empire's political economy in the Atlantic and in comparison to trade in other goods or products.

The Africanization of the Isthmus of Panama

Unlike other trades destined for Spanish America, the demand for African slaves manifested itself very early on, as it was linked to structural changes in the economy from the time of the conquest. African slaves were the involuntary protagonists of a transatlantic trade that decisively transformed the Americas. So much so that, in the words of David Wheat, the population of African origin operated as "surrogate colonists" in Spanish America (Wheat 2016). From the slaves to the free blacks, including the local population of African descent (known as *criollos*), these social actors carried out a multitude of tasks that were vital for the conquest of

Spanish America and the viability of the colony (Vinson 2001; McKnight and Garofalo 2010; O'Toole 2012; Restall 2013; Bryant 2014; Borucki 2015). The region of Panama provides one of the best examples of the importance of the African forced migrants in taking control and developing a Spanish imperial presence in the Americas.

The first African slaves possibly were brought to the Isthmus of Panama in 1508 with the expedition of Diego de Nicuesa (Tardieu 2009, 42). During the twenty years following the foundation of the first Spanish settlements on the isthmus, Nombre de Dios (1508) and Santa María del Darién (1510), the indigenous population was almost entirely wiped out due to violent clashes with European settlers and the arrival of new pathogens. The first expeditions organized from Panama City to Nicaragua and Peru also transported indigenous slaves, thus contributing to the decline of the native Panamanian population. In the opinion of Governor Francisco de Barrionuevo, by 1533 there were only 500 indigenous people left in the area surrounding Panama City (Mena García 1984, 78).

The shortage of indigenous slave labor on the Isthmus of Panama was already evident during the early 1520s, and created a strong demand for forced labor to the area. That demand was met by developing an inter-American slave trade from Nicaragua to the Isthmus of Panama, with indigenous people enslaved as victims (Radell 1976; Sherman 1979; Newson 1982). However, as the demand for slave labor was much higher than the existing supply in Central America, the transatlantic slave trade quickly became the main source for enslaved workers. In 1523 a ship with a cargo of five hundred African captives landed and in 1525 an additional thousand African slaves were brought to the isthmus (Ward 1993, 35). In 1531 the Panama City Council asked the Crown for privileges so that more African slaves could be sent to the region in order to support the colonization process (Jopling 1994, 113–15).

The demand for African slave labor in the region of Panama was especially strong in comparison to other parts of Spanish America. At first, the implementation of systems known as *encomiendas*, for organizing indigenous labor to support the Spanish settlers, was an incentive for the conquistadores of the Isthmus of Panama. However, the number of natives integrated into the Panamanian *encomiendas* was low by comparison with other areas. This meant that, for example, the Panamanian *encomenderos* (those granted control of the *encomiendas*) never reached anything like the power or the control of such large native workforces as their peers in the valleys of Peru. From the mid-sixteenth century the influence of the Panamanian *encomenderos* was in decline, while local government officials and traders stood out as the main local power group (Mena García 1984, 176–245). Moreover, according to some authors, the suppression of indigenous slavery in the mid-sixteenth century did not have any pronounced influence on the local economy and the productive sectors of the colony; nor did the taxes paid by the natives have any notable importance on the tax revenue of the Panamanian Audiencia (Mena García 1984, 324, 325). All these factors show the extent to which African slaves had a prominent role in the establishment of the first colonial structures on the Isthmus of Panama and their subsequent development.

The strong demand for slave labor on the Isthmus of Panama during the first decades of colonization led to an important upsurge in the trade in African captives, which affected the demographics of the isthmus. In a few years the population of African origin had superseded the indigenous population as the main human group in areas under Spanish influence. In 1575 it was estimated that there were about 6,000 African slaves within the Audiencia of Panama. Nearly 2,500 of these were concentrated in Panama City (Mena García 1984, 91). By 1607 the slave population of the city had increased to almost 3,700. Together with the free blacks – about seven hundred and fifty – the population of African origin represented almost eighty percent of the total inhabitants of the city.[2] These numbers registered a steady increase over the years. At the end of the 1620s and the outset of the 1630s, there were several accounts of 14,000 African slaves in the region.[3] By the 1640s, the figure was estimated to be have reached 17,000 (Vila Vilar 1976, 175).

African slaves sustained the transport and service sectors, which were the main industries of the area of Panama. The importance of this region in the geopolitics of the Spanish empire was largely due to its role as a junction connecting Spain and the Atlantic trade routes to South Pacific America. The strategic value of the Isthmus of Panama was inestimable as the first stop for Potosí silver from Bolivia on its global journey to Asia via Spain, whose circulation gave rise to one of the most incisive processes in the emergence of globalization (Flynn, Giráldez, and Von Glahn 2003). In 1561, the Crown and the Seville merchants' guild established an annual convoy, known as the fleets and galleons system, connecting Spain with Cartagena de Indias, the Isthmus of Panama and Veracruz. The fleets and galleons system brought stability to the trade fairs celebrated in Nombre de Dios and subsequently, following the destruction of the town by Francis Drake in 1596, at the new settlement of Portobelo (1597), which became a crucial trading centre where Peruvian and Spanish merchants met (Castillero Calvo 1980; Vila Vilar 1982). The extremely difficult eighty kilometers of mountains, rivers, mudflats and tropical jungle that separated the Caribbean port of Portobelo from Panama City on the Pacific Ocean were negotiated by the Panamanian transporters through the forced employment of African slaves to transport goods and precious metals by mule-pack (Castillero Calvo 1980; Mena García 1984).

As a producer of goods and products, the importance of the isthmus was marginal, both in the Spanish-American colonial economy and in the overall economy of the Spanish empire. However, African slaves were crucial to sustaining the productive activities developed in the rural areas of the isthmus. They were in charge of raising livestock and were employed in the gold mines, the pearl fisheries and the sawmills and in wood harvesting, field work, and the maintenance and upkeep of the roads and the construction of Panama's military defenses (Mena García 1984, 389–400).

The work performed by African slaves in the city of Panama was concentrated in domestic service and the building sector, while free blacks were employed in various trades, from artisans to public notaries, despite the fact that their skin color could be considered a formal disadvantage (Espelt Bombín 2014). For example, in 1650 Manuel Botaccio Grilo, a mestizo, acceded to the post of notary public in Panama City after several years.[4]

The presence of people of African origin in the cities of the isthmus was not only appreciable in terms of their numbers and the activities they developed, but also in the structure and naming of urban developments. For example, in 1607 there were four suburbs or neighborhoods in the outskirts of Portobelo in which the majority of the population was of African origin. The district of Triana was where the king's slaves dwelt and were employed by the local authorities, while it was said that the Carnicería district was inhabited by blacks and people of mixed race. A third suburb was called Guinea, in direct reference to the origin of its inhabitants.[5]

People of African origin in the towns of the isthmus joined and founded religious confraternities through which they engaged in civil and religious activities. In his description of the bishopric of Panama City in 1650, Friar Hernando Ramírez pointed out that of the six existing confraternities in Portobelo, the one of San Pablo had a large membership of people of mixed race and blacks. This also occurred in the town of Natá with the San Sebastián confraternity of the *criollo* slaves and in Panama City with the confraternity of Nuestra del Rosario de negros *congos*, which was established in the convent of Santo Domingo.[6]

Another aspect that shaped the Africanization of the Isthmus of Panama was the expansion of communities of runaway slaves known as maroons. The maroon population developed a parallel society that competed for the natural and economic resources of the isthmus and were especially active from the 1550s through the 1580s (Pike 2007; Tardieu 2009). The so-called Kingdom of Bayano around the Chepo River, was a stronghold of the rebels for decades. According to the contemporary accounts of Alonso Criado de Castilla, in 1575 almost half of the black population of the Isthmus of Panama – around 2,500 inhabitants – lived in maroon communities (Mena García 1984, 52, 426). Faced with the alarming rise of the maroon population, the crown issued a decree prohibiting the sale of slaves on the isthmus for fear that the new captives would swell the ranks of the rebels (Bowser 1974, 63; Pike 2007, 265, 266).

The Transatlantic Slave Trade in the Context of the Spanish Atlantic

The transatlantic slave trade was organized as a very particular business compared to other trades to Spanish America, both in terms of the routes it took and the profile of its merchants (O'Malley and Borucki 2017; Borucki, Eltis, and Wheat 2020). The bulk of the commercial activity between Spain and Spanish America was channeled through the Carrera de Indias. The Carrera de Indias consisted of a circuit of navigation connecting ports on the Spanish mainland – Seville initially and Cádiz from the end of the seventeenth century – and the American ports of Cartagena de Indias, the Isthmus of Panama – Nombre de Dios until 1596 and Portobelo after that – and Veracruz. From the mid-sixteenth to the mid-eighteenth centuries, navigation was organized through a convoy system that operated annually or every two years. Most of the products and goods travelling from Spain to Spanish America, whether they had been produced in Spain or not, travelled through the Carrera de Indias trading system. Therefore, while the Carrera de Indias represented trade routes that ran within the limits of the Spanish empire, the African slave trade to Spanish America surpassed them. As the Spanish empire never developed a system of factories and garrisons in sub-Saharan Africa, the slaves transported to Spanish America were dispatched from territories claimed by other empires of the Atlantic world.

The trans-imperial character of the African slave trade had an impact on the shipping patterns adopted by the slave traders. Slave traders sailed with greater flexibility compared to the merchants who operated through the Carrera de Indias convoy system, which connected established ports once a year at best. Between the 1590s and 1630s, the ports of Cartagena de Indias and Veracruz, and at times Buenos Aires, were the only ones officially authorized to receive slave ships from Africa (Wheat 2011; Schultz 2015; Sierra Silva 2017). The Spanish authorities encouraged adapting the geography of the slave trade to the routes of the Carrera de Indias. However, the difficulties that the authorities had in controlling the navigation of the slave ships meant that the final decision on the port of arrival was in the hands of the ships' captains. On the other hand, the cargo holds on the licensed slave ships that travelled to Spanish America contained many products in addition to the slaves. Soon the official slave trade became a legal cover, with many of these ships carrying more contraband goods than slaves. These trading and shipping practices mirrored the transatlantic and trans-imperial exchanges carried out by vessels involved in the business of slave smuggling. Several documents point to the widespread development and momentum of the illegal slave trade. For example, in 1566 an order was issued from Spain urging authorities throughout the Spanish Caribbean, from Mexico to Venezuela via Panama, to take action against the smuggling of slaves and merchandise by unlicensed Portuguese ships.[7] In this sense, the slave trade facilitated the development of supply chains for trade in slaves and products of various kinds between different regions within the empire and beyond, often regardless of the official trading routes endorsed by the Carrera de Indias.

The profile of the merchants running the African slave trade was characterized by a strong transnational component. The businesses of the Carrera de Indias had a strong presence of foreign products and capital as in assets. The rules and laws of the Carrera de Indias allowed trading in goods produced beyond the borders of the empire, but direct participation of foreign merchants was restricted. Leaving contraband to one side, foreign merchants frequently employed Spanish intermediaries or purchased citizenship that allowed them to participate more directly in official trade. However, the slave trade was very different. From the early days of American colonization, Spanish merchants played a very discreet role in the slave trade and the Crown did not oppose the participation of foreign merchants in this trade. The main protagonists of the slave trade to Spanish America were, on the other hand, merchants who were not even subjects of the empire, such as the Genoese, Portuguese, Dutch, French and English.

The Crown and the authorities in charge of the organization of the commerce and the navigation to Spanish America – the Consejo de Indias in Madrid, and the Casa de la Contratación in Seville – not only accepted the fact that the official trafficking of slaves had become a trans-imperial, transnational and decentralized activity; they also obtained direct income in Spain through the sale of licenses to participate in the slave trade. From the 1520s until the 1630s, the Crown launched a controlled market of licenses to participate in the official slave trade. During most of this period, licenses were issued by the Casa de la Contratación in Seville, while between 1595 and 1640 the marketing of the licenses was outsourced to private companies, all of Portuguese origin. Later on, from the 1660s to the 1740s, this system changed, and monopolies to introduce slaves were leased to specific companies (Delgado Ribas 2013).

Portuguese merchants and their political leaders soon discovered that the demand for African slaves in the Spanish American colonies meant a lucrative and steady business. From 1534, the crown of Portugal officially allowed the direct export of slaves from Cape Verde and São Tomé to Spanish America (Mendes 2008, 66). The interest of the Portuguese Crown in fostering the slave trade to Spanish America complemented the Spanish kings' interest in cooperation with Portuguese slave traders. For instance, in 1541 Charles V signed a contract with the Torres brothers' Portuguese company to send slaves to America, and in 1556 Philip II contracted Manuel Caldeira to import 2,000 slaves from the Cape Verde Islands (Mendes 2008, 74; Delgado Ribas 2013, 17, 18).

Until the mid-seventeenth century, the Portuguese were better positioned than merchants of other origins to take control of this trade in

African captives. In the first place, they were well established in Seville, the main Spanish port from where Atlantic trade and navigation was channeled (Pérez García and Fernández Chaves 2009; Fernández Chaves and Pérez García 2010). They not only had physical access to sources of slavery in Africa and the familiarity necessary to interfere in inter-cultural trade with local leaders, they also had sufficient capital to organize transatlantic expeditions and the human resources to negotiate them through all the traffic segments, from Portugal and Spain to Africa, from there to Spanish America and from Spanish America to the Iberian Peninsula (Studnicki-Gizbert 2007; Green 2012; Hicks 2017). Consequently, from the early decades of the sixteenth century until the 1630s, the supply of slaves to Spanish America was strongly linked to the fate of Portuguese expansion in Africa. The Portuguese factories in Cabo Verde, the Gulf of Guinea and later in Angola were the ports of origin for the ships crossing the Atlantic that provided slave labor for the Spanish colonization of America. As a result, the arrival of different African ethnic groups in Spanish America was tied to the evolution of the Portuguese presence in Africa (Wheat 2011).

The Portuguese and Spanish empires were united under the Habsburg crown between 1580 and 1640. Although the two empires maintained their respective legal entities, laws and traditions, the new political context facilitated the movement of Iberian subjects throughout the combined Atlantic possessions of the two empires (Subrahmanyam 2007). Therefore, participation in the slave trade became the main Portuguese means of access into Spanish American markets. From 1595, the same entrepreneurs who leased out the Portuguese factories in Africa from where the slaves were removed also took control of the slave transport licenses to Spanish America (Vila Vilar 1977). Therefore, for nearly 50 years merchants of Portuguese origin virtually dominated the importation of slaves into Spanish America, from Mexico to Buenos Aires (Assadourian 1966; Newson and Minchin 2007; Eagle 2013; Lokken 2013; Schultz 2017; Sierra Silva 2018). As a trans-imperial activity, the slave trade to Spanish America benefited especially from the union of both empires, boosting its role as a “commodity chain” that created a series of links that would soon prove crucial in the functioning of the empire.

The slave trade to the Isthmus of Panama developed along those lines from the early sixteenth century to the mid-seventeenth century. Within the Spanish American slave trade circuits, the Isthmus of Panama provided a port that became involved in the intra-imperial and inter-American routes. The ships that originated in Africa and had made the transatlantic crossing would sell or deposit their cargoes of slaves along the Atlantic seaboard from whence they were redistributed to the American viceroyalties together with other products. From the 1570s onwards, the port of Cartagena de Indias began to emerge as the main redistributive center for slaves in Spanish America and hosted a growing community of

Portuguese slave traders (Vidal Ortega 2002). Between 1595 and 1640 more than half of all the slaves who were taken to the Caribbean had landed in Cartagena de Indias, some 157,000 people.[8] During this period it is estimated that between 1,000 and 1,500 slaves were taken annually from Cartagena de Indias to Portobelo (Bowser 1974, 78).

In 1607, according to the president of the Audiencia of Panama, the slave trade was described as the richest and most constant trade in the region where "everything is done by means of Portuguese".[9] In that same year, it was recorded that there were thirty-one Portuguese residents in Panama, representing the main community of foreigners in the city, twice as many as the Italians, who constituted the second largest group.[10] To a large extent, slave traders who settled on the isthmus turned out to be agents of companies based in Cartagena de Indias or in Lima. Their work on the isthmus involved coordinating the large slave trade linking those two cities with the Isthmus of Panama as an intermediate stop. However, traders investing in slaves also became involved in other activities, availing themselves of the opportunities the isthmus offered as the focal point for the transshipment of merchandise and precious metals from Peru and Spain (Bowser 1974, 60, 63, 64; Newson and Minchin 2007, 193–95).

The strong Portuguese presence in Spanish America and the remarkable economic dynamism of Portuguese slave traders elicited widespread hostility and misgivings from certain Spanish American merchants. Many local traders perceived the Portuguese as foreigners and as an economic, religious and even a political threat to their interests and the integrity of the empire. For example, the 1607 report that pointed to the iron-fisted control that the Portuguese exercised over the slave trade in Panama highlighted that many of those traders had left the Indies to join forces with other merchants living in the Italian Jewish quarters of Rome and Ferrara and that investigations carried out there by the Inquisition had revealed these Portuguese subjects to be Judaizers.[11]

Mistrust of the Portuguese traders crystalized in the inquisitorial offensive unleashed in Cartagena de Indias (1636–1638), Lima (1635–1641) and Mexico (1642–1649) that put an end to the networks set up by the Portuguese as a result of the slave trade. Most of those accused of being Judaizers were merchants of different ranks, the most prominent being those linked to slave trafficking, such as Manuel Fonseca Enríquez, Blas Paz de Pinto and Juan Rodríguez Mesa, all of them based at Cartagena de Indias, and Manuel Bautista Pérez, based at Lima. Many of these merchants were captured between Panama City and Portobelo, like Jorge de Espinosa, who was arrested in 1635 while trying to buy goods and slaves for 12,435 pesos. A similar fate befell Enrique Lorenzo, who had specialized in the slave trade between Cartagena de Indias and Portobelo, and Luis de Lima, who was an agent for other Peruvian merchants (Quiroz 1985).

The Suspension of Official Slave Trading During the 1640s

Between 1640 and 1651 the official slave trade to Spanish America was suspended (Vila Vilar 1976; Schwartz 1993). The reasons for that suspension further highlight the specific characteristics of the slave trade to the colonies in comparison with the ways through which other transatlantic trades took place. On 1 December 1640, the Duke of Braganza initiated a revolt that sought to remove Philip IV from the Portuguese throne. The monarch also reigned over the Spanish empire. Thus began a conflict between the two Iberian empires that was to continue until 1668, spanning the zenith of the global expansion of the Spanish and Portuguese empires. As news of the uprising in Portugal spread, so too did conjecture about the position that the Portuguese communities would adopt in Spain and its American colonies. At first, no specific measures were taken to expel the Portuguese from the Spanish Indies; however the adoption of certain practices reflected the bellicose situation, such as barring Portuguese ships from mooring at the Spanish American ports on the 1 January 1641.[12] The Crown of Castile did not fill the gap left by the Portuguese by permitting merchants of other nationalities to trade in Spanish America, nor did it allow Spanish merchants to sail directly to Africa to lead the slave trade. This combination of factors implied the suspension of the slave trade to Spanish America, which had been dominated by Portuguese merchants since the end of the sixteenth century.

The war between these empires disrupted the slave trade and further fueled the mistrust, palpable since the 1630s, towards the very dynamic community of Portuguese merchants, often perceived as foreigners, in Spanish America. During the 1640s, the activities of the Portuguese in Spanish America were severely curtailed by the authorities. In the Panamanian case, in May 1645 a royal decree was issued from Spain recommending that the Audiencia of Panama expel Portuguese subjects in Panama City and Portobelo to the interior of the province or, failing that, to Lima.[13] Nevertheless, having carried out their own investigations, the local authorities pronounced that the Portuguese residents did not represent any threat to the interests of the Crown as they did not keep any ties with Portugal.[14] Something similar happened in March 1649, when an edict was issued in the main urban centers of the Isthmus of Panama – Panama, Portobelo, Villa de los Santos and Natá – that the inhabitants of Portuguese origin be identified on "pain of life and loss of their property applied to the Chamber of His Majesty". In total, eighty-seven male adults were counted. Since most of them belonged to the lower-income bracket and there was no suspicion of any commercial links with the Portuguese Empire or the slave trade, none of them was expelled.[15] The truth is that, within this context of war, one of Spain's main interests was to dismantle the Portuguese slave trade networks that included related circular trade links for various products across the two empires between the Iberian Peninsula, Africa and Spanish America. The expulsion of the Portuguese Juan Baeza from Panama City in 1646 and the seizure of his property were justified on the grounds of his business with conationals on the Iberian mainland.[16]

From 1643 the Council of the Indies began to receive letters and briefs from various points in Spanish America specifically referring to the lack of African slaves or including it as one of the main topics. Individuals, councils, presidents of Audiencias and viceroys all described to what extent and how the suspension of official slave traffic affected the day-to-day running of their cities and provinces. The complaints raised by the cities underscored the importance of the slave trade to the different local economies of Spanish America. These reports show the Spanish American economies' incapacity to replace the African workforce, and therefore the extent to which Spanish America depended upon the slave trade, which was necessarily trans-imperial.

The main Spanish American mining centers, which were vital for the functioning of the empire, expressed their concern on numerous occasions. In 1645, the *corregidor* of La Plata y Potosí, don Juan Velarde Treviño Fernández, complained of the lack of black slaves in those areas.[17] Although African slaves rarely worked as silver miners, they were vital in blacksmithing, shoemaking and driving llama trains, among other crafts that supported the mining economy. Two years later another report reached the Council of the Indies, with the request for Buenos Aires to become an official port for the slave trade from which to supply the Potosí area with African forced labor.[18] In 1647, the Audiencia of Charcas estimated 1,000 slaves to be the ideal number to meet the labor needs of the region: in the vineyards, the wheat plantations, the sugar mills and the gold mines of Carabaya (now Peru).[19] Things were not going any better in Mexico. By the summer of 1647, the *corregidores* of Zacatecas and the treasurers of the hacienda of San Luis Potosi had already written at least three letters on the decline in mining activities and the consequent fall in the tax known as the *quinto real* (or "King's fifth") due to the impossibility of bringing new recruits to the mines.[20] A year later, in 1648, the president of the Audiencia of Guadalajara began to insist on the same subject and in 1651 the Viceroy of Mexico requested the dispatch of at least 1,000 African slaves.[21]

The representatives of Cartagena de Indias, the city that had become the main port of destination for African slaves in Spanish America since the late sixteenth century, also showed their discontent to the Crown. The information emanating from Cartagena de Indias was twofold: on the one hand, it indicated a stagnation of agricultural activities in rural areas and mining in the interior areas of Santa Fe and Zaragoza, while on the other hand there were reports focusing on the decline in the port's commercial dynamism and the consequent fall in tax collection.[22] According to the Cartagena de Indias town council, one of the keys to relaunching the slave trade with the participation of local merchants was to formalize the exchanges of merchandise that went hand in hand with the transatlantic slave trade. Their proposal was that the slave ships could leave Cartagena de Indias for the Canary Islands with local products. These would be sold there and exchanged for local wines and other goods to be finally exchanged for slaves on the coasts of Africa. Moreover, Cartagena's council advocated further decentralizing the slave trade by replacing the system of issuing licenses in Spain for slave trafficking with an alternative model of free participation in exchange for the payment of taxes in Spanish America on disembarkation.[23]

The reports written from Lima detail how the viability and endurance of the prosperous Peruvian economy relied on the African slave trade. According to Joseph de los Rios y Barrios, *procurador* for Lima in Madrid, the effects of five years without access to *bozales* slaves (those arriving directly from Africa), were estimated in losses of almost eight million pesos, affecting all types of crops, farms and industries.[24] According to other descriptions, the smallest, most usual type of rural hacienda in Peru required between ten and twelve slaves. Medium-sized holdings could need between fifty and a hundred slaves and the largest ones up to 200.[25] Thus, according to observers from Lima, the annual flow of African slaves needed to satisfy the Peruvian demand distributed between Lima, the Nazca Valley, Arequipa, Cuzco and even Potosi ranged between 1,500 and 2,000 captives.[26]

In the more discrete Panamanian economy, agricultural production and transport were identified as the sectors most affected by the lack of slave labor. By 1645, corn crops, honey production and market crops had completely declined to the point that, according to reports, the price of vegetables had increased threefold. The lack of slaves tending cattle limited meat production to meet the needs of Panama City and Portobelo and the additional high demand each time the fleet of galleons reached the shores of the isthmus. The sawmills had been stripped of manpower, and this reduced labor force also affected the provision of boats and hammocks.[27] Other reports point to a crisis in the maritime sector, both in terms of navigation and the exploitation of marine resources. For example, while forty boats had been involved in fishing at the end of the 1630s, the figure had decreased to sixteen by the middle of the following decade.[28] Slave labor was reported to be crucial for the maintenance of the fortress system in Portobelo and for security in general throughout the isthmus, as the companies in charge of repelling the constant attacks from the maroons relied largely on the contribution of the African slaves.[29]

From a broader perspective, the Panamanian authorities underlined the way in which the lack of slave labor in one region of Spanish America could have repercussions in another. It was reported, for example, that the decline in wheat and corn crops in Peru due to the shortage of African slaves had brought about a fall in flour imports to Panama and had almost doubled the price of bread.[30] The provision of other basic products such as tallow, butter, tobacco, chickpeas, beans and rice had also dropped. To complicate things further, a fire in 1644 had destroyed the food supplies in storage in Panama City.[31] In sum, slave trafficking had provided labor that was fundamental for the manufacture of products and the launching of services that in turn generated other types of businesses in Spanish America and across the empire.

Although the slave trade was officially suspended during the 1640s, some slave merchants continued to cross the Atlantic to supply Spanish America. The fact that trafficking was no longer official makes it difficult, but not impossible, to trace its activities in the archives. In the case of the Isthmus of Panama, in August 1641, the royal officials of the Audiencia of Panama sent 13,250 pesos to Spain obtained from the sale of about forty-four slaves who had arrived from Providence Island.[32] That same year another ship with a cargo of slaves also reached the Isthmus of Panama. Although the arrival of ships with African slaves is not reported for the rest of the 1640s, in 1651 the royal officer Tomás de la Mata Linares acknowledged having seven *criollo* slaves and ten *bozal* slaves. Another royal officer, Sebastián Gómez Carrillo, declared having two *bozal* and seven *criollo* slaves.[33] Probably, those *bozal* slaves were transported to the isthmus while the official slave trade was still suspended.

The arrival of some 5,000 slaves in Spanish America, most of them through smuggling, during the period in which the official slave trade was suspended is documented.[34] Nevertheless, it would seem that many more captives were forced to make the transatlantic crossing.[35] More than an important fall-off in the existing supply of African slaves, this period witnessed a rearrangement of the transatlantic slave trade routes and its protagonists. According to A. M. Caldeira, the figures for slaves exported from Angola (the main source of slaves in Africa for the Portuguese during the seventeenth century) at the beginning and the end of the decade of the 1640s were very similar, around 15,000 and 16,000 slaves per year, with roughly a third more if we include the estimated contraband slave arrivals. Despite the Dutch campaigns in Angola, the Portuguese managed to keep the slave trade to America afloat. In contrast, the destinations of the Portuguese slave ships varied with respect to previous periods. Generally speaking, traffic to Spanish America and more specifically to the Spanish Caribbean came to play a secondary role. Tensions between the Spanish and Portuguese empires, together with increased demand for slaves from the Portuguese-Brazilian ports of Bahia, Pernambuco and Rio de Janeiro as the Dutch were expelled from the region, were determining factors in the change of routes and the shortage of African slaves in Spanish America (Caldeira 2014).

In this context of change, the Spanish-American ports that continued to receive contraband slaves were those which, irrespective of playing a peripheral role in the Carrera de Indias trade route, were more exposed to the transatlantic routes to Africa, like Buenos Aires, or those that were closer to the emerging Dutch and English colonies in the Caribbean, such as Santo Domingo (Moutoukias 1988; Caldeira 2014; Freeman 2020). Moreover, from the 1640s onwards, the Spanish American colonies in the Caribbean also had to compete with the growing demand from English settlers for African slaves to service the burgeoning sugar industry. Although European indentured servants constituted the main workforce employed in Barbados during the 1640s, there was a growing demand for African slaves, which stimulated the activities of the English slave merchants (Downes 1987).

In April 1651, the Crown and the Council of the Indies relinquished their position of prohibiting trans-imperial cooperation for the African slave trade to Spanish America. Pressure from the main Spanish American cities' representatives had influenced the re-opening of official markets and licenses to trade were again sold in Seville. The Spanish authorities prohibited the slave traders departing for Africa from engaging in business with the Portuguese rebels in the region. However, once the ships had left Spain it was almost impossible for royal officials to verify from whom and where the African slaves were bought. After 1651, the slave trade to Spanish America changed considerably compared to the period before 1640. Dutch traders operating from Curaçao became the main transatlantic slave carriers operating in the Caribbean and the leading providers of slaves to Spanish America (Klooster 1998). Thus, the trans-imperial character of the slave trade to Spanish America and its trans-national characteristics intensified as shipping patterns became more decentralized with respect to the metropole.

Conclusions

The African slave trade was one of the first forms of commerce regulated by the Spanish empire at the outset of the conquest of America. Its impact on the globalization of Spanish America was paramount. Millions of African captives were taken to America as slaves in the conquest and development of colonial societies. Their central role in these processes brought about the Africanization of the colony in terms of population and culture. Their importance is evident in the case of the Isthmus of Panama: at the beginning of the seventeenth century up to eighty percent of the population of the region was of African origin. The Spanish American demand for African slaves was linked to the expansion of the colonial economy as a whole, from domestic service to the livestock trade, mining and the construction industry.

The African slave trade developed as a trans-imperial and transnational enterprise that made it very different from other types of commerce with Spanish America. The absence of Spanish trading posts in Africa placed the supply of African slaves in the hands of merchants from other empires. Consequently, the slave trade was a channel of direct contact between Spanish America and other empires that largely escaped the control of the state, despite attempts to regulate it. In comparison with other forms of trafficking, the slave trade was largely decentralized along the Spanish-American coasts. This particular feature, added to the fact that the slave trade went side by side with the exchange of other goods and products, meant that the slave ships developed an intricate network of routes linking not only the main ports of Spanish America but other secondary ports. Meanwhile, the use of African slaves by Spanish-American settlers in various kinds of production activities fueled the development of other trades and trafficking of a different nature.

The trans-imperial, transnational and decentralized character of the slave trade contrasts with the organized trade within the framework of the Carrera de Indias, which, was strongly directed from the homeland, highly centralized and generally intended to restrict the direct participation of foreigners. The existence of these two very different models of transatlantic trade management underscores the diversity of challenges facing the Spanish empire in organizing relations with Spanish America. At the same time, these two models of trade demonstrate the flexibility of the Spanish empire's political economy and its ability to address very different but fundamental problems for the colonization of American territories, such as the constant and growing demand for African slaves.

The characteristics of the transatlantic slave trade to Spanish America also contrast with the classic views on mercantilist policy ideals that European empires would champion in the Atlantic world. In other words, this reality belied the establishment of triangular trade among Europe, Africa and America in an imperial framework, based on the exchange of European manufactured goods, slaves and colonial products in favor of the homeland and from which the merchants of the empire benefited exclusively. However, far from representing the specific characteristics of this case as something unique, such aspects should rather be understood as constitutive elements of the political economy of the Spanish Atlantic as a whole.

Notes

1. This research has received funding from the European Research Council (ERC) under the European Union's Horizon 2020 research and innovation program, grant agreement ERC CoG 648535, "ArtEmpire", which finances its publication in open access. The author is grateful to the editors, Ilaria Berti, Omar Svriz and Bartolomé Yun-Casalilla, for their suggestions and to

Bethany Aram for constant support and insights. Likewise, this chapter has benefited from Routledge's reviewers' input.

2. Biblioteca Nacional de España, mss. 3064, ff. 63r-64r.
3. Archivo General de Indias (AGI), Panamá, Leg. 87. 1-XI-1629; AGI, Panamá, Leg. 49, n. 30. 1-XII-1633.
4. AGI, Panamá, Leg. 50, n. 3. 30-IV-1649; Leg. 57, n. 56. 18-III-1650.
5. Biblioteca Nacional de España (BNE), Mss. 3064, f. 126r.
6. Biblioteca de la Real Academia de la Historia (BRAH), Colección Muñoz, various mss. 66, ff. 275r-286v.
7. AGI, Indiferente General (IG), Leg. 427, Lib. 30, ff. 175v-176r. 12-VIII-1566.
8. www.slavevoyages.org/voyages/FzOj2HX8
9. AGI, Panamá, Leg. 15, r. 8, n. 79. 25-VI-1607.
10. BNE, mss 3064, f. 63r.
11. AGI, Panamá, Leg. 15, r. 8, n. 79. 25-VI-1607.
12. AGI, IG, Leg. 429, Lib.38, f. 181v. 1-I-1641.
13. AGI, Panamá, Leg. 229, Lib. 3, ff. 225v-226r. 15-V-1645; ff. 290v-291r. 7-VIII-1646.
14. AGI, Panamá, Leg. 229, Lib. 3, ff. 335r-335v. 5-VIII-1647.
15. AGI, Escribanía, Leg. 484-A, pieza 1, ff. 152r-172v.
16. AGI, Panamá, Leg. 229, Lib. 3, f. 306v. 14-II-1647.
17. AGI, IG, Leg. 2796. 1645.
18. AGI, IG, Leg. 2796. 1-IV-1647.
19. AGI, IG, Leg. 2796. 4-IV-1647.
20. AGI, IG, Leg. 2796. 5-II-1645; 1-XI-1647.
21. AGI, IG, Leg. 2796, 24-IV-1648; AGI, México, Leg. 36, n. 57. 11-VII-1651.
22. AGI, IG, Leg. 2796. 13-XII-1646, 21-III-1647; 11-V-1647; 20-II-1648; 14-X-1648.
23. AGI, IG, Leg. 2796. 30-VIII-1645; 19-X-1645.
24. AGI, IG, Leg. 2796. 30-VIII-1645.
25. AGI, IG, Leg. 2796. 12-V-1646.
26. AGI, IG, Leg. 2796. 12-V-1646; 5-VII-1647.
27. AGI, Panamá, Leg. 49, n. 87. 12-IX-1645.
28. AGI, Panamá, Leg. 31, n. 46.
29. AGI, Panamá, Leg. 49, n. 87. 12-IX-1645; AGI, Panamá, Leg. 31, n. 46; AGI, IG, Leg. 2796. 1-VII-1647.
30. AGI, Panamá, Leg. 31, n. 44. 12-IX-1645.
31. AGI, Panamá, Leg. 49, n. 87. 12-IX-1645.
32. AGI, Panamá, Leg. 35, n. 52.
33. AGI, Escribanía, Leg. 484-A, pieza 3, ff. 12v-17r, 19v-22v.
34. www.slavevoyages.org/voyages/qb5pOnLh
35. www.slavevoyages.org/voyages/qb5pOnLh

Bibliography

Assadourian, Carlos Sempat. 1966. *El tráfico de esclavos en Córdoba de Angola a Potosí, siglos XVI–XVII*. Córdoba: Dirección General de Publicaciones.

Borucki, Alex. 2012. "Trans-Imperial History in the Making of the Slave Trade to Venezuela, 1526–1811." *Itinerario* 36 (2): 29–54.

———. 2015. *From Shipmates to Soldiers. Emerging Black Identities in the Río de La Plata*. Alburquerque: New Mexico University Press.

Borucki, Alex, David Eltis, and David Wheat. 2015. "Atlantic History and the Slave Trade to Spanish America." *American Historical Review* 120 (2): 433–61.

———, eds. 2020. *From the Galleons to the Highlands: Slave Trade Routes in the Spanish Americas*. Albuquerque: University of New Mexico Press.

Bowser, Frederick P. 1974. *The African Slave in Colonial Peru, 1524–1650*. Stanford, CA: Stanford University Press.

Bryant, Sherwin K. 2014. *Rivers of Gold, Lives of Bondage: Governing Through Slavery in Colonial Quito*. Chapel Hill: University of North Carolina Press.

Caldeira, Arlindo Manuel. 2014. "Angola and the Seventeenth-Century South Atlantic Slave Trade." In *Networks and Trans-Cultural Exchange: Slave Trading in the South Atlantic, 1590–1867*, edited by David Richardson and Filipa Ribeiro da Silva, 101–42. Leiden: Brill.

Castillero Calvo, Alfredo. 1980. *Economía terciaria y sociedad, Panamá, siglos XVI y XVII*. Panamá: Instituto Nacional de Cultura de Panamá.

Delgado Ribas, José María. 2013. "The Slave Trade in the Spanish Imperial System, 1500–1800." In *Slavery and Antislavery in Spain's Atlantic Empire*, edited by Josep Maria Fradera and Christopher Schmidt-Nowara, 13–42. New York: Berghahn Books.

Downes, Andrew. 1987. "The Economics of Transition to the Black Labor System in Barbados, 1630–1680." *The Journal of Interdisciplinary History* 18 (2): 225–47.

Eagle, Marc. 2013. "Chasing the Avença: An Investigation of Illicit Slave Trading in Santo Domingo at the End of the Portuguese Asiento Period." *Slavery & Abolition* 35 (1): 99–120.

Espelt Bombín, Silvia. 2014. "Notaries of Color in Colonial Panama: Limpieza de Sangre, Legislation, and Imperial Practices in the Administration of the Spanish Empire." *The Americas* 71 (1): 37–69.

Fernández Chaves, Manuel Francisco, and Rafael M. Pérez García. 2010. "Las redes de la trata negrera: mercaderes portugueses y tráfico de esclavos en Sevilla (c. 1560–1580)." In *La esclavitud negroafricana en la historia de España siglos XVI y XVII*, edited by Aurelia Martín Casares and Margarita García Barranco, 5–34. Granada: Editorial Comares.

Flynn, Dennis Owen, Arturo Giráldez, and Richard Von Glahn. 2003. *Global Connections and Monetary History, 1470–1800*. Burlington, VT: Ashgate.

Freeman, David. 2020. *A Silver River in a Silver World: Dutch Trade in the Rio de La Plata, 1648–1678*. London and New York: Cambridge University Press.

Green, Toby. 2012. *The Rise of the Trans-Atlantic Slave Trade in Western Africa, 1300–1589*. New York: Cambridge University Press.

Hicks, Mary E. 2017. "Financing the Luso-Atlantic Slave Trade, 1500–1840." *Journal of Global Slavery* 2 (3): 273–309.

Jopling, Carol F., ed. 1994. *Indios y negros en Panamá en los siglos XVI y XVII: selecciones de los documentos del Archivo General de Indias*. Antigua-South Woodstock: Plumsock Mesoamerican Studies.

Klooster, Wim. 1998. *Illicit Riches: Dutch Trade in the Caribbean, 1648–1795*. Leiden: KITLV Press.

Lokken, Paul. 2013. "From the Kingdoms of Angola to Santiago de Guatemala: The Portuguese Asientos and Spanish Central America, 1595–1640." *Hispanic American Historical Review* 93 (2): 171–203.

McKnight, Kathryn Joy, and Leo J. Garofalo, eds. 2010. *Afro-Latino Voices: Narratives from the Early Modern Ibero-Atlantic World, 1550–1812*. Indianapolis: Hackett Pub. Co.

Mena García, María del Carmen. 1984. *La sociedad de Panamá en el siglo XVI*. Seville: CSIC.

Mendes, António de Almeida. 2008. "The Foundations of the System: A Reassessment of the Slave Trade to the Spanish Americas in the Sixteenth and Seventeenth Centuries." In *Extending the Frontiers: Essays on the New Transatlantic Slave Trade Database*, edited by David Eltis and David Richardson, 63–94. New Haven: Yale University Press.

Moutoukias, Zacarías. 1988. *Contrabando y control colonial en el siglo XVII: Buenos Aires, el Atlántico y el espacio peruano*. Buenos Aires: Centro Editor de América Latina.

Newson, Linda. 1982. "The Depopulation of Nicaragua in the Sixteenth Century." *Journal of Latin American Studies* 14 (2): 253–86.

Newson, Linda A., and Susie Minchin. 2007. *From Capture to Sale: The Portuguese Slave Trade to Spanish South America in the Early Seventeenth Century*. Leiden and Boston: Brill.

O'Malley, Gregory E., and Alex Borucki. 2017. "Patterns in the Intercolonial Slave Trade across the Americas before the Nineteenth Century." *Tempo* 23 (2): 314–38.

O'Toole, Rachel Sarah. 2012. *Bound Lives: Africans, Indians and the Making of Race in Colonial Peru*. Pittsburgh: University of Pittsburgh Press.

Pérez García, Rafael M., and Manuel Francisco Fernández Chaves. 2009. "Sevilla y La Trata Negrera Atlántica: Envíos de Esclavos Desde Cabo Verde a La América Española, 1569–1579." In *Estudios de Historia Moderna En Homenaje Al Profesor Antonio García-Baquero*, edited by León Carlos Álvarez y Santaló, 597–622. Seville: Universidad de Sevilla.

Pike, Ruth. 2007. "Black Rebels: The Cimarrons of Sixteenth-Century Panama." *The Americas: A Quarterly Review of Inter-American Cultural History* 64 (2): 243–66.

Quiroz, Alfonso W. 1985. "The Expropriation of Portuguese New Christians in Spanish America, 1635–1649." *Ibero-Amerikanisches Archiv* 11 (4): 407–65.

Radell, David. 1976. "The Indian Slave Trade and Population of Nicaragua during the Sixteenth Century." In *The Native Population of the Americas in 1492*, edited by William M. Denevan, 67–76. Madison: University of Wisconsin Press.

Restall, Matthew. 2013. *Black Middle: Africans, Mayas, and Spaniards in Colonial Yucatan*. Stanford, CA: Stanford University Press.

Schultz, Kara D. 2015. "'The Kingdom of Angola Is Not Very Far from Here': The South Atlantic Slave Port of Buenos Aires, 1585–1640." *Slavery & Abolition* 36 (3): 424–44.

———. 2017. "Interwoven: Slaving in the Southern Atlantic under the Union of the Iberian Crowns, 1580–1640." *Journal of Global Slavery* 2 (3): 248–72.

Schwartz, Stuart B. 1993. "Panic in the Indies: The Portuguese Threat to the Spanish Empire, 1640–50." *Colonial Latin American Review* 2 (1–2): 165–87.

Sherman, William L. 1979. *Forced Native Labor in Sixteenth-Century Central America*. Lincoln and London: University of Nebraska Press.

Sierra Silva, Pablo Miguel. 2017. "Portuguese 'Encomenderos de Negros' and the Slave Trade within Mexico, 1600–1675." *Journal of Global Slavery* 2 (3): 221–47.

———. 2018. *Urban Slavery in Colonial Mexico: Puebla de Los Ángeles, 1531–1706*. New York: Cambridge University Press.

Studnicki-Gizbert, Daviken. 2007. *A Nation upon the Ocean Sea: Portugal's Atlantic Diaspora and the Crisis of the Spanish Empire, 1492–1640*. Oxford and New York: Oxford University Press.

Subrahmanyam, Sanjay. 2007. "Holding the World in Balance: The Connected Histories of the Iberian Overseas Empires, 1500–1640." *American Historical Review* 112 (5): 1359–86.

Tardieu, Jean-Pierre. 2009. *Cimarrones de Panamá: la forja de una identidad afroamericana en el siglo XVI*. Frankfurt: Iberoamericana Editorial.

Vidal Ortega, Antonino. 2002. *Cartagena de Indias y la región histórica del Caribe, 1580–1640*. Seville: Escuela de Estudios Hispano-Americanos.

Vila Vilar, Enriqueta. 1976. "La Sublevación de Portugal y La Trata de Negros." *Ibero-Amerikaniches Archiv* 2 (3): 171–92.

———. 1977. *Hispanoamérica y el comercio de esclavos. Los asientos portugueses*. Seville: Escuela de Estudios Hispano-Americanos.

———. 1982. "Las ferias de Portobelo: apariencia y realidad del comercio con Indias." *Anuario de estudios americanos* 39: 275–340.

Vinson, Ben. 2001. *Bearing Arms for His Majesty: The Free Colored Militia in Colonial Mexico*. Stanford, CA: Stanford University Press.

Ward, Christopher. 1993. *Imperial Panama: Commerce and Conflict in Isthmian America, 1550–1800*. Alburquerque: University of New Mexico Press.

Wheat, David. 2011. "The First Great Waves: African Provenance Zones for the Transatlantic Slave Trade to Cartagena de Indias, 1570–1640." *Journal of African History* 52: 1–22.

———. 2016. *Atlantic Africa and the Spanish Caribbean, 1570–1640*. Chapel Hill: University of North Carolina Press.

2 "The Reader's Information" and *Norte de la Contratación*: The Translation and Circulation of Commercial Information Between Seville and London Around 1700[1]

José Manuel Díaz Blanco

Anyone walking through the busy streets of London in 1702 would find Samuel Crouch's bookshop on a corner between the streets of Pope's Head Alley and Cornhill. The business had a good reputation; before Samuel, it had already been run by Nathaniel Crouch, one of the most prestigious London booksellers of the seventeenth century (Mayer 1994, 1997). So our distracted passer-by could easily have been tempted to venture inside. And had he crossed the threshold and looked at the latest editorial releases, a newly printed book, *The Spanish Rule of Trade to the West Indies*, would have fallen into his hands. The work might well have attracted his attention. What new material did Crouch have to offer? A quick glance at the cover would tell him it was a Spanish work, originally written by José de Veitia Linaje and translated into English by Captain John Stevens (Stevens 1702). It is unlikely that he would recognize the name Veitia, but it is probable that he would be familiar with the name of Stevens, a renowned translator of the best Spanish literature, who on this occasion was presenting not a novel to the English public but a commercial treatise that promised to explain the intricacies of Spanish commercial dealings in the Indies and how products from all over Europe were introduced there. Would he take it home with him?

Let us not answer this question yet. We will see later how successful Crouch and Stevens's company was. For the moment, let us reflect on how remarkable that simple everyday scene was; an anonymous man is out walking, enters a bookshop and is interested in one of the books for sale. Many of the questions posed by our imaginary character would still make sense today – and others, too, that immediately spring to mind. What was that Spanish book that was deserving of translation? Why had it been edited in English? What did it explain about the topic? What interest did the subject raise in countries as different as Spain and England?

DOI: 10.4324/9781003168058-3

Several of these questions, and others, too, await a response. The truth is that historians have shown little interest in the book that Crouch placed on the shelves of his bookshop. And if they have, it has been to revile it. A scholar as clairvoyant as the historian Clarence H. Haring looked upon it with much suspicion. Haring was a fervent admirer of Veitia, and Stevens's version merely inspired his utter indifference. He did not dedicate a single line to it in the main text of his pioneering study on the Carrera de Indias, making space for it only in a very short footnote, with the following adjudication: "the English version by Captain John Stevens, published in London around 1700, is a much abbreviated summary of the original" (Haring 1979, XII). Nothing else? Obviously, Haring was right from one point of view. If you want to know about seventeenth-century Spanish colonial trade and you have access to the two texts, it is always preferable to work with the original rather than with the copy. That is beyond dispute. If, on the other hand, we consider that the copy has an interest per se, it is a different matter altogether. In this case, the series of questions arising from the presence of Stevens's book in London bookshops prevails. Keep asking us for answers.

The following pages will endeavor to provide answers to some of these questions; especially those relating to the introduction of products in America. As we have already stated, Stevens's book reported on Spanish trade in the Indies. But from which perspective? To what extent was it useful to the various English merchants who were trying to introduce merchandise into Spain and its overseas territories? Or what image did it project of the Spanish mercantile system in a country as economically advanced as England? The central idea to which these questions are expected to lead us is the fact that, just as the reception of European products brought about cultural adaptation and change in America, their dispatch also forced Europeans to change their points of view and learn new things.

On the Original Book in Spanish (and a Reader of Special Importance)

Let us begin by talking about the original Spanish book, the one that was later translated into English by Crouch and Stevens. It was *Norte de la Contratación de las Indias*, written by José de Veitia Linaje and published in the city of Seville in 1672. To some extent, *Norte de la Contratación* is a literary tribute to the commercial splendor of the Andalusian capital when it was the port of reference for Spanish colonial trade during the sixteenth and seventeenth centuries. On the other hand, it is also a very personal work in which the virtues of its author, Veitia, shine through, but whose limitations can also be observed (Veitia Linaje 1672).[2]

Veitia was a knight of the order of Santiago, one of the most important military orders in the country, whose members were appointed by the

Spanish monarch. A minister at the Casa de la Contratación, where he worked as a treasury officer, loss appraiser and finally as treasurer. The Casa de la Contratación was one of the institutional organizations that directed Spanish trade with the Indies and *Norte de la Contratación* dealt precisely with the labyrinthine world surrounding it.[3] Veitia, therefore, was writing about something he knew inside out, partially because of the posts he had held there, but also because, while writing his work, he had privileged access to the archives and thus the primary sources of information. It was not so much the views of merchants that were put forward in his writings, but those of the officers who supervised their activities. And he gave more space to the topic of commercial legislation than to its daily practice. Nonetheless, *Norte de la Contratación* was an extraordinary book, which students of the Carrera de Indias have always considered a masterpiece, justifiably ranking it as a classic (Montoto 1921; Solano 1982).[4]

Veitia dedicated his book to Don Gaspar de Bracamonte, Count of Peñaranda and President of the Council of the Indies. Indeed, this was the work of one politician dedicated to another politician, but it talked about trade and its instruments. It was divided into two parts, or rather into "two Books, with the hope that the first would write about everything Political, and Legislative in relation to the *Audiencia Real*, and its Courts. And in the second, military and naval matters" (Veitia Linaje 1672). Indeed, the thirty-seven chapters of the first book deal with the institutional organizational chart of trade in Seville, especially the Casa de la Contratación and the Consulado de Cargadores a Indias, while the twenty-seven chapters of the second volume report on the navies and fleets of the Carrera, the University of Seafarers and the departments within the Casa most closely linked to life at sea.

Norte de la Contratación became a favorite read for businessmen. And in such a cosmopolitan environment we must not suppose that only Spaniards liked it. It did not go unnoticed by the English merchants who settled in Andalusia at the end of the seventeenth century, representing a significant chapter in the history of English commercial expansion of the time. In effect, in the final years of the century British merchants, attracted by the Spanish markets' intrinsic value, began to gain a foothold, which they looked upon as a platform into the markets of the American viceroyalties. During this expansionist movement, they were competing with other merchants, especially the French, who were similarly striving to carve themselves a niche, thus leading to a commercial contest that contaminated the War of the Spanish Succession (Pérez Sarrión 2012). But let us not rush ahead. We will come to the conflict of the early eighteenth century in due course. Let us just state for now, that shortly after the publication of *Norte de la Contratación*, perhaps as early as the 1680s, a community of English merchants was formed in Seville to organize and appoint deputies and consuls (Díaz Blanco 2017).

Around the same time, many Englishmen also settled in Cádiz. In fact, the coastal city overlooking the bay was gaining ground on Seville as the business center of the Andalusian region. The English also formed a cohesive community there, where they held positions such as stewardships and consulates (Carrasco González 1997b, Fernández Pérez 1997). Let us take a closer look at one Englishman in particular. His name was William Hodges and he will be one of the protagonists of our little story. Hodges was born in the middle of the century, around 1645, and became related by marriage to the family of Joseph Hall, a leading London merchant. The young man, probably of humble birth, entered the world of business, where he enjoyed considerable success, amassed a personal fortune and even joined the ranks of the nobility. Shortly after his wedding, around 1680, he settled in Cádiz and remained there for almost two decades. In Cádiz, Hodges became one of the most conspicuous members of the local English community, as described by Samuel Pepys, his illustrious guest (Bédoyère 2006, 240).[5]

Guadalupe Carrasco González has followed the tracks of Hodges in Cádiz. His analysis demonstrates how Hodges built his business career by setting up successive companies that, in turn, were extensions of a parent company established in London (Carrasco González 1996, 1997a). First reports of him were in 1680 when Hodges, newly arrived in Cádiz, was accepted as a partner by Gervasio Resvy. Some years later, in 1686, Resvy returned to England and Hodges, already experienced in Andalusian trade, remained on as the principal partner. His first partner was Cristóbal Hayne, representative of the main company in London; in 1696 Ellis Terrel joined the business, followed by Henrique Bertie in 1700. At this time, although Hodges continued to be a stakeholder, his personal involvement in the business was minimal. According to Carrasco González (1997a, 50), "[T]he experience acquired by the senior partners will allow G. Hodges to return to London and leave his business dealings in Cádiz in their hands".[6] In effect, he used his wealth to financially assist the English government in 1697, in return for which he obtained a baronetcy. Shortly afterwards, around 1700 or 1701, the new nobleman returned to his homeland.[7]

Those twenty years, from 1680 to 1700, left their mark on the Englishman. In a sense, William Hodges really became the Guillermo Hodges referred to by sources in Cádiz. Spanish culture had taken hold of him, planting a seed that was to survive and bear fruit. Among other things, Hodges was a reader of *Norte de la Contratación*. This is demonstrated by various accounts. The first is somewhat vague, even mysterious, and by itself could be considered of little consequence. It refers to one of the many preserved copies of *Norte de la Contratación*, especially some striking handwritten notes that appear on the cover. One of them declared the original owner to be Spanish. It reads "De los libros de. . . " (from the books of), but the name is crossed out and can hardly be seen.

Figure 2.1 Sir William Hodges, baronet. Engraver John Smith, after Godfrey Kneller.

Source: Public domain, via Wikimedia Commons.

The blotting out was due to a change of ownership and it is the name of the new owner that we see written at the top of the cover page where "Wm" is written to the left and "Hodges" to the right.[8] Is it so very intrepid to read it as W[illia]m Hodges and suppose that it refers to that

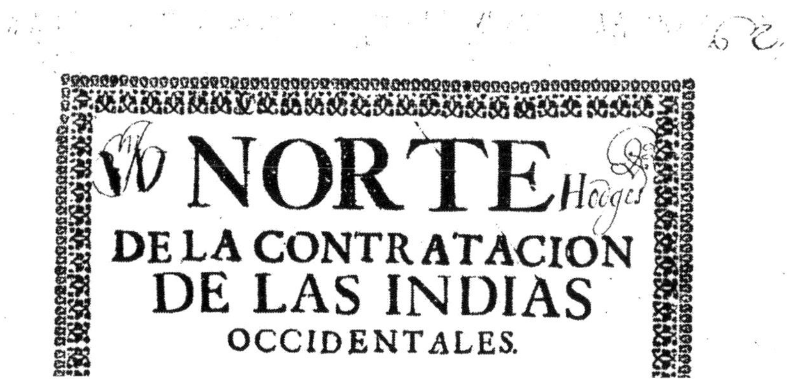

Figure 2.2 *Norte de la Contratación* (cover, detail with William Hodges's signature).

Source: Google Books.

successful merchant established in Cádiz? Without further evidence, it might seem like a hasty conclusion. However, it appears highly plausible in view of the fact that Hodges was one of the promoters of Veitia's text in England, probably the patron who inspired the book published by Crouch and Stevens in 1702, shortly after Hodges returned to England.

On the English Versions (and on the Approach of Their Particular Translator)

Just as *Norte de la Contratación* was dedicated to the Count of Peñaranda,[9] *The Spanish Rule of Trade to the West Indies* was addressed to Sir William Hodges, baronet, the very same Cádiz merchant who had returned to England in 1700 or 1701, at the outbreak of the War of the Spanish Succession.[10] His wealth and title helped him to win an impressive political race, occupying important executive positions in the Bank of England along the way and becoming an elected member of the English Parliament between 1705 and 1710. Like all influential men, Hodges received compliments, but the dedication does not seem accidental. After all, he was the main promoter of the translation of *Norte de la Contratación* and, although it cannot be demonstrated beyond all doubt, it is, however, plausible to think that he actually sponsored the work financially. If so, one could consider him the financial manager of an editorial business in which the bookseller Crouch looked after the commercial side of things and his translator, Captain Stevens, the strictly literary side.

The selection of John Stevens for the task must have seemed quite appropriate to Hodges and Crouch. From his remarkable biography spanning much of the seventeenth and eighteenth centuries, we should mention one of his great hobbies, and indeed his great passion: Spanish culture. Stevens learned Spanish, tirelessly read up on its prodigious literary tradition and was encouraged to translate many of the most significant titles, valuable for their aesthetic quality or their presumable usefulness to an English public. He was known for his translation of *El Quijote* and, enthused by the character, he also provided a version of the apocryphal sequel penned by Alonso Fernández de Avellaneda. He was interested in the picaresque genre and provided British readers with translations of *Estebanillo González*, *La Pícara Justina* and *El Buscón* by Quevedo, an author he idolized and whose satirical work he steeped himself in for a long time. He appreciated legal and historical literature, translating to English the extensive works of Brother Prudencio de Sandoval, Francisco Manuel de Melo and Juan de Mariana. Finally, and logically, he compiled a Spanish-English bilingual dictionary and wrote a Spanish grammar. This vast work, developed systematically over his lifetime, made Stevens one of the princes of British Hispanic studies and undoubtedly the best of his day.[11]

His *Norte de la Contratación* is a work that merits our attention and not the indifference or the contempt that it has sometimes received, not least because he never resigned himself to the arduous exercise of merely passing the text from one language to another. *The Spanish Rule* was not exactly a translation of *Norte de la Contratación* into English, but a version prepared for the English public. In addition to a mere linguistic transfer, this included modifying its contents. "I have not, in the Englishing of this Work, confin'd my self to the Rules of Translation", he wrote (Stevens 1702, "The Preface"). That methodology would have forced him not to eliminate or add anything and he had done both. He acknowledged having taken from the text what he did not consider beneficial or instructive, but he compensated for his audacity by introducing new materials and was fully aware of their great value.

The approach per se was not surprising. Translations in the early modern period differed frequently from what we consider usual today. When transferring a work from one language to another, it was quite natural to introduce changes that involved the elimination or addition of entire passages. The figure of the translator was far more than an expert in languages and became, much more than today, a true cultural mediator, a translator of cultures.[12] In any case, and despite what has already been said, Stevens was not an extreme example of this trend either. His changes did not substantially modify the work of Veitia. They only abbreviated it to make it more manageable, correcting the expansive baroque of the original author. Let us not forget that, fundamentally, Stevens and Veitia were addressing similar audiences and they connected well. Both wrote essentially for the cosmopolitan traders of European commerce, all integrated in worldwide business networks. The difference is that one was

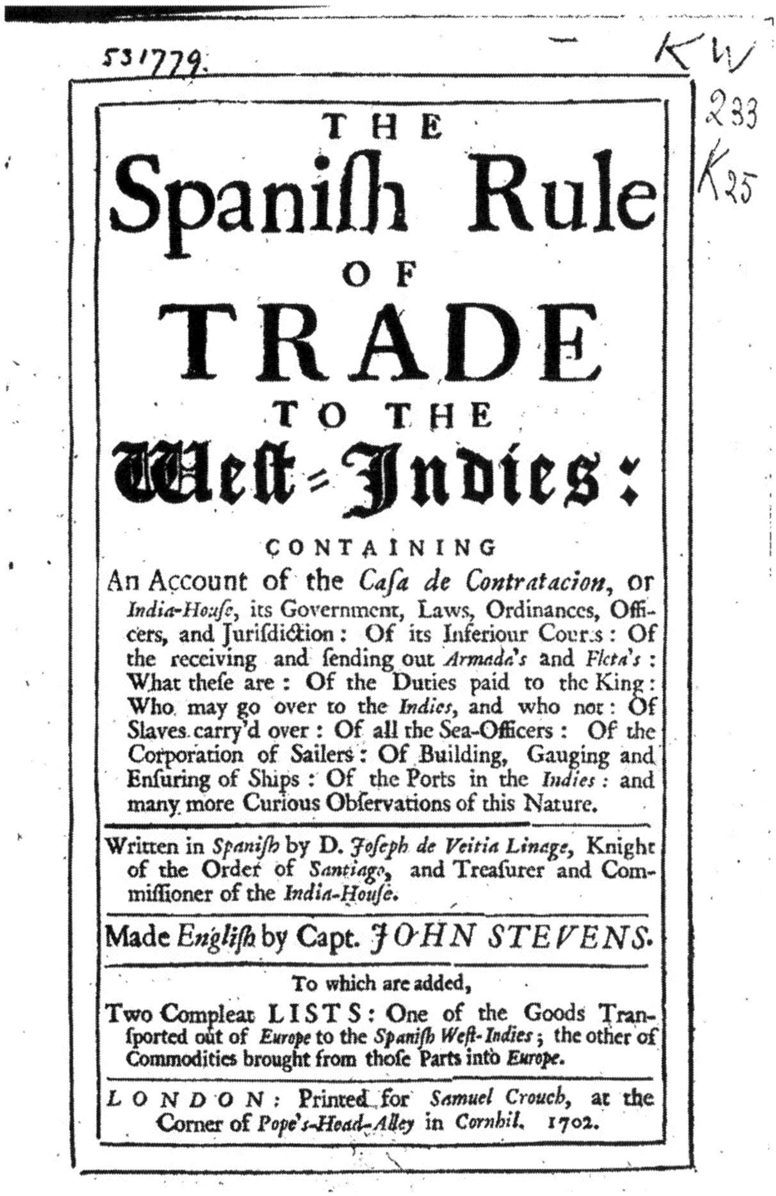

531779.

THE

Spaniſh Rule

OF

TRADE

TO THE

West-Indies:

CONTAINING

An Account of the *Caſa de Contratacion*, or *India-Houſe*, its Government, Laws, Ordinances, Officers, and Juriſdiction: Of its Inferiour Courts: Of the receiving and ſending out *Armada's* and *Fleta's*: What theſe are: Of the Duties paid to the King: Who may go over to the *Indies*, and who not: Of Slaves carry'd over: Of all the Sea-Officers: Of the Corporation of Sailers: Of Building, Gauging and Enſuring of Ships: Of the Ports in the *Indies*: and many more Curious Obſervations of this Nature.

Written in *Spaniſh* by D. *Joſeph de Veitia Linage*, Knight of the Order of *Santiago*, and Treaſurer and Commiſſioner of the *India-Houſe*.

Made *Engliſh* by Capt. *JOHN STEVENS*.

To which are added,

Two Compleat LISTS: One of the Goods Tranſported out of *Europe* to the *Spaniſh Weſt-Indies*; the other of Commodities brought from thoſe Parts into *Europe*.

LONDON: Printed for *Samuel Crouch*, at the Corner of *Pope's-Head-Alley* in *Cornhil*. 1702.

Figure 2.3 The Spanish Rule of Trade to the West Indies (cover).

Source: Google Books (original example: Koninkliijke Bibliotheek, Netherlands)

thinking directly about readers living in Spain and the other about those living in England. Of course, at times some of these were one and the same, as we have seen in Hodges's biography.

Changes became evident even in the title, as you will have already observed. The baroque overtones of the original Spanish version – a metaphor at several levels that presented the book as a compass to guide readers through the wide sea of colonial trade (Veitia Linaje 1672, "Al lector") – was reduced to the sober, less literary, but much clearer *The Spanish Rule of Trade to the West Indies*. The new title was presented in capital letters at the top of a cover abundant in information. Without even opening the book, you could learn a lot about it by reviewing that cover. In the first instance, much of its contents were itemized thanks to a summary that contained:

> An Account of the *Casa de Contratacion*, or *India-House*, its Government, Laws, Ordinances, Officers, and Jurisdiction: Of its Inferiour Courts: Of the receiving and sending out *Armada*'s and *Flota*'s: What these are: Of the Dutes paid to the King: Who may go over to the *Indies*, and who not: Of Slaves carry'd over: Of all the Sea-Officers: Of the Corporation of Sailers. Of Building, Gauging and Ensuring of Ships: Of the Ports in the *Indies*: and many more Curious Observations of this Nature.

Next, the cover informed readers of the work's double authorship. Veitia was presented as the original author, highlighting his noble status as knight of Santiago and his knowledge of the subject as "Treasurer and Commissioner of the India-House". Below, Stevens was recognized as having transferred the text to English, the author of a version that was advertised for sale in Crouch's downtown bookshop containing additional material.

Although not made explicit on the cover, the first addition was the dedication to Hodges, obviously absent in *Norte de la Contratación*. It is characteristically respectful of the conventions of the genre. It starts out with generic reasoning, reminding readers that it had been the privilege of books to come into the world under the protection of powerful patrons. The great princes had welcomed them, but they were not the only ones to show their generosity. "True Worth is not confined to Palaces, nor is Merit only to be found in Courts" was a direct allusion to Hodges, who had surpassed many men of lesser status in charity, generosity and affability, both in Spain and in England, achieving in return the recognition of his noble title that he had earned so long ago. He signed those obsequious words "the most obedient and most humble servant of Hodges, John Stevens" (Stevens 1702, "Epistle Dedicatory").

This was followed by another addition, a preface in which Stevens presented *The Spanish Rule*, explaining the guidelines he had followed to make it attractive to the British reader. He began by alluding to his surprise on discovering the limited bibliography in English on the subject. Many books had been published on the Discovery, the Conquest and the expeditions to the New World, but none delved deeper into the issue of commerce, "a Point of so great Concern" (Stevens 1702, "The Preface"). The situation ought not to be attributed to any secret drive by the Spaniards, argued Stevens, against the prejudices of fairly widespread public opinion. On the contrary, Spaniards had written extensively about their American dominions, without excluding mercantile matters. Of all the Spanish literature on trade with the Indies, Veitia's work was by far the best. It was time to praise *Norte de la Contratación* without ambiguity. Stevens praised the author again for his personal quality and his specific professional experience, and now related in greater detail the contents of the original work. A good way to appreciate the thematic richness of *Norte de la Contratación* is to read the words of this English reader of the 1700s, who did not hide his admiration for the enormous range of topics it managed to address.

As befits all true readers, sincere admiration did not rule out useful criticism. There were many things from the original version that would have no place in the English version of *Norte de la Contratación* and, as we have seen, Stevens had no intention of hiding this. He recognized that, in addition to translating, he had added and deleted many passages, and he explained what he had done. The title was an obvious example. Despite its conceptual complexity, it could be translated reasonably well: *The North Pole, or Star of the Trade to the Indies*. So the change had not been imposed by technical need, but was introduced deliberately. Later, Stevens had no scruples when it came to repeating similar alterations. In his own words, he had summarized Veitia's text, leaving "what was solid and material, without swelling the Volume to a needless bulk with those things that are no way Beneficial or Instructive" (Stevens 1702, "The Preface"). In return, as if seeking to compensate his public for the lost passages, he announced the occasional insertion of new material to fill the gaps from the Spanish version.

Stevens knew the risks of such a procedure. It was no simple task to deal so aggressively with such a complicated text as *Norte de la Contratación*, with all its twists and turns and so difficult to understand even in its Spanish version. In part, he justified his audacity by acknowledging that all his modifications had received "the Approbation of Persons most knowing in these Affairs". This clarification is important. Stevens did not act alone. He communicated with experts in the field, although unfortunately he does not provide us with their names, "not having their Consent to make them Publick" (Stevens 1702, "The Preface"). If this is not a literary device devised by Stevens, then it would appear that the experts wanted to remain anonymous. It can be assumed that these were businessmen, merchants, financiers or administration officials: in short, people from the business world of London with possible political connections. We could shrug our shoulders and accept that their true identity can never be known. But, evidently, that modest reference led to the social circles of William Hodges, if not to Hodges himself.

In fact, those discreet learned scholars received compliments from Stevens comparable to those contained in the dedication to Hodges. They were "Persons of Worth, Integrity and Knowledge, who wanted to give a more accurate Account of these Affairs." They had provided Stevens with all kinds of information and, most importantly, they had placed at his disposal a document worthy of the greatest attention, above all in terms of reporting the goods introduced by Europeans in America. Stevens described it as "a most Exact and Compleat List of all the Commodities transported from all Parts of Europe to the West-Indies; as also of such as those Parts furnish us with "(Stevens 1702, "The Preface").

To the delight of the reader, Stevens reproduced that very complete and accurate list following the preface of his edition. It was divided into two parts; the first detailed the European products that were sent to America and the second, the American products that were brought to Europe. At first glance, the list of American imports to Europe is shorter and does not offer a catalog of regional and local geographic references as consistent and detailed as the former. Whoever wrote that document knew Europe better than America. In fact, it is probable that the author did not know America, but was acquainted with the most significant merchandise that came from there to the English coasts: pearls, emeralds, gold, silver, dye products such as *grana* (cochineal), wood, sugar, cocoa, tobacco, ginger and sarsaparilla. In general, these were precious materials and raw materials for manufacturing, with the inevitable reference to the "pieces of eight", the famous silver coins craved worldwide (Stevens 1702, "The Preface").[13]

"The Compleat List of all the Commodities Transported from all Parts of Europe to the West-Indies" reproduces a range of goods including raw materials and local agricultural products in addition to a very large quantity of manufactured products or exotic foods and condiments, especially Asian spices. On account of its geographic precision, the Compleat List is one of the most relevant documents in demonstrating how the Spanish Carrera de Indias had become a business for a large part of Europe (Everaert 1973, García Fuentes 1980, Oliva Melgar 2007). Northern Europe's commercial and manufacturing superiority was evident. An accelerated demand for goods from the American market came largely from France, the Hanseatic League, Flanders, the Netherlands and England. The England where *Norte de la Contratación* was translated was sending a varied range of goods to the other side of the Atlantic. Textile goods were the flagship of the European secondary sector; however, along with traditional textiles such as silks or twills, there were other more innovative fabrics, such as the *chinescos*, English products that imitated oriental tastes, and calicos, which came from India. England was not only involved in manufacturing; like the Netherlands, it forwarded to America what the East India Company brought from Asia. The Compleat List drew the profile of a world united by maritime routes, where England moved with great virtuosity. It was the seventeenth-century world in which Hodges had been educated.

The Compleat List covered one of the weak points in *Norte de la Contratación*, thus filling a gap in the Spanish version, which spoke only sparingly of something as essential as merchandise, but on which Stevens could give the English public an essential and very complete perspective from Cádiz. Those responsible for *The Spanish Rule* deemed it necessary to bring the text closer to the sphere of merchants and distance it from legal compilations, and this addition reveals their accurate assessment of the strengths and weaknesses of *Norte de la Contratación*. While the dedication to Hodges replaced the dedication to Peñaranda, the Compleat List appeared where Veitia had placed an extensive and fascinating preface (Veitia Linaje 1672, "Al lector"). In these masterful pages, Veitia explained the intention of his work by firstly referring to its title followed by an account of the research carried out in the archives of the Casa de la Contratación, specifying the sources he had handled and the abbreviations that he used when quoting them in the book's marginal notes, where he detailed the location of all the sources that he had used. Veitia's work was exemplary with an impressive modern-style methodology, but the pragmatic Stevens wondered if any Englishman would ever have the opportunity to consult the documents housed in the Casa. Since he could not foresee the existence of the Archivo de Indias, created almost a hundred years later (Heredia Herrera 1992; González García 1995), he concluded that it would be preferable to eliminate the convoluted literary references. In effect, the exceptional marginal notes of *Norte de la Contratación* disappeared in *The Spanish Rule*; or rather, they were transformed, since Stevens both adopted and adapted the concept of marginal notes, using them to provide glossaries of terms that would assist in reading the contents of the main text.

Having eliminated the cumbersome cluster of paratexts (censures, licenses, laudatory sonnets and others), *The Spanish Rule* selectively reproduced the dual structure of *Norte de la Contratación*. The changes mainly affected the first part, of which only twenty-four chapters of the original thirty-seven were incorporated, while all twenty-seven chapters of the second were included. However, that does not mean that the second part appears in its entirety, as published by Veitia, because Stevens eliminated certain passages of the original as he thought fit, thus reducing the length of the chapters. Presumably, like the additions, the removal of sections was not the sole responsibility of the translator. Surely, Crouch, Hodges and those discreet gentlemen who had offered him the missing information had also indicated what was redundant in the text. In effect, it is evident that many of the deleted passages would have had little meaning in an English book. What did English society want to know about the chapel of the Casa de la Contratación? Or what interest could there be in a list of names of all the presidents, official judges and learned judges from the sixteenth century until 1670? Evidently, none.

Whoever cross-checked both texts could easily devise the criteria. However, at the end of the considerably reduced last chapter, Stevens systematically explained the fragmentation patterns of his version of *Norte de la Contratación*. The last warning to readers before closing the book was the following:

> Much more the Author adds in this Chapter, but the greatest part has been already mention'd under the proper Heads; other things there are of no moment, some foreign from the matter, and several instances of what has been done, which was never a Rule, not practiced now. I have thought not to enlarge too much, and therefore omit all that may not be of some benefit or satisfaction.
>
> (Stevens 1702, 367)

Avoiding duplication in terms of topics, avoiding what was not important for an English reader, eliminating what was valid in 1672 but no longer applicable in 1702, making the volume more manageable . . . these were all sensible reasons, which point to Stevens's collaboration with people familiar with colonial trade.

Stevens's book was thus shorter than the original, as stated by Haring (1979, XII), but nonetheless it is a remarkable work from several perspectives. One has to recognize its merits, with a second and a third edition published shortly after the first, around 1711 and again in 1720. The change of title in the 1711 edition can make identification difficult, but it is practically the same work. The volume that Crouch placed that year in the windows of his bookstore was called *The Rule Establish'd in Spain for the Trade in the West Indies*, but it was virtually the same *The Spanish Rule of Trade to the West Indies* of the first and third editions. There were minimal changes to the cover and it had a new prologue "to the reader" (in addition to the original preface, which remained in place). The addition was just a couple of paragraphs, but it was strong in its praise of the work, underlining the veneration that the original Veitia enjoyed in Spain: "A work exceedingly esteem'd in Spain, and is the General Guide of all Spanish Traders to those Parts, as being a genuine Summary of all the Laws that that wise Council in Two Hundred Years time thought fit to establish for the better Conduct of this profitable Trade" (Stevens 1711, "To the Reader"). Now the English reader could enjoy this marvel. And a useful marvel it was.

In addition to the multiple editions, there are other indications of the positive impact of Stevens's work on English society. Some were of

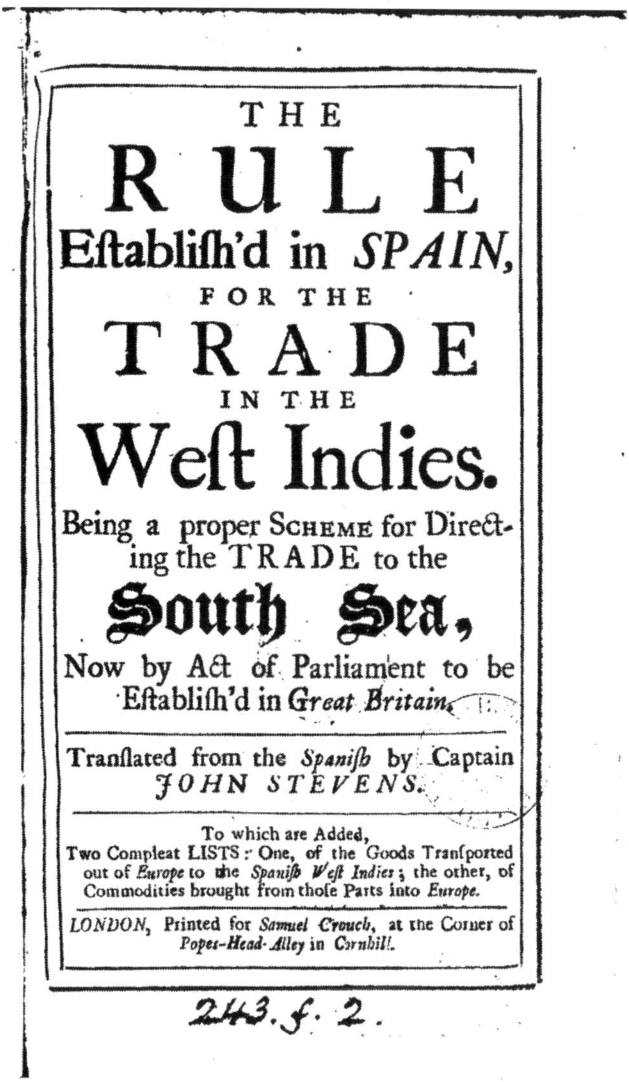

THE

RULE

Eſtabliſh'd in *SPAIN*,

FOR THE

TRADE

IN THE

Weſt Indies.

Being a proper SCHEME for Direct-ing the TRADE to the

South Sea,

Now by Act of Parliament to be Eſtabliſh'd in *Great Britain*.

Tranſlated from the *Spaniſh* by Captain *JOHN STEVENS*.

To which are Added, Two Compleat LISTS: One, of the Goods Tranſported out of *Europe* to the *Spaniſh Weſt Indies*; the other, of Commodities brought from thoſe Parts into *Europe*.

LONDON, Printed for *Samuel Crouch*, at the Corner of *Popes-Head-Alley* in *Cornhill*.

Figure 2.4 The Rule Establish'd in Spain (cover).

Source: Google Books (Original: Bodleian Library)

dubious merit, and in present-day terminology would be called plagiarism. In 1712 a book in two volumes written by Edward Cooke appeared simultaneously in three London bookshops, under the title *A Voyage to the South Sea and Round the World*. Cooke was one of the best English mariners of the early eighteenth century and his book narrated the tale of the Woodes Rogers privateering expedition. The expedition sailed from Bristol in 1708 on the *Duke* and *Duchess*, and did not return to England until three years later (Cooke 1712; Williams 1997). Cooke saw a very varied amount of land. Nevertheless, despite the direct knowledge he acquired, the material he used was to a large extent copied from others, often without mentioning the original author. For example, when Cooke narrated his experiences in Chile,[14] he recalled that there was a beautiful (rather embellished) map of Santiago in *Histórica relación del reino de Chile* (1646) by Alonso de Ovalle. Without compunction, he copied and incorporated it into his work, without the slightest mention of the Creole author and the Roman publishing house which had participated in its creation (Cooke 1712, I, 85). He did the same with the Compleat List, the most valuable addition in the English version of *Norte de la Contratación*. He included it in the introduction to the second volume, remaining utterly silent with regard to any literary debt, but implicitly acknowledging the valuable interest of the information it contained.[15] And this is precisely what the present article is all about: information as a point of interest for trade and politics. Let us conclude by reflecting on this central issue, towards which we have been guided by the apparently insignificant fact of the arrival of a new title to Crouch's London bookshop.

Why Was *Norte de la Contratación* Translated in England at the Beginning of the Eighteenth Century?

John Stevens himself provided us with a good answer to this question. He laconically mentioned that in *The Spanish Rule* he had put "what I thought necessary for the Reader's Information" (Stevens 1702, "The Preface"). This is the key point. Stevens could not have said it better using fewer words: "The Reader's Information". Two really fundamental concepts are clearly stated here: 1) a reader whom he has clearly defined as the recipient of his work and 2) information as a fundamental good that he is providing. The purpose behind converting *Norte de la Contratación* into *The Spanish Rule* is to provide specific information to a specific reader interested in American trade and, especially, in the introduction of products in the New World.

Stevens had a reader in mind: a *model reader*, if we apply the language of semiological analysis (Eco 1999). This is a reader who did not necessarily present restrictive profiles. In fact, the case may well have been quite the opposite. One of the values that Stevens saw in Veitia's work was that it was not directed exclusively at merchants, but offered a legal perspective that could be useful to many other people.[16] However, it is evident that the model reader of the English *Norte* was the prosperous businessman who had met with considerable success in the islands. Stevens, Crouch and Hodges were preparing this work in the hope that it would interest English merchants. If that model reader was not explicitly addressed in *The Spanish Rule*, his identity was revealed in the new prologue of *The Rule Establish'd*. We must bear in mind that it was a small page addressed "to the reader", that same reader for whose information the *Norte de la Contratación* had been translated. Well then, that reader immediately transmutes into the fascinating "Adventurers in the South Sea Trade", before long remembered more soberly as "our own Merchants" (Stevens 1711: "To the Reader"). That publishing company, created by merchants, was targeted at merchants.

Crouch's bookshop was in the heart of the City of London, the economic heart of the country. After the catastrophic fire of 1666, London surfaced from its ashes with all the vigor of the prevailing prosperity, expanding considerably on both banks of the Thames, beyond the city walls that had delimited the central outline of the city since medieval times. Cornhill Street was one of the traditional divisions of London, forming part of one of the routes leading directly to the square of St. Paul's Cathedral. Much money changed hands in and around Cornhill, especially in the famous Royal Exchange, the London merchants' market, and in the Bank of England. It was at places like this where the city's merchants stopped, and Hodges among them. The doors to Crouch's bookstore opened at the corner between Cornhill and Pope's Head Alley, in a prime location right in front of the Royal Exchange.[17] Obviously, Hodges was well acquainted with the business that traded with the best products of the human mind. And there were others like him. It had to be a unique specialist bookstore for merchants, the ideal place to market a book on matters of trade that addressed their interests. *The Spanish Rule* could sell well; Hodges and Crouch, immersed in the publishing world, were fully conscious of this. They saw their opportunity and, in fact, the book ran to a second and a third edition in rapid succession. As expected, the model reader proved to be an effective buyer.

A close examination of the interest of English entrepreneurs in this book leads us to political and economic factors alike. Let us start with the first, which were linked to the international situation in the early eighteenth century. Much of the international agenda of the day revolved around the Spanish monarchy after the outbreak of the War of the Spanish Succession, in 1701. As we know, the initial trigger of the conflict was the question of succession, but many other issues came into play as it developed, including the evolution of Spanish colonial trade, which was of paramount importance for the European powers.

During the War of the Spanish Succession, England and France disputed the balance between their shares of influence on the Carrera de Indias. Getting involved in the conflict was a complicated issue. What gains could be achieved from taking a step forward? In both countries, attempts were made to muster currents of public opinion favorable to intervention. In the case of France, Ana Álvarez López (2008) has demonstrated how the

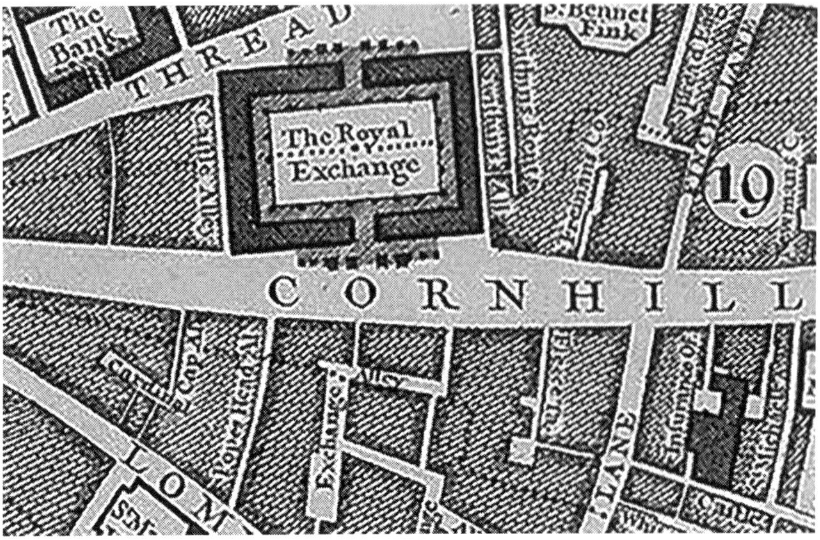

Figure 2.5 Historical map of London by John Rocque (1746, detail of Cornhill–Pope's Head Alley, facing the Royal Exchange).

Source: Public domain, via Wikimedia Commons.

"fabrication" of an "imaginary" in relation to Spain included the affirmation of the rights of Louis XIV to the Spanish throne and the consequent benefits to all of such a conquest. In such sensitive circumstances, a book like *The Spanish Rule* could bring its influence to bear on public opinion, as the *Gazette* or the *Mercure Galant* did in Paris. It had the ability to reinforce the convictions of those who supported entering the war and to subtly overcome resistance from those who held a less favorable view. It was a wake-up call for English involvement in the conflagration that was to divide Europe in the dawn of the eighteenth century. Otherwise, France could end up with too many slices of the pie.

The political background becomes even clearer in *The Rule Establish'd in Spain*. A link to contemporary events should not be assumed in this second case; this is explicitly stated in the work and is related to the founding of the South Sea Company, soon to become a catalyst for the commercial advantage obtained by Great Britain during the Treaty of Utrecht. The company was established in 1711 and in 1713 it benefited from the famous *Asiento de Negros* and the *Navío de Permiso* (Finucane 2016). None of the numerous privileges it enjoyed proved sufficient to avert its resounding crash just a few years later; however, this circumstance was hardly predictable at the outset when the company placed itself right at the heart of English public debate with the publication of different literary works on the issue. With a remarkably modern socio-economic outlook, the editorial landscape became animated in parallel with the political scenario.

One of the outstanding titles was the aforementioned volume by Edward Cooke, written "at this time, when a Trade to the South Sea is so much talk'd of, [and] all Persons are desirous to know wherein that Trade will consist". Similar intentions can be found in *An Account to the Trade in India*, also published in 1711 and sold exclusively by none other than the indefatigable bookseller Samuel Crouch. While the identity of its author, one Charles Lockyer, is somewhat obscure, the work itself clearly depicts the political and economic personality of the United Kingdom at this time, characterized by a marked commercial drive towards Asia and America. Lockyer justified his work, "considering, that Trading Voyages in India are much talk'd of", and very little understood in England" (Lockyer 1711). An invaluable testimony: in England there was much talk about Asian trade, especially in relation to the founding of the South Sea Company, but direct knowledge of the subject was limited. Trade in particular and the economy in general required technical and contextual knowledge, but that know-how could be acquired by learning from others. From whom? Well, from the Dutch, for example, seasoned and famous merchants inside and outside Europe. Lockyer's work included *An Account of the Management of the Dutch in their Affairs in India.* After so many wars at sea, this English willingness to learn from their competitors is somewhat surprising. Nothing could have been further removed from the English alleged cultural insularity.[18]

It was not the Dutch model that Hodges, Crouch and Stevens proposed to their English readers, but the Spanish model. It is interesting to underline this aspect. In England, the Spanish monarchy had been fiercely criticized. The writer, Thomas Mun, who exemplified English economic thought, conveyed the typically negative image of Spaniards. However, the broad and ever-changing British public debate accommodated radically opposing views. As Hispanophiles, Hodges and his team came close to influencing the political *status quo* in 1711 by offering Spanish trade regulations as "a proper Scheme for directing the [English] Trade to the South Sea, Now by Act of Parliament to be Establish'd in Great Britain". What was already established in Spain could be a guide for what was about to be established in the United Kingdom. In a fine display of common sense, the introduction explained why. "As Experience is the Best Mistress, Wise Men will never refuse the Assistance of those, who having been so long time Employ'd in a Business which Interest oblig'd them to Cultivate in the best manner" (Stevens 1711). Here the "Wise Men" were the English and those with experience, the Spaniards. And English wisdom consisted in recognizing that one could and should learn from the Spanish experience in colonial trade.

In any case, the main reason for its success in England was that *Norte de la Contratación* taught the English how that Spanish trade operated.

Whether more or less in favor of its structure, if the English wanted to take part in it, they had to be acquainted with it. And they wanted to become part of it. During the eighteenth century, the British community in Cádiz and Seville grew and strengthened, as did their participation in its trade. So, if you put yourself in the shoes of an English merchant of the time, it is easy to realize the importance of the information offered by Veitia. Although Stevens's work was a condensed version of the original, it included everything that could interest businessmen. The same practical knowledge that Veitia had shared with his Spanish readers could now be enjoyed by their English counterparts. They also needed it, because they were involved in the very same business. The Carrera de Indias was a transnational enterprise. All western Europe participated in it, so it was not only necessary for Spaniards to be well acquainted with it. The English did very well in translating Veitia, since the knowledge he imparted was otherwise difficult to acquire. The best know-how came, of course, from practical experience. But a literary apprenticeship of the kind offered by *Norte de la Contratación* was also enormously valuable. In fact, in the seventeenth century the idea that businessmen should receive considerable theoretical training for the performance of a trade was already widely accepted.

The English translated *Norte de la Contratación* so that anyone who understood the language could acquire certain basic professional notions on subjects as undeniably necessary as the legal requirements when trading with Spanish America, what taxes should be paid, which ports had a leading role in trade routes, what was the formation of the convoys where the merchandise would travel, how the navy protecting merchants operated, what legal guarantees covered mercantile activities, who were the royal officials who supervised and organized it and so forth. Obviously, this was the information that any Englishman needed to know in order to *understand* that trading system and, accordingly, to *participate* in it formally or *circumvent* its rules (should that be what they wished to do).

So the businessman who paused in front of Crouch's bookstore on that day would not only have good reasons for looking at Stevens's work, but also for buying it; he would find valuable information for any reader eager to learn, at least until the business model defined in it ceased to exist, removed by the Bourbon reforms of the eighteenth century, which first mimicked European mercantilist policies with the introduction of the scheme of privileged companies before evolving into what was called the era of Free Trade. Therefore, it is not surprising that the last English edition of *Norte de la Contratación* was issued in 1720. As the work became increasingly outdated, it was no longer interesting and useful.

We come to a close echoing the classic thoughts of John H. Elliott, who contended that while Europe profoundly changed American culture, one must also look at how America changed European culture (Elliott 2015).

To a large extent, this was achieved thanks to the role exercised by the Spanish monarchy as a platform for the circulation of knowledge on a global scale, as recently underscored by Bartolomé Yun-Casalilla (2017). In this book on the American cultural processes of acceptance, adaptation or rejection generated by the arrival of European or Asian products, it seemed appropriate to me to emphasize that the shipment of these goods also generated learning processes among Europeans. Moreover, in relation to Spanish- American markets, it was not only the Spanish who had to face these changes, but merchants from other countries too, including the English.

This short tale of the English translations of *Norte*, apart from providing us with invaluable details about merchants and their tastes, serves above all to exemplify the processes of learning and adaptation necessary to participate in the trade and navigation of the Carrera de Indias. Such processes took place thanks to the intense flow of information and knowledge that characterized the era. What else but this was afoot the day that Crouch placed Veitia's work in his shop window and a determined London reader took notice of it?

Notes

1. Project "Religión, extranjería e identidad europea en la Monarquía Hispánica durante el siglo XVIII: estudio comparativo y análisis de las pervivencias y contrastes" (PGC2018–093799-B-100)" ["Religion, foreigners and European identity in the Hispanic Monarchy during the 18th century: a comparative study and analysis of the survivals and contrasts"], financed by the Spanish Ministry of Science, Innovation and Universities and the European Regional Development Fund (ERDF).
2. Two new printed editions were produced in the twentieth century: Buenos Aires, Comisión Argentina de Fomento Interamericano, 1945, and Madrid, Instituto de Estudios Fiscales, 1981. The latter is a facsimile of the original seventeenth-century edition, many examples of which can now be consulted online. Therefore, we are quoting Veitia's text with its original pagination.
3. While there is no complete monography on this important institution, quite an extensive bibliography exists on the topic, including works by Vila Vilar, Acosta Rodríguez and González Rodríguez (2004), De Carlos Boutet (2003), Iglesias Rodríguez (2017). On the treasury of the Casa, which Veitia headed for more than twenty years, see Donoso Anes (1996).
4. The idea that Veitia's work constitutes a classic is expressed with particular enthusiasm and clarity by García Baquero González (1992).
5. In Pepys's words, "my worthy friends Sir William Hodges with my Lady and family".
6. Nonetheless, as the author explains, the latter company went bankrupt immediately. There is no evidence pointing to the exact relationship between the bankruptcy in 1700 and Hodges's return to London. Did he go back because the company had gone bankrupt or did the company go bankrupt because its main partner was missing? Obviously, such a detailed question is not of major importance, although it could have a certain relevance in the context of understanding why he decided to sponsor the English translation of *Norte*, as we shall see.

7. The title was territorially linked to Middlesex; in 1714 it passed from William to Joseph Hodges and on the death of the latter in 1722 it became extinct: www.leighrayment.com/baronetage.htm
8. A digitized version is available on Google Books: https://books.google.es/ (consulted on 20 May 2018).
9. D. Gaspar de Bracamonte, Count of Peñaranda, was one of the most important politicians in seventeenth-century Spain. He served as diplomatic representative in Münster and as viceroy of Naples, and finally presided over several councils in the court of Madrid. Paradoxically, as happened frequently with Spanish politicians of that time, there is no monographic biography on him, but he is quoted extensively in a wide bibliography on Spain at that time. For an excellent example of this, see Valladares 2016.
10. This duplicity can be perceived in the limited bibliography on Hodges. For Spanish scholars, Hodges is fundamentally a merchant. For British scholars, he is above all a nobleman dedicated to politics, coming from the business bourgeoisie. See the excellent biographical synopsis made by Eveline Cruickshanks and D. W. Hayton at www.historyofparliamentonline.org/ (consulted on 15 May 2018)
11. His biographies situate it between around 1662 and 1726. See Steiner (1970), Santamaría (1992), Murphy (1999 and 2004), Fernández y Cormier (2008). For further details, see the excellent entry on the subject in the *Biblioteca Virtual de la Filología Española*, directed by Manuel Alvar Ezquerra: www.bvfe.es/autor/10730-stevens-john.html. (consulted on 15 May 2018).
12. Studies abound defining the translator as an intercultural mediator. This stems from the so-called cultural turn in translation studies, produced by outstanding works since the 1990s, as discussed in depth in Bassnett 2011/12. For the era of Veitia and Stevens, see Burke 2006.
13. For an updated extensive presentation on the circulation of American goods in the modern era, see Aram and Yun-Casalilla 2014. American gold and silver are American globalized products par excellence, with a broad bibliography ranging from Hamilton 2000 [1934] to more recent contributions in the framework of global history, such as Ibarra and Hausberger 2014.
14. I should like to point out that Cooke's Chilean testimony and in particular his account of the islands of Juan Fernández inspired Daniel Defoe to imagine the famous story of the shipwrecked Robinson Crusoe.
15. This example of the document is reproduced in Cooke (1712, II, X-XVII). Walker (1979, 292–298), reproduces the document based on Cooke's version.
16. This assessment was totally correct, by the way. Veitia was fully cognizant that anyone – not only leading businessmen – who had suffered a setback in their dealings with the Carrera de Indias could sue and plead for justice before the Casa de la Contratación.
17. This is stated in the works marketed by Crouch, beginning with those discussed here, on whose title pages we read: "London: Printed for Samuel Crouch at the Corner of Popes-Head-Alley in Cornhill" (figure 5).
18. Another example of this attitude in the work of Lockyer can be found on the last page, where the printing press included a potentially interesting announcement to the type of readers who had acquired it: "Advertisement. Merchant's Accounts, or the true Italian Method of Book keeping, by Double Entry, approv'd to be the best, and practiced as such by the most eminent Merchants and Exchangers in Europe, are Taught, and the Truth of

each Entry demonstrated. By Charles Snell, Accomptant, at the Free-Writing School, in Foster-Lane, London; Who teaches Young Gentlemen to Write all the usual Hands, and Arithmetick; also Boards such as desire it at his House". While one could learn from the Dutch how to do business with Asians, one could learn lessons in accounting from the Italians.

Bibliography

Acosta Rodríguez, Adolfo, Vila Vilar, Enriqueta y González Rodríguez, Adolfo, coords. 2004. *La Casa de la Contratación y la navegación entre España y las Indias*. Seville: CSIC, Universidad de Sevilla.

Álvarez López, Ana. 2008. *La fabricación de un imaginario. Los embajadores de Luis XIV y España*. Madrid: Cátedra.

Aram, Bethany and Bartolomé Yun-Casalilla, eds. 2014. *Global Goods and The Spanish Empire, 1492–1824. Circulation, Resistance and Diversity*. London: Palgrave Macmillan.

Bassnett, Susan. 2011–2012. "The Translator as Cross-Cultural Mediator." In *The Oxford Handbook of Translation Studies*, edited by Kirsten Malmkjær and Kevin Windle. https://doi.org/10.1093/oxfordhb/9780199239306.013.0008

Bédoyère, Guy de la, ed. 2006. *The Letters of Samuel Pepys, 1656–1703*. Woodbridge: The Boydell Press.

Burke, Peter. 2006. *Lenguas y comunidades en la Europa moderna*. Madrid: Akal.

Carrasco González, María Guadalupe. 1996. *Los instrumentos del comercio colonial en el Cádiz del siglo XVII (1650–1700)*. Madrid: Banco de España.

———. 1997a. *Comerciantes y casas de negocios en Cádiz (1650–1700)*. Cádiz: Universidad.

———. 1997b. "La colonia británica de Cádiz entre 1650 y 1720." In *Monarquía, imperio y pueblos en la España moderna. Vol. I*, edited by Antonio Mestre, Pablo Fernández Albaladejo, and Enrique Giménez López, 331–42. Alicante: Universidad de Alicante.

Cooke, Edward. 1712. *A Voyage to the South Sea and Round the World*. London: B. Lintot y R. Gosling.

De Carlos Boutet, Guiomar, coord. 2003. *España y América: un océano de negocios*. Madrid: Sociedad Estatal Quinto Centenario.

Díaz Blanco, José Manuel. 2017. "Las naciones extranjeras en la Sevilla moderna: ¿hacia un modelo de organización territorial?" In *Economía, política y sociedad en Iberoamérica (siglos XVI-XIX). Actuales líneas de investigación histórica*, edited by Adrián García Torres, Rosa Tribaldos Soriano and Mar García Arenas, 149–68. Alicante: Universidad de Alicante.

Donoso Anes, Rafael. 1996. *Una contribución a la historia de la contabilidad. Análisis de las prácticas contables desarrolladas por la tesorería de la Casa de la Contratación de Sevilla (1503–1717)*. Seville: Universidad de Sevilla.

Eco, Umberto. 1999. *Lector in fabula. La cooperación interpretativa en el texto narrativo*. Barcelona: Lumen.

Elliott, John H. 2015. *El viejo mundo y el nuevo*. Madrid: Alianza.

Everaert, John. 1973. *Le commerce international et colonial des firmes flamandes à Cadix, 1670–1700*. Bruges: De Tempel.

Fernández, Heberto y Monique Cormier. 2008. "A Forgotten Translator and Lexicographer of the Eighteenth Century, Captain John Stevens." *Romanistik in Geschichte und Gegenwart* 14 (1): 73–98.
Fernández Pérez, Paloma. 1997. *El rostro familiar de la metrópoli. Redes de parentesco y lazos mercantiles en Cádiz, 1700–1812*. Madrid: Siglo XXI.
Finucane, Adrian. 2016. *The Temptations of Trade. Britain, Spain and the Struggle for Empire*. Philadelphia: University of Pennsylvania Press.
García Baquero González, Antonio. 1992. *La Carrera de Indias. Suma de la contratación y océano de negocios*. Seville: Algaida.
García Fuentes, Lutgardo. 1980. *El comercio español con América, 1650–1700*. Seville: Escuela de Estudios Hispano-Americanos.
González García, Pedro, coord. 1995. *Archivo General de Indias*. Madrid: Lunwerg.
Haring, Clarence H. 1979. *Comercio y navegación entre España y las Indias en la época de los Habsburgos*. México: Fondo de Cultura Económica.
Heredia Herrera, Antonia. 1992. *La Lonja de Mercaderes. El cofre para un tesoro singular*. Seville: Diputación.
Ibarra, Antonio, and Bernd Hausberger, coords. 2014. *Oro y plata en los inicios de la economía global. De las minas a la moneda*. México: El Colegio de México.
Iglesias Rodríguez, Juan José, coord. 2017. "Dossier: Tricentenario del traslado a Cádiz de la Casa de la Contratación (1717–2017)." *Studia Historica. Historia Moderna* 39 (2): 19–219.
Lockyer, Charles. 1711. *An Account to the Trade in India*. London: Samuel Crouch.
Mayer, Robert. 1994. "Nathaniel Crouch, Bookseller and Historian: Popular Historiography and Cultural Power in Late Seventeenth-Century England." *Eighteenth-Century Studies* 27 (3): 391–419.
———. 1997. *History and the Early English Novel. Matters of Fact from Bacon to Defoe*. Cambridge: Cambridge University Press.
Montoto, Santiago. 1921. *Don José de Veitia Linaje y su libro "Norte de la Contratación de las Indias*. Seville: Centro Oficial de Estudios Americanistas.
Murphy, Martin. 1999. "A Jacobite Antiquary in Grub Street: Captain John Stevens (c. 1662–1726)." *Recusant History* 24: 437–54.
———. 2004. "John Stevens." In *Oxford Dictionary of National Biography*, Vol. 52, 561–62. Oxford: Oxford University Press.
Oliva Melgar, José María. 2007. *El monopolio de Indias en el siglo XVII y la economía andaluza. La oportunidad que nunca existió*. Huelva: Universidad de Huelva.
Pérez Sarrión, Guillermo. 2012. *La península comercial. Mercado, redes sociales y estado en España en el siglo XVIII*. Madrid: Marcial Pons.
Santamaría, José Miguel. 1992. "Captain John Stevens." *Livius* 1: 211–19.
Solano, Francisco de. 1982. *Norte sobre la vida y obra del autor del Norte de la Contratación de las Indias Occidentales*. Madrid: Instituto de Estudios Fiscales.
Steiner, Roger Jacob. 1970. *Two Centuries of Spanish and English Bilingual Lexicography (1590–1800)*. De Hague-Paris: Mouton.
Stevens, John. 1702. *The Spanish Rule of Trade to the West Indies*. London: Samuel Crouch.

———. 1711. *The Rule Establish'd in Spain for the Trade in the West Indies.* London: Samuel Crouch.

Valladares, Rafael, coord. 2016. *El mundo de un valido. Don Luis de Haro y su entorno, 1643–1661.* Madrid: Marcial Pons.

Veitia Linaje, José de. 1672. *Norte de la Contratación de las Indias Occidentales.* Sevilla: Juan Francisco de Blas.

Walker, Geoffrey J. 1979. *Política española y comercio colonial, 1700–1789.* Barcelona: Ariel.

Williams, Glyn. 1997. *The Great South Sea. English Voyages and Encounters, 1570–1750.* New Haven and London: Yale University Press.

Yun-Casalilla, Bartolomé. 2017. "Social Networks and the Circulation of Technology and Knowledge in the Global Spanish Empire." In *Global History and New Polycentric Approaches. Europe, Asia and the Americas in a World Network System*, edited by Manuel Pérez García and Lucio de Sousa, 275–92. London: Palgrave Macmillan.

3 European Imperialism, War, Strategic Commodities and Ecological Limits

The Diffusion of Hemp in Spanish South America and Its Ghost Fibers[1]

Manuel Díaz-Ordóñez

Early globalization owes its existence to sailing ships propelled with thousands of tons of European hemp transformed into cordage and sails. The new American territories could have served to increment its cultivation, increasing what Pomeranz defines as *ghost acreage*, to supply the huge demand for hemp to rig the European fleets. In fact, Spanish-American sources make specific reference to a determined effort to increase its cultivation for use in naval vessels.

On examination, however, we find that the results of measures to encourage the sector fell far short of expectations. Moreover, the numerous historical records of failures and frustrations seem incompatible with the classical explanation of European mercantilist resistance to transfer this agro-industrial activity to the American colonies. Therefore, it seems reasonable to broaden the focus of our investigation to include other scientific disciplines, such as botany and agronomy, in order to present a revised view of the limited introduction of hemp cultivation in Spanish South America.

Hemp: A Strategic Input in the Global History of Consumption

Hemp was a very important commodity for European national economies, given its use in such a wide range of productive sectors, including agriculture, beginning with the cultivation of the hemp plant, but also in livestock, construction, transport, textile manufacturing and, most importantly, as the predominant material in the sails and rigging of the European ships of the day. It was the widespread use of hemp as the main article of naval rigging that was the determining factor in the production of this plant, and its processing industries became a strategic axis of imperial economic policy in the modern era. Its characterization as the predominant fiber in the manufacture of naval rigging

DOI: 10.4324/9781003168058-4

(Díaz-Ordóñez 2006a, 2009), meant that hemp became a fundamental imperial strategic commodity from the fifteenth to the nineteenth century. Its study also provides us with a timely opportunity to analyze the paths through which hemp migrated across the lands of Asia and Europe, its subsequent passage to the American colonies and later to Oceania.

This approach should provide us with a more global understanding of complex processes by observing them as *commodity chains*, which, in the words of Terence Hopkins and Immanuel Wallerstein, would gather together interorganizational networks clustered around hemp (Hopkins and Wallerstein 1986, 159). In this sense, a greater understanding of the peculiarities of the cultivation of this raw material is required, including the edaphological, climatic and environmental constraints characteristic of its agricultural production, in order to quantify the labor force required for its harvest and its subsequent connection to the commercial networks involved in its distribution to manufacturing centers and its transit onwards as an industrial item to its distribution and consumer markets. A critical issue is the fact that these networks of the distribution of hemp and its manufactured articles would become global, because the ships whose rigging and sails were made with it were also entrusted with transporting it to America, when the Europeans discovered that it did not exist in the native biota of America or Oceania (Díaz-Ordóñez 2005).

The production of hemp involves a complex agro-industrial system in which very diverse and distinctive operations are combined, including picking, harvesting, preparation and industrial transformation. For this reason, it seems appropriate that we should give an account of its global expansion on the basis of its strategic nature and its *entangled history*. In doing so we observe how the conditioning factors underlying the existence of the new territories under European imperial dominion underwent processes of economic transformation, which at the same time influenced the political and economic measures adopted by their respective homelands.

Our argument focuses on analyzing the extent of Spanish resistance to moving the hemp agro-industry (cultivation and manufacture) to Spanish South America. If such resistance existed, this would back the argument in favor of the economic policy of mercantilism of the time, which defended restricting and even prohibiting American manufacturing, while the new territories were to be employed solely for the purpose of obtaining raw materials. Conversely, if these reservations in relation to the development and production of hemp in America did not exist, we could say that as a commercial activity with the production of rigging, sail and wick, it received differential treatment in comparison with other European manufacturing sectors (such as textiles, footwear, books, iron and steel, etc.) that were controlled by governments to defend their metropoles' domestic industrial sectors.

A second question, linked to the first, leads us to ask if the Spanish could take advantage of the new American territories to increase the area of cultivable land in the peninsula itself for the agricultural production of a strategic product such as hemp. This was a concept defined by Kenneth Pomeranz for which he coined the term *ghost acreage*, to explain how Europeans of the modern era disposed of additional arable land in the colonies and increased their capacity for economic growth (Pomeranz 2000). Continuing with this line of argument, while *ghost acres* allowed the Spanish colonizers access to more soil for cultivation – in this case of hemp – the new American biota also permitted them to become acquainted with, experiment and consume new raw materials (Pomeranz 2000, 275; De Vries 2001, 431–33). And so the question arises: were the Spanish able to profit from plants and vegetables from that new ecological reserve in order to replace European hemp?

America: Ghost Acreage to Replace the Cultivation of European Hemp?

Chronological evidence of hemp, and specifically the species *Cannabis sativa* L., dates far back in the environmental history of our planet (Edwards and Whittington 1992, 85). Scientific studies place its biological origin in Central Asia (Faeti, Mandolino, and Ranalli 1966, 367), in an area close to the Turpan Depression (Mukherjee et al. 2008, 483), from which it would have spread towards eastern Europe (Riera, López-Sáez, and Julià 2006, 127) during the first millennium before the Christian era and continued its expansion through southern Europe during the first centuries CE.[2] Since the Middle Ages, hemp has been used in different human activities and industries, transformed and manufactured as ropes, sacks, fabrics, livestock feed in its seed form, and in oils for manufacturing, medicinal derivatives and so on.

Our understanding of hemp as a global product entails a number of issues that we deem essential to the research at hand. In the first instance, hemp became a strategic commodity during the early Modern Age, because it was the essential product in the manufacture of maritime rigging for the military and merchant fleets that began connecting the world from 1500 onwards and whose numbers increased spectacularly.[3] This increase in total displaced tonnage also prompted the proportionally astronomic growth in European hemp used in the manufacture of sails and rigging (Díaz-Ordóñez 2009, 601–6). Secondly, until the mid-nineteenth century, the Russian Empire was the predominant European hemp producer (Díaz-Ordóñez 2016, 96–99), with vast crops in present-day Ukraine, Belarus, the Baltic Republics and part of Poland. This Russian preponderance is mainly explained by the climatic and soil conditions of some of the regions dominated by the Tsar. The production of industrial hemp requires land, preferably in temperate and cold climates, which benefits from average annual rainfall of around 635 to 760 millimetres, and where the seeds are sown at dawn in temperatures of 6–8 °C. Such conditions can be easily met in the great plains of Belarus and Ukraine, with a humid continental climate (Dfb in the Koppen-Geiger classification), in which those ideal sowing temperatures are reached by the second half of March, which allowed farmers to plant the land very early and allowed the vegetative growth of hemp to last for more than a hundred days before the summer harvest. This fact also allowed Belarusian or Ukrainian crops to present a high percentage of fiber. The outcome was a significant increase in yield per surface unit, but also a better-quality final product.

This great production of fiber was transported along the Russian river basins to the Baltic ports, such as Narva, Riga, Kaliningrad or St. Petersburg, from where it was distributed across western Europe, with the help of English and Dutch merchants (see Map 3.1). Thirdly, in relation to the latter, the European wars of early modern times altered commercial circuits, thus activating waves of hemp promotion policies in the Western powers and their overseas territories (Díaz-Ordóñez 2017, 72–75).

This complicated scenario, which combined the strategic necessity of the overseas empires to stock up on essential materials to maintain connections with the new territories dominated since the fifteenth century, and the overbearing role of the Russian empire as a supplier, drove the European powers to explore new agro-industrial possibilities in their new peripheries. The solution would have been obvious if the Europeans had found hemp either cultivated or in its wild form in the new American territories or, failing that, had encountered alternative fibers to European hemp for the manufacture of rigging and sails. The second possibility, having established the biological absence of hemp in these parts, would be for the empires to establish hemp agricultural development policies in the new territories, as they became successively incorporated into their domains. Both possibilities link back to the concept of Pomeranz's ghost acreage (Pomeranz 2000, 275). However, although historiography has discussed alternative ghost acreages and their impact on economic growth (Vries 2001, 434–36), either in the form of an increase in arable land or, alternatively, the possibility of resorting to new and alternative supplies and products that could be consumed in England, in particular, or in Europe, in general, it seems reasonable to assume that, in any case, the empires exploited the possibilities offered by the new peripheries. But in the case of hemp, and any prospective substitute raw materials, there is no clear indication of the American territories offering any such resource. First, the Spanish colonizers, and later the English, explored the possibilities offered by the American biotas, but without reaching any decision on new fibers to incorporate into the catalog of commodities that could be transformed into rigging and sails. In initial contacts between Old and New World, the writings of the Spanish explorers mention

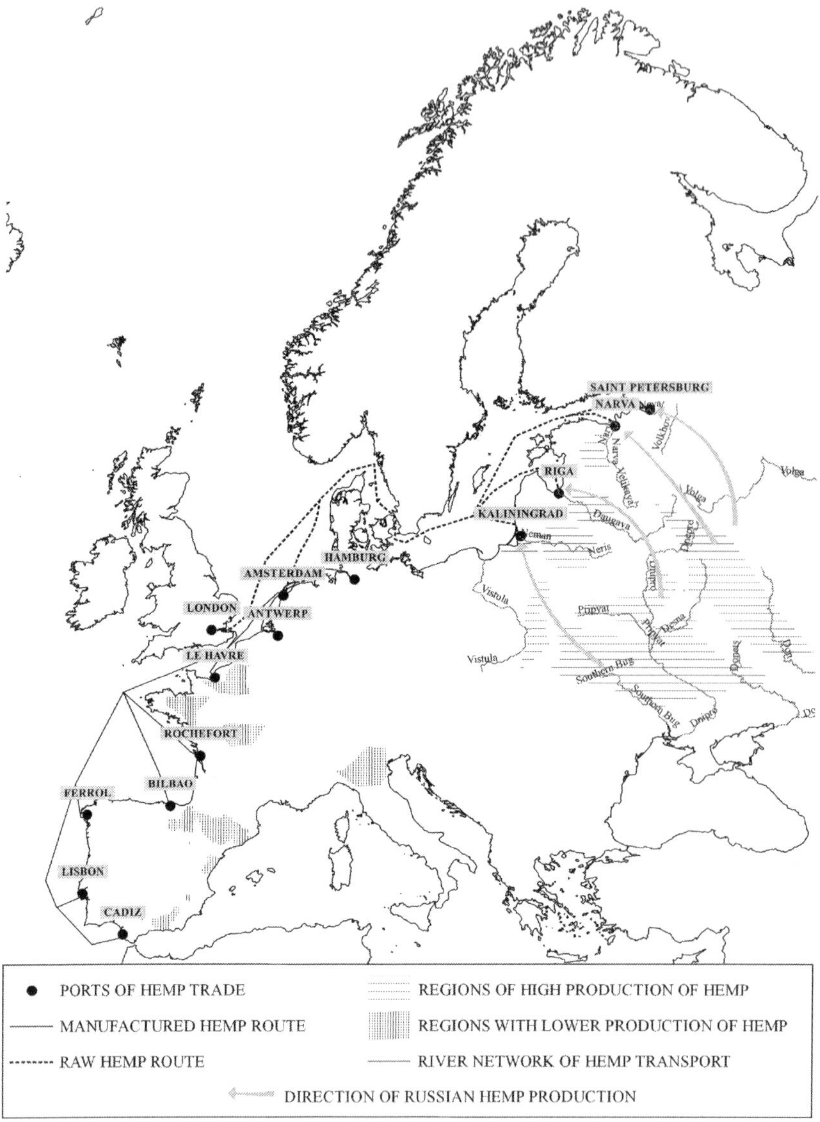

Map 3.1 Russian Hemp Routes and Manufactured Distribution in the Early Modern Age in Europe.

Source: prepared by the author from sources and bibliography. Software GIS QSIG 2.18.4.

the plant species used by the Indians of the Caribbean islands (Cuba, San Juan de Puerto Rico and Jamaica). Among these, they highlighted the use of certain species of vines and lianas (climbers) called *magueys* and *damahaguas* (also known as *majagua*), a *Malvacea* of the hibiscus genus.[4] For its part, the *maguey* (known as *pita, cabuya, fique, mezcal,* etc.) was the plant most used in various pre-Columbian human activities and manoeuvres. Some chroniclers speak of its extended use among the settlers of central Mexico (*Agave americana*)[5] and the *henequen* (*Agave fourcroydes*) on the Yucatecan coast, in Costa Rica (Fernández 1889, 17) and in Ecuador (Velasco 1833, 1:41–42). Finally, in Paraguay, the use of *chaguar* or *caraguatá* (*Bromelia hieronymi*) fibers was identified among the indigenous *Wichi* and across present-day Argentina and Bolivia.[6]

The existence of these plants that the natives had used for generations before the Europeans' arrival could have led the newcomers to decide to replace hemp with some of them. Nevertheless, none of these plant species clearly replaced European hemp in the manufacture of rigging, but rather served as effective complements to the logistical needs that the Europeans faced in their incursion, occupation, settlement and constitution of an economic system of dominion over the new continent. While a preference for European hemp for rigging remained, this was not the case with sail-making, for which Spaniards readily employed the fabrics manufactured by the indigenous people of Cajamarca and Chachapoyas since pre-Columbian times. With the arrival of the Iberian settlers in these regions, the natives adapted their traditional manufacturing forms to the standards of European rigging. This adaptation required natives to adjust their traditional economies to the newcomers' needs in order to supply a distribution network linking the manufacturing zones to the markets, ports and naval facilities of the Spanish Pacific (Góngora 1970, 453; Juan and Ulloa 1826, 87; Cooney 1979).

However, the production of rigging with American fibers turned out to be much more complicated. Let us, therefore, analyze the interaction between imperial needs and the availability and adequacy of these plant alternatives. From a chronological perspective, the Spanish colonizers first had to meet the rigging demands of the ships bound for the new territories. As dominion over the American continent became increasingly consolidated, the need for these goods increased ostensibly, because in addition to the demand from ocean-going vessels, this now extended to the coastal and river vessels operating along the American coasts. Subsequently, the consolidation of Spanish economic dominion in the new territories would also affect the growth of merchant fleets in America and, simultaneously, the military squadrons that had to defend them (Armada de Barlovento in the Caribbean or the Armada del Mar del Sur in the Pacific) (Pérez and Torres 1987). These commercial and military fleets required naval construction and maintenance centers, such as the Havana arsenal, the Guayaquil and Coatzacoalcos shipyards and the San

Blas naval station, all reliant on supplies of rigging made with European hemp, dispatched in the vessels of the Carrera de Indias. In fact, the contract to supply processed hemp to the American colonies became a very profitable business for Spanish manufacturers and merchants after 1500, as evidenced by the participation of leading productive organizations such as the Seville cord-makers' association, bidding for the contract to supply rigging to the Carrera in the sixteenth century.[7]

Contemporary correspondence and reports lead us to believe that under Spanish dominion, American fibers normally played a complementary role to European hemp in the manufacture of naval rigging. Nevertheless, American fibers could replace European hemp when the Spanish fleets entered crisis mode, due to possible delays in the arrival of hemp from Europe, or local stock shortages in the American warehouses. It was when crisis situations presented themselves that *pita* and *henequen* were supplied to complete the rigging of the ships attached to the fleet of the Viceroyalty of Peru (Romero and Contreras 2006, 154). Similarly, in 1573, Lorenzo Martínez de la Madrid, mayor of Valencia (current Venezuela), in his exposition recommending that the king create an Armada del Mar del Sur to protect the Spanish Pacific, also argued that the ropes and cables necessary for the cordage of the ships' rigging should be made from *pita* (Cappa 1894, 42). Furthermore, he suggested that major repairs to the rigging of the Spanish ships arriving in the Philippines could be effected, in part, with *abroma* fibers (*Abroma augusta* L.), *Calamus* or sweet flag (*Acorus calamus L.*), and coconut fiber (Cappa 1894, 54). The possibility of using *pita* as a complementary commodity along with European hemp for naval rigging facilitated the development of agro-industrial production centers, such as the one established in the Ecuadorian region of Jaén (under the jurisdiction of the Real Audiencia of Quito). The relevance of this manufacturing enclave is clear because of the connection it generated between the production and the consumption of cordage, textiles and sacks in nearby towns, cities and ports (Torres de Mendoza 1868, 9: 379). These active exchanges between *pita* producers and the consumption of articles for Spanish imperial needs are described in texts such as the *Relación General de las Poblaciones Españoles del Perú* by Juan de Salazar y Villasante (Cappa 1894, 94). According to the author, the shipyard in Guayaquil benefited from its geographic proximity to the island of Puná, where the indigenous population had specialized in manufactures made with *pita* since pre-Columbian times and benefited from the huge demand for yarns, cordage and textiles generated at the Spanish naval installation from the middle of the sixteenth century. This activity continued to develop in the 1730s (Juan and Ulloa 1826, 62). As a final example of the use of American *pita* to complement European hemp in Spanish South America's naval facilities, in 1795 the San Blas settlement recorded an annual consumption of this Mexican fiber of around 55 tons (Mosk 1939, 172).

The fact that the benefits of the *ghost American fibers* – to paraphrase Pomeranz – were not fully exploited, leads us to question the reasons behind this decision: was it solely due to European resistance to altering their customs or consumer habits, as occurred with other crops such as wheat, grapes or olives? Sources do not clearly point to a rejection of American plant fibers for exclusive reasons of consumer traditions, European tastes or resistance to change. On the contrary, Spanish reports generally present fairly precise comparisons detailing the final characteristics of articles manufactured with American plants, compared with those of European hemp. In other words, the Spanish colonizers were not reluctant to use what was available in terms of native plants for the manufacture of cordage and textiles. In fact, we know that American cotton was widely used in the sails of Spanish Pacific-going ships. This seems to point to the fact that the Spaniards were eminently pragmatic and practiced a degree of technical objectivity in their decision-making. The tests carried out on American fibers (resistance, traction, impermeability, etc.) manufactured as rigging showed, according to the results recorded at the time, that European hemp was far superior. The sailors and scientists, Jorge Juan and Antonio de Ulloa, rated the rigging and canvas made with *pita* in the shipyard in Guayaquil as far inferior to that brought from Spain, so it was only used to rig the smaller vessels (Juan and Ulloa 1826, 62). Similar technical opinions were voiced about the *pita* made at the San Blas station at the end of the eighteenth century.[8] This qualitative differentiation of the fibers used in the Old and New World for their characteristics of greater resistance and tolerance has been discussed in some works, which emphasize that the lack of technical development in the production process would have determined the relatively low quality of American fibers compared to those produced in Europe (Alston, Mattiace and Nonnenmacher 2009, 104–5).

Technical appraisals, which estimated the *pita* to be inferior, were repeated with the parthenium weed (*Parthenium hysterophorus*), with a series of experiments carried out in Mexico around 1778, which concluded with the impression that the cordages manufactured with this plant had barely half the resistance of similar ones made with European hemp.[9] There are numerous reports underscoring the difficulties and the fact that the fibers extracted from the plants lacked sufficient quality and strength. A similar picture is presented for *henequen*, which could not compete with European hemp in terms of resistance throughout the modern era. *Henequen* was criticized for its low endurance in humid environments to the point of being disqualified for use in Spanish naval rigging.[10] In addition, *henequen* production was very limited; first, until the invention of the mechanical harvester in the United States and its distribution in Mexico in the first half of the nineteenth century, and, second, by the invention and implantation of mechanical scrapers in textile mills in the second half of the nineteenth century (Evans 2013).

These machines facilitated more profitable extraction of the *maguey* fibers and, at the same time, improved the quality of the articles manufactured from this vegetable. Both inventions led to what, in the words of some authors, became known as the *henequen boom* in Mexico during the second half of the nineteenth century (Alston, Mattiace, and Nonnenmacher 2009, 106).

The Introduction of Hemp to Spanish South America: Prohibition or Advocacy? Sixteenth Through Nineteenth Centuries

Having established the moderate impact of the use of *alternative ghost fibers* on Spain's requirements for major strategic naval equipment, the second way in which Pomeranz defined imperial dominions' extraordinary contribution, in terms of the greater availability of arable land, bears scrutiny. Some scholars and primary sources suggest that European mercantilism subjugated the American economies to protect the old continent's markets and manufacturing sectors (Mörner 1990). Without engaging in that debate or providing new evidence regarding the peculiarities of the Spanish empire's mercantilist model, it seems necessary to discuss how true or applicable this image of mercantilism proves with respect to the expansion of hemp cultivation in America.

Referring specifically to hemp, the idea that Spain had also curbed American economic possibilities in order to defend peninsular agricultural and manufacturing interests has been put forward repeatedly since the beginning of the nineteenth century. Among others, German geographer Alexander von Humboldt criticized the excessive control that Spanish colonizers imposed on the American hemp economy. Although Humboldt qualified this negative view of Spanish hemp policy in America in different editions of his works (Humboldt 1836, 373–75) with an explanatory note detailing the significant measures taken to promote the cultivation of European fiber in Mexico over the last quarter of the eighteenth century (Serrera Contreras 1974), for him, Spain had preferred to see the American population consume Asian products carried aboard the Manila galleons or European products rather than to encourage the manufacture of goods in America. More specifically, he explained that the Council of the Indies had hampered cultivation of hemp and the manufacture of hemp and textiles in Spanish America, and that only the arrival of the Bourbon reformers in the eighteenth century eventually permitted some degree of relaxation in its control (Humboldt 1822, 2: 376). However, our sources call into question Humbolt's depiction of this prohibitionist attitude on the part of the Spanish government and paint quite a different picture. It would appear that the Spanish monarchy endorsed and financed the physical transfer of the plant species to

America, encouraged its cultivation in all its domains and fostered the creation of hemp manufactures from the early 1500s.

The very evidence of European hemp's physical transfer to America transcends political decisions and gives us an idea of the logistical needs imposed by the complex transatlantic voyage. The seeds of *C. sativa* plant species (*cañamones*) were used to feed birds and some pack animals (donkeys, mules and horses) transported aboard the first ships that explored the Caribbean and later, the American continent. The first news of the plant's physical transfer with a view to its cultivation in the New World dates from 1513, with the dispatch of twenty kilograms of hemp seeds. As indicated in the texts of the provisions and royal writs, Spanish establishments should obtain the hemp they needed to cultivate and process it on the new continent. The documents also express the desire that the indigenous people become involved in the production of hemp-derived manufactured goods, underscoring their importance for the empire and for the local economy. In short, the royal provisions would appear to form part of a more ambitious plan that envisaged a certain degree of self-sufficiency in strategic hemp materials as imperial explorations and expansion in America progressed (Rio Moreno 1991, 299; Iglesias Gómez 2008, 268; Campos 2012). Similar dispatches were recorded in 1514 (with seeds sent aboard the fleet Pedrarias Dávila commanded), 1520, 1532,[11] the writ of 1537[12] and that of 1545 (Council of the Indies 1681, 117), which for some time was considered to be the initial date of the physical migration of European hemp to America;[13] and finally the writ of 1554.[14]

Spanish sources highlight the difficulties faced by the first American hemp crops, emphasizing their limited extension, low profitability and poor acceptance among the native work force as well as the Spanish *encomenderos* (Gerhard 2000, 11). Efforts to foment the agro-industrial development of hemp originated from the royal officials, such as the president of the Real Audiencia de Nueva España Sebastián Ramirez de Fuenleal (J. de Torquemada 1615, 664), and even from members of the church (Zavala 1987, III: 60; FJ de Torquemada 1983, III: 307) who thought that the production of hemp and the manufacture of processed fiber could provide a suitable occupation for large numbers of natives. However, these measures do not seem to have achieved success. Of course, competition from other European produce for immediate consumption – mainly the production of wheat, wine and oil – was an important conditioning factor and to a considerable extent dictated certain preferences with regard to the use of land and the Indian work force (Crosby 1986). Furthermore, the Spaniards had to face crucial environmental problems, since the climate of many of their American dominions strongly differed from the ideal continental humid conditions of Belorussia and the Ukraine. Many regions of New Spain, New Granada and

Peru were close to the equator and the daily lowest temperatures rarely got down to 10°C.

Hemp's poor development on Mexican soil meant that the rigging required by the Spanish empire continued to be supplied by the homeland[15] (Díaz-Ordóñez 2019, 191–93). Nevertheless, the growing demands of Spanish settlement in the New Word in terms of construction, transport and navigation once again triggered measures to promote American hemp in the last quarter of the century. A notable example of such measures entailed the assignment of royal lands in New Spain to a lace maker, Martín Jiménez, from 1575 for the purpose of sowing hemp.[16] These efforts appear to have been unsuccessful, according to contemporary sources, such as the texts of Horacio Levanto, who blamed their failure on an American preference for Asian fabrics over those made with Mexican hemp (Levanto 1620, 1). At the end of the sixteenth century, hemp harvests in Spanish America were very limited and widely dispersed, with hardly any in Mexico and Chile (Foster 1996, 72). The earliest crops, located in the vicinity of Mexico City, gradually began to disappear after 1600 and the only remaining major focus of hemp production in the new century was in Chile.[17]

Apart from the modest Mexican and Chilean harvests, hemp production was practically nonexistent in the remainder of Spanish America. Sources indicate a complete absence of the crop in Panama, Ecuador, Colombia and Peru.[18] With the end of the Twelve Years' Truce in 1621, the Spanish empire began to suffer a major crisis due to the lack of Russian hemp arriving at the Cantabrian ports (Díaz-Ordóñez 2017, 72–74; Goodman 2001, 199). The Dutch and English merchants, who had been supplying the Spanish ports with such articles produced in Russia, would now and for several decades be enemies of the empire. The shortage triggered the reactivation of measures to promote the plantation of hemp in America, with the monarchy giving continuous instructions to the Council of the Indies and the American officials of the Río de la Plata, Paraguay and the Viceroyalty of Peru (Díaz-Ordóñez 2017, 74). In 1626, these orders were extended to Chile (Díaz-Ordóñez 2017, 74), where extensive crops already existed since the last quarter of the previous century. Some Spanish *encomiendas* on the outskirts of Santiago, in particular those located in Valparaiso region (Quillota[19] and La Ligua[20]), had specialized in the cultivation of hemp and had developed manufacturing industries for the process of hemp-derived products, including wick, cordage and rope for construction and transport and rigging for Chilean and Peruvian ships. These regions had the advantage of having a Mediterranean-type climate, but with continental influences, which permitted farmers in the Valparaiso region to sow hemp at temperatures below 10°C, therefore allowing the plants to grow for several weeks until harvest.

Two decades later, around 1640, most of the crops in Spanish South America had not grown, either geographically or quantitatively, except for the hemp planted in Chile. Thus, the Chilean harvests became an important resource enabling the empire to overcome the problem of having to supply strategic products from Europe to these areas, which were both geographically remote and at war, while Spain was struggling to meet domestic demand. Chilean hemp, transformed into wick, essential for the operation of short- and long-barrel firearms, and the manufacture of rigging for the boats operating in the Pacific, guaranteed dominion over the region and its defense. In the first decades of the seventeenth century, the manufacture of rope wicks became an important economic resource for the Chilean *encomiendas*,[21] enabling them to meet the persistent and considerable demands of the Spanish military forces defending the Mapuche frontier. It ended up developing into an important regional market, linking Chile with the Viceroyalty of Peru, with the sale of Chilean articles such as rigging and cordage for mining and for urban construction, in addition to the rope wick for troops stationed there (Quiroz 2010, 183). This connection between Peruvian demand and the Chilean supply of hemp is also revealed with the growing number of applications from 1600 onwards for licenses to go to the Indies from people involved in Spanish hemp manufacture, demonstrating that the sector was acquiring appreciable relevance in the Chilean economy (Díaz-Ordóñez and Rodríguez-Hernández 2017, 9). The intensity of this Chilean-Peruvian connection is underscored by the flow of financial settlements between the Royal Savings Banks of Lima and Santiago which refer to payments of regular annual purchases of rigging and rope destined for the officers of the viceroyalty from 1646 (Marichal 2017; Alcedo 1788, 4:61).

In 1627, the governor of Chile, Luis de Córdoba y Arce (1625–1629), recognized the central strategic and economic role of Chilean hemp production within the Spanish defense system (Díaz-Ordóñez and Rodríguez-Hernández 2017, 12). He stated that the ninety-two tons of hemp produced annually by Chile were concentrated in the fields around La Ligua and Quillota.[22] In 1636, his successor at the head of government, Francisco Laso de la Vega, argued that the harvest could be increased if the port of Valdivia was integrated as an export platform, with the establishment of new plantations in the adjacent rivers (Díaz-Ordóñez and Rodríguez-Hernández 2017, 13). Just a decade later, in 1645, the Audiencia of Chile estimated the annual hemp harvest to be lower, situating it between sixty-nine and eighty tons, but nevertheless sufficient to meet the demands for rigging the ships operating in the Pacific. He contended that if the monarchy committed to purchasing the crop in advance it could boost the production of hemp in Chile and increase the harvest to 500 tons per year, given the favorable climate and physical characteristics of the region. The Audiencia added that the decrease in indigenous labor force and the Portuguese rebellion of 1640, which reduced the slave trade in Buenos Aires and created a deficit of slave labor to attend to the sowing, harvesting, preparation and manufacture of so many crops, would dictate the final figure (Díaz-Ordóñez and Rodríguez-Hernández 2017, 14). These quantities coincide with later information, such as the *arbitrista* project of 1644, put forward by the rancher Martín de Espinosa and Santander (Góngora 1970, 53–54) who estimated that, if supported, the sector could grow to about 345 tons per year.

Chile's strategic role as supplier of hemp to the Spanish Pacific was closely linked to the region's economy and especially to the empire's defense. The port of Valdivia as a dispatch center for hemp wares provides a cogent example of its importance. However, indigenous conflicts or the presence of rival European fleets, such as the 1646 rumors announcing the presence of a Dutch squadron like the one Hendrick Brouwer commanded years before, accelerated the shipment of defensive materials, in particular wick and rigging.[23] This strategic economic activity had considerable impact on Chilean society as a whole, as it strengthened the connection between the Indians and the *encomiendas* or *estancias* and obliged them to undertake activities completely foreign to their tradition. And on many occasions this gave rise to cases of abuse on the part of the Spaniards in charge of these establishments and complaints of the overexploitation of the Indians assigned to them (Barros Arana 1890a, 4: 420). At the same time, Chilean hemp products became a bargaining chip in the purchase of services sold by the monarchy (Díaz-Ordóñez and Rodríguez-Hernández 2017, 15) and were widely used by Chilean merchants and producers as barter in the purchase of Asian and Spanish products that reached the Peruvian markets (du Biscay 1943, 82).

But to what extent did this South American production of hemp serve Spanish imperial global needs? As discussed, it would appear that it served to meet regional demands in the Pacific, although it was not viewed as a solution on a global scale for Spain partly due to production costs in Chile; but, more importantly, the elevated cost of its carriage to the peninsula (freight, insurance, loading and unloading, etc.) rendered it inadvisable. However, the fact that the South American production could not be used as ghost acreages for the Spanish empire dictated a new connection with the Spanish mainland, because from the 1720s the crown was obliged to once again instigate measures to promote the cultivation of hemp in traditional fiber-producing regions, such as La Rioja and Granada (Goodman 2001, 204–6).

In the first decades of the eighteenth century, as shown in Map 3.2, Spanish South America continued to show a marked presence of hemp cultivation in Chile and its contrasting absence in the rest of its geographical landscape (Juan and Ulloa 1826, 84; Cooney 1979, 105). However, even in Chile Spaniards failed to obtain abundant harvests, especially in the area around Valparaiso, due to the belligerence of the natives who had not been subjugated (Juan and Ulloa 1826, 47). Although we have not been able to quantify Chilean hemp production for the eighteenth century, it seems that it did not increase above the approximate ninety

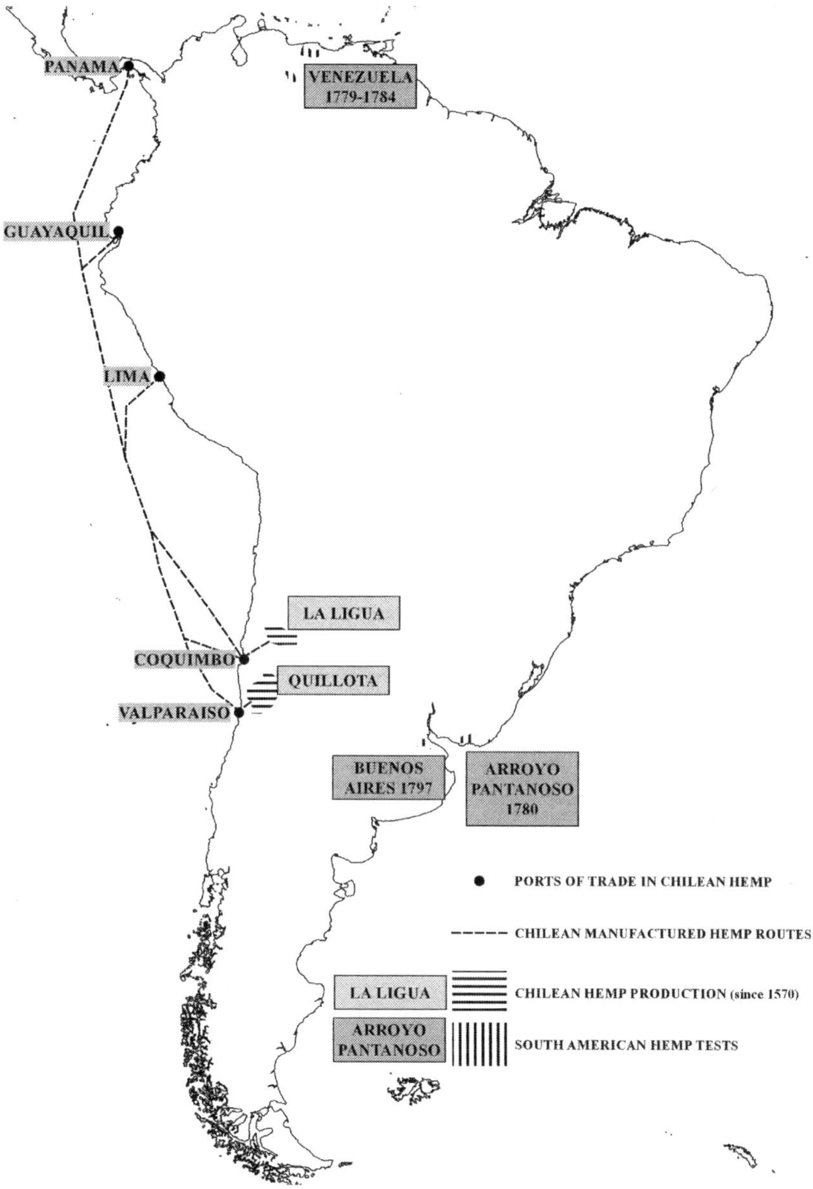

Map 3.2 Distribution of Goods Manufactured from Hemp in Spanish South America (1570–1800) and Places of Cultivation.

Source: prepared by the author from sources and bibliography. Software GIS QSIG 2.18.4.

tons per year, which Governor Córdoba mentioned in his reports for the previous century (Barros Arana 1890a, 4: 302). The Jesuit establishments had spread in the region, and by the end of 1767 they operated a vertical production structure, from the sowing of hemp to the manufacture of rigging and wick (Barros Arana 1890b, 6: 252). Around 1780, according to the authors of the time, Chile continued to produce less than one hundred tons per year (Arteta de Monteseguro 1783, 137). The quality of its sowings was so well recognized by the Spanish authorities that, in 1796, seeds of this hemp were sent to New Spain (Serrera Contreras 1974).[24] However, the importance of the hemp economy persisted with the end of Spanish dominion. Accordingly, within the framework of the Chilean emancipation movement of 1818, the independence faction offered Great Britain the export of its hemp harvests at very low prices in exchange for support in the conflict against the Spanish government (Barros Arana 1890c, 12:47).

Conclusion: Towards an Ecological Explanation

During the whole colonial period Spanish settlers in South America managed to establish the constant cultivation of hemp only in specific areas in Chile. The case of hemp contradicts the mercantilist thesis that defended European versus American economic prioritization, presenting two key arguments: first, the Spanish empire, far from promoting its prohibition or limitation, put in place measures to support the plant's migration and agro-industry in America; second, continuous experiments were carried out to obtain *alternative ghost fibers*, given the existence of different plant species in the American biota (*pita, henequen, maguey* and *caraguatá*), while it is true that the Spanish authorities had to conclude that these could not compete with European hemp on account of its very distinctive technical characteristics suitable for the construction of rigging. The use of cotton, woven by the inhabitants of Cajamarca and Chachapoyas, in the manufacture of sails destined for Pacific ships is the best example of Spanish duality in the strategic supply of these materials in America: tested and integrated into the supply of naval equipment for the region and, at the same time, replacing the scarce supply of European hemp canvas imported from Spain. In short, this overall context coincides with Pomeranz's concept of colonial *ghost acreage*.

While the ships sailing in the Spanish Pacific were supplied with this Chilean production of hemp and the sails made with native American cotton, the Atlantic continued to suffer a marked shortage of these manufactured goods required in shipbuilding. For this reason, an establishment such as the naval dockyard of Havana, which launched more than one hundred ships during the eighteenth century, continued to depend on the rigging and sail mostly made with Russian hemp at factories located at the Spanish mainland ports of Ferrol and Cadiz. The limited Spanish success with hemp on American soil brings us closer to the concept of connected stories, in which the motherland, which had previously acted as the driving force of this agricultural development in its overseas possessions, was forced, partly by the difficulties it faced as a result of interruptions in the supply of Russian hemp brought about by European wars, to reactivate policies of national agricultural development that ended up altering the agrarian landscapes of large areas of domestic Spanish territory, such as La Rioja and Granada.

Our current research will try to clarify why Spanish authorities were unable to secure adequate hemp crops in America, while they managed to increase its production on the Peninsula (Díaz-Ordóñez 2016, 2006b). At the time, some observers blamed Indians who had "no instruction in the matter, no knowledge of the plant, no idea to form the spinning machine, and weave".[25] But this explanation seems inadequate as many practitioners and experts in the field, who could have trained the natives, obtained licenses in Spain to travel and settle in the Indies. In the eighteenth century, the dispatch of technical instructions to guide the farmers in their harvesting activities intensified. Therefore, hemp's failure to prosper in southern Spanish America derived from neither a lack of Spanish interest nor farmers' poor agricultural knowledge in the New World. The ecology of hemp itself suggests further explanations for its limited spread in America. Political, commercial and social considerations may have influenced the growth of hemp less than other requirements, including light, climate and soil, may have influenced. As has been pointed out, the conditions of the sowing temperature, which benefited the Russian territories of Belarus or Ukraine, seem to have harmed the Spanish in their American enterprise. Hence, environmental contexts and ecological constraints require more attention in the future.

Notes

1. This research has been carried out within the framework of the project HAR2014–53797-P "Globalización Ibérica: Redes entre Asia y Europa y los cambios en las pautas de Consumo en Latinoamérica" [Iberian Globalization: Networks between Asia and Europe and Changes in Consumption Patterns in Latin America] financed by Ministerio de Economía y Competitividad, Spain, of which the principal investigator is Bartolomé Yun-Casalilla.
2. Bouby 2002, 89–92; Kroll 2001; Wild 2002, 7.
3. Romano 1962, 575; Unger 1992, 248; Van Zanden 2000, 82; Maddison 2001, 77; Aldcroft and Sutcliffe 2005, 36.
4. López de Velasco 1894, 95; Sánchez Valverde 1862, 66; Benítez 2013.
5. Zorita 1909, 1:128; García Icazbalceta 1858, 1:244; La Renaudière 1844, 40.
6. Charlevoix 1910, 1:42; López de Velasco 1894, 551; Napp 1876, 273.
7. Archivo General de Indias (hereafter AGI), Indiferente, 443, L.35. Cordmakers' guild to the officials of the Casa de la Contratación. Madrid; 25 October 1689.
8. AGI, Indiferente, 101. Capellán de San Blas; Mexico, 19 June 1792.

9. AGI, Indiferente, 100. Andrés Gómez Moreno a José de Gálvez; Madrid, 12 November 1778.
10. Archivo Histórico Nacional (hereafter AHN), CODICES, L. 729. Indies dictionary of government and legislation. C. Tom. I (CAB- CER). Voz Cáñamo.
11. Puente y Olea 1900, 416; Iglesias Gómez 2008, 268; Rio Moreno 1991, 166.
12. AHN, CODICES, L. 729. Indies dictionary of government and legislation. C. Tom. I (CAB- CER). Voz Cáñamo.
13. Dewey 1913, 291; Mosk 1939, 171; Hill 1983, 56; Small and Marcus 2002, 284.
14. AHN, CODICES, L. 729. Indies dictionary of government and legislation. C. Tom. I (CAB- CER). Voz Cáñamo.
15. Archivo General de Notarías de Ciudad de México (Hereafter AGNCM), SDHN/371, Notary 1, Vol. 8, Leg. 4. 11 October 1563.
16. AGNCM, SDHN/5224, Notaries Office 1, Vol. 9, Leg. 12, 421/421v. 12 January 1575.
17. Díaz-Ordóñez and Rodríguez-Hernández 2017, 7; Díaz-Ordóñez 2005.
18. Serrano y Sanz 1908, 170; Torres de Mendoza 1868, 9:291 and 428; Cobo 1891, II:418; Díaz-Ordóñez 2017, 77.
19. Díaz-Ordóñez 2005; Keller and Silva Castro 1960, 24; Alcedo 1788, 4:356; Gay 1862, 15.
20. Góngora 1970, 25; Contreras Cruces 1999.
21. Errázuriz Valdivieso 1881, 1:411; De Ramón 1960, 90.
22. AGI, Chile, 19, R. 7, N. 69. Luis de Córdoba y Arce; Concepción, 1 February 1627.
23. AGI, Audiencia of Chile, Leg. 11. Santiago de Chile, 24 May 1646
24. AGI, Indiferente, 1559. Viceroy of New Spain to Viceroy of Peru; Mexico, 12 January 1796.
25. Royal Heritage. Royal Library, Manuscripts II/622, f. 82v-84v

Bibliography

Alcedo, Antonio de. 1788. *Diccionario geográfico-histórico de las Indias Occidentales ó América: es á saber : de los reynos del Peru, Nueva España, Tierra-Firme, Chile y nuevo reyno de Granada : con la descripcion de sus provincias, naciones, ciudades, villas, pueblos, rios, montes, costas, puertos, islas, arzobispados, obispados, audiencias, virreynatos, gobiernos, corregimientos, y fortalezas, frutos y produciones ; con expresion de sus descubridores, conquistadores y fundatores: conventos y religiones: ereccion de sus catedrales y obispos que ha habido en ellas : y noticia de los sucesos mas notables de varios lugares: incendios, terremotos, sitios, é invasiones que han experimentado, y hombres illustres que han producido*. Vol. 4. Madrid: En la Imprenta de Manuel Gonzalez.

Aldcroft, Derek Howard, and Anthony Sutcliffe. 2005. *Europe in the International Economy, 1500 to 2000*. Cheltenham: Edward Elgar.

Alston, Lee J., Shannan Mattiace, and Tomas Nonnenmacher. 2009. "Coercion, Culture, and Contracts: Labor and Debt on Henequen Haciendas in Yucatán, Mexico, 1870–1915." *The Journal of Economic History* 69 (1): 104–37.

Arteta de Monteseguro, Antonio. 1783. *Discurso instructivo sobre las ventajas que puede conseguir la industria de Aragón con la nueva ampliación de puertos . . .* En Madrid: Imprenta Real.

Barros Arana, Diego. 1890a. *Historia general de Chile*. Vol. 4. Santiago: Jover.
———. 1890b. *Historia general de Chile*. Vol. 6. Santiago: Jover.
———. 1890c. *Historia general de Chile*. Vol. 12. Santiago: Jover.
Benítez, Fernando. 2013. *Los indios de México IV*. Vol. IV. México, D.F.: Ediciones Era.
Biscay, Acarette du. 1943. *Relación de un viaje al Río de la Plata y de allí por tierra al Perú: Con observaciones sobre los habitantes, sean indios o españoles, las ciudades, el comercio, la fertilidad y las riquezas de esta parte de América*. Buenos Aires: Ed. Alfer & Vays.
Bouby, Laurent. 2002. "Le Chanvre (Cannabis Sativa L.) : Une Plante Cultivée à La Fin de l'âGe Du Fer En France Du Sud-Ouest ?" *Comptes Rendus Palevol* 1 (2): 89–95. https://doi.org/10.1016/S1631-0683(02)00015-5.
Campos, Isaac. 2012. *Home Grown: Marijuana and the Origins of Mexico's War on Drugs*. Chapel Hill: The University of North Carolina Press.
Cappa, Ricardo. 1894. *Estudios críticos acerca de la dominación española en América. Parte tercera. Industria naval*. Madrid: Librería Católica de Gregorio del Amo.
Charlevoix, Pierre-François-Xavier de. 1910. *Historia del Paraguay*. Vol. 1. Madrid: Libreria General de Victoriano Suarez.
Cobo, Bernabé. 1891. *Historia del Nuevo Mundo*. Edited by Marcos Jiménez de la Espada. Vol. II. Seville: Imp. de E. Rasco.
Consejo de Indias. 1681. *Recopilacion de leyes de los reynos de las Indias: mandadas imprimir, y publicar por la Magestad Catolica del rey Don Carlos II. Nuestro Señor: va dividida en quatro tomos, con el indice general, y al principio de cada tomo el indice especial de los titulos, que contiene*. En Madrid: Por Julián de Paredes.
Contreras Cruces, Hugo. 1999. "Servicio Personal y Economía Comunitaria En Los Cacicazgos Indígenas de Aconcagua Durante El Siglo XVII, 1599–1652." *Diálogo Andino* 18: 121–51. www.academia.edu/2063705/Servicio_personal_y_econom%C3%ADa_comunitaria_en_los_cacicazgos_ind%C3%ADgenas_de_Aconcagua_durante_el_siglo_XVII_1599-1652.
Cooney, Jerry W. 1979. "A Colonial Naval Industry: The 'Fabrica de Cables' of Paraguay." *Revista de Historia de América* 85: 105–26.
Crosby, Alfred W. 1986. *Ecological Imperialism: The Biological Expansion of Europe, 900–1900*. Cambridge and New York: Cambridge University Press.
De Ramón, Armando. 1960. "La Encomienda deJuan de Cuevas a La Luz de Nuevos Documentos 1574–1583." *Boletín de La Academia Chilena de La Historia* 62: 52–107.
Dewey, Lyster H. 1913. 'Hemp'. In *Yearbook of The United States Department of Agriculture*, 283–346. Washington, DC: Government Printing Office.
Díaz-Ordóñez, Manuel. 2005. "El Cáñamo y La Corona Española En Ultramar: América y Filipinas (Siglos XVI-XVIII)." *Revista de Historia Naval* 90: 45–60.
———. 2006a. "El Empleo Del Esparto En La Cordelería Naval Española de La Antigüedad Hasta El Siglo XVIII." *Tiempos Modernos, Revista de Historia Moderna* 5 (14). www.tiemposmodernos.org/tm3/index.php/tm/article/view/70/102.
———. 2006b. "Si En La Comisión de Marina Te Vieres. . . : Las Dificultades Salariales y de Promoción de Un Técnico Comisionado de La Armada Real En El Setecientos." *Revista de Historia Naval* 24 (95): 71–88.

———. 2009. *Amarrados al negocio: reformismo borbónico y suministro de Jarcia para la Armada Real (1675–1751)*. Madrid: Ministerio de Defensa, Secretaría General Técnica.

———. 2016. "La comisión del cáñamo en Granada. Sustituir la dependencia báltica como estrategia defensiva del Imperio español en el siglo XVIII." *Vegueta: Anuario de la Facultad de Geografía e Historia* 16: 93–123.

———. 2017. "Los Pros y Los Contras de La Guerra Como Motor de La Globalización Del Cáñamo En América En El Siglo XVII." In *Comercio, Guerra y Finanzas En Una Época En Transición (Siglos XVII-XVIII)*, edited by Antonio José Rodríguez Hernández, Julio Arroyo Vozmediano, and Juan Antonio Sánchez Belén, 61–90. Valladolid: Ediciones Castilla.

———. 2019. "Las nuevas periferias americanas en la circulación de cáñamo y jarcia para la construcción naval militar española en el siglo XVIII." *Magallanica* 6 (11): 181–212.

Díaz-Ordóñez, Manuel, and José Antonio Rodríguez-Hernández. 2017. "Cannabis sativa y Chile (1577–1700): un insumo al servicio del imperio." *TEMPUS Revista en Historia General* 6: 1–21. https://idus.us.es/xmlui/handle/11441/68891.

Edwards, Kevin J., and Graeme Whittington. 1992. "Male and Female Plant Selection in the Cultivation of Hemp, and Variations in Fossil Cannabis Pollen Representation." *The Holocene* 2 (1): 85–87. https://doi.org/10.1177/095968369200200111.

Errázuriz Valdivieso, Crescente. 1881. *Seis años de la historia de Chile: (23 de diciembre de 1598–9 de abril de 1605) : memoria historica escrita en cumplimiento de los estatutos universitarios*. Vol. 1. Santiago de Chile: Imprenta Nacional.

Evans, Sterling. 2013. *Bound in Twine: The History and Ecology of the Henequen-Wheat Complex for Mexico and the American and Canadian Plains, 1880–1950*. College Station: Texas A & M University Press.

Faeti, V., G. Mandolino, and P. Ranalli. 1966. "Genetic Diversity of Cannabis Sativa Germplasm Based on RAPD Markers. Plant Breed." *Plant Breeding* 115 (5): 367–70. https://doi.org/10.1111/j.1439-0523.1996.tb00935.x.

Fernández, León. 1889. *Historia de Costa Rica durante la dominación española 1502–1821*. Madrid: Tip. de M. Ginés Hernández.

Foster, Erich. 1996. "History of Hemp in Chile." *Journal of the International Hemp Association* 9 (3): 72–7.

García Icazbalceta, Joaquin. 1858. *Colección de documentos para la historia de México*. Vol. 1. México: Librería de J. M. Andrade.

Gay, Claudio. 1862. *Historia física y política de Chile: según documentos adquiridos en esta república durante doce años de residencia en ella y publicada bajo los auspicios del Supremo Gobierno*. T. 1 Agricultura. Paris: En casa del autor.

Gerhard, Peter. 2000. *Geografía Histórica de La Nueva España 1519–1821*. México: UNAM.

Góngora, Mario. 1970. *Encomenderos y estancieros: estudios acerca de la constitución social aristocrática de Chile después de la conquista : 1580–1660*. Santiago de Chile: Universidad de Chile, Sede de Valparaiso, Area de humanidades, Departamento de historia.

Goodman, David. 2001. *El Poderío naval español: historia de la armada española del siglo XVII*. Translated by Juan Pedro Campos. Barcelona: Península Ediciones.

Hill, Robert J. 1983. "Marijuana, Cannabis Sativa L." *Regulatory Horticulture. Weed Circular* 9 (1–2): 57–66.

Hopkins, Terence K., and Immanuel Wallerstein. 1986. "Commodity Chains in the World-Economy Prior to 1800." *Review* (Fernand Braudel Center) 10 (1): 157–70. www.jstor.org/stable/40241052.

Humboldt, Alexander von. 1822. *Ensayo político sobre el reino de la Nueva-España*. Vol. 2. 4 vols. París: Casa de Rosa.

———. 1836. *Ensayo político sobre Nueva España*. Perpiñán: Librería de Lecointe.

Iglesias Gómez, Laura María. 2008. *La Transferencia de Tecnología Agronómica de España a América de 1492 a 1598*. Madrid: Ministerio de Industria, Turismo y Comercio. Oficina Española de Patentes y Marcas.

Juan, Jorge, and Antonio de Ulloa. 1826. *Noticias secretas de América*. London: Imprenta de R. Taylor.

Keller, Carlos, and Raúl Silva Castro. 1960. "Los orígenes de Quillota." *Academia Chilena de la Historia*, Boletín 26 (61): 97–130.

Kroll, Helmut. 2001. "Literature on Archaeological Remains of Cultivated Plants (1999/2000)." *Vegetation History and Archaeobotany* 10 (1): 33–60. https://doi.org/10.1007/PL00013368.

La Renaudière, Philippe François. 1844. *Historia de Méjico*. Barcelona: Imprenta del Imparcial.

Levanto, Horacio. 1620. *Memorial sorbe [sic] el trato de la China con Nueua España, y estos Reynos dirigido al Señor Don Fernando Carrillo . . . Presidente del . . . Consejo de Indias*. s.l.: s.n.

López de Velasco, Juan. 1894. *Geografía y descripción universal de las Indias: desde el año 1571 al de 1574*. Madrid: Establecimiento Tipográfico de Fortanet.

Maddison, Angus. 2001. *The World Economy a Millennial Perspective*. París: OECD.

Marichal, Carlos. 2017. "Cajas de La Real Hacienda de La América Española." *Base de datos histórica. Cajas de La Real Hacienda de La América Española*. 2017. http://realhacienda.colmex.mx/.

Mörner, Magnus. 1990. "Economía Rural y Sociedad Colonial En Las Posesiones Españolas de Sudamerica." In *Historia de América Latina*, edited by Leslie Bethell, 3:122–47. Barcelona: Crítica.

Mosk, Sanford A. 1939. "Subsidized Hemp Production in Spanish California." *Agrihist Agricultural History* 13 (4): 171–75.

Mukherjee, Ashutosh, Satyesh Chandra Roy, Subir De Bera, Hong-En Jiang, Xiao Li, and Cheng-Sen Li. 2008. "Results of Molecular Analysis of an Archaeological Hemp (Cannabis Sati)." *Genetic Resources Crop Evolution* 55: 481–85. https://doi.org/10.1007/s10722-008-9343-9.

Napp, Ricardo. 1876. *La República Argentina*. Buenos Aires: Impreso por la Sociedad Anónima.

Pérez-Mallaína Bueno, Pablo Emilio, and Bibiano Torres Ramírez. 1987. *La Armada del Mar del Sur*. Seville: Escuela de Estudios Hispano-Americanos.

Pomeranz, Kenneth. 2000. *The Great Divergence: China, Europe, and the Making of the Modern World Economy*. Princeton, NJ: Princeton University Press.

Puente y Olea, Manuel de la. 1900. *Los trabajos geográficos de la Casa de Contratación*. Seville: Escuela Tipográfica y Librería Salesianas.

Quiroz, Francisco. 2010. "Industria urbana y rural en el Perú colonial tardío." In *Compendio de historia económica del Perú III: la economía del período colonial tardío*, by Magdalena Chocano, Cristina Mazzeo, and Ramiro Flores, edited by Carlos Contreras, 3:169–221. Historia Económica 7. Lima: Banco Central de Reserva del Perú y IEP Instituto de Estudios Peruanos.

Riera, Santiago, José Antonio López-Sáez, and Ramón Julià. 2006. "Lake Responses to Historical Land Use Changes in Northern Spain: The Contribution of Non-Pollen Palynomorphs in a Multiproxy Study." *Review of Palaeobotany and Palynology* 141 (1–2): 127–37. https://doi.org/10.1016/j.revpalbo.2006.03.014.

Rio Moreno, Justo Lucas del. 1991. *Los inicios de la agricultura europea en el nuevo mundo 1492–1542*. Seville: ASAJA-Seville: Caja Rural de Huelva : Caja Rural de Sevilla.

Romano, Ruggiero. 1962. "Per Una Valutazione Della Flotta Mercantile Europea Alla Fine Del Secolo XVIII." *Studi in Onore Di Amintore Fanfani* 5: 573–91. Milán: Giuffré, A.

Romero, Emilio, and Carlos Contreras. 2006. *Historia económica del Perú*. Lima: UAP y Fondo Editorial UNMSM.

Sánchez Valverde, Antonio. 1862. *Idea del valor de la isla española de Santo Domingo*. Santo Dominuo [sic]: Imprenta nacional.

Serrano y Sanz, Manuel. 1908. *Relaciones históricas y geográficas de América central*. Madrid: V. Suárez.

Serrera Contreras, Ramón María. 1974. *Cultivo y manufactura de lino y cáñamo en Nueva España, 1777–1800*. Seville: Escuela de Estudios Hispano-Americanos de Sevilla.

Small, Ernest, and David Marcus. 2002. "Hemp: A New Crop with New Uses for North America." In *Trends in New Crops and New Uses*, edited by J. Janick and A. Whipkey, 284–326. Alexandria: ASHS Press.

Torquemada, Fray Juan de. 1983. *Monarquía Indiana*. Vol. III. México: Instituto de Investigaciones Históricas/UNAM.

Torquemada, Juan de. 1615. *I^a parte de los veynte y un libros rituales y monarchia yndiana: con el origen y guerras de los yndios occidentales, de sus poblaçones, descubrimiento, conquista, conuersion y otras cosas marauillosas de la mesma tierra : distribuydos en tres tomos*. Seville: Matías Clavijo.

Torres de Mendoza, Luis. 1868. *Colección de documentos inéditos relativos al descubrimiento, conquista y organización de las antiguas posesiones españolas de América y Oceanía*. Edited by Archivo General de Indias. Vol. 9. Madrid: Imprenta Frias y Compañía.

Unger, Richard W. 1992. "The Tonnage of Europe's Merchant Fleets, 1300–1800." *The American Neptune* 52: 247–61.

Van Zanden, Jan Luiten. 2000. "Early Modern Economic Growth: A Survey of the European Economy (1500–1800)." In *Early Modern Capitalism*, edited by Maarten R. Prak, 69–87. Londres: Routledge. http://depot.knaw.nl/2252/.

Velasco, Juan de. 1833. *Historia del reino de Quito en la América Meridional (1789)*. Vol. 1. Quito: Imprenta del Gobierno.

Vries, P. H. H. 2001. "Are Coal and Colonies Really Crucial? Kenneth Pomeranz and the Great Divergence." *Journal of World History* 12 (2): 407–46.

Wild, J. P. 2002. "The Textile Industries of Roman Britain." *Britannia* 33: 1–42.

Zavala, Silvio Arturo. 1987. *El servicio personal de los indios en la Nueva España*. Vol. III. México: El Colegio de México, Centro de Estudios Históricos; El Colegio Nacional.

Zorita, Alonso de. 1909. *Historia de la Nueva España*. Vol. 1. Madrid: Librería General de Victoriano Suárez.

4 Spanish Women as Agents for a New Material Culture in Colonial Spanish America[1]

Amelia Almorza Hidalgo

Introduction

From the perspective of global history, various authors have explained how migratory networks and economic relations and consumption patterns connected distant areas of the world long before the twentieth century. This creation of an interconnected geographical space thanks to the circulation of people, objects and ideas was especially striking in the case of the Spanish empire during the early globalization of the sixteenth century (Subrahmanyam 1997; Gruzinski 2006; Aram and Yun-Casalilla 2014). The emigrants who travelled to America in search of better living conditions were key agents in the construction of the Spanish empire and had a fundamental impact on the economic and social structures of the New World. Family letters conserved along with the travel licenses to the Indies make it possible to analyze the instructions that Spanish women received from their husbands about the goods – most of them textiles – that they would take to America. Thus, this chapter sets out to link transatlantic family migration networks to the movement of European products and the creation of a demand for these products in the colonies. To date, the impact of colonization on the American economy generally has been analyzed in terms of the violent actions that occurred during the Spanish conquest and the role of the state and the Church in the creation of a new market. The large mercantile companies that mobilized enormous capital in the Carrera de Indias (the navigational route of the Indies) have also received considerable attention. However, the development of American markets and changes in consumer behavior were determined by the presence of the first Spanish settlers and their processes of social mobility, as they created consumer groups of reference within the process of colonial social stratification (Bauer 2001, 82). The circulation of people and goods from the sixteenth century onwards had a fundamental impact on the creation of a global consumer market (Yun-Casalilla 2014, 280). Spanish women also played an important role as exporters of certain models of consumption and behavior, which they transmitted through the goods they included in their luggage. This

DOI: 10.4324/9781003168058-5

chapter analyzes the material culture linked to the migration of Spanish women to America in particular and the important role it played in the creation of a demand for certain European products in America, and ultimately, in generating widespread trade in European textiles.

Material Culture in Emigrants' Family Letters

In the sixteenth and the first half of the seventeenth century a total of 450,000 emigrants undertook the voyage to Spanish America with the aim of settling and prospering in the new territories (Mörner 1976). Women and extended families featured in large numbers in the migration chain (Almorza Hidalgo 2018). This family migration was made possible thanks to the circulation of people – merchants, clergy and sailors – between Spain and America, transatlantic networks and family correspondence. Some well-established, prosperous emigrants sent letters from America to their relatives in Spain inviting them to join them and gave specific instructions for the trip, which were included in the licenses to travel to the Indies.[2] The letters that have survived were written between 1540 and 1616, with the largest number dating from 1571 to 1594, which coincides with the greatest incidence of family migration. The bulk of these letters (150) were written by men in America to their wives. The letters came mostly from the American capitals (Mexico, 146 letters; Lima, 94 letters) and other cities like Cartagena, Puebla, Panama and Potosí, the urban centers with the largest populations of Spanish origin (Otte 1988, 11). The socioeconomic origin of the emigrants was very varied, although neither the most marginal groups nor those of the highest social status feature in this correspondence. Few mention their trade, but those who do are artisans, laborers, soldiers, miners, merchants, clergy and officials of the vice regal administration (Otte 1988, 14–21).

Of the 650 letters published by Enrique Otte, most of those addressed to women contain precise indications for the journey. These letters were produced in the context of a migration chain, in which a male member of the family (husband, father or brother) had travelled before, and once settled and having achieved a certain level of prosperity, then asked his wife, children or siblings to follow him. Most of the letters to women are addressed to the wives of emigrants in America, followed in second place, by their sisters, who are invited to travel so that they too can enjoy the wealth of their emigrant brothers. Accordingly, family reunification took place in the Indies (Almorza Hidalgo 2010). Because of the enormous dangers the trip posed for women, the letters often contain detailed information on how their travel should be organized. Such instructions scarcely feature in the letters addressed to men. The women to whom the letters were addressed lived mostly in Seville, as many families had settled in the city, attracted by its economic growth and the possibility of moving to America (Almorza Hidalgo 2018).

Some men who managed to prosper in America sent sums of money to finance their families' travel expenses, usually fifty to one hundred pesos (Otte 1988, 25). Where to send this money, how to invest these sums and how to organize the journey were included in the correspondence. In this way, they sent information on the processing of the travel license at the House of Trade (Casa de la Contratación) or the Council of the Indies (Consejo de Indias). In addition, family members (especially women) were advised to join a travelling group, and to be in the company of trustworthy people making the journey from Seville to America.

Passage on the Spanish fleets was usually financed by family members who had already emigrated, through signed deeds whereby they undertook to make payment on the arrival of their relations in America.[3] Moreover, some emigrants sent money to finance the trip and provisions for the crossing, which were the responsibility of each passenger. Food packs were prepared in Seville, and had to include water, oil, vinegar and wine, as well as large quantities of biscuit, dried fruit, chickens, pulses, bacon and spices (Otte 1988, 29; Mena García 2004).

The entire journey entailed a heavy investment for the passengers, as the ticket cost at least twenty ducats per adult in the 1580s, plus the additional cost of provisions and other travel expenses. To that effect, emigrants had to sell all their properties before embarking, which they added to the sums sent by relatives from America. But not all emigrants received financing for the trip. For example, Alonso Herojo wrote from Tunja (Nueva Granada) to his wife in 1587 yet did not send her money. Instead, he promised to provide for the family upon arrival: "Sell all that you have and come to these lands with your children and mine [. . .] when you come here, you will find the table set and the bed made, and if you come naked, you will not lack the mercy of God who is great, as I will clothe and honor you with my person and money, because what I have I do not want except for your children and mine".[4] Significant travel costs led many emigrants to seek hire as the servants of other passengers in order to pay for their passage (Elliott 2006, 95).

In other cases, the necessary resources were sent to undertake the journey. For example, in 1574, the Spaniard Alonso Ortiz, who had settled in Mexico, wrote up to four letters to his wife Leonor Gonzalez urging her to join him, as he was beset with a judicial process in which he was being prosecuted for living separately from her.[5] In order to facilitate his wife's trip, with the help of a contact, Juan de Castro Ribera, who was travelling to pick up his own wife, he sent 150 pesos of common gold (in *8-reales* coins) to prepare for the trip, and a power of attorney in which he committed up to 200 Castilian ducats to pay for the entire travel group (his wife and children with other possible relatives) upon arrival in Mexico.[6]

When men sent money for the trip, it was sometimes intended for the purchase of products to take to America – mainly textiles in the form of clothing. They also included requests for working tools or household goods. These were mainly sent in the early years of colonization, when there was a greater shortage of Spanish products, or from less populated areas where European products arrived in much more limited supply. Sebastián de Pliego, for example, wrote to his wife from Mexico in 1581 requesting her to bring with her a series of household items such as a "good frying pan and broiler, a large ladle and a spoon [. . .] a wire mesh cooking basket, as well as plates and bowls, and a kettle".[7] Furniture does not feature largely, although requests for beds were common, mainly with *guadamecíes*, hides tanned in Cordoba that were highly sought after throughout America (Otte 1988, 31). The hides could also be used in the decoration of the house: a certain Gaspar Viera from Chiapas wrote to his wife in 1595 sending her quite a small sum of money with the following instructions: "The outfits you wear should be honorable, made of silk and gold, because that is the most suitable. I should also like you to bring in a drawer eight hides from Cordoba, large silver-plated figures; with this alone your house will be fully furnished".[8] There are also occasional requests in this correspondence for chairs, especially sedan chairs: "an armchair for you to come from Veracruz to here".[9] Finally, although very rarely, there are requests for food products, such as oil, wine or spices (saffron, pepper, clove and cinnamon).

The products most in demand in emigrants' letters were textiles, which were given the generic name of "Castilian clothes" (*ropa de Castilla*). The male settlers who managed to send sums of money for the purchase of products made specific requests regarding the clothes to be worn by the women who were to join them. There are detailed descriptions of such clothes purchases in up to twenty-five letters, and in others there is mention of separate instructions about the textiles to be bought in Seville, although these are not conserved in the licenses: "The money will be distributed as follows: 100 pesos to pay for leaseholds and any other debts you may have and the other 100 pesos for provisions and the other 100 for clothing, according to the recital that accompanies this. [. . .] I shall pay for the shipping costs, and they'll give you a cabin in which you shall travel at your pleasure".[10] The amounts sent for the purchase of clothes were generally around one hundred pesos (sometimes 140 or 150 pesos, and 400 pesos in only one instance), which was approximately the same amount assigned for payment of the trip, including cargo charges, provisions and other expenses. The importance given to the clothes they should take with them was such that Bartolomé de Morales indicated in his letter that the money sent for the preparation of the trip was for the purchase of clothing; what was left over could be invested in provisions, and not the other way around: "Madam, the 100 pesos should be mainly for the purchase of clothing, because here clothes are expensive, and what is left over will be for provisions".[11]

Dress appears in letters as an incentive inciting women to travel and presented as proof of the wealth and well-being awaiting them in America:

"I have very pretty dresses for when you come and a household fit for a king".[12] It could also be an excuse for not undertaking the journey, if one lacked the required wardrobe for the trip: "And if you have but a few dresses, do not feel ashamed because I shall provide these here with the help of God".[13] Sometimes the man excused himself for not sending money, arguing that he had not found trustworthy intermediaries:

> I see what you say in your letters, and I would very much like to find a person to take you a hundred pesos, with which to dress yourself, but I have not been able to find anyone honest and true, to whom I could give them. [. . .] I am not sending the money, because with two hundred more you will dress much better here, and even if naked, you and your daughter should travel on the fleet.[14]

There were a series of circumstances that explained the requests to purchase Castilian clothes to take to America. The primary reason was the high price of these goods in the New World, so it was very convenient to buy them in Seville before travelling: "Bring everything you can, because here they cost an arm and a leg".[15] The goods shipped on the Carrera de Indias acquired a high price in America due to transatlantic shipping charges, including transport and duties.[16] Not only that, strong demand for European textiles meant they became increasingly scarce and were sold at exorbitant prices: "If you come to this land, bring shirts and dresses, the rest is here in such abundance that there could not be more".[17]

On the other hand, goods were selected in the context of long-distance and definitive emigration, which meant a long trip fraught with danger and discomfort, with limitations on the luggage that could be transported. Passengers to the West Indies were issued a license to carry personal baggage without having to pay transit fees (*almojarifazgo*). Some people could afford to travel in small cabins, but most passengers travelled on deck on top of their belongings, which were stored in boxes or bundles.[18] If the luggage was very heavy, it was necessary to pay for the boxes to be loaded and unloaded. Upon arrival at an American port, passengers had to pay the cost of the journey to their destination. Those travelling to Peru had to cross the isthmus and to continue along the Pacific coast, which meant additional transport costs. Therefore, generally speaking, the only goods that could be transported were those that were costly in America, relatively easy to transport and compensated for the costs involved.

The selection of objects that emigrants chose to take with them on the journey was significant and was related to the expectations of a better life in America. The men who managed to send money for the purchase of products were craftsmen, urban workers or small-scale businessmen who were successful after years of hard effort. Being able to reunite their family was proof of their prosperity and women had a fundamental role to play in socially representing the status they achieved. On the other hand, women travelled with the expectation of living a more comfortable life in America. The clothing included in luggage was fundamental for their integration into the New World, so that the acquisition of textiles in the process of Atlantic emigration took on considerable relevance.

In this sense, research on gender and material culture has pointed out how, in the case of women, movable property had an outstanding value in the modern era in terms of personal wealth, since it could be handed down to successive generations, and it was more stable and personal than real or monetary property that was generally in male hands. A woman's wardrobe was an item of property accumulated over a lifetime during which a woman's social position changed from single to married and widowed and represented a certain stability (Cavallo 2000). Throughout, clothing appears as a key element in the construction of the female identity, generating a narrative of its own, as an important form of property for women. In the case of emigration to America, the female wardrobe fulfilled different needs. Textiles were the most easily transportable goods in the limited space available for luggage on the transatlantic crossing.[19] Moreover, clothes were seen as assets that could be sold and turned into money in case of need, thanks to the huge demand for European textiles in American cities, and the resulting high prices. In 1592, for example, Sebastián Gómez Altamirano complained that he was finding it difficult to get rich, on account of the misfortunes suffered during his trip: "It was necessary when I arrived in the Indies to sell the garments that I brought with me, to remedy my way".[20] That is to say, the sale of his wardrobe had allowed him to face the difficulties encountered on arrival in America, but on the other hand, with its urgent sale he had lost the possibility of using it as an initial business investment.

Clothing had an additional series of benefits for the emigrant woman and her living prospects in America. Emigration was an opportunity to build a new life and defend a certain status achieved. In this process, women's dress and adornments were a fundamental element in the process of building new identities in America. The importance of female attire was even more decisive in the case of single women who travelled in search of the possibility of an advantageous marriage.[21] The wardrobe of unmarried women was a key preparative element with a view to marriage (Stanley 2016, 453). So, the widow Leonor García declared that she

> goes to that land out of a desire to travel and to stay there and she goes with her three daughters, with an exemption of up to 200 pesos on the customs tax known as the *almojarifazgo*, on the grounds of her need to transport a considerable amount of luggage because she had three daughters to marry in accordance with their *quality* (status).[22]

There were frequent requests from migrant women for exemption from the *almojarifazgo*, on the grounds that they needed to take more luggage than allotted, on account of their status.

A woman's attire was not only personal property, it also reflected her family's status and position, and therefore interested the husband as well, as evidenced by money transfers to finance women's wardrobes, with instructions on what to buy. Therefore, an emigrant woman's luggage was not only made up of the clothes she had previously owned, but it often included an important purchase of textiles before embarking on the voyage. In some cases, we find precise indications that all previously owned goods were to be sold, and new clothes bought. In this sense, Sebastián de Pliego indicated to his brother in 1581: "First of all [...] sell everything you have there, as well as what is at home; sell off all the canvasses you can, and buy linen; bring all that you can and a few more balls of linen, for use in your home".[23] An emigrant who could not send money for new clothes might send instructions on the most valuable clothes to be transported – above all, linens and clothes that were in good condition. In 1596, for example, Juan de Mercado wrote from Cartagena to his wife in Seville that she should travel with her children, and he told her: "And don't bring bulky clothes, just a box or two of dresses and linens, because the rest will cost more to bring than their worth here".[24] According to explicit guidelines in the correspondence, clothes were to be purchased in Seville.[25] The city of Seville had experienced spectacular economic growth throughout the sixteenth century, as a result of the Carrera de Indias. Workshops and craft stores supplied not only local demand but also exports to the Indies. In addition, the cities of Seville and Cadiz were connected to the main European textile production circuits (France, Flanders and Italy) for the shipment of products to America. These textiles were handled by large-scale merchants, but private individuals also had access to this trade through warehouses and private retail stores (Lorenzo Sanz 1979). Purchases of this nature made just before the trip in preparation for future settlement in the New World involved investing in outfits of greater quality and splendor than the dresses they used to wear in Castile. They therefore implied a reframing of identity with a view to an improvement of their status in America, where emigrants expected to live in better conditions than in Spain.

The requests for textiles that appear in correspondence were mainly for manufactured clothing, that is, garments made by tailors in Seville. Only three letters make requests for rolls of textiles to be manufactured later in America. The author of one of these was Alonso Zamora, who wrote to his wife from Santa Fé de Bogotá. In addition to the list of dresses that she had to buy in Seville, he asked her "to also buy some *ruán*,[26] maybe two pieces, and a piece of *holanda*,[27] and some silk, for sewing here".[28] The other two requests came from la Puebla de los Ángeles (Mexico), which had a large community of textile craft workers from

Brihuega (Toledo) (Altman 2000). In 1571 Diego de San Llorente wrote to his wife in Seville and told her that he was sending 150 pesos, and with it she should

> buy the things that I tell you as follows, because these will be required in your home; that is, a bed upholstered with high-quality *guadamecí* [embossed leather], nine *varas* [approximately twenty-five feet][29] of satin in brownish or orangey hue, one *vara* [2.8 feet] of brown or purple velvet, a piece of silk *burato*, another of silk and wool, ten *varas* [twenty-eight feet] of black taffeta, and two *varas* [5.6 feet] of fine black satin, some pillows and a good quality bed cover.[30]

The clothes to be bought are often divided into two types: lower-quality dresses intended for travel, and finer dresses for life in America. From Guatemala, Francisco de Mesa sent instructions for his sister's trip:

> And in Seville you will be able to dress as an honest maiden: for the journey two dresses, one colored and the other of plain black velvet, a velvet *saya*,[31] and a Turkish (*turca*) and satin *jubón*[32] all plain, without embellishment, and a colored dress for the journey with a gold *pasamanillo*.[33]

Alonso de Zamora, mentioned earlier, advised his wife:

> [I]f you come, sell all the things you have for decorating the home, take to Seville no more than the clothes that you and your daughter are wearing, and two blouses each, that you will buy better and cheaper in Seville, and you will not have to be laden with clothes and weighed down [. . .] so, as I say, with only one dress each you have more than enough for Seville; these will be with green skirts [*faldellines*] and green braids, [. . .] cloaks [*capotillos*], and your hats, and these you can keep for the sea. A pair of well-made *jubones* made of *holanda* to go with the green dresses. In Seville you will dress in the same style as here: each with a black taffeta gown, and another in brown satin [. . .]; you will buy two rugs, one big and one small, and three blue velvet cushions.[34]

Other listings are much more modest, but nevertheless include investments in quality fabrics. The most sought-after products were *sayas* (dresses) and cloaks made of silk textiles: satins, velvets and taffeta. These fabrics were expensive products that required careful processing, and do not seem to have been worn before or during the voyage. Velvet was the most expensive product and was mainly used for mantles, which were largely produced in Segovia. Taffeta, another silk fabric cheaper than velvet, was generally brightly colored and one of the most popular textiles.[35] Juan de Ribera wrote from Lima to his brother-in-law Rodrigo Díaz, a dyer in Seville, who travelled with the whole family:

> The money I send to you is only for dresses [. . .] and so you will make garments for yourself and for all the ladies, and if it cannot be velvet, let it be taffeta, because in this land nothing else is used. [. . .] They will come in pieces, and understand, my lady, that in these parts they look not so much at the person but how she is attired.[36]

Other frequently requested garments were shirts for men and blouses for women, usually made with *ruán* or *holanda*. In 1590 one man wrote to his sister: "Try to bring all the money you have, having spent it on silk garments for yourself which are very expensive here and that God knows you deserve [. . .] and some shirts and linen which are cheaper over there".[37] Similarly, María de Carranza in Mexico wrote to her brother in Seville with instructions for the journey telling him to bring "as much white dress cloth as you can, as it is very costly here".[38]

These requests were also determined by what was being worn by the various groups of Spaniards in America, which was influenced by the Spanish clothing introduced by emigrants, as well as by the climatic conditions of each locality. From Panama, Pedro Gallegos wrote to his wife, stating: "[Y]ou shall buy the dresses you have to bring for the voyage in Seville, and these should be light and honest, because the land here is warm".[39] From Mexico, a certain Bartolomé de Morales cautioned his wife: "Do not bring any *anascote* cloak [woolen stuff], as in these parts what is used is *burata*,[40] nor woven cloth, I mean skirts, just for the sea-crossing, and a *ropilla de balleta*".[41] As we can see, tastes adapted to the American context.

On the other hand, we find that the fabrics requested had to be bright in color (in the case of taffeta and satins) or black in the case of velvets.[42] The reason for this was that European clothes should stand out in quality and texture, as opposed to the coarser clothes and dark colors used by the poorer population. There are also suggestions that women should buy beads and trinkets, dressy hats, shoes (*chapines*),[43] and adornments and complements to dress up their outfits for festive days or special occasions. For example, although the hosier Roberto de Burt does not have the capital to order velvets or taffeta for his wife, he does ask her to wear blouses, a shiny cloak, *chapines* (shoes) and hair ornaments, which would stand out as small luxury objects in America:

> Endeavor to bring nice gifts. Whatever you can buy with the silver you have, good blouses and headdress and a sleek cloak, for nothing else is worn in this city, however poor the person is, and other trinkets, fine shoes and footwear (*servillas* and *chapines*), good quality hair adornments, for these are much used. As for dresses, these shall

> be made here [. . .] And do not forget to purchase a lady's hat with pretty feathers, which is to be given to a lady who asked me for it".[44]

There is a marked difference between female and male clothing in the requests included in these letters, the latter being much more brief. Andrea Lopez, for example, who offered her two sisters marriages in Mexico, told them to wear: "a *saya* gown and *ropa de tamete* (*estameña*)[45] with gilt edging (*pasamano*), a light bodice, a sleek cloak, a dress and skirt and bodice (*ropa, saya y jubón*) in black taffeta adorned with necklets (*soguillas*), blouses, ruff necks (*gorgueras*) and headdresses, as fitting". In contrast, she tells her brother Agustín López to wear "a *sayo* [man's garment] and cape and black cloth boots and doublet, a cap and shirts".[46]

In addition to clothing fabrics, there were frequent requests for canvas or linen, mainly to be made into household linens such as sheets, tablecloths and napkins. "And if you want to bring some money to start out with, bring it in goods. [. . .] And if there is much canvas there that is homemade, it will prove gainful, and it will be a start to begin with".[47] The use of linen textiles for home decoration was common in sixteenth-century Spain and America (Boyd Bowman 1973, 351). Taffeta and velvet were also requested to decorate the home, so that curtains, bedspreads and cushions could be made and chairs upholstered. Some requested that these household items should be manufactured in Spain. Thus, in addition to beds and *guadamecís*, there were frequent requests for embroidered velvet cushions or even rugs for the *estrados*, a sort of dais within the main room of the home set aside for women, which was where they received visitors. Writing from Chimbo (Ecuador), Juan de Fuero explained to his son that he should

> bring all the linens that you have at home, because here they are highly esteemed, and the women should come well dressed in silk, because here it is very expensive, and bring six velvet colored cushions and a good carpet, so that these 700 ducats are spent on what is necessary, leaving enough for the journey to Nombre de Dios, as there I will have money to pay your passage and transport to where I am.[48]

Some letters point out that the menfolk who had been in America for many years started to decorate and prepare their houses only just before the family arrived, or they expected the women to do so on arrival. Although they had been settled in the New World for several years, only the arrival of the women allowed them to create a domestic setting, along Castilian lines. Diego de Espina told his wife in Seville:

> Take note, madam, that you merely have to buy what is necessary for your dress and provisions, as here you will find every household

> service, beds and table newly made, that I am now beginning to welcome you here on your arrival. Yours to the death.[49]

The richest and most detailed lists related to the daughters (or sisters) who were called over to marry in the Indies, and whose appearance should be as good as possible. One of the most explicit sets of instructions is that sent by Francisco Ramirez Bravo, a rich miner from Nochtepec (Mexico), who summoned his daughter for marriage.[50] To this effect, the daughter had to make an entrance that would impress the local population, and for this reason he instructed her to bring

> three silk dresses, decorated skirts [*basquiñas*] of velvet and polished satin, as is customary; for the crossing a deep-red dress, over-skirt [*basquiña*] and *turca*, two silk cloaks, fine velvet shoes [*chapines*], a taffeta hat with gold braid and feathers, small cloak of black decorated damask, with its smart golden edging, whatever headdresses you wish, so that you look well dressed and attractive, because here you are famed for your looks, and there will be many looking on. [. . .] The armchair for my daughter must be adorned in velvet.

He also told her to wear some jewels such as earrings, rings and a chain with her *agnus dei*.[51] The clothing and fabrics worn by migrant women were therefore a family investment, aimed to demonstrate and reinforce a certain status in the Indies. This was an investment made in expectation of a new life in America.

Spanish Clothes and Social Mobility in Colonial America

The emigrants sought to reproduce in America the way of life of the European elites. One of the various means of achieving this was through the goods they consumed, which had a fundamental impact on the economic model they developed in the colonies (Elliott 2006). One of the most important of these consumer goods was textiles. In colonial society, clothing and material culture were fundamental elements in the construction of identities and in the structuring of social groups (Bauer 2001; Presta 2010), where status was demonstrated through appearance (Graubart 2007, 128). In the cities with the highest concentration of inhabitants of Spanish origin and where the social origin of the new arrivals could at times be unclear, self-reinvention was very possible with the necessary economic and social resources. In this sense, having the capital to invest or employ in businesses was important, but so too was the material culture that permitted newcomers to build a certain identity. In the make-up of the colonial world, which occurred in a context of violence and where goods of Spanish origin were valued over what was produced locally, textiles from Europe had a fundamental role. Thus, there was enormous demand for textiles from Spain, not exclusively Spanish-made, but of the style worn in Spain, which also included foreign products. In fact, there was an important trade in European textiles to America, from the end of the sixteenth century and throughout the seventeenth century (Oliva Melgar 2003).

In the first decades of colonization, this was a very dynamic society, partly on account of the constant migratory waves not only of Spaniards but also of the indigenous and African populations. These migrations gave rise to a reconfiguration of social categories, and during this process the Spanish emigrants tried to become part of the colonial elite or to improve their status with respect to their former situation in Spain. The clothing worn by emigrants played a fundamental role in the process of building a new life after the journey, which began on landing. This is what Eugenio de Salazar tells us about the trip he made with his family in 1573. Arriving in Santo Domingo, after a most uncomfortable journey, he described a flurry of activity in:

> opening boxes in great haste, taking out clean shirts and new dresses, everyone looking so elegant and stylish, especially some ladies from our village who came out from below deck [. . .] so well-coiffed, curled, coiled and arranged, that they looked like granddaughters of those who were on the high seas.
>
> (Martínez 1999, Appendix 3, 299)

Several sixteenth-century chroniclers ridiculed the fact that many emigrants claimed to be of a higher status than they were prior to their arrival in America. For example, Buenaventura De Salinas accused the Spaniards of inventing distinguished backgrounds on the voyage to the New World:

> When they land in Panama, the Chagres River and the South Sea baptize them, and give each one the title of *Don*: and on arrival at this City of Kings (Lima), they are all dressed in silk, descend from Don Pelayo, and from the Goths, and Archgoths, go to the Palace, claim to have incomes and trades, and in the Churches form two columns, like the Colossus of Rhodes, and order masses to be said for the soul of El Cid.
>
> (Salinas y Córdoba 1630, 1957, 246)

Here he was referring to how Spaniards arrived in America claiming high social rank based on their lineage relating them to old Christians, including the leaders of the *Reconquista*. External symbols were also employed to this end such as the title of *don* and luxury consumer goods. Chroniclers highlighted the luxurious garments worn in the main American cities, and especially the clothing worn by women. In the case of Lima, Francesco Carletti pointed out, "It is indeed remarkable to see the greatness and splendor of the dress worn by the wives of the Spaniards" (Carletti 1606, 1976, 48). According to Pedro de León Portocarrero, women "dressed ostentatiously and expensively; all generally wear silk and very rich fabrics and velvets of gold and fine silver. They wear thick gold chains, pearl necklets, rings, chokers, diamond bands, emeralds, rubies and amethysts" (León Portocarrero XVII 1958, 39). This excessive luxury was also apparent in Mexico, described by Thomas Gage: "Both men and women wear excessive attire, more silk than cloth. Precious stones and pearls only increase their vain ostentation" (Gage 1648, 56).[52] These descriptions give an account of the country's wealth, and therefore of its elite. The wealth of a particular group was commonly exhibited through the women's dress in the new colonial elites, to the scandal of contemporary moralists (Almorza Hidalgo 2015).

Emigrants consciously used clothes as a strategy to simulate belonging to a higher social category, as can be clearly seen from family correspondence. From Cartagena de Indias, Diego de Saldaña wrote to his wife asking her to join him, and told her that when she arrived in Seville "take something from home and dress everyone very honestly. . . . For, as you know, where people are not known, they are honored for their dress".[53] Cristóbal de Montalvo wrote to his mother-in-law in Seville telling her that he had a daughter in Lima, whom her mother "should bring dressed in a manner that those who don't know her think she is the daughter of some important man".[54] In a context of growing *mestizaje*, people began to dress "Spanish style" and in European fabrics in order to differentiate themselves from others who could not rise to such levels.

To varying degrees the colonization process produced a change in the style of dress of all social groups. Thus, indigenous populations were sometimes forced to alter their traditional dress. On other occasions, changes in modes of production and new markets led to new styles (Bauer 2001, 110; Presta 2010). In the new colonial town centers, the growing population began to absorb large quantities of textile manufactures. In order to take advantage of these markets, the *obrajes* (textile mills) were founded, whereby indigenous labor was employed through the *encomienda*. The coarser and poorer-quality textiles they generally produced were used by the lower classes (Miño Grijalva 1991). Nevertheless, some cloth industries managed to produce quality textiles that achieved regional circulation in America: the Puebla cloths, which were sold in the Viceroyalty of Mexico and even in Peru before their prohibition, and the Quito cloths, which acquired a certain quality and were sold throughout Peru (Bauer 2001, 110). Sebastián Carrera wrote to his wife from Lima that "everyone dresses in clothes made here, and a dress doesn't last more than a year, because so much dust eats the clothes".[55] Quality fabrics from Europe, which marked a clear social differentiation, were therefore highly prized and costly: "The land here is abundant in food, but goods from the homeland are expensive".[56]

The high price of Spanish clothing, which made the Atlantic textile trade viable, was maintained thanks to the circulation of silver, mainly in the second half of the sixteenth century. The city of Lima represents a clear illustration of this phenomenon. With an estimated population of 25,000 Spaniards at the beginning of the seventeenth century, the city became a major consumer of textiles and luxury products.[57] Thus, according to the historian Juan Bromley, by 1630 there were fifty shops of the guild of hats and silk-workers, eighteen *obrajes* of hat-makers, fifty tailor shops, and thirty "shops of clothes from the land", in addition to other weavers whose number is not given (Bromley 1959, 285). In the sixteenth and seventeenth centuries European textiles were the goods in highest demand, consumed primarily by the colonizers and Creoles, who demanded quality products for which they paid high prices.[58] This merchandise was distributed in the *calle de los mercaderes* (merchant's street), which around 1630 had, according to the description of the chronicler Buenaventura De Salinas,

> more than twenty stores and more than two hundred shops and public stalls, where every year from five to six million [pesos] of Castilian cloth are traded, and one million or more [pesos] invested in clothing from Mexico and China that are brought in for sale.
>
> (Salinas y Córdoba 1630, 1957, 238)

The city of Lima became a great consumer center for luxury goods, linked to the creation of the new elite and the availability of silver from the Potosí. The chronicler Poma de Ayala accurately described the flows of the Carrera de las Indias, when he referred to the port of El Callao: "From the Indies silver stops there, from Castile clothing stops there".[59]

This American economic growth favored the arrival of new emigrants, who took advantage of the trip to do business using clothes from Spain. In the second half of the sixteenth century, a large number of writs were issued granting an exemption from the *almojarifazgo* tax to people who were going to populate the Viceroyalty of Peru, which meant that they would not have to pay tax on the goods they took to America.[60] In order to boost the arrival of new emigrants to populate the territory, passengers were allowed to carry a certain amount of goods for their own consumption that would be free of taxation. The families of artisans and small merchants obtained an *almojarifazgo* exemption of 200–400 pesos, while royal officers who were going to occupy positions in the viceroyalty obtained exemptions of up to 1,500 or 2,000 pesos. In 1550, Alonso de Madrid, a *borceguinero* (leather boot manufacturer), obtained an *almojarifazgo* exemption worth 200 pesos, as he was travelling to Peru with his wife, children and household.[61] This prerogative, understood as being for settlers, helped them enormously if they could bring the products required to reflect their status, which were mainly textiles and some furniture.

These permits were also used to transport goods to America that could be sold on arrival, without paying transatlantic transport taxes. Fraud became so widespread that in 1549 the king issued a warrant to Peruvian officials "to charge those persons who, having received a royal grant of a certain sum in *almojarifazgo* tax, proceeded to sell it".[62] Thus, products carried on the voyage were not only for personal consumption but also represented a great opportunity for doing business in the Indies. This initial investment permitted emigrants to raise significant capital, with which to start a business and a new life in Peru: "Sir, you will be successful with your few bits and pieces, because I believe they will increase well, being useful in some things that are worth little over there and worth a lot here".[63] In 1587 Celedón Favalis complained of not having invested money in clothes during his trip to Peru, which would have allowed him to start good businesses and become very rich: "I was misfortunate in not succeeding to bring with me even a mere 600 ducats employed in certain things with which without a doubt I would have made more than 3,000 pesos, and would have meant becoming rich forever".[64]

The conquistadores of Peru became involved from very early on in the Spanish clothing trade business and started the first dispatches of capital to invest in European products in Seville, which would be shipped to America for sale.[65] In the second half of the sixteenth century, trading companies emerged that were run by Peruvians who were able to invest large sums of capital (Vila Vilar 1991). Family correspondence also reflects this mercantile activity; from Cartagena Francisco del Barco wrote: "I am sending to Spain two thousand gold pesos, worth three thousand ducats; these are to be invested in Seville and [the benefit] to be brought here".[66]

Aside from the professional merchants, a large part of the Spanish population was involved to a greater or lesser extent in the business of buying and selling goods, and even in sending money to Panama or Seville for the purchase of clothes that would later be sold in Peru. Diego de Ocaña, a Jeronymite friar who arrived in America in 1599, described his surprise to find that in Lima "everyone is an investor and everyone is a merchant".[67]

In the creation of these trade circuits in which emigrant families participated, the information sent in the correspondence about the specific products in demand in the American markets was crucial. For example, the aforementioned Celedón Favalis wrote to his father, Simón Favalis, in Madrid:

> The merchandise that is good for this land are goods from Milan. [. . .] Silk stockings and colored silks are also very good

> merchandise for here, as long as they are not black or brown or white [. . .] Segovia hats also sell for a very good price. [. . .] Anything that comes from Castile is sold for a good price, as long as it is not a trifle or a bead, which used to be worth a lot here. Mr. Juan Giménez del Río has told me that he will send to you a list of the things that are saleable and very profitable, so that you may be aware of what is on offer.[68]

Also from Lima, Alonso de Villadiego made a large order of fabrics from Segovia, *holandas*, velvets, silks, Toledo trimmings (*pasamanería*), taffeta and short silk stockings. He also asked for goods from Milan and highlighted the success of silk stockings and colored silks, as well as hats and black plumes.[69] Silk seems to be one of the products in highest demand and most expensive in the capital. The letters underline that the clothes must be of superior quality; "Try to use all the money that you have to bring silk clothes, that are costly here, and stuff of shirts and linens that are cheaper over there".[70] Products that did not sell could even be returned to Spain.[71]

The products that the merchants indicated in their letters corresponded with the textiles that the emigrants were requested to bring with them. For example, Alonso de Villadiego wrote to his nephew, the merchant Tomé Sánchez de Guzmán, whose arrival he was awaiting in Lima, and asked him to bring the following textiles:

> You will be able to employ your estate in the following merchandise, which is a highly successful business here with many advantages, because here they do not have enough:
>
>> Black *paño ventidoseno* [woolen cloth] of Segovia de Gumiel, Black *raja* [woolen cloth] from Segovia or Las Navas. [. . .] Thin *holandas*, [. . .] Black velvets of 1- ½ naps [*pelo y medio*], Loose silks, Toledo trimmings [*pasamanería*] and taffeta, And short silk stockings. And with these extraordinary things, those who come here shall be said to produce earnings and it is a safe business.[72]

These textiles (velvets, linens, silks) coincide with the products detailed for the Indies fleet destined for Peru in the second half of the sixteenth century (Olivera Alegre 2005). Also, the textiles involved in family trade coincide with those analyzed by Peter Boyd Bowman in the inventories of the merchants of Puebla de los Angeles (Mexico) in the mid-sixteenth century (Boyd Bowman 1973), which indicates that the emigrants had quite precise information about the Spanish clothing in demand in America, and moreover that they themselves played a fundamental role in creating this demand.

Conclusions

During the colonial era a relatively homogenous culture developed throughout the Americas, based on social stratification and consumer patterns associated with social mobility (Bauer 2001). This process was shaped by Spanish emigrants who travelled to the New World full of expectations about a new life and equipped with goods to facilitate their settlement. Most of the women and family groups emigrated to America between 1540 to 1620 (Almorza 2018). These Spaniards, and especially the womenfolk, transported consumption patterns and social behavior that had a fundamental impact on colonial society and economy.

Requests for silks, satins, velvets and taffeta, as well as *ruán* and *holandas*, in addition to embroidered cushions or leather-upholstered beds from all corners of the Spanish colonies, initiated a global process in the sixteenth century. Aware of the strong demand and the high prices that these products fetched in America, settled Spaniards became involved in the Spanish clothing business via the Carrera de Indias. They sent information through letters or lists of the products to be purchased to relatives who subsequently travelled to join them, involving the family in the transatlantic transport of goods, and favoring the creation of a trade networks among private individuals that escaped the appraisal and control of the Crown. In the context of the first phase of globalization and in the case of Spain, we can determine how the movement of people (geographically and socially) was closely linked to the movement of goods. It also gave rise to large-scale trade in European textiles from Seville that were distributed in America where they were mainly purchased by the emerging elites, but also by the middle-class urban groups (Earle 2001; Phillips 2003).

Notes

1. This research was made possible thanks to the project HAR2014–53797-P "Globalización Ibérica: Redes entre Asia y Europa y los cambios en las pautas de Consumo en Latinoamérica" [Iberian Globalization: Networks between Asia and Europe and Changes in Consumption Patterns in Latin America] financed by Ministerio de Economía y Competitividad, Spain, of which the principal investigator is Bartolomé Yun-Casalilla.
2. The letters included with the licenses to the Indies have been published by Enrique Otte (Otte 1988). Werner Stangl has revised several editions of collections of private letters of the Spanish Empire (Stangl 2013).
3. Payment on arrival was in operation until at least the early seventeenth century. Sergio Rodríguez Lorenzo carried out a study of the contracts of passage deposited in the Archivo Histórico Provincial de Sevilla, Sección Protocolos Notariales (Rodríguez Lorenzo 2017).
4. Otte 1988, letter 372. Letter from Alonso Herejo to his wife Teresa González, in Reina (Tunja 1587).
5. As part of the population policy, several laws were passed to prevent the abandonment of women by their menfolk and to promote family reunification in

the Indies (Almorza Hidalgo and Rojas García 2015). Jane E. Mangan has analysed family relations in Atlantic Spanish America, their role during the emigration to Peru and how different types of families were created in the colony, incorporating indigenous, mestizos and Afro-Peruvians (Mangan 2016).

6. Otte 1988, letters 50–55. Letters from Alonso Ortíz (Mexico) to his wife Leonor González (Zafra, Badajoz), 1574. Leonor González finally travelled to Mexico in 1575 (Archivo General de Indias (AGI), Indiferente, 2056, N.77).
7. Otte 1988, letter 174. Letter from Sebastián de Pliego (Puebla, Mexico) to his wife Mari Díaz, in Mecina de Buen Varón (Granada).
8. Otte 1988, letter 254. Letter from Gaspar Viera (Ciudad Real de Chiapas) to his wife Cecilia Rodríguez Verdugo.
9. Otte 1988, letter 154. Letter from Luis de Córdoba (Puebla, Mexico) to his wife Isabel Carrera, in Seville, 1566.
10. Otte 1988, letter 19. Letter from Juan López de Sande (Mexico) to his wife Leonor de Haro, in Triana (Seville), 1568.
11. Otte 1988, letter 42. Letter from Bartolomé de Morales (Mexico) to his wife Catalina de Ávila, in Constantina (Seville), 1573.
12. Otte 1988, letter 36. Letter from Juana Bautista (Mexico) to his sister Mariana de Santillán (Seville), 1572.
13. Otte 1988, letter 89. Letter from Hernán Ruiz (Mexico) to his wife Mariana de Montedoca (Seville), 1584.
14. Otte 1988, letter 66.
15. Otte 1988, letter 17. Letter from Antonio de Blas (Mexico) to his wife Leonor Bernal (Sanlúcar), 1566.
16. Peter Boyd Bowman ascertained that the price of European textiles in Mexico increased by almost 200%, due to transatlantic transportation costs and Carrera de Indias fees. (Boyd Bowman 1973, 338).
17. Otte 1988, letter 70.
18. Otte 1988, letter 174. Letter from Sebastián de Pliego (Puebla, Mexico) to his brother, 1581. Otte 1988, letter 300, Letter from Diego de Virués (Nombre de Dios, Panama) to his wife Ana López de León (Seville), 1559.
19. Amy Stanley has analysed the wardrobe of women from the rural world who migrated to cities linked to domestic service in Japan in the nineteenth century, highlighting its value as an easily transportable item that could be sold and a key element in creating the identities of migrants (Stanley 2016).
20. Otte 1988, letter 365. Sebastián Gómez de Altamirano (Antioquía, Nueva Granada) to the graduate Francisco de Tena, in Campanario, 1592.
21. A large number of women who travelled to America in the sixteenth century were single (Almorza Hidalgo 2018).
22. AGI, Lima, 565, L3, 186 v.
23. Otte 1988, letter 174.
24. Otte 1988, letter 356. Letter from Juan de Mercado (Cartagena) to his wife María de Cárdenas (Seville), 1596.
25. Otte 1988, letter 319: "In Seville you dress in the way that is customary here".
26. The *ruán* was a textile named after the city of Rouen (France), and could be woollen or linen fabric. It was cheaper than other fabrics and normally used for skirts or household goods (curtains, sheets or tablecloths) (Boyd Bowman 1973, 347). Eufemio Lorenzo highlights the strong presence of French textiles (*angeos* and *ruán*) transported from Seville to the Indies in the sixteenth century (Lorenzo Sanz 1980, 157).

27. *Holanda* was "the most costly of sixteenth century linens, used to make fine kerchiefs, quilts, pillows, bedsheets, shirts and tunics for those who could afford quality fabrics" (Boyd Bowman 1973, 346).
28. Otte 1988, letter 319, Alonso Zamora from Santa Fé de Bogotá to his wife in Almaguer (Toledo).
29. The Castilian *vara* was a standard unit of length of approximately 2.8 feet (Boyd Bowman 1973, 336).
30. Otte 1988, letter 157. Letter from Diego de San Llorente (Puebla, Mexico) to his wife Luisa Sánchez, in Seville, 1571
31. *Saya* could be a skirt (non-elite women) or a dress (Bernis 2001, 221). Women would wear a shirt, *saya* and cloak when they left the house.
32. The *jubón* was a kind of doublet to be wear over the skirt (Bernis 2001, 217).
33. Otte 1988, letter 247. Letter from Francisco de Mesa (Guatemala) to his mother, Isabel Chaves, in Baena (Córdoba), 1585.
34. Otte 1988, letter 319. The women's clothes for journeys in the sixteenth century were as described in the letter, a green dress and a small cloak to wear with a hat (Bernis 2001, 46).
35. According to the dictionary of Sebastián de Covarrubias: "Taffeta: fine silk cloth, pronounced thus from the noise it makes when one is clothed in it, making the sound *tif, taf*. For its onomatopoeic form" (Covarrubias 1611). Silk fabrics, velvets, satin and taffeta, highly demanded among the Spanish elite, had different qualities and prices (Bernis 2001, 277).
36. Otte 1988, letter 443. Letter from Juan de Ribera (Lima) to his brother-in-law Rodrigo Díaz, dyer, in Seville, 1575.
37. Otte 1988, letter 497. Letter from Diego Hurtado (Lima) to his sister Juana Hurtado, in Seville, 1590.
38. Otte 1988, letter 181. Letter from María de Carranza (Puebla, Mexico) to her brother Hernando de Soto, in Seville, 1589.
39. Otte 1988, letter 298. Letter from Pedro Gallegos (Panama) to his wife María Jiménez, in Llerena (Badajoz), 1594.
40. *Burato* was a textile of silk or wool and silk, normally used for women's cloaks (Bernis 2001, 280).
41. Otte 1988, letter 42. Letter from Bartolomé de Morales (Mexico) to his wife Catalina de Ávila (Constantina, Seville), 1573.
42. Otte 1988, letter 376. Alonso Ramírez Gasco (Trinidad) to his son and son-in-law Juan García Ramírez and Pedro Sánchez de Corrales, in Villanueva de Alcardete (Toledo), 1577.
43. *Chapines* were the classic elite Spanish women's shoe in the early modern period, a high sandal made of cork and leather and covered in velvet (Bernis 2001, 271).
44. Otte 1988, letter 476. Roberto de Burt, stockinger, to his wife Ana Franca. Los Reyes, 1583
45. *Estameña* in early modern Spain was a silk cloth, commonly used in skirts (*basquiñas*) (Bernis 2001, 280). According to Sebastián de Covarrubias, *ropa* was the loose cloth to wear over the dress, which was tight to the body (Covarrubias 1611). Thus, the *ropa* could be worn over the shirt and *saya* or *jubón*.
46. Otte 1988, letter 49. Letter from Andrea López de Vargas (Mexico) to his sisters (Jerez de la Frontera, Cadiz), 1577.
47. Otte 1988, letter 59. Mexico, 1574, letter to his brother, inviting him to send the nephews.
48. Otte 1988, letter 414. Letter from Juan Fuero (San Miguel de Chimbo, Ecuador) to Juan Fernández Resio (Cuenca), 1587.

49. Otte 1988, letter 516. Letter from Diego de Espina (El Callao) to his wife María Sánchez (Seville), 1597.
50. Nochtepec was a mining enclave near Taxco (Province of Guerrero) (Enciso Contreras 1999).
51. Otte 1988, letter 216. Letter from Francisco Ramírez Bravo (Nochtepec, Mexico), to his daughter Doña Isabel Bravo (Lepe, Huelva), 1582. The *agnus dei* was a small religious figure of a sheep, representing Jesus Christ, that was also used as an amulet (Covarrubias 1611; and Aram 2001, 274).
52. Peter Boyd Bowman also mentions several sixteenth-century accounts which describe the Mexican population's excessive use of silk (Boyd Bowman 1973).
53. Otte 1988, letter 351. Letter from Diego de Saldaña (Cartagena) to his wife Águeda Martínez (Villanueva de Alcardete, Toledo), 1590.
54. Otte 1988, letter 524. Letter from Cristóbal de Montalvo (Trujillo) to his mother-in-law Margarita de Ayala (Seville), 1590.
55. Otte 1988, letter 425. Letter from Sebastián Carrera (Lima) to his wife, 1558.
56. Otte 1988, letter 511, Letter from Juan Delgado de Salido (Lima), to his father, Juan Aguado, in Alcobendas (Madrid), 1599.
57. Bernabé Cobo estimates that at the outset of the seventeenth century Lima had 61,000 inhabitants, made up of 25,000 Spaniards, 30,000 Blacks and 6,000 Indians (Bromley 1959).
58. According to Gleydi Sullón, a significant share of this clothing trade with Spain was in the hands of the Portuguese (Sullón 2016).
59. Poma de Ayala 1615–1616, fol. 1034, "*Ciudad*".
60. On the *almojarifazgo* of the Indies: Lorenzo 1980, 363.
61. AGI, Lima, 566, L.6, F.248R, 1550.
62. AGI, Lima, 566, L.6, F.175V, 1549.
63. Otte 1988, letter 423. Letter from Alonso del Castillo (Lima) to his father, 1557.
64. Otte 1988, letter 487. Letter from Celedón Favalis (Lima) to his father, Simón Favalis (Madrid), 1587.
65. Rafael Varón Gabai analyzed the businesses of the Pizarro family in Peru in the sixteenth century (Varón Gabai 1994).
66. Otte 1988, letter 330. Letter from Francisco del Barco to his siblings Antón Rodríguez and Catalina González (Las Casas de Millán, Cáceres), 1575.
67. Ocaña 1605, 64.
68. Otte 1988, letter 487, 1587.
69. Otte 1988, letter 497. Letter from Diego Hurtado (Lima) to his sister Juana Hurtado (Seville), 1590.
70. Otte 1988, letter 497.
71. Otte 1988, letter 277. Letter from Hernando de Cantillana (Panama) to his wife doña Magdalena de Cárdenas, in Seville, 1575. Hernando de Cantillana sent his wife clothes that had been on the market for sale in Lima for sixteen years.
72. Otte 1988, letter 479. Letter from Alonso de Villadiego to his nephew Tomé Sánchez de Guzmán, a merchant in Salamanca (Lima), 1584.

Bibliography

Almorza Hidalgo, Amelia. 2010. "Sibling relations in Spanish emigration to Latin America, 1560–1620." *European Review of History: Revue europeenne d'histoire* 17 (5): 735–52.

———. 2015. "Género y conflicto social en las primeras descripciones del Virreinato del Perú (siglo XVII)." In *Comercio y cultura en la Edad Moderna. Actas de la XIII Reunión Científica de la Fundación Española de Historia Moderna*, edited by Juan José Iglesias Rodríguez, 2.569 2.581. Seville: Universidad de Sevilla.

———. 2018. *"No se hace pueblo sin ellas". Mujeres españolas en el Virreinato de Perú: emigración y movilidad social (siglos XVI – XVII)*. Madrid: CSIC, Universidad de Sevilla, Diputación de Sevilla.

Almorza Hidalgo, Amelia y Reyes Rojas García. 2015. "Los expedientes de vida maridable del Archivo General de Indias: análisis de un caso de estudio." In *América en la burocracia de la monarquía española. Documentos para su estudio*, edited by Jaqueline Vassallo y Noelia García, 111–30. Córdoba: CIECS CONICET, Bruges.

Altman, Ida. 2000. *Transatlantic Ties in the Spanish Empire: Brihuega, Spain and Puebla, Mexico, 1560–1620*. Stanford, CA: Stanford University Press.

Aram, Bethany. 2001. *La reina Juana. Gobierno, piedad y dinastía*. Madrid: Marcial Pons.

Aram, Bethany, and Bartolomé Yun-Casalilla, eds. 2014. *Global Goods and the Spanish Empire, 1492–1824. Circulation, Resistance and Diversity*. Houndmills, England: Palgrave Macmillan.

Bauer, Arnold J. 2001. *Goods, Power, History. Latin America's Material Culture*. Cambridge: Cambridge University Press.

Bernis, Carmen. 2001. *El traje y los tipos sociales en El Quijote*. Madrid: Ediciones El Viso.

Boyd Bowman, Peter. 1973. "Spanish and European Textiles in Sixteenth Century Mexico." *The Americas* 9 (3) (January): 334–58.

Bromley, Juan. 1959. "La ciudad de Lima en el año 1630." *Revista Histórica* 24: 268–317.

Carletti, Francesco. 1976. *Razonamiento de mi viaje alrededor del mundo (1594–1606)*. México: Universidad Nacional Autónoma de México.

Cavallo, Sandra. 2000. "What did Women Transmit? Ownership and Control of Household Goods and Personal Effects in Early Modern Italy." In *Gender and Material Culture in Historical Perspective*, edited by Moira Donald and Linda Hurcombe, 38–53. London: Macmillan Press.

Covarrubias Orozco, Sebastián de. 1611. *Tesoro de la lengua Castellana o española*. Madrid: printer Luis Sánchez.

Earle, Rebecca. 2001. "Two pairs of Pink Satin Shoes!!; Race, clothing and identity in the Americas (17th – 19th centuries)." *History Workshop Journal* 52: 175–95.

Elliott, John. 2006. *Imperios del Mundo Atlántico. España y Gran Bretaña en América (1492–1830)*. Madrid: Taurus.

Enciso Contreras, José. 1999. *Taxco en el siglo XVI: sociedad y normatividad en un real de minas novohispano*. México: Council of Zacatecas.

Gage, Thomas. 1648. *The English – American his travel by sea and land, or, A New survey on the West Indies (1610–1656)*. London.

Graubart, Karen B. 2007. *With Our Labor and Sweat: Indigenous women and the construction of colonial society in Peru, 1550–1700*. Stanford, CA: Stanford University Press.

Gruzinski, Serge. 2006. "Mundialización, globalización y mestizajes en la Monarquía católica." In *Europa, América y el mundo: tiempos históricos*, edited by Antonio Feros and Roger Chartier, 239–62. Madrid: Marcial Pons.

León Portocarrero, Pedro de. 1958. *Descripción del Virreinato del Perú: crónica inédita de principios del siglo XVII*. Rosario, Argentina: Universidad Nacional del Litoral.

Lorenzo Sanz, Eufemio. 1979. *Comercio de España con América en la época de Felipe II. Tomo I, los mercaderes y el tráfico indiano*. Valladolid: Servicio de Publicaciones de la Diputación Provincial de Valladolid.

———. 1980. *Comercio de España con América en la época de Felipe II. Tomo II, la navegación, los tesoros y las perlas*. Valladolid: Servicio de Publicaciones de la Diputación Provincial de Valladolid.

Mangan, Jane E. 2016. *Transatlantic Obligations: Creating the Bonds of Family in Conquest – Era Peru and Spain*. New York: Oxford University Press.

Martínez, José Luis. 1999. *Pasajeros a Indias. Viajes trasatlánticos en el siglo XVI*. Madrid: Fondo de Cultura Económico.

Mena García, Carmen. 2004. "Nuevos datos sobre bastimentos y envases en armadas y flotas de la Carrera." *Revista de Indias* 64 (231): 447–84.

Miño Grijalva, Manuel. 1991. "La manufactura colonial: aspectos comparativos entre el obraje andino y el novohispano." In *El sistema colonial en la América Española*, edited by Heraclio Bonilla, 103–53. Barcelona: Crítica.

Mörner, Magnus. 1976. "Spanish emigration to the New World prior to 1810: A report of the state of research." In *First Images of America: The Impact of the New World on the Old*, edited by Fredi Chiapelli, 737–81. Berkeley: University of California Press.

Ocaña, Diego. 1605. *Relación del viaje de Fray Diego de Ocaña por el Nuevo Mundo (1599–1605)*. Archive of the University of Oviedo. http://digibuo.uniovi.es/dspace/handle/10651/27859.

Oliva Melgar, José María. 2003. "La participación extranjera en el monopolio y el consulado de Indias en el siglo XVII." *Rábida* 22: 53–66.

Olivera Alegre, Gloria. 2005. "Las mercancías textiles en el Virreinato del Perú del siglo XVI: calidad y necesidades." *Cultura* 23 (19): 359–77.

Otte, Enrique. 1988. *Cartas privadas de emigrantes a Indias. 1540–1616*. Seville: Consejería de Cultura. Junta de Andalucía.

Phillips, Carla Rahn. 2003. "Mercado, modas y gustos: los cargamentos de ida y vuelta en el comercio atlántico de España." In *España y América: un océano de negocios. Quinto Centenario de la Casa de la Contratación, 1503–2003*, 187–202. Madrid: Sociedad Estatal de Conmemoraciones Culturales.

Poma de Ayala, Felipe Guamán. 1615–1616. *Nueva Crónica y buen gobierno* [on line]. Digital Research Center of the Royal Library, Copenhagen, Denmark. www.kb.dk/permalink/2006/poma/info/en/frontpage.htm

Presta, Ana María. 2010. "Undressing the Coya and Dressing the Indian Woman: Market Economy, Clothing, and Identities in the Colonial Andes, La Plata (Charcas), Late Sixteenth and Early Seventeenth Centuries." *Hispanic American Historical Review* 90 (1): 41–74.

Rodríguez Lorenzo, Sergio. 2017. "El contrato de pasaje en la carrera de indias (1561–1622)." *Historia Mexicana* LXVI (3): 1479–571.

Salinas y Córdoba, Buenaventura De. 1957. *Memorial de las historias del Nuevo Mundo (1630)*. Lima: Universidad Nacional de San Marcos.

Stangl, Werner. 2013. "Un cuarto de siglo con 'Cartas privadas de emigrantes a Indias'. Prácticas y perspectivas de ediciones de cartas transatlánticas en el imperio español." *Anuario de Estudios Americanos* 70 (2): 703–36.

Stanley, Amy. 2016. "Maidservants' Tales: Narrating Domestic and Global History in Eurasia, 1600–1900." *The American Historical Review* 121 (2): 437–60.

Subrahmanyam, Sanjay. 1997. "Connected Histories: Notes towards a Reconfiguration of Early Modern Eurasia." *Modern Asian Studies* 31 (3): 735–62.

Sullón, Gleydi. 2016. *Extranjeros integrados: portugueses en la Lima Virreinal, 1570–1680*. Madrid: CSIC.

Varón Gabai, Rafael. 1994. "Negocios y gobierno de los Pizarro del Perú. Un ensayo de interpretación." *Histórica* XVIII (2): 417–34.

Vila Vilar, Enriqueta. 1991. *Los Corzo y los Mañara: tipos y arquetipos del mercader con América*. Sevilla: Escuela de Estudios Hispano-Americanos.

Yun-Casalilla, Bartolomé. 2014. "The Spanish Empire, Globalization, and Cross-Cultural Consumption in a World Context, C.1400–1750." In *Global Goods and the Spanish Empire, 1492–1824. Circulation, Resistance and Diversity*, edited by Bethany Aram and Bartolomé Yun-Casalilla, 277–305. Houndmills, England: Palgrave Macmillan.

Part II

Food and Empire

5 The Introduction of Poultry Farming to the Indigenous People of the New Kingdom of Granada, Sixteenth and Seventeenth Centuries[1]

Gregorio Saldarriaga

Introduction

While the exchange of products between different parts of the world, especially after 1492, interested anthropologists and historians throughout the twentieth century (Foster 1962; Carcer and Disdier 1955), it was with the classical works of A. W. Crosby, *The Columbian Exchange* (1973), *Ecological Imperialism* (1986), and *Germs, Seeds, and Animals* (1993), that the subject was given a more comprehensive appraisal, highlighting both the ecological and demographic impact of these exchanges. In Crosby's work and in subsequent studies the introduction of animals plays an important role, with special emphasis on cattle herds large and small (Del Río Moreno and López and Sebastián 1998, 1999; Melville 1994; Gómez 2016; Castaño 2019), as their breeding produced changes in ecosystems and even in the conditions of the different areas where they were introduced.

In general, scant attention has been paid to the introduction of birds, especially poultry, in America.[2] This may be because their ecological and geographical impact was not as evident as that of cows, sheep and pigs. However, their presence should not be underestimated for two reasons: a) chickens had an important place in the European diet in the early modern age, as dietary treatises acknowledged chicken as a meat that provided sustenance, and it was delicate in flavor, as well as healthy. It was therefore prescribed for the sick, and deemed suitable for the upper echelons of society. It is worth recalling that between the end of the Middle Ages and the beginning of the modern era foods were considered suitable for certain people according to their position in society;[3] b) the profound socio-economic and cultural impact of their introduction, given that their geographical spread extended beyond that of sheep and goats. Chickens also had a greater presence than pigs and cows in the homes of different social groups. Cows and pigs were present throughout the continent, but did not feature to the same extent as chickens in the homes of the natives, people of color and Spaniards, one of the reasons being that poultry could be raised in relatively confined spaces and with

DOI: 10.4324/9781003168058-6

minimum effort, while raising pigs and cattle demanded a far greater economic investment.

This chapter studies the introduction and spread of birds in the New Kingdom of Granada, concentrating on how this occurred in indigenous settlements, from the sixteenth to the mid-seventeenth century. We will focus our attention on the imperial administrative mechanisms that sought to impose breeding among the indigenous population, the contradictions between royal officials arising from this enforcement and more importantly, the way in which indigenous communities reacted to the presence of these animals. In order to achieve this objective, special attention will be given to the different forms of production, distribution and consumption of breeding birds. But this chapter will also analyze the way indigenous poultry activities, due to the availability of cash derived from them, had an impact on other products' consumption. Although the research of this last aspect is not easy, due to the bias of the sources generated by the *visitas de la tierra* (the inquiries on the different regions promoted by the Spanish authorities), which are mostly inexpressive about the consumption of these goods, this double approach is important for a better understanding of the way the indigenous populations took advantages of these new activities.

Tributes, *Congrua* and Religious Payments

As noted by Colmenares, within the *encomiendas* taxation through the payment of tributes went through several stages. At first, it was unregulated and depended on the will of the Spaniards and the economic capacity of the indigenous population. From 1542, the Crown insisted that the governors and bishops should start placing a value on the villages, although not many records of these processes have survived.[4] A centralized tax regulation began to emerge with the establishment of the Audiencia of Santa Fe in 1550; especially with the land *visitas* (inspection visits carried out by royal civil servants, or *visitadores*, in some particular territories) that verified the living conditions of the natives and the appraisals of their tributes conducted by the *oidores* (judges) of the Audencia from 1555 onwards. From the moment these visits began, the *oidores* were given the title of visitors. In 1590, when Antonio González was president of the Audiencia, the *encomenderos* lost their absolute monopoly over native labor. From then on they could reserve only some of the natives from their *encomiendas* to do specific work for them. The others could be hired by other people for different types of activities (Colmenares 1999, 136–55). Anyone who was hiring had to refer to the *corregidor de indios* (administrative official) to arrange work with the indigenous (at least from 1593 onwards, when the institution was created). For our purposes here it is important to take this process into account, as it demonstrates how relations between the indigenous peoples and the dominant society started out with the exclusive intermediation of the *encomenderos*, and how this changed over time as other types of commercial relations became institutionalized.[5]

Tributes varied from one region to the next because a basic tenet of the Crown was that each town would pay according to its possibilities and what it could produce. They also varied according to the appraisals and reassessments. However, from the 1550s onward, once the tribute system was established, it was maintained across all the provinces of the New Kingdom of Granada that men between the ages of seventeen and fifty-four who were not nobles (*caciques* and captains) were obliged to pay tributes on the various products for which they had been appraised, twice yearly, by the feast of St. John and by Christmas.[6]

The visiting *oidores* did not set the rate uniformly in all the provinces of the New Kingdom of Granada; there were areas where taxes were established from the first visits (1555), while others had to wait until later in the sixteenth century. In spite of this, given the dietetic importance of chickens, taxes on these birds were already in place in many towns prior to the establishment of official taxation by the Audiencia,[7] in compliance with the Burgos Laws (1512) which ordained that each village was to receive twelve hens and one rooster, for their personal benefit.[8]

We do not know whether this ruling was fully implemented, but it appears likely that the hens were soon distributed among the Indians. An early example of this is the governorship of Cartagena, where taxation was established in general terms by the governor and bishop prior to the visits of the *oidores*. Unfortunately, no copies of the amounts imposed as payment have been found. Our only reference is the testimonies that in 1569 gave an account of the tributes that the Indians paid. The indigenous people of Pihón and Tameme indicated that they carried hens and aboriginal partridges (*Colinus cristatus*) to the house of their *encomendera*, Constanza de Heredia. In the relationship between Indians and *encomendera*, taxes and commercial figures became intertwined. The *encomendera* sometimes paid two *reales* for the hens, when each Indian delivered eight hens, while on other occasions she paid barely three *reales* to each carrier, or four *pesos for* 40 partridges. It is probable that for deliveries of a higher value she paid for the goods, and she paid the transport only for lower-valued deliveries.[9] After 1569, the visitor Melchor de Arteaga, *oidor* of the New Kingdom of Granada, established that each taxpayer would give two hens a year, and that twenty taxpayers would have to clear, lumber and burn a *fanega* (measure of land) for sowing corn. The governor of Cartagena, Pedro Fernández de Busto, wrote in 1571 that the levy was high for hens; six years later, the Bishop of Cartagena, Brother Dionisio de los Santos, put forward the same argument. Both proposed removing hens from taxation in order to increase agricultural work. The bishop's proposal was to increase corn production, while the governor was in favor of cassava and corn, although quantities were not specified.[10] According to the governor, the Audiencia's appraisal was damaging to the indigenous people because they had never seen a chicken in their lives, which, of course, was an exaggeration, given that the 1569 visit already states that the Indians were paying taxes on hens. However, this statement could be interpreted as an indication that the model had not yet been firmly introduced among the Indians and was still proving to be quite a burden.

The role of partridges in the system of tributes, as mentioned in connection with Doña Constanza de Heredia and her *encomienda*, must be taken into account. When President Antonio González assessed the province in 1590, he ordered, among other things, that each taxpayer should pay a hen and two partridges per year.[11] It would seem that he took heed of the plea made by the bishop and governor some years before, because he reduced the number of hens by half, although he did not implement the change as they had suggested. González was particularly careful not to affect the city of Cartagena's supply system, which attracted a substantial share of the province's production. This explains why in many of the ordinances he drafted for the *encomiendas* he acted merely as a legitimator, maintaining existing uses and customs in the governorship (Saldarriaga 2011, 236). It made sense that partridges were chosen instead of hens (or along with them), because, although their culinary and dietetic characteristics were very similar (Huarte de San Juan 1976 [1575], 248 and 334), the manner of procuring them was completely different. Hens involve breeding, while securing partridges meant hunting for them in the woodlands at a certain time of year, an activity that took about a week.[12] In the testimonies recorded by the visitor Juan de Villabona y Zubiaurre during his visit to Cartagena between 1609 and 1611, some residents reported that partridge hunting was difficult for the natives and those without experience had to resort to buying partridges.[13] It is tempting to think that the requests to eliminate partridge taxation were influenced by the increase in poultry among the Indians. However, the same witnesses argued that hens should also be removed from taxation, not because they were in short supply, but because those available were for their own use; they too advised an increase in taxes on corn to compensate for this reduction.[14] Nevertheless, Villabona y Zubiaurre considered that only the partridges ought to be exempt from taxation.[15] This visitor's decision offers further insight into two aspects of the appraisals: 1) the *visitadores'* observations were not always dictated by the natives' possibilities of making payment, but were mediated through negotiation with the traditions of the region and the Crown's political and economic policy; 2) there was a desire to implement a working model that corresponded with Christian life: it was not so much that partridge hunting was viewed as unsuitable, but it was deemed preferable that these country folk should be involved in raising animals or cultivating crops, which was the role the indigenous communities played within this hierarchical society (Norton 2015, 58–59).

Tribute payments were generally set at two hens for each Indian; one had to be paid on the feast of St. John and the other at Christmas. Sometimes a fixed quantity was imposed, lower than the number of taxpayers, but in any case it involved a large quantity of birds. This was the case of the taxpayers of the Sibundoy valley, whose tributes were assessed at 900 hens in 1570 by the visitor Garcia de Valverde, in spite of the fact that the men of tax-paying age totaled 1,371.[16]

The introduction of hens was so prevalent that between the turn of the century and the 1630s, certain villages indicated that they could pay part of their tribute in hens. Some asked for all or a large part to be paid in poultry; others even proceeded to exchange payment[17] of some of their taxes with hens.[18] One of the reasons for this is illustrated by the indigenous people of Siquima and Manoa. According to Pedro Combi, although they produced many things, these villagers preferred to pay with hens and chickens, because they were available in their own homes.[19] This indicates the extent to which poultry-keeping had become a domestic activity among the natives. Other towns did not offer any explanation for why it suited them to pay their tribute in hens, but had proceeded directly with the changeover. Such was the case of the town of Guatica, in the Popayán province; since 1623 they had changed from paying half a *fanega* of corn to the Protector of Indians, to giving him a chicken, arracachas (*Arracaccia xanthorrhiza*), bananas and yucas. A report by Francisco Tuza indicates that in 1619 a locust plague in the area not only affected harvest that year, but also the possibility of growing corn in following years (although the reason for this is not explained). They went from cultivating an area for the *encomendero* of ten *almudes* – divided into two crops a year – with the help of a plow pulled by oxen, to sowing twenty *almudes*, without the help of the oxen and in low areas and cane fields.[20] That is to say, the locust plague had scaled up the natives' work growing corn, making it harder for them to comply with their tax obligations. Switching from corn payments to arracachas, bananas and yucas made sense, as these were farming activities that did not directly compete with corn during the sowing or the harvesting season. Likewise, hens involved work, but without the complexity of growing corn, since raising poultry was a domestic activity incorporated into the natives' daily lives.

Aside from those who explicitly asked to pay their tribute in hens, it is clear that the integration of poultry in the daily life of the indigenous peoples was a reality in almost the entire New Kingdom of Granada. This is demonstrated by the fact that, except for Cartagena and the Panches towns, the indigenous peoples did not seem to have problems with paying tributes with hens nor did they complain to the visitor about this aspect of their tax. The complaints arose when eggs and hens were forcibly taken from them, and paid at lower prices than their value.[21]

The indigenous people also had to give poultry to their parish priests, as part of the income from their ecclesiastical office; this emolument was called a *congrua*. The first appraisals in 1555 ordered them to supply the priest with ten birds a week – five hens and five roosters. On the days when meat consumption was forbidden, natives had to give the priest twelve eggs and fish each day.[22] In 1576, the fixed amounts were set, through ordinances, for the towns of the Tunja and Santa Fe regions. The number of hens was reduced, with the stipulation that priests had to receive three per week from the indigenous. However, the number of eggs rose to twenty on vigil days and during Lent when fish also increased to "three fish canes" (about fifteen fish).[23] From then on the rule was maintained throughout the sixteenth century without any major changes in the number of hens.[24] There were variations in the number of eggs, however; for example in Ubaté, according to the testimony of *cacique* Juan Neabascaguya in 1592, on Fridays and Saturdays they gave sixty eggs to the parish priest. According to another testimony presented in 1594 by *cacique* Don Alonso Meagam, the inhabitants of Siminjaca gave forty eggs every Friday and Saturday.[25] Some parish priests tried to stretch their *congrua* with the help of the young people attending their doctrine classes, by forcing them to do manual labor, hunt animals or collect vegetables (López Rodríguez 2001, 131–34). The parish priests in Teusaca, for example, in addition to receiving the stipulated amount, used to ask the youngsters for more potatoes and eggs, which they had to take from their homes, and they also sent them out to hunt rabbits and birds for them.[26]

The burden that this *congrua* represented for the towns is striking. It is true that in most cases it was not a year-round obligation, because it had to be paid only while the priest was in the locality. There were very few villages in the New Kingdom of Granada with doctrinal instruction twelve months in a row; the normal period was three months for a small town or six for a medium-sized town. However, three months of instruction for a small town meant about thirty-six hens and 240 eggs, while in a large town the amounts doubled. In larger towns, payment rotated by *parcialidades*, the various groups that existed within the town, each headed by a captain.[27] The people of Caqueza and Ubatoque, congregated in a single town, had doctrine instruction all year round and took turns with their monthly payments. The only time of year when instruction stopped was Lent, when the priest went to Santa Fe. On his return, he asked them for the hens, eggs and corn for the time he was absent (López Rodríguez 2000, s. 47, 48, 32).

The *congrua* was not the only religious tax that the natives had to pay; at the very least they also had to make payments for papal bulls (Hernández Méndez 2006; Benito Rodríguez 1996), brotherhoods, tithes and religious services.[28] In 1594 the *cacique* of Suta stated that the papal bulls had to be paid by the indigenous who lived in the town as well as by those who had fled from it.[29] In this particular case, they paid with money obtained from farm produce. In other towns without money or gold dust, such as Momil and Perina in the governorship of Cartagena, they paid the parish priest three hens for each papal bull.[30] The natives also paid for religious services, mainly marriages and baptisms. The Indians were not supposed to be charged for these services; this probably explains why in their testimonies they indicated that these payments were voluntary. Depending on the region and time, the charges varied from one chicken for a christening, to four hens for a wedding, or just one, but cooked or roasted.[31]

Towns handed over a substantial number of hens to the Spaniards through tributes paid directly to the *encomenderos* and various payments to the Church and its members. However, it is also clear that poultry activity had transcended the raising of a few hens and had developed into the business of poultry farming. In other words, it had become an activity from which the Indians obtained economic benefits. This came about because they had learnt how to take ownership of poultry rearing and because the Crown became interested in the activity since the last decade of the sixteenth century. By this time the indigenous productive system had already been transformed, and the indigenous producers had gained entry into the markets with the birds they supplied directly from their henhouses, without the mediation of the *encomendero*. Thus, in 1590, in the province of Cartagena, Antonio González prohibited *encomenderos* from contracting from the Indians more hens than they needed for their own households. The tribute itself was not altered by this limitation, because it had already been fixed by the appraisals, but the ruling seriously curtailed purchases by the *encomenderos* from the Indians. This curbed the monopoly previously exercised by the *encomenderos* and allowed the Indians to freely negotiate the selling of hens with other buyers. Failure to comply with these regulations led to the suspension of an *encomienda* for two years.[32]

Production Units

Before moving on to the markets, it is worth pausing for a moment to consider production mechanisms and regulations. The initial delivery of poultry to the Indians is not clearly documented and there is a lack of sources apart from the order, laid down by the Burgos Laws of 1512, to give twelve hens and one rooster to each town. It is unclear how the initial arrangement was implemented in the New Kingdom; the operation is as blurred and lacking in documentary evidence as all tax obligations prior to the enactment of the New Laws of 1542 and the visits and appraisals of the New Kingdom of Granada. However, what was clearly stated was the number of birds to be delivered, not how production was to be organized; besides, in its initial stages it was clear that hens were only for the benefit of the natives and should not be taken by the Spaniards. To gain a better understanding of the process of introducing poultry-rearing practices in indigenous populations, let us look at how this was stipulated for the Spanish settlements, although, as we shall see, this was not always explicit. For example, the first rulings handed down for Santa Marta mentioned the breeding animals, such as cows and pigs, but hens did not feature, as they were included under the generic term of 'other breeding animals' (Friede 1955, 76). In those early years there did not seem to be any Crown ruling on how to establish the breeding of these animals.

The first regulation appeared only in 1573, in the "Ordinances for the Discovery, New Population and Pacification of the Indies", specifying the breeding animals and the amounts that the inhabitants of the new settlements should have. Ordinance 89 specified that, in addition to other animals, each resident was to have six hens and one rooster. Comparing this ruling with the Burgos Laws, there were two obvious differences. On the one hand, in relation to the number and proportion of hens to roosters, the Burgos document stipulated twelve to one, while the ordinance stated six to one. On the other hand, in the Burgos document the figures were for an entire town, while in the ordinance figures were for each head of household residing in a town. Although there are divergences between the two regulations, these are understandable because of the different parameters addressed.

Years later, in 1601, when visiting the towns of Balsa and Fontibón de Ulata – having departed from Pamplona – Antonio Beltrán de Guevara, *corregidor* and senior judge in Tunja, brought in a ruling to ensure that the Indians would have eggs and birds to sell. He ordered that each resident should have six hens and one rooster, while the *caciques* and governors should have ten hens and one rooster.[33] The reason for the difference is not evident in the order prescribed by Beltrán de Guevara, although one might assume that it combined elements of business and hierarchical logic: the fact that the principals had more than the other residents strengthened their authority, as it gave them greater prestige.

It is probable that the criteria applied by Beltrán de Guevara had been also met in the other indigenous towns under the jurisdiction of the city of Tunja. When the *oidor* Juan de Valcárcel visited Tequia in 1635, the *cacique* don Pedro testified that some men had six hens, while others had ten.[34] His testimony does not clarify whether some had more on account of their political position or simply as a result of their own endeavors. The latter may be the reason, because, according to the same *cacique*, every indigenous subject had two or three mares, and some of them even ten or twenty sheep,[35] and traded with Spaniards from the large estates or from Tunja. Aside from the question of whether trading interfered with the idea of social differentiation that the Spaniards were attempting to impose with chicken breeding, the interesting thing is that the henhouses continued to have six or ten hens. However, with Valcárcel's visit that pattern changed, because he demanded that each Indigenous man in a town should have twelve hens and one rooster.[36] This standardized increase in the number of hens was intended to ensure that the Indians would always have hens, chickens, capons and eggs to sell to travellers.

The provisions of 1603 and 1635 regarding the number of hens have one element in common: they did not deal with the tribute system, but with creating the means whereby the indigenous people could supply a market away from the *encomienda* system. The Crown sought to ensure that indigenous subjects were directly involved in the poultry trade, or at least that they could trade without the mediation of the *encomenderos*, thereby reinforcing the practices of a Westernized model of life, while restricting the power of the *encomenderos*.

Despite the lack of initial information on the introduction of chicken breeding among the natives, at least in terms of production units, the presence of poultry rearing gradually increased in the villages, with hens being reared by individuals rather than collectively. In the first instance, the number of henhouses per village expanded, followed by an increase in the size of the henhouses. As the indigenous people went from a productive model that sought to satisfy fiscal and religious obligations to one that fed the market, the daily life of the indigenous people was transformed in terms of work, productivity and income.

Trade and the Poultry Market

Indigenous peoples could sell hens, chickens, capons, roosters and eggs in their own towns and villages, or they could sell them elsewhere. In indigenous towns located at the intersections of roads or waterways, travellers were the most recurrent purchasers. In the center of the Audiencia, some towns, like Motavita, Cómbita, Susa and Suta, combined the selling of products with horse rentals for passengers, meeting the needs of the people travelling between Santa Fe, Villa de Leiva and Tunja. In towns like Tibitó, various products were sold, not within the town itself, but on the *camino real* that connected the Spanish settlements.[37] There are records of these activities from the late sixteenth century until 1638, but it is likely that they continued throughout the colonial period.

In the towns of the province of Cartagena, goods were supplied to passengers travelling within the governorship or to other provinces; transport was essentially by river for those making the journey to or from the province of Antioquia or the center of the Audiencia. Unlike in the intermediate towns between Tunja and Santa Fe, there was very little diversity in the merchandise offered to travellers, as it was almost entirely restricted to hens and eggs. At most, ducks occasionally appeared.[38] This shows that the productivity of some towns in the central highlands was more diverse in comparison to others areas in the New Kingdom of Granada, which translated into relative prosperity that became evident at the beginning of the seventeenth century. However, production in the towns of Cartagena should not be overlooked, as here there are two aspects worth considering: first, the indigenous demographic density of the Cartagena province was lower than that of Santa Fe and Tunja; second, passenger traffic to or from Cartagena was intense, given that this was the most important port in the New Kingdom of Granada and one of the main ports of the American Atlantic during the sixteenth and seventeenth centuries. Therefore, a relatively low population had to supply the needs of an elevated number of travellers, so the indigenous groups of Cartagena did not have the luxury of diversifying their commodities for selling; it is clear they could have more products for paying taxes, but this was forced by the power of the *encomenderos*, but Indians did not sell these other products for their own interest.

On the other hand, in areas where traffic was less intense and there were hardly any travellers to buy chickens and hens, as was the case for the Indian villages located along the road to Cartago or Carrapa on the border between Antioquia and Popayán governorships, the problem faced by indigenous populations was not related to production, but to lack of demand.[39] In other towns within the jurisdiction or in the mining area of Antioquia, they found a way of selling their hens but it is not clear that their customers were the travelling public.[40]

The other alternative was to sell hens, chickens and eggs in the town to people looking to buy in large numbers, unlike the travelling public who usually purchased on a retail basis. Large-scale buyers then moved on to cities and mines to sell their purchases. According to Fray Pedro Simón, at the beginning of the seventeenth century the Darién Indians, who were not under Spanish domination, sold 1,000 hens to a resident of Cartagena, who in turn sold them in that city (Simón 1982, 261 and 494). Around 1610, the local *encomendero* Diego de Mesa, bought a hundred birds – hens, chickens and pullets – from the Indians in his town of Cince to take to Zaragoza.[41] In part, this was the kind of practice that the Crown sought to avoid by limiting the number of hens that an *encomendero* could contract with the town under his stewardship. However, the business was sufficiently lucrative for these limitations to be respected. *Encomenderos*, overseers and parish priests bought hens or exchanged them for products, and then sold them at a considerable profit.[42]

In addition to selling hens in the town and its surroundings, the natives were in the habit of heading out to sell in cities, mines, or other indigenous towns. For reasons that may have been linked to tax pressure, low population density, the constraints of *encomenderos* and managers or the fact that local sales had used up their entire production capacity, the towns of the Cartagena province did not sell their products outside their own settlements. Clearly they travelled to Cartagena to take the hens to their *encomenderos*, but they did not do so for their own benefit. In contrast, in another area with a low density of indigenous people, such as the mining west, within the province of Antioquia and the north of the Popayán province, the indigenous inhabitants used to take their hens to the cities and mines to sell them to Spaniards, other natives or people of color. Whether in cities or mines, it appears that chickens played a prominent role in trade, but were not the only goods for sale; soap, cane syrup, corn, beans, pigs and ducks were also sold, among other items. In the regions of Arma and Anserma, although the mines were less prosperous than those of Antioquia, some of the towns gained a certain level of wealth, and even had their own pack animals (oxen or domesticated cows) to transport all these products.[43]

The Eastern mining town of Montuosa, in the Pamplona district, provided an attractive market for hens reared by Indians in the nearby villages.[44] Prices were much lower than in the mines of Antioquia: a hen was sold for two *tomines* and a chicken for one, a price that was twelve times lower than in Zaragoza. Some of the hens destined for Zaragoza were raised in the towns of Cartagena, where they already had a higher value than at the Montuosa mine. The absence of bird-producing villages in the vicinity of Zaragoza, in a province where supply was already under pressure due to high demand, meant that prices in Zaragoza were much higher than those in the Pamplona mines.

In the center of the Audiencia, and especially in towns around Santa Fe and Tunja, there was a thriving poultry trade from the late sixteenth century to the mid-seventeenth century. It was also extremely varied on account of the number of different trading centers. Of all the regions of the New Kingdom of Granada, this one was the most frequently inspected in the colonial period and consequently more information exists about this region than others. Perhaps, this larger quantity of information available could distort comparisons.

Not all urban centers in the province of the New Kingdom of Granada attracted indigenous poultry production to the same degree. For example, the emerald mines of Muzo did not constitute a market for poultry, but this was not due to a lack of interest in trade, as Indians took wheat flour for sale there.[45] For the Ubaté merchants, hens were a means to buy the wheat, which, once ground and sieved, was taken to Muzo. Unfortunately it has not been possible to find a suitable explanation as to why the indigenous merchants opted for this particular course of action. Tunja was not an attractive destination for Indian free enterprise either, unlike Santa Fe, where the indigenous people of Bogotá, Cájica, Cueca, Engativa, Fontibón, Gachencipá, Neusa, Sopono, Taguencipá and Usaquen came to sell their birds.[46] Other Spanish towns and villages that purchased birds from indigenous merchants were Villa de Leiva and Honda, Mariquita, San Sebastián de las Lajas and Vélez.[47]

Other places that purchased birds from the indigenous traders were some of the larger indigenous towns in the municipalities of Santa Fe and Tunja, such as Duitama, Sogomoso, Tunjara, Ubaté and Zipaquirá.[48] Archaeological and ethnohistorical studies have revealed that prior to the arrival of the Spaniards, there were markets in various settlements in Muisca territory (Langebaek 1987, 20, 91; Langebaek 2008, 81–88). The prevalence of the markets is not our primary interest, but rather the incorporation of hens and eggs as products for sale. These were not the only products of European origin on sale; some of the villages that took their hens there also transported wheat, sheep and wool blankets.[49] However, hens were the only item for sale in all the markets. Unfortunately, it is not possible to determine who the buyers were, or the final destinations of purchased products. As "European" products were highly coveted in Spanish society, one can reasonably assume that they would later feed into the trade channels of towns, cities and mines, or that they could also be used for indigenous consumption.

Consumption and the Use of Hens

So far we have shown that the indigenous peoples of the New Kingdom of Granada had incorporated the rearing and selling of hens into their daily activities, with certain regional variations explained by demography, the productive systems and the existing commercial networks in each of the provinces. This last section takes a closer look at two aspects of the integration of hens into the lives of the natives. Firstly, we will focus on the products that the Indians obtained through the sale of the birds. Secondly, we will attempt to discover whether hens became part of the diet in poultry-producing villages. This section also explains how the introduction of hens affected consumption habits of the indigenous people.

What indigenous persons purchased with the profits from selling chickens and hens does not always appear explicitly in visits records; however, references do appear in all the regions of the New Kingdom of Granada mentioned in this chapter. No records have been found prior to 1590, which is understandable, as it was only then that the Crown stimulated production for the purpose of selling, and also limiting the number of hens that the *encomenderos* could buy. From the 1590s until the mid-seventeenth century, in all consigned deals, clothing appears to be the main item bought with the money obtained from the sale of poultry (or through barter, which was less frequent). Sometimes, indigenous persons received canvas or they bought specific pieces of clothing (shirts, blankets and *nagua* skirts). In addition, they bought tools and occasionally pigs and unspecified products for their "sustenance". They also reported that with this money they paid their taxes.[50]

As it is difficult to determine what was included under the generic term "sustenance", let us focus on aspects with more precise information. Many of the items purchased after the selling of hens had a strong

Spanish component, having been introduced into indigenous lives as part of the process of Christianizing their behavior. Dress played a very important role here. We know that blankets were objects of exchange in pre-Spanish times and that this continued under colonial rule, more so because they were part of the tributes paid by some towns. However, in these testimonies there are only two references to blankets; the rest mention other types of garments, and clothes are referred to in a more global sense, which seemed to follow Westernized logic in relation to clothing. Ultimately, one of the major transformations was the integration of the indigenous peoples into a money-market mentality, where they sold local products in high demand in order to buy specific goods that they did not produce, or to fulfill the fiscal obligations imposed by the Crown.

It is often difficult to determine whether chicken was eaten occasionally or whether it became part of the everyday diet of indigenous peoples, because of the manner in which the information was recorded. In some cases, it is very clear that chicken was not incorporated into the local diet; for example, in the province of Cartagena at the beginning of the seventeenth century, certain towns raised them for their *encomendero* or for the travellers, but when it came to eating, indigenous people preferred fish, iguanas or turtles.[51] This resistance could be interpreted as a question of traditional taste versus new products. This echoes an idea expressed by Spaniards in the mid-sixteenth century but less often at the beginning of the seventeenth century: that the Indians of the Atlantic coast and those living on the riverbanks did not appreciate meat, and that their entire protein consumption came from fish.[52] Furthermore there is the idea of a clash between different productive systems: while fish, iguanas and turtles are obtained through hunting or fishing, hens are produced through breeding or buying. Nonetheless, we must also bear in mind that in terms of production they were not opposites but complementary to one another, since both were carried out in parallel: one (hens) was for external consumption; the other (fish) for home consumption. One might venture that choice had partly to do with production limitations or the high demand for hens among the Spanish population. After all, it was far more profitable to sell what was generating an income and to eat what was less economically viable. This is why, in the same region, in towns that were not located at a crossroads or were too far from a city, where demand was lower indigenous people lost their appeal as poultry suppliers but began to eat chicken as part of their diet.[53]

Some towns in the west and the center of the New Kingdom had sufficient hens for themselves and for sale, while in a few others the hens were only for their own consumption.[54] Several other towns said nothing about whether they used them for their own consumption or not. By not explicitly stating that they did not, but without indicating alternative sources of protein, as some coastal towns had done, it can be assumed that hens were incorporated into their diet, although maybe not on an everyday basis. Unfortunately, there are no references to the ways in which chicken was cooked, so we cannot determine whether they followed Spanish culinary practices or traditional indigenous methods. Would they have realized that in the humoural belief, poultry was recommended for certain types of diseases?[55] It is likely that such reports may have reached them, even indirectly, because in some communities with sick people among them, the *encomenderos* provided suitable food to restore them to good health, including, for example, chickens and hens.[56]

Conclusions

In 1670, the graduate Antonio de Guzmán y Céspedes explained his advances in the process of the pacification and discovery of Chocó. He reported that, around 1665, he had established friendly relations with the *cacique* Don Pedro Daga:

> And on my first voyage to this province I enjoyed a feast and discovering that they did not breed hens and speculating the cause, I discovered that this was because the Spaniard did not discover them by the crowing of the rooster and having removed this distrust I brought them hens from down-river to breed and distribute among the people and on that occasion there were many who told me that all of them had been bred for me.[57]

Apart from the crowing of the roosters, it is worth noting that the breeding of these animals implied a reduction in the mobility of the villagers, since they could no longer move collectively with ease, which left them at the mercy of the Spanish advance. The adoption of poultry farming by the indigenous people led to their inevitable integration into the sedentary model of Spanish life. It also reveals how the operation functioned: the hens were not given to the natives as a gift, but as a remunerative, tributary and trade obligation.

Trade integration did not come from breeding poultry alone. At the end of the day, other products – wheat and horses, pigs and cattle – also made it possible, as well as the hire of labor, both individually and collectively. However, in the production of goods, only hens benefited from a Crown decree ordering that all towns were to have them as part of their farms. This ultimately turned out to be the case, not with all towns, but with almost all of them. There were many towns that had pigs or cows; but they were not at all as widespread as hens, at least within the indigenous communities. The introduction of some crops generated profound changes in the practices of indigenous peoples: in particular, sugarcane and wheat. But there were obvious differences. Wheat, for example, was imposed as a tax obligation on some towns, but not in terms of the profits they obtained from it. In addition, wheat was grown only in certain cold highland regions of the New Kingdom of Granada and Popayán. So, while relevant from an economic perspective, wheat-growing was not a widespread activity among the Indigenous community. Finally, according to the testimonies we have, Indians did not eat large quantities of wheat breads, even in the producing areas, preferring bread made from corn. In other words, wheat was a colonial product that they cultivated and traded but did not eat. Sugarcane had a greater impact on the lives of the Indians, partly because cane was grown on almost all soils across the New Kingdom of Granada and because its use in sweets, in *guarapo* (sugarcane juice) and the sweetening of *chicha* (a drink made from corn) transformed their consumer habits and social behaviour. However, since the end of the sixteenth century, the Crown had prohibited the Indians from working in the mills, because of the dangers posed to their health. In spite of this, many Indians worked in sugar production, although not as many as those involved in the rearing and trade of hens (Saldarriaga 2015, 2017).

For the indigenous peoples of the New Kingdom of Granada, this integration into the model of Spanish life through poultry rearing meant that they not only learned how to work in a particular way, but also how to insert themselves into commercial networks that exposed them to greater interaction with nonindigenous groups. This trade offered them access to products in exchange for hens or purchasing capacity with the money obtained from their sale. Undoubtedly, this market integration transformed consumer patterns and cultural patterns of behavior. With greater product specialization, they progressively lost the habit of producing certain goods which they had previously manufactured for themselves. Clothing is an example of this, for as some records noted, what they obtained with the sale of chickens and hens was used for the purchase of clothing. The cotton they cultivated was not sufficient to make their clothes, only enough for their *chinchorros*, as in the case of Cince.[58] It is clear too that the Christian model of decorum exerted a degree of pressure in terms of dress. There are many examples of other elements that could be obtained with the comforts afforded by the hens, such as, for example, a papal bull, a baptism and even a wedding, all practices of a Christian way of life.

Breeding and poultry trading represented one side of the colonial system. Not only was a practice imposed, but a network of elements was generated around it, rendering it more complex. Thus, what began as an enterprise to meet tax obligations evolved into an activity that satisfied the commercial needs of Spanish society. Meanwhile, those in charge of rearing these birds had to adopt a certain way of life, with new and increasing needs and demands, the more hens they raised. This was a system of farming that imposed a change that was not only economic and productive but fundamentally social and cultural.

Notes

1. This article stems from studies commissioned by the University of Antioquia during a post-doctoral stay at Villa I Tatti, the Harvard University Center for Italian Renaissance Studies, and carried out within the framework of the project HAR2014–53797-P "Globalización Ibérica: Redes entre Asia y Europa y los cambios en las pautas de Consumo en Latinoamérica" [Iberian Globalization: Networks between Asia and Europe and Changes in Consumption Patterns in Latin America] financed by Ministerio de Economía y Competitividad, Spain, of which the principal investigator is Bartolomé Yun-Casalilla.
2. Some works on the introduction of hens in America: Heyden and Velasco 1996; Molina Londoño 2002; Ferreira Vander Velden 2012; and Norton 2015.
3. Slavin 2009; Méndez 1991 [1553], 145; Grieco 1996, 2010, 2013, 151–52; Huarte de San Juan 1976 [1575], 248; García Marsilla 2013; Sorapán de Rieros 1616, 144.
4. AGI, Santa Fe 228, N. 1, f.1r; N. 1A, f. 1r.
5. There are classic works on the *encomienda* system in the New Kingdom of Granada providing an account of how they functioned and their transformation: Ruiz Rivera 1975; González 1992 and Colmenares 1997. In recent years there has been renewed interest in studying the *encomienda* system. See Gamboa Mendoza 2010, Gómez 2014, and Quiroga Zuluaga 2010.
6. González 1964, 460. The rule of not collecting tributes from Indians older than this was not always adhered to, as occurred in the province of Santa Marta, AGI, Santa Fe, 230, N. 37A, ff. 1v, 5v.
7. AGN, Colonia, Visitas de Santander, t. 2, d. 7, f. 476v.
8. Laws of Burgos 1512.
9. AGN, Colonia, Visitas de Bolivar, t.8, d. 8, ff. 910 r and v, 912v and 913r.
10. AGI, Santa Fe, 228, N. 10, f. 2r; N. 10A, f. 3r.
11. AGN, Colonia, Visitas de Bolívar, t. 1, d. 1, f. 53r and ff.
12. AGN, Colonia, Visitas de Bolívar, t. 2, d. 1, f. 35t, 42v, 185v, 272r; Visitas de Bolívar, t. 8, d. 8, f. 909v; Visitas de Bolívar, t. 9, d. 1, f. 27v and ff.
13. AGN, Colonia, Visitas de Bolívar, t. 1, d. 1, f. 362v.
14. AGN, Colonia, Visitas de Bolívar, t. 1, d. 1, f. 360r, 362v, 363r and 365r.
15. AGN, Colonia, Visitas de Bolívar, t. 1, d. 1, f. 414v.
16. "Visita, cuenta, descripción y tasa de los naturales del valle de Sibundoy, encomendado en el capitán Rodrigo Pérez, vecino de Pasto" [Transcripction by Juan Friede], *Anuario Colombiano de Historia Social y de la Cultura* 4 (1969): 123–130, 125.
17. Such exchanges consisted in valuing a particular tributary product and exchanging it for another product with a similar or comparable value. This was not an officially approved practice, but was usually mediated unofficially by negotiation between *encomendero* and *cacique*, or even with the *corregidor*, as seen in one particular case in the village of Guatica.
18. AGN, Colonia, Visitas de Antioquia, t. 2, d. 1, f. 28v; Visitas de Boyacá, t. 1, d. 5, f. 421r; Visitas de Cundinamarca, t. 1, d. 1, f. 40v.
19. AGN, Colonia, Visitas de Cundinamarca, t. 10, d. 4, f. 470r.
20. AGN, Colonia, Visita de Cauca, t. 6, d. 1, f. 25r y v.
21. AGN, Colonia, Visitas de Bolívar, t. 2, d. 1, f. 184r.
22. "You shall give to the said clergyman for every four months four bushels of corn and every week ten birds five females and five males and for the days that are not of meat you shall give every day twelve eggs and fish and every

day a basket of chicha and firewood to burn and grass for his horse if he has one and in Lent we order you not to send the hens but the said fish and eggs for the time that the said priest is in residence. " AGN, Colonia, Visitas de Cundinamarca, t. 5, d. 6, f. 958r.

23. AGI, Patronato, 196, R 8, f. 2r. The priests' *congrua* was complemented in the statutes of Tunja with a weekly load of potatoes, which were also provided by the Indians. In addition to that were twenty loads of corn, twenty rams and three pigs, given by the *encomendero* annually. That same year, in the visit to Chusbita, this ruling was maintained for chickens, eggs and fish, but varied with respect to other commodities the *encomenderos* had to deliver twelve bushels of wheat and twenty of corn. AGN, Colonia, Visitas de Boyacá, t. 17, d. 10, f. 787.
24. AGN, Colonia, Visitas de Boyacá, t. 17, d. 1, f. 100v; Visitas de Cundinamarca, t. 4, d. 8, f. 877r.
25. AGN, Colonia, Visitas de Cundinamarca, t. 5, d. 2, f. 222r; Visitas de Boyacá, t. 17, d. 7, f. 532r.
26. According to the testimony of Antonio Sayuara, *cacique*, the only parish priest who never ordained this was the Franciscan friar Pedro Aguado, one of the most important chroniclers to write about the New Kingdom of Granada in the sixteenth century. AGN, Colonia, Visitas de Cundinamarca, t. 5, d. 3, f. 576v.
27. AGN, Colonia, Visitas de Boyacá, t. 17, d. 1, f. 100v.
28. The Crusade Bulls were documents that the Church sold periodically on the pretext of financing crusades to conquer holy lands, which promised indulgences to the buyer; the brotherhoods were the congregations that gathered together to pay devotion to a sacred image, to celebrate its feast day, and carry out certain acts of solidarity; the tithes represented a proportional payment on what was produced that all Catholics had to pay to the Church. Due to questions of royal patronage, in Spanish America collection of this payment fell to the officials of the Crown who in turn auctioned it to individuals.
29. AGN, Colonia, Visitas de Boyacá, t. 17, d. 5, f. 301v-303r.
30. AGN, Colonia, Visitas de Bolívar, t. 1, d. 1, f. 190v.
31. Gamboa Mendoza 1999, 147; AGN, Colonia, Visitas de Antioquia, t. 2, d. 1, f. 21r y d. 20, f. 748; Visitas de Cauca, t. 4, d. 1, f. 26r; Visitas de Cundinamarca, t. 9, d. 2, f. 452r.
32. AGI, Patronato 196, r 24, f. 3r.
33. AGN, Colonia, Visitas de Santander, t. 3, d. 13, f. 631r; Visitas de Santander, t. 7, d. 7, f. 729r.
34. AGN, Colonia, Visitas de Boyacá, t. 1, d. 5, f. 456r.
35. It could be by accident, but one should point out that point 89 of the *Ordenanzas para la población* stipulated that each resident should have "twenty sheep from Castile".
36. AGN, Colonia, Visitas de Boyacá, t. 1, d. 5, f. 571; Visitas de Boyacá, t. 11, d. 1, f. 3r; for the English, in the Middle Ages the ratio was one rooster for fifteen hens, although it does not appear to have been rigidly fixed, Slavin 2009, 41.
37. AGN, Colonia, Visitas de Boyacá, t. 14, d. 11, f. 793r; Visitas de Boyacá, t. 19, d. 15, f. 978v y 982v; Visitas de Cundinamarca, t. 10, d. 2, f. 276r; Visitas de Cundinamarca, t. 12, d. 3, f. 369r; d. 9, f. 824r.
38. AGN, Colonia, Visitas de Bolívar, t. 3, d. 5, f. 692v; t. 4, d. 4, f. 532v; t. 10, d. 1, f. 26r.
39. AGN, Colonia, Visitas de Cauca, t. 3, d. 9, f. 586v; d. 10, f. 612v

40. AGN, Colonia, Visitas de Antioquia, t. 3, d. 2, f. 273r; Visitas de Cauca, t. 3, d. 11, f. 646r; d. 17, f. 933v.
41. AGN, Colonia, Visitas de Bolivar, t. 10, d. 2, f. 198r y v; Visitas de Antioquia, t. 3, d. 2, f. 202v; AGI, Santa Fe, 71, N. 8, f. 1r.
42. AGN, Colonia, Visitas de Bolivar, t. 2, d. 1, f. 29r y 185r.
43. AGN, Colonia, Visitas de Antioquia, t. 2, d. 16, f. 474r; Visitas de Cauca, t. 1, d. 4, f. 908v y 915; t. 2, d. 2, F. 295r; d. 3, f. 431r; t. 6, d. 1, f. 20v, 26, 50r y 58v; d.2, f. 374v; d. 3, f. 624r.
44. AGN, Colonia, Visitas de Boyacá, t. 9, d. 1, f. 218r; Gamboa 1999, 250.
45. AGN, Colonia, Visitas de Boyacá, t. 17, d. 7, f. 546r; Visitas de Cundinamarca, t. 5, d. 2, f. 224v.
46. AGN, Colonia, Visitas de Cundinamarca, t. 1, d. 2, f. 298r; d. 3, f. 455r y 466r; t. 5, d. 1, f. 62r; t. 7, d. 2, f. 172r y 179v; t. 8, d. 5, f. 637r; t. 12, d. 8, f. 715r; d. 10, f. 1005v.
47. AGN, Colonia, Visitas de Cundinamarca, t. 6, d. 6, f. 595v; Visitas de Santander, t. 2, d. 13, f. 559; Visitas de Santander, t. 3, d. 2, f. 361r.
48. AGN, Colonia, Visitas de Bolívar, t. 4, d. 12, f. 967v y 968r; Visitas de Cundinamarca, t. 1, d. 5, f. 777r; t. 6, d. 8, F. 858r; t. 10, d. 3, f. 396r; t. 12, d. 8, f. 715r.
49. They also took products such as agave, beans, corn, potatoes, papas and cassava, as well as cotton blankets and clay vessels.
50. AGN, Colonia, Visitas de Antioquia, t. 3, d. 2, f. 273; Visitas de Bolívar, t. 2, d. 1, F. 29r; t. 4, d. 4, f. 532v y 533r; d. 5, f. 672v; t. 10, d. 2, f. 197v; Visitas de Cundinamarca, t. 2, d. 2, f. 246v; Visitas de Cauca, t. 1, d. 4, f. 908v; volume 2, documento 2, f. 295r; t. 4, d. 1, f. 26r, f. 29r y v; t. 6, d. 2, f. 374v; Visitas de Cundinamarca, t. 3, d. 6, f. 817r; Visitas de Santander, t. 3, d. 2, f. 361r y 383r.
51. AGN, Colonia, Visitas de Bolívar, t. 3, d. 5, f. 692v; Visitas de Bolívar, t. 4, d. 4, f. 532v, 533r, 535v; d. 5, f. 672v.
52. AGN, Colonia, Visitas de Bolivar, t. 3, d. 5, f. 692v; t. 4, d. 2, f. 320r; d. 4, f. 532v, 533r, 535v; t. 10, d. 5, f. 856v.
53. AGN, Colonia, Visitas de Bolívar, t. 4, d.2 f. 320r.
54. AGN, Colonia, Visitas de Antioquia, t. 2, d. 16 f. 474r; Visitas de Cauca, t. 1, f. 540r, 544v; t. 3, d. 11, f. 646r; d. 17, f. 933v; Visitas de Cundinamarca, t. 2, d. 4, f. 758v; t. 3, d. 3, f. 529r.
55. Huarte de San Juan 1976 [1575], 248, Sorapán de Rieros 1616, 45, 135, 141 and 144, Farfán 1944 [1592], Libro segundo, cap. quinto, f. 104v, Méndez Nieto 1989 [1607], 58.
56. AGN, Colonia, Visitas de Cundinamarca, t. 1, d. 2, f. 304r; Visitas de Santander, t. 1, d. 1, f. 29r y 32r.
57. AGN, Colonia, Caciques e Indios, t. 11, d. 11, f. 857v.
58. This includes fishing nets as well as a kind of light hammock. AGN, Colonia, Visitas de Bolívar, t. 10, d. 2, f. 197v.

Bibliography

Benito Rodríguez, José Antonio. 1996. "Historia de la Bula de Cruzada en Indias." *Estudios Históricos-Jurídicos* XVIII: 71–102.

Castaño, Yoer. 2019. *Eslabones del mundo andino. Comercio, mercados y circuitos pecuarios en el Nuevo Reino de Granada y la Audiencia de Quito 1580–1715*. Medellín: Eafit.

Carcer y Disdier, Mariano. 1955. *Disertaciones sobre la papa (patata) y la batata (patata), rectificación histórica*. México: UNAM.

Colmenares, Germán. 1997. *Encomienda y población en la provincia de Pamplona*. Bogotá: Universidad de los Andes.

———. 1999. *Historia económica y social de Colombia*. Bogotá: Tercer Mundo.

Del Río Moreno, Justo, and Lorenzo López y Sebastián. 1998. "Hombres y ganados en la tierra del oro: Comienzos de la ganadería en Indias." *Revista complutense de Historia de América* 24: 11–45.

———. 1999. "La ganadería vacuna en la isla Española (1508–1587)." *Revista complutense de Historia de América* 25: 11–49.

Farfán, Agustín. 1944 [1592]. *Tractado breve de medicina*. Edición facsimilar. Colección de incunables americano siglo XVI, volumen X. Madrid: Cultura hispánica.

Ferreira Vander Velden, Felipe. 2012. "As galinhas incontáveis. Tupis, europeus e aves domésticas na conquista no Brasil." *Journal de la société des américanistes* 98 (2). https://doi.org/10.4000/jsa.12350

Foster, George M. 1962. *Cultura y conquista. La herencia española de América*. Veracruz: Universidad Veracruzana.

Friede, Juan. 1955. *Documentos inéditos para la historia de Colombia*. Tomo I. Bogotá: Academia Colombiana de Historia.

Gamboa Mendoza, Jorge Augusto. 1999. *Fuentes documentales para la historia colonial pamplonesa. Visitas a la provincia de Pamplona (1570–1778)*. Pamplona: Universidad de Pamplona.

———. 2010. *El cacicazgo muisca en los años posteriores a la Conquista: del sihipkua al cacique colonial, 1537–1575*. Bogotá: ICANH.

García Marsilla, Juan Vicente. 2013. "Alimentación y salud en la Valencia Medieval. Teorías y prácticas." *Anuario de estudios medievales* 43 (1): 115–58.

Gómez, Mauricio. 2014. "Indios contra encomenderos en tierra de frontera. Antioquia a inicios del siglo XVII." *Trashumante. Revista Americana de Historia Social* 3: 8–26.

———. 2016. "Cerdos y control social de pobres en la provincia de Antioquia, siglo XVIII." *Anuario Colombiano de Historia Social y de la Cultura* 43 (1): 31–59.

González, Álvaro. 1964. "Encomiendas, encomenderos e indígenas tributarios del Nuevo Reino de Granada en la primera mitad del siglo XVII." *Anuario Colombiano de Historia Social y de la Cultura* 2: 410–530.

González, Margarita. 1992. *El resguardo en el Nuevo Reino de Granada*. Bogotá: El Áncora.

Grieco, Allen J. 1996. "Alimentation et classes sociales à la fin du Moyen Âge et à la Renaissance." In *Histoire de l'alimentation*, edited by Jean-Louis Flandrin and Massimo Montanari, 479–90. Paris: Fayard.

———. 2010. "From rooster to cocks: Italian Renaissance fowl and sexuality." In *Erotics Cultures of Renaissance Italy*, edited by Sara F. Matthews Grieco, 89–140. Farnham and Burlington: Ashgate.

———. 2013. "What's in a Detail: More Chickens in Renaissance Birth Scenes." In *Renaissance Studies in Honor of Jospeh Connors*, Vol. II, edited by M. Israëls and L. Waldman, 150–54. Florence: Officina del libro.

Hernández Méndez, Rodolfo Esteban. 2006. "Acercamiento Histórico a las Bulas de la Santa Cruzada en el Reino de Guatemala." *Boletín AFEHC*, no. 16. http://afehc-historia-centroamericana.org/index.php?action=fi_aff&id=355

Heyden, Doris, and Ana María L. Velasco. 1996. "Aves van, aves vienen: el guajolote, la gallina y el pato." In *Conquista y comida. Consecuencias del encuentro de dos mundos*, coord. by Janet Long, 237–53. México: UNAM.

Huarte de San Juan. 1976 [1575]. *Examen de ingenios para las ciencias*. Edición preparada por Esteban Torre. Madrid: Editora Nacional.

Langebaek, Carl. 1987. *Mercados, poblamiento e integración étnica entre los muiscas, siglo XVI*. Bogotá: Banco de la República.

———. 2008. "Dos teorías sobre el poder político entre los muiscas. Un debate a favor del diálogo." In *Los muiscas en los siglos XVI y XVII. Miradas desde la Arqueología, Antropología y la Historia*, edited by Jorge Gamboa, 81–88. Bogotá: Universidad de los Andes.

López Rodríguez, Mercedes. 2000. "El tiempo de rezar y el tiempo de sembrar: el trabajo indígena como práctica de cristianización durante el siglo XVI." *Anuario colombiano de Historia Social y de la Cultura* 27: 27–67.

———. 2001. *Tiempos para rezar y tiempos para trabajar. La cristianización de las comunidades muiscas durante el siglo XVI*. Bogotá: ICANH.

Melville, Elinor. 1994. *A Plague of Sheep: Environmental Consequences of the Conquest of Mexico*. Cambridge: Cambridge University Press.

Méndez, Cristóbal. 1991 [1553]. *Libro del ejercicio corporal y de sus provechos por el cual cada uno podrá entender qué ejercicio le sea necesario para conservar su salud*. México: Academia Nacional de Medicina.

Méndez Nieto, Juan. 1989 [1607]. *Discursos medicinales*. Salamanca: Universidad de Salamanca, Junta de Castilla y León.

Molina Londoño, Luis Fernando. 2002. *La avicultura en Colombia*. Bogotá: Fenavi.

Norton, Marcy. 2015. "Human-Animal Relationships and the Columbian Exchange." *American Historical Review* 120 (1): 28–60. https://doi.org/10.1093/ahr/120.1.28.

Quiroga Zuluaga, Marcela. 2010. "La encomienda entre los pueblos de la provincia de Paez en el siglo XVII." *Fronteras de la Historia* 15 (1): 85–107.

Ruiz Rivera, Julián Bautista. 1975. *Encomienda y mita en Nueva Granada*. Seville: Escuela de Estudios Americanos de Sevilla, Consejo Superior de Investigaciones Científicas.

Saldarriaga, Gregorio. 2011. *Alimentación e identidades en el Nuevo Reino de Granada, siglos XVI y XVII*. Bogotá: Universidad del Rosario.

———. 2015. "El trigo en el Nuevo Reino de Granada, siglos XVI y XVII: imposición y establecimiento de un eje alimentario entre las poblaciones indígenas." In *Una obra para la historia: homenaje a Germán Colmenares*, edited by Diana Bonnett, 57–84. Bogotá: Universidad del Rosario.

———. 2017. "Trabajo y vida indígenas en los trapiches del Nuevo Reino de Granada, 1576–1674." *Anais do Museu Paulista* 25 (1): 149–68. http://dx.doi.org/10.1590/1982-02672017v25n0106.

Simón, fray Pedro. 1982. *Noticias historiales de las conquistas de Tierra Firme en las Indias Occidentales*. Tomo VI. Bogotá: Banco Popular.

Slavin, Philip. 2009. "Chicken Husbandry in Late-Medieval Eastern England: *c.* 1250–1400." *Anthropozoologica* 44 (2): 35–56.

Sorapán de Rieros, Juan. 1616. *Medicina española contenida en proverbios vulgares de nuestra lengua*. Madrid: Martín Fernández Zambrano.

"Visita, cuenta, descripción y tasa de los naturales del valle de Sibundoy, encomendado en el capitán Rodrigo Pérez, vecino de Pasto." 1969. Transcription by Juan Friede. *Anuario Colombiano de Historia Social y de la Cultura* 4: 123–30.

6 Gifts, Imitation, Violence and Social Change

The Introduction of European Products in the First Decades of the American Conquest[1]

Luis Miguel Córdoba Ochoa

Introduction

The introduction of goods of European origin into the New World was channeled in ways that differed greatly from the typical market mechanisms of the Renaissance. American communities had developed practices in the exchange of goods that were not controlled by the exchange value but governed in many cases by the symbolic or religious value attributed to certain goods. Spaniards considered the natives to be naive to give gold or precious stones in exchange for ironmongery, but for the Indians precious stones had an almost sacred value, hence their willingness, for example, to trade their goods for the green glass marbles that the Spaniards took to Yucatan and Mexico. The Indians possibly believed that they were jade or turquoise, stones coveted by the Mayan and Mexican privileged classes and nobility.

Given these circumstances, the Iberians recognized that in order to acquire indigenous goods it was necessary to continue using violence, but also barter or ransom, elegant ways of describing forced exchanges of goods. The market penetration of European goods, food and animals in America not only brought about changes in the clothing and dress habits of the natives and their consumption of new foods but also profoundly altered their daily life and social structures. In the decades after the dethronement of Moctezuma and Atahualpa, the rapid incorporation of European products occurred in conjunction with strategies by the native elites to preserve their privileges by adopting peninsular customs and practices. The new *caciques* or *kurakas* appointed by the Spaniards as intermediaries to collect tribute payments, who lacked legitimacy in the eyes of the natives, were among those who sought feverishly to appropriate Spanish uses and customs to lay the foundations of a new legitimacy, which was nevertheless traumatic and contested by the old *caciques*.

From almost the first Spanish incursions into Mexico and the Andes, allied native elites made political use of the consumption of European goods. The process of the conquest gave way to a readjustment in the

DOI: 10.4324/9781003168058-7

identities of the indigenous governors who survived Spanish penetration. In some cases, a singular aspect of this readjustment was expressed in the strategic use of Spanish clothing, adornments and utensils in a context that resignified identities. The forcible imposition of European goods was not the only means for their diffusion in the New World, for indigenous elites also sought to make visible their consumption of such goods for reasons of social harmony.

The assimilation of European products in the Americas can hardly be understood solely from the perspective of economic history, and in fact the expression "exchange of goods" conceals the violence that hallmarked the use of European products in America.[2] In addition to the violence associated with the imposition of wheat cultivation instead of corn, for example, there were also constant deliberations about the desirability or detriment of the use of European goods by the natives. The assimilation of some of them, such as knives or iron axes, the rapid introduction of chickens or the importance given to breeding Spanish cattle in regions such as the peninsula of La Guajira, were facts that did not, however, imply the acceptance of Spanish dominion. Their use was generally selective, and, as was well known in Chile, for example, the most successful resistance was led by indigenous people who had been educated in close contact with Spaniards.

The following pages seek to explain how the penetration of the first European goods in the New World oscillated between violence and the agreements and forced exchanges that provided the Indians with useful products, as well as other objects which for the Spaniards were mere trinkets but, to their surprise, were highly appreciated by the natives for religious and symbolic reasons. Likewise, we shall analyze how the Spanish invasion triggered processes of emulation and ostentation among sectors of the native population that sought to maintain their pre-Spanish status or on the part of the newly imposed *caciques* who saw the incorporation of European clothing and customs as a means of legitimizing their recently acquired governing role.

The conquest of America dislocated the social hierarchies of the two sides in conflict. The mining exploitations as well as successful participation in military and repopulation campaigns in the New World facilitated the social promotion of Spaniards with humble socio-economic origins. Collaboration with the Europeans allowed indigenous people who did not belong to the Mexican or Andean elites to occupy privileged places in local communities whose highest social layers were almost destroyed. Europeans and natives alike turned to the ostentatious consumption of the goods of both worlds to reaffirm their unexpected fortunes. This problem will be analyzed in the last part of the chapter, which considers the history of social practices that influenced the enjoyment of goods and the factors that accelerated cultural transfers in the years after the conquest.

Ransoms and the First Dissemination of European Goods in the Caribbean

The consumption of goods of European origin by the native peoples of the New World was not alien to the violence that marked the invasion of the continent. Even those European products that reached the native communities as a result of peace agreements carried the signs of violence.

These first goods were brought by Spaniards to the Caribbean islands and the province of Tierra Firme for their own sustenance and comfort, or because the Crown had ruled accordingly. Early evidence indicates that a constituent part of the laws governing the creation of Spanish settlements was to ask the first founders to transport European seeds and animals to the Caribbean to create a food environment similar to the one they had at home. The Crown issued royal decrees ordering the destruction of the settlements of the Taíno people, thus forcing them to live in villages similar to the first Spanish towns and cities on the islands. These rulings were designed to facilitate the evangelization and control of these peoples and the management of indigenous labor in the mines. The Spanish settlers were entrusted with the daunting task of making them believe that they would be better off there than in their ancestral lands.[3]

Instructions for the loading of the first caravels seemed to respond to initial reports about the islands' limitations in terms of providing sufficient foodstuffs to meet the expectations of the settlers, as can be observed in the list of provisions for the four ships prior to their departure for the Caribbean in1495.[4]

The ledgers that Dr. Sancho de Matienzo wrote up as treasurer of the Casa de Contratación between 1503 and 1521 confirm that in the following years such initial brief indications about the foods to be shipped turned into exhaustive lists of all kinds of goods. The Casa de Contratación behaved as if every ship that left for the Americas was another ark destined to repopulate a wasteland (Mena 2004, 237–78; Ladero 2008; Vila Vilar and Lacueva Muñoz 2012).

From the beginning the Crown encouraged the practice whereby soldiers heading to the Americas would take with them European food, seeds and animals, and as news of the discoveries told of the magnitude of the new lands, instructions were also given for the expeditions to carry household goods (Mena 1996, 25). In the case of Spaniards permitted by the Crown to carry out campaigns of conquest only if they took with them a number of horses, cattle, pigs, goats, sheep and seeds and lived in settlements there, it would appear that the possibility of building their lives in the New World without Mediterranean food and goods was ruled out from the very beginning.

As for the language of the first writs and the stipulations aimed at imposing a new order on the lives of the Indians, a linguistic sophism was used that legitimized the looting of the indigenous communities. As exploitation steadily became the order of the day, it was recounted as if the Spaniards were allowing the Indians to feed themselves, and for this reason the expression "you will give to the Indians" became common, in allusion to the fact that with the imposition of tribute payments and forced labor in the allotments they would be allowed to retain part of what they themselves had produced. While the settlers in principle looked down on the quality of food in the new territories, the officers in the homeland contrived to imply that only by the grace of the agents of the Crown were the indigenous people able to feed themselves (Saldarriaga 2011).

Instructions given to the Hieronymite fathers stated that once the natives were taken to the places where they would be forced to live,

> you must distribute among the residents of the place giving to each of them the smallest piece of land to plant trees and other things, and make bundles for them and their entire family more or less in accordance with the quality of the person and the size of that family.[5]

Once the destruction of the native settlements had concluded, the Spaniards, in this case the Hieronymites, were vested with the power to assign plots of land to the dispossessed. This operation of destroying and populating according to Spanish criteria was based on the idea that there were no civilized manners of living on the islands and that it was therefore lawful to not only alter traditional urban planning but also the islanders' mode of dress and the kind of food they ate (Pagden 1988).

News of episodes of famine and the death of Spaniards in the Caribbean gave rise to new laws for the transport of European foods to the New World. In 1513, Pedro Arias Dávila, from Segovia, an outstanding figure in the wars of Granada and the taking of Orán in 1509, was named governor of Castilla de Oro, the present-day Panama. The instructions he received in August of that year prior to taking up office ordered him to bring farm hands and *trimesino* wheat seeds and barley to sow the land. The seeds would have to be transported carefully to prevent them from being damaged in transit, so that if they did not germinate this would not be on account of any defect in the grains but because the soil and climate were unsuitable (Medina 1913, 52). Moreover, it was ordained in 1518 that Spanish cattle should be introduced in the new settlements where the natives had been moved, having been uprooted from their native settlements.[6]

The creation of Spanish settlements in the Caribbean replicated in many ways the same differential and hierarchical patterns that characterized the stratified society in the homeland, although the wealth of the West Indies gave rise to displays of ostentatious consumption that were a source of astonishment for the newcomers. In 1513 the early settlers' lack of moderation in relation to their clothing, household and food was already well known and therefore Pedrarias was ordered to enforce the ruling that prohibited excesses in dress, as many in the Caribbean had ended up impoverished as a result of dressing like rich courtiers (Medina 1913, 51). Six months later, however, the king authorized Pedrarias and his wife Isabel de Bobadilla to dress in gold, silk and brocade. In this way, it was evident at a glance that he was the governor, whose clothes had to shine brightly in the distance under the Panamanian sun (Medina 1913, 57). Despite numerous sumptuary laws, the different attempts to limit conspicuous consumption in America were rarely successful. Rather, vicarious consumption, that bombastic excess, was a hallmark of the Spaniards in the Indies and fits well with the cultural processes of emulation in general (Veblen 2014).

The experiences of famine in the Darién region from 1510 onward emphasized how European foodstuffs were held in high esteem by individuals who proclaimed that their consumption made them feel they were still Christians. Vasco Núñez de Balboa, the leader who made the South Sea known to the Spaniards, illustrates the sense of loss brought about by the lack of familiar goods from the peninsula, when he wrote to the king on 20 January 1513 that he and his men had been shamefully treated in Hispaniola as if they were not Christians, and that on many occasions they appreciated finding a basket of corn more than a basket of gold (Medina 1913, 131; Aram 2008). In order to obtain the native foods and the gold that allowed them to buy expensive supplies from the Iberian Peninsula, the Spaniards in Darién resorted to a practice that was decisive in introducing European goods to the indigenous towns. This consisted in arranging peace agreements with the natives, who on numerous occasions were forced to collaborate with the Spaniards or put up with awkward truces not involving submission. Usually both parties exchanged goods to endorse peace, which paved the way for even those Indians who had most fiercely resisted the Spanish occupation, such as the Mapuches or Chichimecas, to receive Spanish food, clothing, weapons and utensils (Ruiz 2010; Favaró, Merluzzi, and Sabatini 2017).

Exchanging Goods Under the Peace Agreements

In the Darién province, Balboa made strategic use of food exchanges with the indigenous people to secure their support, but without entirely giving up on *aperreamientos* (slaughtering of natives by using dogs) and other killings. Goods from Castile allowed him to forge important alliances with communities which, in exchange for gold, pearls, food or slaves, could obtain knives and iron axes, whose advantages over their traditional stone weapons were evident (Fernández de Oviedo Tomo III [1851–1855] 1992, 212).

Balboa explained that the arrival of Pedrarias Dávila as governor in 1514 caused serious damage to the network of alliances he had created in previous years, and thanks to which the Indians had revealed to him the existence of the South Sea. Writing to the king in January 1513 on the strategies he used in achieving the collaboration of the indigenous population, he explained: "Principally I have sought, wherever I have gone, to ensure the Indians of this land are very well treated, not allowing them be harmed in any way, treating them truthfully, giving them many things from Castile to attract them to our friendship" (Medina 1913, 130). In October 1515 he explained how, on account of the damage caused by Pedrarias's men, the natives "who in former times used to come out on the road with presents for the Christians now come out to attack them" (Medina 1913, 139).

In a report written in 1518 the lawyer Alonso de Suazo explained that when Balboa was travelling through the governorship of Castilla del Oro, the Indians were waiting for him with food, "for he was winning over the land little by little with much wisdom and common sense". Balboa's meetings with the *caciques* generally involved a banquet in which foodstuffs were exchanged and alliances were renewed (De Suazo 2000, 91–92). However, Balboa spared no form of violence in forcing the natives to collaborate. Thus, the gifts that paved the way to the consumption of Spanish goods bore the undeniable hallmark of the violent relations between indigenous and newcomers. The level of brutality is illustrated in an incident involving the conquistador Hernán Cortés, who ordered that Moctezuma's first emissaries be lined up in chains and that the Spanish troops' largest cannon should be fired before their eyes. Before they had time to recover from their fear and shock he proceeded to offer them wine and food (León Portilla 2014, 34).

The testimony of Gaspar de Espinosa, mayor of Castilla del Oro, provides a grim account of Spanish subjects who waged a campaign of raids against the indigenous people that included setting fire to entire villages and executions designed to spread terror, burning the Indians alive, tearing them apart with dogs, hanging and shooting them. He also recorded that "two were killed with gunpowder shot, to frighten the Indians even more" (Medina 1913, 157). To stop these attacks, the *caciques* agreed to make peace, as did the *cacique* Chiarna, in the region of Comogre, who agreed to meet with Espinosa. Regarding this forced peace, Espinosa wrote that Chiarna

> was given the best treatment that I and my companions could give, and rather as a token of appreciation and to forge our friendship we played a game of jousting with canes; and ate and drank provisions from Castile, bread and wine and other things together with me, gave him a shirt and cap and other trinkets from Castile; it was all so peaceful that there were comings and goings without any fear.
>
> (Medina 1913, 155)

Another *cacique*, Chiribuque, agreed to meet up with Espinosa to agree on peace terms, "for the bitter war we fought". According to Espinosa, the *cacique* was received with

> much love, good will and excellent treatment, so that while we were there, everything that the *cacique* wanted was given to him including Indians that had been taken, as well as things from Castile, knives and hooks and combs and caps; and he ate and drank with me and engaged in conversation with everyone as if he were a Christian.
> (Medina 1913, 157)

The peaceful atmosphere that Espinosa described may appear dubious. Nevertheless, his narrative shows that Spanish goods, either because of their obvious utility or the exoticism they conferred upon their new native owners, had the eventual effect of offering arguments to the natives who favored negotiations with Spaniards with a view to taking advantage of the said goods, their food and their animals.

The exploration of Castilla del Oro served to consolidate the dispatch of goods with the armadas destined for the governorship, part of which were purchased to exchange for precious metals or other objects from the Indians. In 1519, for example, the king ordered the Casa de Contratación to buy cheap gifts so that Governor Lope de Sosa would give them to the *caciques* and chief Indians of Castilla de Oro in order to garner their goodwill, because numerous accusations of Spanish ill-treatment had been received from Panama.[7] The Armada led by Gil González Dávila to Panama in 1521 had fabrics on board worth 78,000 *maravedís*, which were used for the trading of goods with the indigenous people (Medina 1913, 186).

Marbles or glass beads were frequently given by the Spaniards to the Indians. In 1517 in Yucatan they realized that these were highly valued by the Maya and then by the Nahuas. The Spaniards traded them for gold or food without totally understanding the particular regard for these trinkets displayed by these Indians, who were the most sophisticated native community they had come across. It would appear that these beads, especially the green ones, were taken for jade or turquoise beads. Jade was a semiprecious stone produced in Yucatan, but like turquoise, which came from the present-day states of New Mexico and Arizona, its use was confined to the privileged sectors of Mayan and Aztec nobility. Both stones had been objects of great value since the era of the Olmecs. They were associated with the mythological goddess of running water, Chalchiuhtlicue, as well as life and fertility (Melgar 2010, 155–68). Years later Bernal Díaz del Castillo understood the mistake, which proved fatal for the Mexica people, because the precious stones known as *chalchihuites*, that is, jade and turquoise, were given as gifts to the indigenous nobility as a gesture of peace, but the Spaniards never fully realized the significance of the humble glass marbles. The symbolic effect of Cortés and his men handing out marbles on their way to Tenochtitlan was recorded in the following report given by Diego Muñoz Camargo, when he wrote that

> the natives called Hernando Cortes *chalchiuh* captain, which is rather like saying captain of great esteem and courage, and this is the meaning given, because the *chalchihuitl* is emerald green in color, and the emeralds are seen by the natives as something very precious, and so they compared the person of Cortés to these stones, calling him *chalchiuh* captain, comparing the good Spaniard to *chalchihuites* and emeralds, as in "emerald captain" or "highly prized knight", by calling him a *chalchiuh* captain *par excellence*.
>
> (Muñoz 2013, 174)

In addition to handing over goods as part of their agreements with the Indians, the Spaniards would invite them to festivities to celebrate peace between the two groups. Although these feasts sometimes lacked food from the homeland, they always insisted that bread and wine be served, the natives' appreciation of the latter being used to good advantage by the Spanish.[8] Although fear often forced such encounters, they allowed the natives to obtain goods such as axes and iron knives, which gave them an advantage over their own native rivals. Nonetheless, these banquets in celebration of peace did not imply a cessation of the violence that characterized relations between Spaniards and natives. On the contrary, a banquet to celebrate peace could conclude in a calculated massacre.[9]

For this reason there was an air of caution when Spaniards and Indians shared food. An early example of this occurred on the island of Hispaniola following the uprising led by the *cacique* Don Enrique (or Enriquillo) against the Spaniards, which began in 1519 and lasted for more than twelve years without being brought under control. Enriquillo was a Ladino and had been baptized, having been raised by the Franciscans in the city of Santo Domingo and thus very familiar with Spanish ways. Faced with his successful resistance, Charles V sent Francisco Barrionuevo to Santo Domingo in 1533 with orders to subdue him if it proved impossible to agree on peace terms. Having made his way with a small troop to the region where Don Enrique had taken refuge, Barrionuevo told him that the king had ordered that if he made peace he would be well treated and his men would not be persecuted. In their first meeting Barrionuevo and Enriquillo embraced "with a lot of pleasure, and holding hands, they went to sit" on a cotton blanket. Then about seventy of Enriquillo's Indians embraced Barrionuevo one by one. Barrionuevo showed him the king's letters and those of the Audiencia assuring him peace, and Enriquillo gave his word he would do the same. Later, Spaniards and

Indians ate together, but Enriquillo retired to have lunch with his wife. In the afternoon there were fresh promises of peace and a brief exchange of goods between the soldiers and the Indians. That night some of them ate together, but Enriquillo again withdrew to his own quarters.[10] Gonzalo Fernandez de Oviedo recounted that the Spaniards believed that he refrained from eating with them for fear of betrayal. Earlier, in 1529, Enriquillo had rejected an offer of sheep and pigs from the president of the Audiencia of Santo Domingo Sebastián Ramírez de Fuenleal as an attempt to agree on peace.

When Barrionuevo returned to his caravel he sent Enriquillo wine, oil and biscuits (De Suazo 2000, 369). Shortly afterwards, the *cacique* and his men went to the village of Açua to make sure that the peace agreement would be maintained. There were about twenty-five Spaniards on horseback and other soldiers with whom the Indians repeated the ritual of exchanging hugs. Later there was a banquet during which they shared the food that the Spaniards had supplied: chickens, capons, hams, veal, as well as the best bread and wine that could be obtained. All ate together "with much pleasure and rejoicing, but Don Enrique did not eat or drink anything," although, according to Gonzalo Fernández de Oviedo, they begged him to do so (Fernández de Oviedo Tomo I [1851–1855] 1992, 136).

The reasons for distrusting the Spanish banquets or offerings were evident. The attraction and taste for European food also proved lethal for slaves of African descent who fled from their masters, the Cimarrons, or for the indigenous people who were captured or killed following such invitations from the Spaniards.

One such case occurred in Panama as a result of the creation in the Darién region of a fortified Cimarron enclosure by a notorious fugitive slave leader known as King Bayamo in 1552 (De Aguado 1957, IV, 103–132). Bayamo was in command of 300–500 Africans who had escaped from slavery and taken refuge in a mountain fort which was proving impregnable to the Spaniards. Pedro de Ursúa from Navarre was appointed to put an end to this threat. Ursúa's strategy was to negotiate with Bayamo and his men, making them believe that they could maintain their independence. Ursúa set up camp in front of the fortress to which the Cimarrons were invited and offered gifts to persuade them of the Spaniards' good intentions. But all was not as it seemed. Ursúa had previously sent his lieutenant Francisco Gutiérrez with "jars of wine mixed with poison or venom, and with certain merchandise and things from Spain with which to deceive and attract that mob with gifts and flattery, with native cunning and double-dealing" (Aguado 1957, IV, 121).

Fray Pedro de Aguado narrated that Ursúa explained to his soldiers, who were astonished by this lavish display of friendship to the Cimarrons, that the Spanish troops were unable to take the bastion of the former slaves and accordingly, under the guise of a good deal, he would invite Bayamo to eat and drink, and intoxicate him and his men with the poisoned wine in order to secure his capture and kill the main rebels (Aguado 1957, IV, 125).

On the first day that Bayamo and some of his men went to Ursúa's camp they were given food and drink and they stayed overnight. The next day Ursúa gave Bayamo "a cap of good green fine cloth and two shirts of *ruán* cotton and a bonnet and a machete, and to the black captains who accompanied him, each was given the same shirts of *ruan* cotton and stout breeches and colored caps" (Aguado 1957, IV, 126).

Although the Cimarrons were offered wine laced with venom, it did not appear to have the desired effect, and for that reason Francisco Gutiérrez returned to Nombre de Dios for more gifts, wine and poison. His return was celebrated by the Spaniards and by the Cimarrons because they received more gifts and were invited to more banquets by the soldiers, who managed to persuade them to leave their enclosure and go to the Spanish settlement (Aguado 1957, IV, 127).

With the new supply of wine doctored with venom, Ursúa offered a banquet. Bayamo came with forty men, to whom the poisonous drink was given because "there were two people in charge of pouring wine for the guests: one had a bottle with clean wine for the Spaniards and the other a pitcher with the doctored wine for the blacks". After the banquet Ursúa led the Cimarrons to his chamber, where he gave them shirts and machetes and a cup of poisoned wine before sending them on their way. Finally, as Bayamo's few remaining men made their way in, the Spaniards began to stab them while at the same time offering them shirts. Although Bayamo himself became aware of the deceit, he was seized by Ursúa's soldiers, who took advantage of the inebriated state of the Cimarrons and their bewilderment at the capture of their leader. With Bayamo in his power, over the following two months Ursúa tricked him into bringing about the return of the Cimarrons who had fled, with the promise of building a town on the river Francisca, near Nombre de Dios. Once reunited, Ursúa took them to Nombre de Dios. Bayamo was sent to Lima, from where he was sent by the viceroy as a prisoner to Spain. The presentation of gifts, first employed in the wars between Christians and Muslims, took on a new and valuable role in securing agreements with the native population of the New World. However, the dramatic ending to the tale of Bayamo and his men revealed their more lethal side.

Ostentation and Emulation

The processes of conquest in the New World led to the creation of an elite group known as the *beneméritos*. As a reward for their activities in deposing ethnic lords and subjecting native societies to the *encomienda* system, to servitude and different forms of covert slavery, they were able to rise in social status in relation to the limitations imposed by a lowly birth within the feudal system of the Iberian Peninsula. A distinctive element of these New World elite groups was their ostentation and their ability to provide food and lodgings to a large clientele, just like the nobility in the homeland (Domínguez 2012).

The first shipments sent by the Casa de Contratación for the Caribbean islands included the necessary foodstuffs for the sustenance of the Spaniards, but also luxury goods. In the hurly-burly of the island of Hispaniola in the first years of the sixteenth century, the acquisition of these articles served to highlight differences in fortune. Henceforth, the desire for luxury goods that led to the capture and plundering of the precious metals of the Native American communities resulted in elite groups of conquistadores, *encomenderos* or miners emulating Gargantua in their levels of consumption. The merchants of Seville soon turned this circumstance to their own benefit and began to ship luxury objects that allowed the elite of the New World to demonstrate in their homes, at their dining-tables and in their personal attire that they been touched by the magic finger of fortune. Close to this group were the members of the clergy.

The conquest brought about a social mobility that also gave rise to high levels of consumption of luxury European goods among the upper echelons of the Spaniards in America. These goods arrived legally in the Caribbean but the transatlantic network was also used to guarantee the supply of luxury goods to the Indian elite and officials.

In the new Caribbean cities, however, this desire for ostentation was somewhat restricted by the high prices of Spanish products. In 1545 the Italian traveller Galeoto Cey explained that the residents of the city of Santo Domingo – especially the women – were lavish in their dress, which is why most of them were heavily indebted, since they bought everything in instalments and never finished paying off their debts (Cey 1995, 10).

Extravagance as a symbol of supremacy implied that, in addition to the need to consume certain widely used goods and foodstuffs, the more privileged residents needed to acquire luxury clothing and a wide repertoire of goods that would endorse their place of privilege. When Cortés was elected captain-general by his men in Veracruz, he changed his outfits for more luxurious ones "and put on his plume of feathers with his medal and a gold chain and velvet clothing laced in gold, just like a brave and hard-working captain" (Díaz del Castillo 1986 [1632], 33).

Ostentation in dress, which was originally adopted by the Spanish captains to distinguish their superiority, was also used as a testimony of their hierarchical ascendancy in trading with the natives. Cortés had a carved hip-joint armchair brought to him and wore a string of knotted diamonds and a crimson cap with the medal of St. George when he received the dignitaries sent by Moctezuma.[11] The first samples of Spanish clothing that arrived in Tenochtitlan came from Cortés himself because to each Moctezuma emissary he gave two *holanda* shirts and blue diamonds. In addition, he sent the *tlatoani* "a glass goblet from Florence carved and gilded with many woodland and hunting scenes, three *holanda* shirts, and other items" (Díaz del Castillo 1986 [1632], 67). After his triumph over Pánfilo de Narváez's men, Cortés dressed in orange to receive them in a hip-joint armchair. These details of Cortés's attire were recorded thanks to the extraordinary memory of Díaz del Castillo, but they were also echoed by the indigenous chroniclers, who included drawings in their codices. He sought to establish his power in battle, but also to dramatically emphasize his superiority in meetings with the ambassadors of Moctezuma and the Mexican ruler himself, as can be seen in representations of Cortes in Book XII of the Florentine Codex, which deals with the conquest of Mexico. There we find a drawing of him on his ship, seated on his hip-joint armchair as he received the dignitaries who offered him a headdress and other gifts from Moctezuma.[12]

The drawings of the Florentine Codex recreated the first contacts between Mexicas and Spaniards, although they were done in the mid-sixteenth century. The details with which the informants of Fray Bernardino de Sahagún represented the Spanish clothes, arms and headdresses are a testimony to the attention that the Mexicas paid to the Spaniards' clothing and goods. The rank conferred on Cortés and his successors by their clothing and the use of hip-joint armchairs was a common theme in the manuscripts and codices of New Spain. Thus, in the Osuna Codex, drafted in 1556, the viceroy Don Luis de Velasco and the *oidores* of Mexico were depicted in their respective hip-joint armchairs dressed in the dark doublets, leggings and caps typical of the Habsburgs.[13] Likewise, there is a drawing of the viceroy, handing over the staffs of justice to the indigenous sheriffs who would act in his name. They were still not wearing Spanish clothing and the only attribute that identified them with the Spanish world was the staff of justice.

However, one of the drawings of the Osuna Codex does show indigenous people wearing Spanish clothing. In it four natives are walking behind another Indian on horseback carrying the magnificent and emblematic standard of the eagle on a cactus plant. The text indicates that these were armed Mexican *tenochcas*, who were marching on a campaign to Florida. Illustrating the rapid assimilation of Spanish customs and dress, they are no longer attired in the native clothing with which they are represented in the Florentine Codex; here they are dressed in Spanish attire, with doublet, leggings and feathered hats. Moreover, they are no longer carrying the well-known *macuahuitl* Aztec weapons, but the steel swords of the Spaniards. The indigenous conquest of Mesoamerica, as the joint campaigns carried out by the Spanish with their native allies have been called, amplified the processes of adoption of European goods, weapons and food among the latter (Oudijk and Restall 2008).

The alliances coordinated by Cortés, Pizarro and the other Spanish captains proved decisive for these indigenous allies in acquainting themselves with European food and Spanish clothes, utensils and weapons. The elites who retained their privileged rank in the native world after the conquest did so because they accepted the new religion, although conversion did not necessarily imply a rupture with their old beliefs. However, the indigenous nobility began to acquire Catholic prints and images to exhibit them, if possible, in specially designated places, as indicated by indigenous wills and testaments.

In Mesoamerica and in the Andes some of the most obvious consequences of Spanish dominion were the creation of taxation mechanisms, the distribution of *encomiendas*, the persecution of native beliefs and the direct or covert enslavement of the indigenous people in areas producing precious metals. In all of these processes the indigenous people came into contact with European goods in numerous ways, either because they were forced to grow cereals such as wheat, or to raise European cattle, or they simply found it more convenient to use Spanish tools and welcomed the arrival in their kitchens of new European meats and fruits. The early exchanges of goods that lay the foundations for alliances between Spaniards and Indians in the period from 1520 to 1550 gave way to a broad and rapid distribution and assimilation of European goods, but not without the loss of thousands of lives and a wealth of cultural knowledge.

The adoption of European goods was not automatic. There was a long selection process that related to previous cultural traditions, strategies of adaptation or survival in the face of the new conditions of the sixteenth century and the search for recognition and legitimacy. The *caciques* and native elders saw the use of these new clothes, the consumption of new foods, the rejection of their native beliefs and the acquisition of images, furniture and Spanish utensils as a means of endorsing their position of privilege in the context of Spanish domination.

In the regions where the most far-reaching Westernization processes took place, the history of the introduction of Old World utensils and goods shows that there were goods that were immediately accepted for their obvious utility, such as knives or axes. In addition, the religious orders' persistent campaigns to convert the natives to Catholicism was the reason why they began to acquire prints, paintings and sculptures of Jesus, the Virgin and the saints to decorate their homes, as demonstrated in sixteenth-century indigenous wills and testaments. In 1551, for example, Anna Tabales Mazata, an inhabitant of the town of San Juan Atlangatepec, declared in her will that she left her heirs "a Lady of Sorrows, a Saint Michael, a Saint Francis, a Saint Anthony, a Christ the Saint, two boxes, two blankets, two underskirts for work, thirty-nine sheep and a dark horse, saddled and schooled" (Rojas Rabiela, Rea López, and Medina Lima Vol. 2 1999, 94).

Rivalry between the different religious orders in the process of evangelization resulted in the erection of chapels and churches at the expense of indigenous labor. In the case of Mexico City, Alonso de Zorita explained that more than twenty monasteries had been built, that there were villages with more than ten churches and that "each neighborhood and each leader wanted to have a church of its own" (Zorita 2011, 247) One of the consequences was an increase in Church revenue thanks to the legacies and alms donated by the dying. As a final act, wealthy Indians exhibited their wealth and the diversity of their assets by handing over valuable legacies to fraternities, churches and monasteries. Terrified by hellfire preaching, suitably reinforced with pictures, paintings and frescoes depicting the suffering that awaited souls in hell or purgatory, and perhaps the conviction that occupying prominent positions at the head of communities demanded munificence in donations to the Church seems to have induced the natives into believing that their largesse would be well received only if they donated cattle or goods of European origin to the churches and confraternities (Wobeser 2012, 1311–48).

This was the case of Ana de Santa Barbara, chief *cacique* of Santo Domingo Tepexi de la Seda, who made her will in 1621. In it she ordered that the Funeral Mass be held with the body present and a deacon, a subdeacon and offerings of bread, wine, three rams and three goats. A year after her death, eight masses were to be said with bread, wine and rams. When she died, fifty goats were to be given to the confraternity of Our Lady of the Rosary and three pairs of mules were to be sold so that the vicar could buy a new crown for the Virgin. Fifty goats would also be given to the confraternity of the Santo Entierro de Cristo Nuestro Señor (Rojas Rabiela, Rea López, and Medina Lima Vol. 3 1999, 106–8). This extravagance reflected the belief that one's passage through purgatory could be shortened through mass and donations, and such acts of posthumous generosity were a confirmation of the Church's success in convincing the Indians that the punishments of the afterlife could be alleviated, especially with the bequest of European goods.

Christian Indians Dressed as Spaniards

Native hierarchies were disrupted by the conquest; nonetheless, the Spanish republics in the New World varied considerably from domestic models. Civil wars in Peru, the decision of the Crown to restrict the power of the *encomenderos* and the promotion of governors, *corregidores* and *oidore*s who imposed new clients to replace the former elites of the conquest were some of the factors that elevated subjects without merit to positions of privilege. Likewise, the decline in taxpayers, especially noticeable at the end of the sixteenth century and the early years of the seventeenth century, reduced the earning power of the heirs of the first *encomenderos*, while merchants held onto a substantial share of the Indian riches.

In his *Nueva Corónica y Buen Gobierno*, whose last adjustments were probably made in 1598, Poma de Ayala provided extensive information on the disruption of the hierarchies that affected Spaniards and Indians alike and how, in his opinion, they were turning the world upside down. When referring to the *corregidores* of the viceroyalty of Peru, whose earnings stemmed largely from compelling the natives of their districts to acquire Spanish merchandise, Poma de Ayala described them as persons who lived with little fear of God and enriched themselves at the expense of the Indians. They appointed Indians without rights of origin as governors in charge of collecting the tributes (Poma de Ayala Tomo I, 1980 [1615], 365). Poma de Ayala attributed these changes in indigenous governance to a relaxation of the hierarchies observed by the *corregidores* in their personal lives, which he depicted in one of his drawings entitled "That the *corregidor* invites to eat at his table lowly people, Indian *mitayos*, mestizos and mulattos and honors them". In the drawing a mestizo, a people of mixed race and a tributary Indian are seated at the table of a *corregidor* who seems to be offering a toast to them. Poma de Ayala criticizes the collapse of traditional hierarchies represented by a banquet at which individuals of such different condition were treated as equals. He notes that the *corregidor*,

> being a titled lord from his ancestors, sits at his table to eat, invite, talk and drink, play with people, uncouth ruffians and robbers, thieves, liars, louts and drunks, Jews and Moors, lowly people, Indian *mitayos*, and reveal his secrets to them; and holds conversation with these mestizos and mulattos and blacks, and in this life there are many of these men and women.
>
> (Poma de Ayala Tomo I 1980 [1615], 375–76)

Eating-places, where class differences were most obvious both in the hierarchized Quechua society and in the Spanish world, had become areas of confusion where honor was being lost and differences disappearing. Poma de Ayala reproached the fact that mestizos, people of mixed race and tributary Indians shared a table with a Spanish *corregidor*, but equally disapproved of priests dismissing the former *kurakas* who attended to their interests and instead invited to their tables "drunks, lowly Indians, mestizos, mulatos [sic], in order to rob the Indians" (Poma de Ayala Tomo II 1980 [1615], 46). He explained the close relationship between the clergy and these individuals as part of a strategy to plunder the Indians to the very last, since the main *caciques* sought to protect their taxpayers from excessive charges, but when replaced by the "lowly Indians", as Poma de Ayala called them, the priests were free to demand the payment of unlimited quantities of "wheat and corn, potatoes and mutton, hens, chickens, eggs, bacon, lard, tallow, chili, salt, chaff, dried corn, dried potato, quinoa, beans, lima beans, chickpeas, beans, fish, shrimp, lettuce, cabbage, garlic, onion, coriander, parsley, peppermint and other trifles, food and fruit, firewood, grass" (Poma de Ayala Tomo II 1980

[1615], 13). This list shows how, in the late sixteenth century, Andean dining tables served a mixture of European and American food as a result of the Spanish settlers, and how the Indians were compelled to grow plants brought from the peninsula and raise pigs, chickens, rams and cattle.

Poma de Ayala wrote the *Nueva Corónica* to denounce the abuses committed by the Spaniards, and also by the mestizos, whom he considered to be a plague. He described in crude terms the constant violence endured by the Indians in the viceroyalty of Peru that constituted the central resource used by Spaniards to establish the great money-making machine of the Andean world that filled the coffers of the Crown.

Tax obligations to *corregidores* and priests forced the production of European goods and the need to maintain the government's role in the indigenous world under Spanish dominion compelled the main *caciques* to convert to Christianity by integrating themselves into the congregations and confraternities. By the end of the sixteenth century, the desire to emulate the Spanish was leading the caciques to dispense with their native dress, to dress like at the Spanish style in order to differentiate themselves from the rest of the native population. While in the early years following the conquest one of the few Spanish elements carried by the *caciques* who acted as intermediaries for the Spaniards were the staffs of justice that the *corregidores* gave them, in the space of just a few decades their style of dress had changed as a strategy to reaffirm their legitimacy before the Crown (Gómez 2017, 107–41).

The Indian Christians described by Poma de Ayala were the product of a rapid cultural transformation focused essentially on maintaining their privileges and protecting their communities. For this reason, he had no compunction in comparing them with the Spaniards of Castile, affirming that they knew "all the crafts, artifices, benefits", since they were singers of plainchant, musicians who played the organ, the *vihuela*, the flute and the trumpet, scribes of the council and notaries, mayors, bailiffs, painters, woodworkers, sculptors, gilders, tailors, shoemakers, carpenters, blacksmiths, chair-makers and silversmiths, and skilled in multiple other trades in the Hispanic world. Furthermore, they knew how to fire shotguns and use other weapons like swords, daggers and halberds. They played "in every game like Spaniards"; they were great horsemen, animal tamers and bullfighters.

In the eyes of Poma de Ayala the Indians acquired significance because they became Christians, because they learned Spanish trades and because they were loyal to the king. In their attire they closely reflected the clothes worn by Spaniards. For this reason Poma de Ayala wrote that the principal *cacique*

> has to dress like a Spaniard with a difference, not cut off all his hair but have it cut to ear level, wear a shirt, collar, doublet and boots,

> with shirt and coat, hat and sword, halberd and other weapons like a lord, with horse and mules.

Moreover, he had to behave like a Spaniard when eating and sleeping; had to learn Latin; and know how to write, count and file suits (Poma de Ayala Tomo II 1980 [1615], 156–59).

Shortly after Poma de Ayala concluded his work, the Hieronymite friar Diego de Ocaña travelled throughout Peru and wrote a detailed manuscript about his trip. In describing the clothing of the Indians on the coast of Peru, he explained that they wore hats like Spaniards and that the *caciques* "wear a doublet and shoes and stockings, a ruff and a Spanish-style suit" (Ocaña 2010, 113). In Potosí the Spaniards who owned the ninety silver mines exhibited their wealth in their dress, but so did Indians of both sexes. The Society of Jesus had created a confraternity of the Child Jesus, made up of rich Indians, who paraded through the streets of the city carrying candles weighing five pounds and clothed in fine silks and velvet "better than the Spanish" (Ocaña 2010, 272).

Chroniclers like Poma de Ayala, Ocaña and others demonstrated – a fact corroborated by the study of indigenous testaments – that the uses, clothing and goods of Spanish origin in the native population were first introduced by the *caciques*, *kurakas* or ethnic gentlemen. In regions where the Spanish defeated the resistance forces and held sway through force of arms, the native elites sought their social reproduction at the price of becoming rapidly hispanized, which entailed adopting Catholic practices and Spanish clothing and acquiring goods of European origin such as furniture, weapons, pictures, books, decorative objects, jewelry, fabrics and tools. However, probably following the example of their masters, indigenous people of limited means also sought to possess European goods, as recorded in their wills.

These documents indicate that as the seventeenth century progressed, native dwellings in the main American cities featured mestizo table linen, bedclothes and furniture. In Santa Fe de Bogotá, for example, the indigenous people owned dresses that came from the region, such as brush-painted blankets from the Bogotá savannah, cotton fabrics from the warm lands of the Magdalena River, corsets, girdles and ponchos from Peru and Quito, Indian chairs, petticoats from Castile, breeches, mattresses, shirts and dressing tables from Rouen, blue plates from Talavera, caskets from Flanders, Dutch dressing tables and hats from Castile (Rodríguez 2002). Their testaments indicate that one way in which the natives demonstrated their wealth was through the acquisition of European goods, whose mention never went unnoticed in the document. As in New Spain or Peru, wills were drawn up by the indigenous in Santa Fe to pave the way for the salvation of their souls after death through bequests and donations to the Church for the celebration of Masses, and also to protect the testators' heirs.

Conclusions

The last wills and testaments of the natives, whereby they donated lands, cattle, paintings, jewels or capital to the Church, to the confraternities and to the religious orders, provide evidence of how ferocious indoctrination campaigns by the Church and the threat of divine punishment after death struck terror among the populace; hence the need for testators to preserve and expand their social capital with the generosity of their posthumous donations that earned them respectability in their own communities and in Spanish circles. Thus, without resorting to ostensible violence, missionary campaigns succeeded in persuading the indigenous communities to donate – apparently of their own free will – an enormous quantity of goods received on a daily basis by the Church thanks to testamentary bequests. It was as if a safe pass to avoid hell could be achieved mainly with indigenous lands and with Spanish cattle, and the addition of jewelry and religious images. This seemed to imply that in the long term the strategies of the richest native elites of New Spain and Peru for the acquisition of land, livestock and capital were devised on the basis that on their death the main beneficiaries would be the Church rather than family members. In regions where subjection by the Spanish seemed inevitable, the role of ecclesiastical preaching ended up indirectly endorsing the acceptance of European goods.

The new conditions imposed by the Spanish favored the introduction of European goods and customs to the Indian population, usually involving some form of violence. The native elites of the regions where Spanish governance was imposed found that the consumption and display of European goods afforded a new attribute to their privileged status. In these cases, the violence that characterized the introduction of the first European goods and their use by the Indians gave way to their acceptance and accumulation by *caciques* and *kurakas* as a strategy not to be swept aside after the upheaval produced by the conquest. Fear of the afterlife and the need to show off with European goods were new experiences for indigenous leaders. The incorporation of European objects did not, however, imply a rejection of attributes pertaining to their native identity. In many cases, the exhibition of wealth represented by cattle or European goods did not involve a break with their indigenous past; on the contrary, the fact that the *caciques* could show off their fortune with European cattle, for example, could be viewed as proof that they belonged in their own right to the line of rulers whose origins predated the arrival of the Spaniards. However, European goods profoundly altered the societies of the New World, either because they had been forced upon them through violence or as part of a Spanish strategy to create new needs that would be paid for in the future with precious metals. Even the groups that succeeded in frustrating Spanish domination radically modified their social practices by acquainting themselves with the breeding of cattle or lambs, as happened in the peninsula of La Guajira. There, as in other regions, what we might call a resistance economy developed that sought to prevent the establishment of new Spanish settlements. Nonetheless this resistance never brought about a complete break in contact with the Iberians or with other Europeans, since they were already well accustomed to using their goods. This is indicated in the statement given to a Spanish ensign by the Indians in the service of the *cacique* Martín Boronata in La Guajira in 1624. A series of assaults on landowners in the city of Riohacha in which *guajiros* seized the cattle that the Spaniards had placed on their ancestral lands triggered a campaign of harassment and persecution that forced the clans of the savannas near Riohacha to constantly move from one place to another. Arguing for the need for a truce, the *guajiros* told the ensign Francisco Riveros

> that the Indians were very afraid, that they were shaking when they heard that the soldiers were coming and that they could no longer kill cows and that [*cacique*] Aritama and his brother Martín [Boronata] said that they wanted to come to their ranches because they cannot do without the whites as they do not have axes, or yarn, or *chengue* and their children and their women are crying with starvation.

Undoubtedly the *guajiros* could live without the Spaniards, but this testimony indicates that, although they could prevent the expanding power of the settlers in their land, they were seriously affected by the products and livestock that they brought to the region, as occurred in other border areas. In effect, the impact of European goods in the New World was palpable even without the Spaniards themselves being present in the indigenous communities.

If, as has been pointed out, violence accompanied the first diffusion and uses of European goods in the New World, powerful internal forces also led the communities themselves to become interested in acquiring them. One such factor was that the conquest opened the way for the Spanish to appoint new *caciques* or *kurakas*, who often did not belong to the old pre-Hispanic elites, yet seem to have found in European clothing and in the consumption of Spanish foods a means to legitimize their new social and political condition. These new leaders and the ancient elites who kept their ranks proved the first to acquire hats, bonnets, capes, swords, stockings, shoes and other Spanish clothing. By the 1560s it seemed inexcusable that a member of the Mexican ethnic elite did not have a room in his home with Spanish religious images, as becomes evident in probate inventories and wills.

Were native identities lost due to the consumption of these goods? Not necessarily. The outcome was rather an aggregate that made the identity attributes of the indigenous people more complex. The world that Poma de Ayala described with despair was that of subjects who he considered upstarts, whether they were Spanish or indigenous, because they exceeded the status or hierarchical limits of their respective societies. One of the most obvious expressions of this situation was manifested in the consumption of goods, in food and clothing. Therefore, it is necessary to delve into the study of social practices of consumption in the post-conquest era to understand how such consumption was not only the result of Spanish imposition; it was also associated with the search for identity and of individual and collective affirmation in a society that was marked by violence.

Notes

1. This article falls within the framework of the project HAR2014–53797-P "Globalización ibérica: redes entre Asia y Europa y los cambios en las pautas de consumo en Latinoamérica" [Iberian Globalization: Networks between Asia and Europe and Changes in Consumption Patterns in Latin America] financed by Ministerio de Economía y Competitividad, Spain, of which the principal investigator is Bartolomé Yun-Casalilla.
2. Referring to the importance of violence in the spread of European goods across the New World, Bartolomé Yun-Casalilla says that rather than speaking of intercultural dialogue we should speak of intercultural violence (Aram and Yun-Casalilla 2014, 294).
3. *Colección de Documentos Inéditos relativos al descubrimiento, conquista y organización de las antiguas posesiones españolas de América y Oceanía* Tomo XXIII 1875, 314.
4. It was ordered that they should carry 180 *cahices* (seed measure) of wheat, fifty *cahices* of barley, sixty wine barrels, ten tons of vinegar, sixty tons of oil, 650 pieces of bacon, fifty quintals of figs, dried fish, thirty *cahices* of chickpeas, 360 quintals of cake, six mares, four donkeys and two asses, four female calves and two male calves, one hundred heads of small livestock, 200 hens, one hundred pigs, rabbits, sugar, almonds and rice. In addition, it was determined that rice and wheat seeds be taken for Hispaniola. Four kegs of rooted vine shoots were also transported for planting on the island. *Colección de Documentos Inéditos relativos al descubrimiento, conquista y organización de las antiguas posesiones españolas de América y Oceanía* Tomo XXIV 1875, 15.
5. *Colección de Documentos Inéditos relativos al descubrimiento, conquista y organización de las antiguas posesiones españolas de América y Oceanía* Tomo XXIII 1875, 315.
6. Thus, in the Indian villages of Hispaniola of more than 300 inhabitants there would have to be ten or twelve mares, 500 cows and 500 pigs. Each Taíno house should have twelve chickens and one rooster. *Colección de Documentos Inéditos relativos al descubrimiento, conquista y organización de las antiguas posesiones españolas de América y Oceanía* Tomo XXIII 1875, 310–31. This practice that began in the Caribbean spread across the continent. The *reductions* of indigenous peoples consisted in the systematic destruction of pre-Spanish settlements and removal of their former inhabitants into Indian towns that replicated the orthogonal layout of Spanish towns and cities.
7. Archivo General de Indias, hereafter AGI. Panama, 233, L.1–467

8. Martín Camacho, protector of natives of the Audiencia of Santa Fe, said that the Indians who were forced to serve the Spaniards on the Magdalena River had such a taste for Spanish wine that "the son forgot the death of his father and the father the death of his son and the woman the death of her husband". AGI. Santa Fe, 96, 5ª. Letter from Martín Camacho to the king. 1602.
9. On the political meaning of banquets in Spain during the sixteenth century, see Pérez Samper 1997, 53–98.
10. Fernández de Oviedo, [1851–1855] 1992, Volume I, book V, chapter VII.
11. Díaz del Castillo [1632] 1986, 64. The blue diamonds were possibly glass of Venetian origin.
12. The Codex can be consulted at the Laurentian Library and this image in particular at the following address: www.wdl.org/es/item/10623/view/1/19/
13. Also known as *Pintura del gobernador, alcaldes y regidores de México* Dating from 1565, it has been digitalized by the National Library of Spain at the following address: http://hdl.loc.gov/loc.wdl/wdl.7324

Bibliography

Aguado, Fray Pedro de. 1957. *Recopilación Historial.* Introducción, notas y cometarios de Juan Friede. Bogotá: Biblioteca de la Presidencia de Colombia.

Aram, Bethany. 2008. *Leyenda negra y leyendas doradas en la conquista de América. Pedrarias y Balboa.* Madrid: Marcial Pons.

Aram, Bethany, and Bartolomé Yun-Casalilla, eds. 2014. *Global Goods and the Spanish Empire, 1492–1824. Circulation, Resistance and Diversity.* Houndmills: Palgrave Macmillan.

Cey, Galeotto. 1995. *Viaje y descripción de las Indias. 1539–1553.* Estudio preliminar, notas e índices de José Rafael Lovera. Caracas: Fundación Banco Venezolano de Crédito.

Colección de Documentos Inéditos relativos al descubrimiento, conquista y organización de las antiguas posesiones españolas de América y Oceanía. Tomo XXIII. 1875a. Madrid: Imprenta de Manuel G. Hernández.

Colección de Documentos Inéditos relativos al descubrimiento, conquista y organización de las antiguas posesiones españolas de América y Oceanía. Tomo XXIV. 1875b. Madrid: Imprenta de Manuel G. Hernández.

Díaz de Castillo, Bernal. 1986 [1632]. *Historia de la conquista de la Nueva España.* Introducción y notas de Joaquín Ramírez Cabañas. México: Editorial Porrúa.

Domínguez Ortiz, Antonio. 2012. *Las clases privilegiadas en el Antiguo Régimen.* Madrid: Akal.

Favarò, Valentina, Manfredi Merluzzi, and Gaetano Sabatini, eds. 2017. *Fronteras. Procesos de integración y conflictos entre Europa y América (siglos XVI-XX).* Madrid: Fondo de Cultura Económica.

Fernández de Oviedo, Gonzalo. [1851–1855] 1992. *Historia General y Natural de las Indias.* Tomo I y III. Madrid: Biblioteca de Autores Españoles.

Gómez, Mauricio Alejandro. 2017. "Prendas de vestir, circulación e identidades. Un rasgo de la cultura material de los indios urbanos en el Nuevo Reino de Granada (1550–1650)." In *Comunicación, objetos y mercancías en el Nuevo Reino de Granada. Estudios de producción y circulación*, edited by Nelson F.

González Martínez, Ricardo Uribe, and Diana Bonnett Vélez, 107–41. Bogotá: Universidad de los Andes.

Ladero Quesada, Miguel Ángel. 2008. *Las Indias de Castilla en sus primeros años. Cuentas de la Casa de Contratación (1503–1521)*. Madrid: Editorial Dykinson.

León-Portilla, Miguel. 2014. *Visión de los vencidos. Relaciones indígenas de la conquista*. México: Universidad Autónoma de México.

Medina, José Toribio. 1913. *El descubrimiento del Océano Pacífico. Vasco Núñez de Balboa, Hernando de Magallanes y sus compañeros. Tomo II, documentos relativos a Núñez de Balboa*. Santiago de Chile: Imprenta Universitaria.

Melgar Tisoc, Emiliano Ricardo. 2010. "Una relectura del comercio de la turquesa: entre yacimientos, talleres y consumidores." In *Caminos y mercados en México*, edited by Janet Long Towell and Amalia Attolini Lecón, 155–68. México: Universidad Autónoma de México.

Mena García, María del Carmen. 1996. "Dependencia o autoabastecimiento. La lucha por la supervivencia en los primeros años de la colonización de Tierra Firme." *Revista del Caribe* (25): 45–53.

———. 2004. "La Casa de Contratación de Sevilla y el abasto de las flotas de Indias." In *La casa de la Contratación y la navegación entre España y las Indias*, edited by Enriqueta Vila Vilar, Antonio Acosta Rodríguez y Adolfo L. González Rodríguez, 237–78. Seville: Consejo Superior de Investigaciones Científicas; Universidad de Sevilla.

Muñoz Camargo, Diego. 2013. *Historia de Tlaxcala*. Tlaxcala: Universidad Autónoma de Tlaxcala.

Ocaña, Diego de, fray. 2010. *Viaje por el Nuevo Mundo: de Guadalupe a Potosí, 1599–1605*. Madrid: Iberoamericana-Vervuert.

Oudijk, Michel, and Mathew Restall. 2008. *La conquista indígena de Mesoamérica. El caso de don Gonzalo Mazatzin Moctezuma*. Puebla: Instituto Nacional de Antropología e Historia, Universidad de las Américas Puebla.

Pagden, Anthony. 1988. *La caída del hombre natural*. Madrid: Alianza.

Pérez Samper, María de los Ángeles. 1997. "Fiesta y alimentación en la España moderna: el banquete como imagen festiva de abundancia y refinamiento." *Espacio, tiempo y forma. Serie IV, Historia Moderna* (10): 53–98.

Poma de Ayala, Guamán. 1980 [1615]. *Nueva Corónica y buen gobierno*. Tomos I y II. Transcripción, prologo y notas y Cronología de Franklin Pease. Caracas: Biblioteca Ayacucho.

Rodríguez Jiménez, Pablo, ed. 2002. *Testamentos indígenas de Santafé de Bogotá. Siglos XVI-XVIII*. Bogotá: Alcaldía Mayor de Bogotá,.

Rojas Rabiela, Teresa, Elsa Leticia Rea López, and Constantino Medina Lima. 1999a. *Vidas y bienes olvidados. Testamentos indígenas novohispanos*. Vol. 2. México: Ciesas.

———. 1999b. *Vidas y bienes olvidados. Testamentos indígenas novohispanos*. Vol. 3. México: Ciesas.

Ruiz Guadalajara, Juan Carlos. 2010. "Capitán Miguel Caldera y la frontera Chichimeca: entre el mestizo historiográfico y el soldado del rey." *Revista de Indias* 70 (248): 23–58.

Saldarriaga, Gregorio. 2011. *Alimentos e identidades en el Nuevo Reino de Granada, siglos XVI y XVII*. Bogotá: Universidad del Rosario.

Suazo, Alonso de. 2000. *Cartas y memorias (1511–1539)*. Prólogo, edición y notas de Rodrigo Martínez Baracs. México: Conaculta.

Veblen, Thorstein. 2014. *Teoría de la clase ociosa*. Madrid: Alianza Editorial.

Vila Vilar, Enriqueta, and Jaime J. Lacueva Muñoz, eds. 2012. *Mirando las dos orillas: intercambios mercantiles, sociales y culturales entre Andalucía y América*. Seville: Fundación Buenas Letras.

Wobeser, Gisela von. 2012. "Certezas, incertidumbres y expectativas en torno a la salvación del alma. Creencias escatológicas en Nueva España, siglos XVI al XVIII." *Historia Mexicana* 61 (4): 1311–48.

Zorita, Alonso de. 2011. *Relación de la Nueva España I*, Edición, versión paleográfica, estudio preliminar e índice onomástico de Ethelia Ruiz Medrano y José Mariano Leyva. México: Cien de México.

7 Rice Revisited From Colonial Panama

Its Cultivation and Exportation[1]

Bethany Aram and Manuel Enrique García-Falcón

In the sixteenth century cultivated rice and West African cultural influence reached the Isthmus of Panama, where they remain prominent to the present day. The contemporary ubiquity of rice (sometimes cooked in coconut water) at meals and a popular children's fable, *The Little Mandinga Cockroach*, testify to the enduring legacy of cultural and culinary exchange. The Caribbean tale, whose endearing Panamanian version has been compared to *Romeo and Juliet* (Sinan 1974), features a young female cockroach who finds a coin while sweeping the steps of her house and uses it to purchase ribbons to adorn her hair. Seeing the little cockroach so attractive, a bull, a dog, a cock and, finally, a dapper mouse ("el Ratón Pérez") propose marriage to her before the little cockroach agrees to marry the well-attired mouse. The following day, after straightening up her house, the little Mandinga sets a pot of rice with milk to boil before going to the river to collect water. Although the Mandinga cautions her husband against dipping into the pot of rice, in her absence el Ratón Pérez succumbs to temptation, falls into the pot and meets his death. The Mandinga's loss precipitates a chain of calamities: in sympathy, a pigeon clips her wing, the queen cuts off her leg, the king abandons his crown, the river dries out and so on (Lyra 2018). In short, the mishap of el Ratón Pérez reveals his dependence, like that of many others, on the Mandinga and disrupts the social order, highlighting the perils as well as the possibilities of cultural mixture.

The Little Mandinga Cockroach has been told for centuries in regions largely elided by the "Black rice" debate (Hawthorne 2003, 2010a; Eltis, Morgan, and Richardson 2010; Bray et al. 2015). Yet the arguments that Carney developed with reference to present-day Senegambia and eighteenth-century South Carolina, like those of Hawthorne with respect to Guinea-Bissau and Brazil, hold important implications for the sixteenth- and seventeenth-century Spanish Main. Carney seeks to recover the agency of enslaved Africans, particularly women from the Senegambia region, in the transfer and adaptation of the skills and knowledge essential to cultivate, harvest, husk, prepare and consume rice (Carney 1998, 2001).

DOI: 10.4324/9781003168058-8

While enabling South Carolina's planters to develop a new product, Carney argues that slaves of African origin who raised rice established cultural continuities with their traditional forms of subsistence and initially obtained nutritional and other benefits, such as increased autonomy. Adding nuance to Carney's observations, Hawthorne differentiates between the sophisticated and productive riziculture that the Mandinga developed in inland Senegambia, where they benefitted from access to iron, and rice cultivation along Guinea Bissau's coasts and rivers, practiced by less centralized ethnic groups including the Bran, Floup and Biafada (Hawthorne 2003, 2010b, 152) or, alternatively, the Baga and the Nalu (Fields Black 2008). Indeed, the diversity of rice-producing systems in West Africa may have facilitated adaptation of rice cultivation to Cape Verde and, subsequently, Spanish America, where it became a means of subsistence for groups of enslaved as well as free Africans who adapted traditional and adopted new agricultural and dietary practices.

Important reasons emerge for including the sixteenth-century Isthmus of Panama in the global history of rice. Beginning in the sixteenth century, the increasing majority of this precocious rice-growing and exporting region's inhabitants from West Africa entered into contact with other Africans and indigenous peoples of a variety of "nations" as well as with different groups of Europeans. One of the chief criticisms of Carney's thesis – the fact that more Africans from rice-growing regions fell victim to the trans-Atlantic slave trade before than after the 1670s (Eltis, Morgan, and Richardson 2010), points to the need to examine material and technological transfers from West Africa to the Americas during this earlier period and before the rise of large-scale plantation slavery in North America and Brazil. Slaves from the rice-growing regions of Upper Guinea, mainly Senegambia and Sierra Leone, constituted between 75–100% of those shipped to the Americas before the late 1500s, when Angola became the place of departure for most American-bound slaves (Wheat 2016, 23).

Rice in the sixteenth- and seventeenth-century Greater Caribbean, including the Spanish Main, may be relevant for additional reasons. More than one century before enslaved labourers from Senegambia reached South Carolina or the Maranhão, maroons from the same regions appear to have cultivated and consumed rice on the Isthmus of Panama, where they transferred knowledge of the grain to other Africans and native Americans. The sixteenth-century context provides the possibility of considering technological and cultural transfers, as well as gender roles and hybridization, with reference to African and American-born cattle herders and rice growers who overcame slavery. Two of Panama's maroon communities, fortified in the hills of Portobelo and the Chepo (Bayano) river basin in the 1570s, negotiated their freedom with the Spanish Crown, whose strategic interests in the region required the support of free Blacks. To some extent, the maroon experience could have mitigated the "deculturating" effect of enslavement (Hawthorne 2015), without precluding other forms of exploitation, including military service and tribute. Finally, the isthmus's geographical importance facilitated complex cultural transfers, transformations and adaptations, involving Africans of multiple ethnicities, different indigenous groups, European adventurers and all of their American-born offspring of diverse parentage.

The riziculture developed on the Isthmus of Panama and in the Caribbean may have influenced the transfer of knowledge and technologies to cultivate, process and consume the cereal from the coast of upper Guinea to other parts of America. Indeed, the maroon experience offers fresh perspectives on issues of agency, power and hybridization informed by (and relevant to) the "Black rice debate". It also permits a distinction between early modern globalization, represented by access to rice and other new products where they previously had been unknown, and the rise of market-oriented production, which entailed a later, separate process in most areas of the world. The role of rice on the early modern Isthmus of Panama, moreover, invites attention to matters of basic nutrition and survival that arise alongside and even before those of economic (or proto-capitalist) development. In this context, understanding the role of women, seeds and knowledge from Senegambia requires an assessment of the impact of an early convergence of peoples and products from four continents on the Panamanian crossing in light of the quantity, quality and diversity of the food resources they could cultivate and consume.

Exploring the alimentary implications of the Columbian exchange (Crosby 1973, 1986), Rebecca Earle has elucidated Spanish conquistadores' attempts to maintain their own traditional food supplies in line with humoural medicinal beliefs, in order to keep themselves strong and to distinguish themselves from Amerindians. She has, moreover, shown that Europeans' belief in the disruptive nature of dietary change supported their understanding that the health of enslaved Africans would improve if they were able to consume familiar foods (Earle 2012, 54–59). Such humoural beliefs, alongside slave traders' and owners' attempts to ensure their captives' survival and productivity, encouraged the transfer of crops from the western coast of Africa to the Greater Caribbean well before they reached North America. Rice, millet and yams numbered among the foodstuffs that most commonly accompanied and fed enslaved Africans shipped across the Atlantic (Newson and Michin 2007).

Recent attention to historical foodways and culture on the Isthmus of Panama, a strategic bridge between North and South America as well as between the Atlantic and Pacific Oceans, has shown little interest in rice. While the domestication and varieties of corn (Piperno 2017), as well as the spread of cattle (Castro Herrera 2004), have attracted more attention, the exogenous origins of bitter manioc and especially plantains – celebrated as a "national food" (Castillero Calvo 2010) – have inspired heated debates.[2]

A comparative lack of scholarly interest in Panama's rice parallels the only recent emergence of research on its African communities (Tardieu 2009; Piqueras y Laviña 2015; Laviña et al. 2015) and persistent dearth of early modern women's and gender history regarding the region. Thus, the study of rice can benefit from and contribute to knowledge of the African diaspora as well as gender history.

Finally, in conjunction with other foods, rice offers a new angle to examine the impact of the Columbian exchange and early globalization on the different populations involved. The proliferation or, to the contrary, disappearance and restriction, of dietary options and practices becomes crucial to consider the possibility of cultural as well as biological survival and hybridization, including the extent to which groups and individuals could resist, benefit or suffer from the alimentary revolution. The positions espoused in the current literature range from a view of a diversification of available foods and nutrients (Jiménez and Cooke 2001; Castillero Calvo 2006; Aceituno and Martín 2017) to one of a progressive homogenization of dietary options (Martín and Rodríguez 2006; Saldarriaga 2011a), depending upon the sources available and informing the research underway. Thus the present chapter will consider the debated presence and impact of other products, such as plantains and yuca, the reliance on corn, and, finally, the expansion of bovine livestock and mule teams, to assess and to contextualize the role of rice in the region.

Food, Conquest and Survival

Deeply rooted global histories of rice converged in sixteenth-century America, as illustrated in Map 7.1. Thousands of years before the Common Era, the domestication of rice from wild species took place independently in Asia and Africa. In Central and South America, the wild species *Oryza glumaepatula, O. alta, O. latifolia* and *O. grandiglumis* predated Europeans and Africans.[3] In the Old World, the most famous species, *O. sativa*, was domesticated in the Pearl River basin of Zhujiang, China between 11500 and 6200 BCE (Huang et al. 2012) and subsequently spread to the Ganges, Tigris and Euphrates river basins, as well as that of the Nile, and through North Africa, where the Greeks and Romans encountered it (Medina et al. 1996). At the same time, at roughly 1000 BCE, a wild species of rice, *O. barthii*, underwent a separate process of domestication in the upper Niger River delta, to produce the species *O. glaberrima*, which extended along the coast and rivers of the Senegambia region in West Africa (Linares 2002, 2011; Wang et al. 2014). Under the Roman Empire, traces of *O. glaberrina* and *O. sativa* probably reached the Iberian Peninsula, where Islamic rule encouraged a more systematic cultivation of *O. sativa* by the eleventh century in regions such as Valencia and Seville (Hernández Bermejo and Garcia Sánchez 2008).

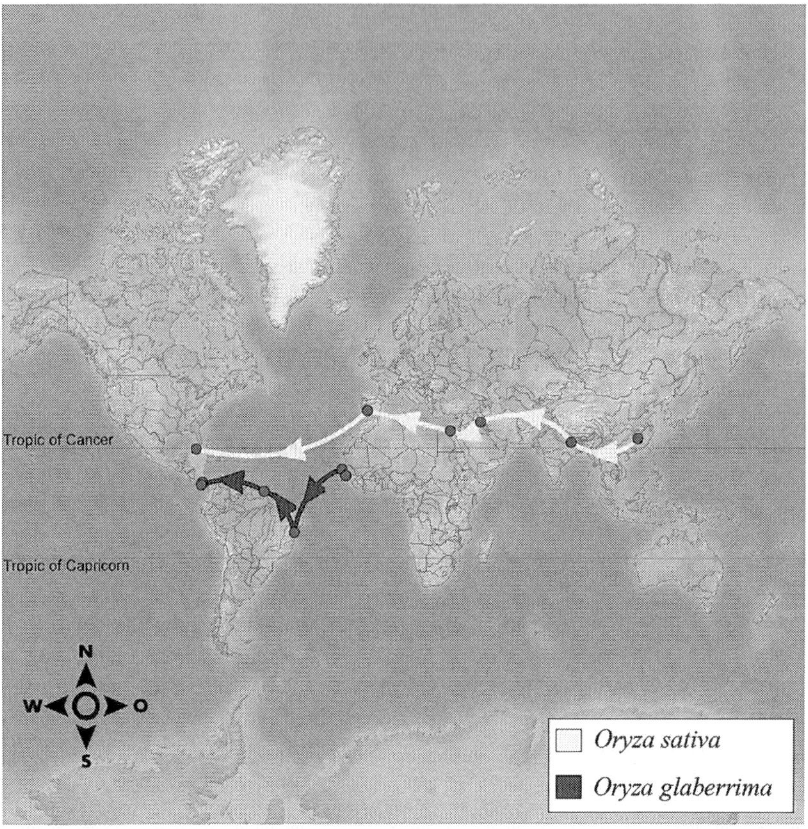

Map 7.1 The Global Circulation and Cultivation of Rice.

Source: designed by Manuel Enrique García-Falcón using stepmap.com.

The global spread of rice encompassed multiple species and itineraries (Portères 1960). In the early sixteenth century, *O. sativa* would have reached the Caribbean and mainland America on ships from Seville and *O. glaberrima* on vessels sailing from the coast of Guinea as well as the Cape Verde Islands. After mid-century, *O. sativa* also reached America across the Pacific on the Manila-Acapulco galleons (Gasch-Tomás 2015). The consumption of rice during sea voyages, especially those originating in Asia or Africa, and the subsequent circulation of any surplus, gave rice planters and consumers on the Spanish Main a variety of options. *O. glaberrima*, shipped in unshelled (plantable) as well as husked or clean (edible) form, proved more durable and resistant to salinity. The finer grains of *O. sativa*, on the other hand, were favored by more sporadic, elite consumers.

Sources also testify to the elite consumption of Asian rice in colonial America. The Jesuit José de Acosta noted in his *Historia Moral y Natural de Indias* (1589) that the most select grains of rice reached sixteenth-century Peru and New Spain from China. The cargo of the Manila galleons typically included clean as well as unshelled rice (Bernabéu 2012, 300; Bonialian 2016, 12), as did trans-Altantic slave voyages from the coast of Africa (Carney 2004, 10), carrying milled rice for consumption as well as rice in the husk that could be milled on board or planted in the case of any surplus upon arrival. Such practices would explain botanical evidence of *O. sativa* as well as *O. glaberrima* observed in the region of El Salvador (Portères 1960). Environmental conditions (particularly salinity) as well as cultural inclinations may have led Panama's first rice farmers to prefer *O. glaberrima*, in counter distinction to elite consumers. Indeed, elite consumption of *O. sativa* did not preclude free workers' cultivation and consumption of *O. glaberrima*. Europeans may have been reluctant to consume *O. glaberrima*, which, conversely, could have sustained groups of West Africans and Native Americans in times of hunger.

The introduction of rice in the Americas entailed a complex, multidirectional process involving Atlantic as well as Pacific trade. Archaeologists and historians, while increasingly explicit about the limitations of the sources consulted and methodologies applied, agree that the Isthmus of Panama, with an estimated pre-Hispanic population of 150,000–200,000 inhabitants, found it diminished by 90% in the twenty years following contact with Europeans and Africans (Cooke et al. 2003; Castillero Calvo, 2010). The devastation wreaked by unfamiliar pathogens, warfare and coerced labour was exacerbated by the demands of the conquest of Peru after 1531. Paleo-ecological evidence has been interpreted to confirm the view of a sudden drop in population possibly preceding and certainly exacerbated by contact with Europeans, pointing to an abrupt cessation of large-scale slash-and-burn farming on the isthmus and its reforestation, probably in the early sixteenth century. The resurgent forests, if a boon for shipbuilding, would recede gradually before the rise of Pacific navigation, demographic recovery and the proliferation of cattle on the isthmus (Castro Herrera 2004). Plants, animals and peoples were uprooted and relocated on an unprecedented scale, with different degrees of utility from the imperial perspective and, therefore, visibility in the sources.

Scholars also agree on the overwhelming importance of corn – whether "panified" and thus acceptable to Europeans or consumed in less labor-intensive and more liquid forms such as chicha, masato or mazamorra (Saldarriaga 2011b) – for subsistence in the region. On the other hand, scholars debate the presence (or absence) of manioc and bananas on the isthmus before European contact. According to Alfredo Castillero Calvo, the plantain for cooking flourished on the isthmus well before Europeans arrived with the Guinea, or African, banana (Castillero Calvo 2006,

488–93). This understanding of the roots of a national dish, based on early Spanish testimonies, while contrasting with the view of geneticists, highlights the importance of human uses of the flora, beyond records of its mere presence. People consume "male" and "female" bananas differently: one food had to be baked or fried, while the other could be eaten directly from the tree. In the sixteenth century, the maroons of Bayano, in particular, cultivated large banana plantations, as well as corn, yuca, sweet potatoes and other vegetables (Aguado 1913 [1581], 114, 130).

While the banana has inspired controversy, the opposite, if less explicit, difference has arisen regarding manioc (*Manihot esculenta*), also known as yuca or cassava. Archaeologists have recorded evidence of domesticated yucca on the isthmian land bridge, along with corn, from pre-ceramic times, thousands of years before European contact (Dickau, Ranere, and Cooke 2007). Yet one of the region's leading historians has argued that Europeans introduced yucca in the area from the coast of present-day Venezuela (Castillero Calvo 2006, 433–43, 452).[4] The use and consumption of sweet yucca, which the natives of Darién planted with corn, differed remarkably, from the toxic root cooked and ground to make cassava bread on Hispaniola. Sweet yuca supposedly nourished natives and Africans more than it did Europeans, who demanded "bread" in times of blight or hunger. In this sense, Gregorio Saldarriaga has emphasized the dependence of early Spanish settlements on the labour of indigenous women who prepared and amassed the available carbohydrates, especially corn in the case of Tierra Firme, into bread (Saldarriaga 2011a). Bitter plantains and sweet yuca, while providing essential calories and nutrients, largely remained outside the scope of urban and imperial regulation.

While recording an extraordinary diversity of flora and fauna, newcomers to sixteenth-century Tierra Firme depended upon corn as well as native labor and know-how to plant, harvest and process it. As Carmen Mena has argued, hunger played a crucial role: Vasco Núñez de Balboa confessed that hunger had forced his men to value a kernel of corn more than a nugget of gold (Mena García 1997). Yet such warnings reached the Iberian Peninsula too late to save more than 700 of the settlers who embarked with Pedrarias Dávila in 1513 and succumbed to hunger, illness and death within months of reaching Tierra Firme (Andagoya 1986 [1544], 86).

Before founding the city of Panamá, Dávila charged his alcalde mayor, Gaspar de Espinosa, with exploring its Pacific hinterland in order to secure a supply of corn.[5] A slave uprising in 1535 followed a similar strategy, involving men of sub-Saharan African origins: Juan Marinero, Pedro Manicongo, Juan Zape, Cristóbal Gelofe (or Wolof, owned by Espinosa himself), Francisco Tumbador, Juan Valenciano, Hernando Portugués, Francisco Capitanejo, Damián (whose master, Juan Portugués, perhaps also of sub-Saharan African origin, claimed to have lived more than 100 years[6]), and a *morisco* (converted Muslim), Pedro Canario, among others. They were slaves with previous experience as domestic servants, fishermen, stablemen and lumberjacks on Hispaniola and/or the Iberian Peninsula. Their contradictory testimony, some of it extracted under torture, articulated a plot to seize corn and native women (as well as men, in some accounts) from Espinosa's ranch, among others, to cross the Chepo River, and to plant the corn ("hacer sus rozas y maizales") in the countryside.[7]

The would-be rebels' survival, like that of their masters, depended upon the appropriation of corn and indigenous women, adaptation and cultural exchange. While plotters planned to consume fish as well as corn, their testimony makes no mention of yuca, bananas or rice. A supply of corn, on the other hand, had become essential. It was considered property whose theft would have exacerbated the consequences of rebellion. Newcomers to the isthmus, whether born in Europe, Africa or America, may have consumed bananas and yuca, as available, but sought to appropriate corn.

Unlike corn, rice reached mainland America in the Armada of 1513, if not before. Carmen Mena García's study of the Armada's dispatch indicates that its provisions for 800 men (consumed by some 1,500) included 3,000 *quintals* of *bizcocho* (cake), 15,000 *arrobas* of (wheat) flour and 12,000 *arrobas* of wine, yet only fifty *arrobas* of rice purchased from the merchant Diego de Ervás in Seville.[8] As Mena notes, additional provisions to send thirteen *fanegas* of wheat, each of a different variety, suggest that the Crown retained hopes that one of them might grow in the region. Rice, on the other hand, appears in smaller quantities, as did almonds from Huelva (Mena García 1998, 375, 404), as if intended for medicinal purposes. Upon reaching Tierra Firme, merchants and officials allegedly made a profit by selling remaining staples at abusive prices. According to the officials' testimony, hungry colonists purchased "oil and wine and medicine and honey and rice and almonds, and many other things of that quality, at very high prices due to all of their great need".[9]

Widespread starvation and illness in the colony may have been one factor that led the Crown to offer incentives for farmers to emigrate to Castilla del Oro after 1519.[10] These *labradores y trabajadores* were promised free passage, medical attention, provisions until they could grow their own food and even pigs and cattle if they were married and travelled with their spouses.[11] Further incentives for farmers included twenty years of exemption from the *alcabala* and other taxes, seeds, tools and, remarkably, bonds (or *juros*) offered to the first farmer able to grow or to collect silk, spices (cloves, ginger, cinnamon) or rice.[12] The crown preserved the illusion of having approached the East Indies, a land of abundant silk, spices and rice.

Meanwhile, the demand for corn increased on the isthmus. New animals competed with humans to consume it. The impact of livestock, especially cattle and mules, on the region's food supply can be summarized as divergent: the widening availability of cattle made beef the cheapest source of calories available in the sixteenth and seventeenth centuries, to the point that a hen cost much more than a cow (Castillero Calvo 2006, 456). On the other hand, a reliance on convoys of 500–1,200 mules to transport silver across the isthmus periodically limited the supply of corn available for human consumption during the *trajín*, or trans-isthmian crossing when the mules fed on corn, leading to extreme scarcities in 1570–71 (Castillero Calvo 1980, 21). These shortages may have catalyzed the human consumption of and adaptation to other foods like beef and rice.

African Towns, Cattle and Rice

Cattle-raising and rice growing proved complementary in upland as well as swampy regions of Senegambia, which the animals grazed and fertilized during the dry season (Carney 1993, 19; Fields-Black 2008, 45). The Wolof and the Mandinga, known for raising livestock as well as rice, may have transferred knowledge of such complementarity to Panama's Pacific coast, where cattle and rice flourished in the sixteenth century (Jaén Suárez 1981, 48; Castillero Calvo 2010, 111). However successful, both species' adaptation to the region took place progressively and irregularly, with dramatic consequences for the land's inhabitants.

The alimentary stress and periods of hunger suffered on the isthmus stemmed from competition for corn among natives, Africans, Europeans and mules. Another problem, recognized from the early sixteenth century and exacerbated by the death or flight of natives as well as enslaved Africans, entailed a lack of inhabitants able and willing to farm the land. The population on this strategic military and economic lifeline of the Spanish Empire, which swelled with the arrival of the galleons and annual (later biannual) fairs, demanded yet failed to produce important quantities of food. Indeed, the perpetual shortages and high prices of basic foodstuffs on the isthmus influenced the Spanish crown's decision to establish peace with its maroon or runaway Black communities, who had provided crucial support to Francis Drake and other English corsairs in the 1570s.

The royally authorized process of "pacification" or "reduction" of these communities undertaken from 1579 through 1582, led by Panama's Royal Tribunal and documented extensively in the official archives, entailed the strategic foundation of two towns of free Blacks. In exchange for loyalty and military service to the Crown, the inhabitants of these towns received "letters of freedom" as well as livestock and seed. Through a series of negotiations with the Royal Tribunal and its representatives, the new settlers were encouraged to plant and to raise food for themselves as well as the cities of Nombre de Dios, in proximity to Santiago el Príncipe, where the maroons from the hills of Portobelo agreed to settle in 1579, and Panama, some three leagues from the town of Santa Cruz, where the Royal Tribunal progressively sought to relocate its former opponents in the vicinity of the Bayano or Chepo River in 1582 (see Map 7.2).[13] The progress of both settlements, as well as the rosters of their inhabitants, normally including Christian first names and African ethnonyms, suggest that their experiences on the isthmus and leadership, more than ethnic origins or affiliations, influenced these communities' alimentary strategies, abilities, and willingness to raise certain products, particularly cattle and rice.

After years of preying upon trans-isthmian travelers and trade, in June 1578, the Portobelo rebels led by Don Luis Mozambique decided to accept the King of Castile's offer and to support his rule against corsairs and runaway slaves in exchange for their own freedom as well as land. At Panama on 30 June 1579, Luis Mozambique and the "Black men and women of diverse nations under his command", pledged obedience to the Spanish crown in exchange for amnesty for crimes committed and letters of freedom for themselves as well as their wives and children. In order to establish a settlement, the Royal Tribunal offered Luis Mozambique and his company the savannah and hills of Chelibre, between the warehouse of Cruces and the Chagres River "with its rivers, grasses and watering places, with everything annexed and convenient to it", six and a half to seven leagues from Panama City.[14] After visiting the land offered, however, Luis Mozambique and his *maestre de campo*, Pedro Zape, reported "that the said site of Chelibre was not conducive to the health and growth of the said Blacks, being fields and swamps and lacking hills, which were most important for their farming and planting."[15]

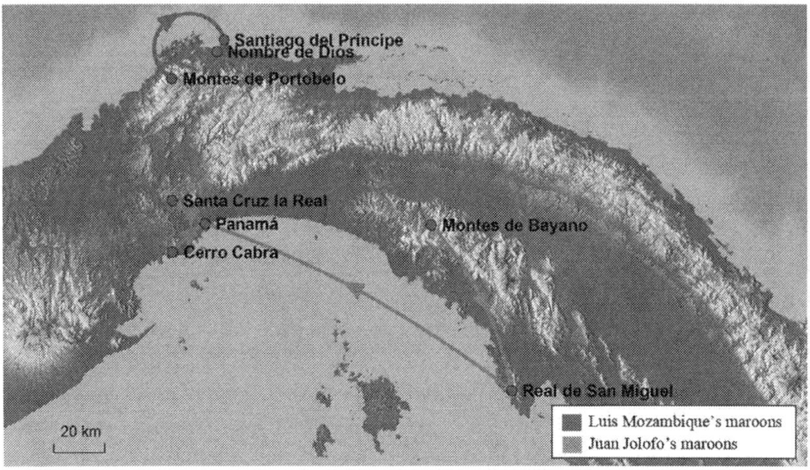

Map 7.2 Maroon Groups in Tierra Firme and Their Settlements, 1579–1582.

Source: designed by Manuel Enrique García-Falcón using stepmap.com.

In light of these objections, the Royal Tribunal offered the former rebels of Portobelo an alternative settlement next to the Fonseca River, near the Spanish city of Nombre de Dios, with a military garrison of thirty soldiers, given its situation on the Caribbean coast. The town, founded as Santiago del Príncipe in September 1579, agreed to plant eight bushels of corn to sustain the garrison each year as well as to raise poultry. The Crown provided hens and fruit trees for the new settlers' sustenance and profit, encouraging them to raise pigs and cattle, while cultivating fruit trees and, particularly, banana fields. Finally, the settlers agreed to assist the Crown against corsairs as well as the Cimarrons of Bayano, who continued to oppose the Spaniards.[16]

Royal officials reported promising developments within one year after the foundation of Santiago del Príncipe. According to one witness interviewed in August 1580, the new settlers were already selling poultry, swine and corn in Nombre de Dios, where such goods had previously been scarce or excessively expensive. According to the garrison's governor, moreover, the former rebels of Portobelo, and especially the Congo men among them, provided effective support against the Bayano rebels and could encourage them to submit to royal authority.[17]

In spite of the governor's prediction, the Cimmarons of Bayano, identified with the Congo nation, proved some of the last to resist Spanish authority. On 20 January 1582, the Royal Tribunal oversaw the foundation of a settlement of some of the former Bayano rebels in the region previously offered to those of Portobelo. Seven captains from Bayano, Juan Jolofo (or Wolof), Antón Mandinga, Pedro Ubala, Juan Angola, Bartolomé Mandinga, Juan Cazanga and Pedro Zape, agreed to settle with their followers to the west of Panama, where they were transferred by sea from Bayano. After disembarking at the mouth of the Río Grande, the captains, visibly pleased with the terrain, founded another settlement, Santa Cruz.[18] The Crown gave the newcomers 3,000 cattle, foodstuffs and seed, forgoing payment on them until the population could sustain itself.[19]

Efforts to establish towns of Black farmers in Santiago del Príncipe and Santa Cruz produced a remarkable amount of information about their members. A comparison of the lists of the first inhabitants of each settlement, established in 1580 and 1582, respectively, facilitate a number of comparisons. The registered population of Santiago del Príncipe, led by Luis Mozambique and Pedro Zape, included 97 men, women and children of diverse African and Creole origins. The list compiled at the town's founding on 6 October 1580 appears to be the most complete, in spite of the reported absence of some of the community's members in Panama city and in the war on Bayano.[20] The population of Santa Cruz, in contrast, numbered 181 inhabitants upon its foundation on 20 January 1582, and grew to 274 individuals with the arrival of additional settlers in March and April. Beyond the size of these communities, their most significant difference appears to have been their relations with indigenous populations: the maroons of Portobelo, settled at Santiago del Príncipe, included American-born creoles or *criollos del monte*, particularly children, but no Indians. On the other hand, the maroons of Bayano who went to Santa Cruz included a number of natives and offspring of Africans and natives, termed *zambahijos*. The influx of natives into Santa Cruz in March and April 1582 became so considerable that royal officials authorized another settlement, San Antonio de Padua, on the other side of the river, for Indians who wished to live in proximity to Santa Cruz. Men initially constituted the majority of settlers at Santiago el Príncipe and Santa Cruz (61% and 62%, respectively, at the founding of each town). In the case of Santa Cruz, however, relations with natives appear to have mitigated the sex imbalance.[21]

Most of the new settlers' ethnonyms pointed to origins or antecedents from Upper Guinea (approximately 86% of the population of Santa Cruz and 81% in Santiago del Príncipe), with different appellatives registered for the partners in almost all of the couples at Santiago, and inner-ethnic unions possible only in a minority of cases where men and women shared the same ethnonyms at Santa Cruz. The most common ethnonyms among the first inhabitants of Santiago and Santa Cruz proved "Biafra" (sixteen in Santiago and thirty-one in Santa Cruz) and "Zape" (twenty-seven in Santiago and thirty-two in Santa Cruz). The slightly higher percentage of former maroons from Upper Guinea in Santa Cruz, however, reflects a much more significant number of male and female Mandinga, Wolof and Nalu in the Bayano group. Whereas Santiago included only one male and no female Mandinga, nine male and two female Mandinga witnessed the foundation of Santa Cruz. Another factor influencing the election of lands to settle or crops to plant appears to have been each community's leadership: Luis Mozambique led his followers to Santiago, while Juan Wolof commanded other captains at Santa Cruz, including Antón Mandinga and Bartolomé Mandinga. Other settlers reported ethnonyms including Congo, Angola or Terranova, including a group from Bayano that chose to settle in Santiago rather than Santa Cruz.[22]

African antecedents as well as American experiences in and out of slavery shaped the communities' preferences and choice of leaders. The maroons of Portobelo elected to reside in the hills outside Nombre de Dios, whereas the Bayano group embraced swampy riverbeds and marshes in the Chagres River basin. Marsh landscapes, undoubtedly familiar to the Mandinga and Wolof, also favoured the cultivation of rice.

Conditions and goods offered to the settlers at Santa Cruz reflected negotiations, exchanges and agreements with their captains, led by Juan Jolofo, the designation of common lands and resources, and the distribution of other plots among the former rebels. On 11 February 1582, the royal judge Alonso Criado de Castilla met with the Bayano group's leaders and agreed that the Crown would receive one-third of the crops the new settlers cultivated on common lands, "be they of maize, sugar, cotton, rice, beans, or other vegetables".[23] Several months later, concerned that the new settlers appeared more inclined to festivities than labour, Criado de Castilla met with the same captains to set a minimum for the common yield due to the Crown at thirty bushels of "dry seed" that would be harvested beginning in September, and repeated that this one-third of the harvest should apply to all of the seeds planted on the common lands "as are beans, rice, cotton, sugar cane, yuca, potatoes, and any other fruits planted, excepting the fields and plantations that each [settler] would plant privately, which would be his, without owing anything to the King".[24] Common plots may have facilitated the collaboration and exchange of knowledge among Mandinga and other planters, which would have been essential for successful rice cultivation. Rather than adopt a monoculture, the settlers reportedly cultivated a variety of African and American plants, in addition to raising chickens, cattle and pigs, and hunting local deer.

One motive for celebrations at Santa Cruz may have been the arrival of another captain, Antón Tiguere, who spoke Spanish well enough to declare that he was no Christian, with a population described as "thirty soldiers" and "of the Congo nation". Following Tiguere's arrival, royal officials interviewed all of the captains at Santa Cruz in an attempt to ascertain how many rebels remained in Bayano. The obligatory questions involved in official legal proceedings led these same captains, all of them described as "Ladino" (Spanish-speaking) to relate aspects of their own life histories on the isthmus. As a boy, Juan Jolofo reported, he had fled Nombre de Dios for the mountains of Bayano, where he had led "his own population (pueblo) . . . of blacks of diverse nations, as are the Wolofs, Berbesies, Nalu, and Biafra" for more than twenty-seven or thirty years; Antón Mandinga related that he had been a captain in Bayano for ten years, governing "a population of the Mandinga nation" before deciding to lead seventy-one soldiers, "black men and black women (soldados piezas negros e negras)" to Santa Cruz. Pedro Ubala reported that he had governed a "black people of the Biafra nation" in Bayano for thirteen years; Juan Angola likewise recalled living thirteen years in the hills of Bayano, and reported leading more than forty Blacks, without specifying their nations; during some twenty-six years in the mountains, Juan Nalu recalled that he had risen to the status of captain under Juan Jolfo; Pedro Zape registered having commanded "a Zape population under his charge and orders" for fourteen years; and Juan Cazanga claimed to have led his own group for two years after following Antón Mandinga for twelve. The captains agreed, moreover, on reporting that only fifteen or sixteen rebels remained in Bayano, identifying their leaders as Mazatamba or Alonzo Cazanga (Wheat 2016, 62) and Diego Congo, and excusing their absence by alleging they might not have received notice of the royal amnesty.[25]

Ten years after the foundation of Santa Cruz, the observations of another royal judge from Panama indicate that the settlement retained an important degree of autonomy. Without reaching the levels of production that the crown would have liked, the judge reported that the inhabitants of Santa Cruz, an estimated one hundred black men and their wives, "raise fowl, maize, rice, yams, potatoes, and other foodstuffs more abundantly than in their land." These agriculturists sold enough goods to purchase tools and clothing at Panama City, yet refused to produce more, according to the judge, who labeled them lazy, and argued that "they could even be rich if they would work". The settlement's strategic importance obliged the Crown to allow the Santa Cruz community to regulate its own sustenance and production.[26]

With reference to the organization of Santa Cruz, Tardieu and Wheat have argued that maroon communities formed associations based on African ethno-linguistic origins and affinities. However, unlike the population of Santiago, that of Santa Cruz included an important and growing number of female and male Indians, as well as the offspring of Indian and African relations. The settlers of Santa Cruz reported a significant number of unions with indigenous women as well as the ensuing presence of mixed (African-Indian, or *zambo*) offspring in their community. Hence the differences between the maroons of Portobelo and those of Bayano reflected specific, decade-long struggles for survival in opposition to the crown of Castile as well as decade-old and, as Wheat has pointed out, plural and malleable, ethnic affiliations. Their leaders' biographies as well as their rosters of inhabitants point to very different experiences in America that informed the choices of the groups offered royal amnesty.

These communities' decision or refusal to cultivate rice and other foodstuffs depended on a series of factors, including socio-cultural roots, the land and workforce available to each group as well as previous experiences in Africa, on the isthmus and elsewhere in the Caribbean. Much the same could be said for the possibility of technological and cultural transfers, and even cultural exchange, within and among ethno-linguistic groups, including specific indigenous populations. Even when rice was planted, as in Santa Cruz, it was only one product among many chosen and raised primarily for subsistence.

The Price of Rice

Rice emerges in the documentary record during royal negotiations with the maroons of Bayano when they settled in Santa Cruz. Following attacks by Francis Drake and other corsairs who found support in the maroon communities, the Spanish Crown sought to win them over by offering freedom, land and supplies to the former rebels who agreed to settle and assist the Crown against corsairs as well as escaped slaves. The accounts of the expenditures involved in this "pacification" punctuated and followed an important military effort. They reflect the diverse resources available on the isthmus, as well as, potentially if less directly, the interests and capabilities of the different groups involved. One of these groups, the maroons of Bayano, had inhabited the delta of the Bayano or Chepo River, which flowed into the Pacific Ocean south of Old Panama City. This area and its surrounding hills had also been the goal of the slaves who fled Old Panama in 1535.

Upon agreeing to settle in Santa Cruz, the Bayano maroons received edible as well as unhusked rice from the crown. The royal tribunal spent fifty-two pesos for two bushels (*fanegas*) of clean rice for the settlers' consumption and another twenty-four pesos on two bushels of rice in the husks, "for the Blacks reduced to the service of His Majesty among the maroons of Bayano to plant", along with another two bushels of clean corn, at five pesos per bushel, deposited at the ranch in the Cerro Cabra hills, not far from Santa Cruz.[27] In these accounts, a bushel of edible rice cost more than five times the equivalent amount of corn. The price of rice – even before it was cleaned and hand milled – clearly limited the amount available in 1582.

In the right hands, rice flourished. Reports compiled in 1607 from geographical surveys undertaken in previous years mention abundant rice on the isthmus. The 1607 "Description of Panamá and its Province" listed corn, rice and beans as grown in the region, with corn yielding 100 seeds to every seed planted, and rice and beans even more. While the area produced some 50,000 bushels of corn each year, only rice grew abundantly enough to be exported. According to this account, "Blacks and Indians" planted corn and rice at the beginning of the wet season in March or April each year. The rice, planted on the banks of swamps, reportedly yielded an annual surplus exported to Peru in some 500 earthen jugs (*botijas* of approximately five litres) worth three pesos each (BN Ms. 3064, "Descripción de Panamá" 1607, *Relaciones Históricas y Geográficas de América Central* 146–48, 170–74).[28]

A contemporary description of the viceroyalty of Peru, likewise elaborated from geographical questionnaires, noted the difficulty of cultivating Spanish products on the Isthmus of Panama, due to its great humidity. At the same time, the description highlighted the importance of corn, claiming that one bundle planted yielded a harvest of 200 bundles, as well as the abundance of inexpensive livestock and presence of tropical fruits (bananas, guavas and mameys) that did not grow in Peru. The description noted, moreover, the availability of fish and poultry, even if "the best and most important [resource] they have is the pearl fishery, from which they extract a good sum every year", while adding, almost as an afterthought, "a lot of rice is also gathered" ("Descripción del Virreinato del Peru", c. 1607, 117; Lewin 1958). Rather than grouping rice with other general foodstuffs, it was mentioned only after profits from pearls, which also depended upon African labor (Tardieu 2008).

The cultivation of rice along Panama's Pacific coast is also mentioned in the report that Captain Diego Ruiz de Campos compiled for the Crown in 1631. According to Ruiz de Campos, rice was grown in the Cerro Cabra hills near Old Panama as well as in the Caymito and Chiriquí River deltas. In those locations, Ruiz de Campos described rice being grown along with other crops, including bananas, sweet potatoes, yuca or beans, and in the presence of animals including cattle, pigs and chickens. Finally, Campos noted the mixed (European, African and American) ancestry of the peoples inhabiting these rice-growing regions.[29]

Although mentioned in the accounts of 1607 and 1631, rice was not noted in the report compiled by the *maestreescuela* of Panama's cathedral, Juan Requejo de Salcedo, in 1640. Requejo did explain, however, that corn and yuca, unlike wheat and barley, were grown in the region and made into tortillas, "which is the bread that the land gives". The cleric referred to bananas as "the sustenance of Blacks", while admitting that they were "eaten by many Spaniards, not for sustenance, but for pleasure ('regalado'), and noted the abundance of good fish and shellfish in the region including clams along the shore, although different from those of Castile (Requejo Salcedo 1640, 73–76). The possibility that different groups consumed foods in distinct ways – either for sustenance or "recreation" – suggests that only a portion of the population may have found nourishment in the consumption of rice, as opposed to corn. Hence the possibility of exporting surplus rice – but not corn – from the region. Most consumers on the isthmus remained dependent upon corn, with or without rice.[30]

The exportation of rice to Peru probably responded to the need to provision ships and to feed African slaves sent south from Panama. Silver, wheat and wine then made the return trip from Peru to Panama, notwithstanding campaigns against the supposed health hazards of Peruvian wine that were designed to protect trans-isthmian and Andalusian commercial interests (Castillero Calvo 2006, 430–32). There emerges a complex panorama of locally produced and imported carbohydrates, with corn most visible and rice occasionally overlooked in the sources.

Conclusions

The different species of rice that reached the sixteenth-century Isthmus of Panama highlight the importance of the choices maroon farmers made for their own and others' sustenance. Although price series are not available for this period, the sale of only a minimal part of the rice the "reduced" settlers produced would caution against any overreliance upon records of sales. On the rare occasions when the sale or purchase of rice is recorded, the variety of rice (*O. sativa* vs. *O. glaberrima*) and its intended consumers (cloistered nuns vs. slaves reshipped to Peru), become crucial variables. Whatever the price of rice in Panama, the price of not cultivating and consuming it could have been greater.

The history of rice appears crucial to assess the effect of early globalization on the Isthmus of Panama as well as the impact of peoples and goods settling in or crossing the isthmus during the period of early modern globalization. It also points to the decisive roles and decisions of free Blacks of African and Creole origins who agreed to settle and to raise food for themselves as well as the importance of strategic, urban population centers including Panama and Nombre de Dios/Portobelo. The Crown's need for loyal subjects and dependence upon them militated against the imposition of any single crop or market-oriented production. Since the nineteenth century, industrial processing techniques, which *O. sativa* withstands better than does *O. glaberrima*, have led to the global extension of "Asian" (white) at the expense of "African" (red) rice, which is cultivated only residually today. Hence industrialization has reduced the domesticated varieties of rice available to (but not necessary embraced by) individuals of diverse origins. Cultural admixture, while seductive, entailed clear perils. Not only el Ratón Pérez but the colonial order depended upon the Mandinga's skills and knowledge.

From the standpoint of the global spread of rice, there remains the question of whether the convergence of continents upon and across the isthmus led to an expansion or reduction of dietary and socio-cultural options. The response is yes to both, which highlights a paradox of early globalization. An increased variety and abundance of foodstuffs coincided with scarcities and privations. Resources multiplied, exceeded only by the demands upon them.

Notes

1. This research has received funding from the European Research Council (ERC) under the European Union's Horizon 2020 research and innovation programme ERC CoG 648535, which finances its publication in open access. The authors are grateful to Richard Cooke, Rebecca Earle, Alejandro García Montón, Jorge Motta, Leonor Motta, Ira Rubinoff, Gregorio Saldarriaga, Bartolomé Yun-Casalilla, and Routledge's anonymous reviewer for their suggestions.
2. The final session of ArtEmpire's first International Conference, in Panama on 21 April 2017, featured an exchange between Richard Cooke and Alfredo Castillero Calvo of contrasting positions on the origins of the banana.
3. Evidence of pre-Hispanic rice cultivation recently found at the archaeological site of Monte Castelo (the Amazon) (Hilbert et al. 2017) points to the need for further studies in order to elaborate a clear map of pre-Hispanic and modern varieties of rice in the New World.
4. Under Philip II, the *regidor* Alonso de Luque requested a monopoly on *cazabe* bread. AGI, Panamá 236, King Philip to Alonso de Luque, 21 December 1573.
5. Securing a supply of maize and other provisions to permit the foundation of Panama numbered among the merits that earned Espinosa a coat of arms.

AGI, Panamá 233, L. 1. f.393–394v, Don Carlos to *licenciado* Gaspar de Espinosa, 5 March 1524.

6. AGI, Patronato 92, N.2, R.1, f. 6v-7v, "Testimonio de Juan Portugues en la probança de Nuflo de Villalobos", 10 March 1529.
7. AGI, Justicia, 364, f. 306–648v. The isthmian population, whether of African, European or local origins, depended upon maize, and increasingly meat, to survive. Defending the "good treatment" of the natives he claimed in *encomienda*, Pedro de los Ríos asserted that he had purchased maize and pigs for their consumption. AGI, Justicia 1043, "Probanza de Pedro de los Rios contra Pedrarias de Avila", 18 February 1533.
8. A leap in the price of rice in Seville between 1519 (489 *maravedíes/quintal*) and 1563 (1,360 *maravedíes/quintal*) appears significant (Mena García 1998, 379, 388, 397).
9. AGI, Patronato 193, R.3, N.2, "Fe del cargo y data de Alonso de la Puente hasta en fin de diciembre de 1515" and AGI, Patronato 193, R.3, N. 3,"Testimonio de como Alonso de la Puente demandó al factor los derechos de la hacienda de Su Alteza", 18 January 1516.
10. AGI, Panamá 233, f. 246v-247v, King Charles to Lope de Sosa, 5 July 1519.
11. AGI, Panamá 233, L. 1, f. 246v-247v, 247v-248, King Charles to Lope de Sosa and to his officials on Hispaniola, 5 July 1519.
12. AGI, Panamá 233, L. 1, f. 230v-231v, Royal decree, 15 May 1519. The King would encourage rice production on Hispaniola as late as 11 March 1573, AGI, Santo Domingo 868, L. 3, f. 5v.
13. With the general offer of amnesty and freedom, the other maroons registered included four or five men and women led by Francisco Berbesí in Cerro de Cabra (outside Panama City, on the road to Natá), who reportedly settled in Panama City, where they worked to earn their living.
14. AGI, Panamá 46, N. 1 and AGI, Patronato 234, R.1, f. 292–295, Acta de "reducción y vasallaje" de Don Luis Mozanbique y los negros cimarrones de Santiago el Príncipe, 30 June 1579, and "Ordenanzas para la reducción y asentamiento de los negros de Santiago del Príncipe", 20 September 1579.
15. ". . . que el dicho sitio de Chelibre no era tal qual convenía para la salud y aumento de los dichos negros, por ser sávanas y ciénegas y ser falto de montes que era lo mas principal para sus labranzas y sementeras". AGI, Panamá 46, N. 1, "Ordenanzas para la reducción y asentamiento de los negros de Santiago del Príncipe", 20 September 1579.
16. AGI, Panamá 46, N.1 and AGI, Patronato 234, R.1, f. 292–295, op cit.
17. Opponents of the reductions and expenses they entailed included the accountant Juan de Vivero, who feared that an uprising of Tierra Firme's large Black population could threaten the kingdom "with greater ease than the Moriscos of Granada". AGI, Panamá 33, N.121, Letter of Juan de Vivero, contador de Tierra Firme, 23 May1581.
18. AGI, Patronato 234, R.6, N.2 f.392, "Testimonio de los Autos . . . en la Real Audiencia de Panamá cerca de la paz y reducción y población de los negros de Bayano poblados en la villa de Santa Cruz la Real", 20 January 1582.
19. AGI, Panamá, 33, N.129, Royal decree for the officials on Tierra Firme, 8 May 1584.
20. AGI, Patronato 234, R.6, f. 297v–303v, "Relación de personas de Portobelo asentados en Santiago del Príncipe," 6 October 1580.
21. AGI, 234, R.6, N.2, f. 427v–428v, "Asiento de indios en San Antonio de Padua," 11 February 1582.
22. AGI, Patronto 234, R.6, N.2, image 449v and ss, Population of Santa Cruz la Real, 4 April 1582.

23. AGI, Patronato 234, R.6, N.2, f. 430–431, "Tributo acordado con el asentamiento de Santa Cruz la Real," 11 February 1582.
24. ". . . la dicha tercia parte del comun sea por lo menos 10 hanegas de senbra dura y de ay arriba por manera que la roza del comun de la qual se ha de pagar la dicha tercia parte sea de 30 hanegas de senbra dura y desde arriba [461] y lo mismo se ha y se entienda no solo del mayz que senbraren como dicho es, mas de todos los demas frutos que cogieren en lo que senbraren por via de comunidad como es frijoles, arroz, algodon, caña dulze, yuca y patata e otros qualesquier frutos que senbraren porque de todos ellos han de acudir y pagar con la dicha tercia parte excepto en las rozas e sementeras que cada uno hiziere para si en particular, porque estas han de ser suyas syn pagar dellas ninguna cosa a su magestad". AGI, Patronato, R.6, N.3, f. 457–461, "Asiento y capitulación que el señor doctor Alonso Criado de Castilla dio a los negros Cimarrones reducidos de Bayano", 5 April 1582.
25. AGI, Patronato 234, R.6, f. 438–445, Testimony of the maroon captains, 1 April 1582.
26. "Crian aves, maiz, arroz, ñames, patatas y otros géneros de mantenimientos en más abundancia que en su tierra. . . . Venden en esta ciudad de las aves y mantenimientos que crian lo ques les basta para herramientas y vestidos, y aun serian ricos si travajasen, mas son flojos y holgazanes. No guardan ni quieren más de aquello que gastan, e sustentase este presidio de tanta costa por no dar lugar a que estén más negros huidos deste reyno y de Cartagena . . ." AGI, Panamá 14, R.4, N.27, Letter of the judge Lic. Antonio de Salazar to the King, 14 June 1589.
27. AGI, Contaduría 1459, R.1, f. 4–4v, "Purchases for Bayano's War", October 1582 (transcribed in Jopling 1994, 394–95).
28. BN Madrid, MS. 3064, "Descripción de Panamá y su provincia (1607)," in *Relaciones Históricas y Geográficas de América Central* (Madrid: Libería General de Victoriano Suñarez, 1908), 170.
29. BN Madrid, ms. 9573, "Relación sobre la costa panameña en el Mar del Sur por el capitán Diego Ruiz de Campos (1631)," f. 11, en *Colección de documentos inéditos sobre la geografía y la historia de Colombia* (Bogotá: J.J. Pérez, 1892), 25.
30. In 1579, Gaspar Rodríguez, the native chief on the Isle of the Pearls, sold royal officials corn for the war on Bayano on the condition that the proceeds would be used to purchase tools and cloth his people required and that the maize would be returned to him upon request. AGI, Contaduría 1459, R.1, f. 4–4v.

Bibliography

Aceituno, Francisco Javier, and Juan Martín. 2017. "Plantas Amerindias en la Mesa de los primeros Europeos en Panamá Viejo." *Latin American Antiquity* 28 (May): 127–43. https://doi.org/10.1017/laq.2016.9.

Acosta, José. 2003 [1589]. *Historia natural y moral de las Indias*. Madrid: Biblioteca Virtual Universal.

Aguado, Fray Pedro. 1913 [1581]. *Historia de Venezuela*, II: 99–123. Caracas: Imprenta Nacional.

Andagoya, Pascual de. 1986 [1544]. *Relación y documentos*. Edited by Adrián Blázquez. Madrid: Historia 16.

Bernabéu, Salvador, and Catia Brilli. 2012. "A bordo del Galeón de Manila: la travesía de Gemelli Carreri." *Anuario de Estudios Americanos* 69 (1): 277–317. https://doi.org/10.3989/aeamer.2012.1.11

Bonialian, Mariano. 2016. "La Seda China en Nueva España a principios del Siglo XVII. Una Mirada Imperial en el Memorial de Horacio Levanto." *Revista de Historia Económica/Journal of Iberian and Latin American Economic History*, 1–25. https://doi.org/10.1017/S0212610915000385.

Bray, Francesca, Peter Coclanis, Edda Fields-Black, and Dagmar Schafer, eds. 2015. *Rice: Global Networks and New Histories*. New York: Cambridge University Press.

Carney, Judith A. 1993. "From Hands to Tutors: African Expertise in the South Carolina Rice Economy." *Agricultural History* 67 (3): 1–30.

———. 1998. "The Role of African Rice and Slaves in the History of Rice Cultivation in the Americas." *Human Ecology* 26 (4): 525–45.

———. 2001. *Black Rice. The African Origins of Rice Cultivation in the Americas*. Cambridge, MA: Harvard University Press.

———. 2004. "'With Grains in Her Hair': Rice in Colonial Brazil." *Slavery and Abolition* 4 (1): 1–27.

Castillero Calvo, Alfredo. 1980. *Economía terciaria y sociedad. Panamá, Siglos XVI y XVII*. Panamá: Impresora de la Nación/INAC.

———. 2006. *Sociedad, Economía y Cultura Material. Historia Urbana de Panamá La Vieja*. Panamá: Imprenta Alloni.

———. 2010. *Cultura Alimentaria y Globalización. Panamá, Siglos XVI a XXI*. Panamá: Editora Novo Art.

Castro Herrera, Guillermo. 2004. "Ganado y Galeones: Elementos para una historia ambiental de Panamá." *Anuario IEHS: Instituto de Estudios Histórico Sociales* 19: 191–230.

Cooke, Richard, Luis Alberto Sánchez Herrera, Diana Rocío Carvajal, John Griggs, and Ilean Isaza Aizpurúa. 2003. "Los Pueblos Indígenas de Panamá durante el siglo XVI: Transformaciones Sociales y Culturales desde una Perspectiva Arqueológica y Paleoecológica." *Mesoamérica* 45: 1–34.

Crosby, Alfred W. 1973. *The Columbian Exchange. Biological and Cultural Consequences of 1492*. Westport, CT: Greenwood.

———. 1986. *Ecological Imperialism: The Biological Expansion of Europe 900–1900*. Reprint. Cambridge: Cambridge University Press.

"Descripción de Panamá y su provincia". 1908 [1607]. *Relaciones Históricas y Geográficas de América Central*, 137–70. Madrid: Librería General de Victoriano Suárez.

Dickau, Ruth, Anthony J. Ranere, and Richard Cooke. 2007. "Starch Grain Evidence for the Pre-ceramic Dispersals of Maize and Root Crops into Tropical Dry and Humid Forest of Panama." *PNAS* 14 (9): 3651–56.

Earle, Rebecca. 2012. *The Body of the Conquistador: Food, Race and the Colonial Experience in Spanish America, 1492–1700*. Cambridge: Cambridge University Press.

Eltis, David, Philip Morgan, and David Richardson. 2010. "Black, Brown, or White? Color Coding American Commercial Rice Cultivation with Slave Labor." *The American Historical Review* 115 (1): 164–71. https://doi.org/10.1086/ahr.115.1.164

Fields-Black, Edda L. 2008. *Deep Roots: Rice Farmers in West Africa and the African Diaspora*. Bloomington: Indiana University Press.

Gasch-Tomás, José Luis. 2015. "Mecanismos de funcionamiento institucional en el imperio hispánico. El comercio de los Galeones de Manila y el Consulado de comerciantes de México en la década de 1630." *Revista de Historia Jerónimo Zurita* 90: 55–74.

Hawthorne, Walter. 2003. *Planting Rice and Harvesting Slaves. Transformations along the Guinea-Bissau Coast, 1400–1900*. Portsmouth, NH: Heinemann.

———. 2010a. *From Africa to Brazil. Culture, Identity, and an Atlantic Slave Trade, 1600–1830*. New York: Cambridge University Press.

———. 2010b. "From 'Black Rice' to 'Brown': Rethinking the History of Risiculture in the Seventeenth- and Eighteenth-Century Atlantic." *American Historical Review*, 151–63.

———. 2015. "The Cultural Meaning of Work: The 'Black Rice Debate' Reconsidered." In *Rice: Global Networks and New Histories*, edited by Francesca Bray, Peter Coclanis, Edda Fields-Black, and Dagmar Schafer, 279–90. New York: Cambridge University Press.

Hernández Bermejo, Esteban, and Expiración García Sánchez. 2008. "Las gramíneas en Al-Andalus." *Ciencias de la naturaleza en Al-Andalus. Textos y estudios VIII*. Madrid: Consejo Superior de Investigaciones Científicas.

Hilbert, Lautaro, E. G. Neves, F. Pugliese, S. B. Whitney, M. Shock, E. Veasey, C. A. Zimpel, and J. Iriarte. 2017. "Evidence for mid-Holocene rice domestication in the Americas." *Nature Ecology and Evolution* 1 (11): 1693–98.

Huang, Xuehui, Nori Kurata, Xinghua Wei, Zi-Xuang Wang, Ahong Wang, Quiang Zao et al. 2012. "A Map of Rice Genome Variation Reveals the Origin of Cultivated Rice." *Nature* 490 (7421): 497–501.

Jaén Suárez, Omar. 1981. "Nuevos hombres y ganado y su impacto en el paisaje geográfico panameño entre 1500 y 1980." In *Hombres y ecología en Panamá*. Panamá: Editorial Universidad de Panamá, Smithsonian Tropical Research Institute.

Jiménez, Máximo, and Richard Cooke. 2001. "Análisis Faunístico de Los Restos Excavados En Las Casas de Terrín (Panamá La Vieja): Una Aproximación a La Dieta y a La Ecología." *Arqueología de Panamá La Vieja*, 89–116.

Jopling, Carol F., ed. 1994. *Indios y negros en Panamá en los siglos XVI y XVII: selecciones de los documentos del Archivo General de Indias*. Antigua, Vermont: Centro de investigaciones regionales de Mesoamérica.

Laviña, Javier, Tomás Mendizábal, Ricardo Piqueras, Guillermina I. De Gracia, Marta Hidalgo Pérez, Maritxell Tous, Rubén López, and Jordi Tresserras. 2015. "La Localización de La Villa de Santiago Del Príncipe, Panamá." *Canto Rodado: Revista Especializada En Temas de Patrimonio* 10: 125–48.

Lewin, Boleslao [c. 1607] 1958. *Descripción del virreinato del Perú. Crónica inédita de comienzos del siglo XVII*. Rosario: Universidad Nacional del Litoral.

Linares, Olga F. 2002. "African Rice (Oryza Glaberrima): History and Future Potential." *Proceedings of the National Academy of Sciences* 99 (25): 16360–65. https://doi.org/10.1073/pnas.252604599.

———. 2011. "Deferring to Trade in Slaves: The Jola of Casamance, Senegal in Historical Perspective." *History in Africa* 14 (1987): 113–39.

Lyra, Carmen, ed. 2018. "La Cucarachita Mandinga." *Cuentos de mi Tía Panchita.* Consulted April 8, 2018. *https://albalearning.com/audiolibros/lyra/cucarachita.html*

Martín, Juan Guillermo, and Félix Rodríguez. 2006. "Los moluscos marinos de Panamá Viejo. Selectividad de recursos desde una perspectiva de larga duración." *Canto Rodado* 1: 85–100.

Martín, Juan Guillermo, Javier Rivera Sandoval, and Claudia Rojas Sepúlveda. 2009. "Bioarqueología. Su Aporte al Proyecto Arqueológico Panamá Viejo." *Canto Rodado* IV: 117–44.

Medina, Xavier, R. Alonso, Juan José Álvarez, L. Álvarez Sala, Josep Bernabeu-Mestre, Francisco Grande Covián et al. 1996. *La Alimentación Mediterránea: Historia, Cultura, Nutrición.* Institut Català de la Mediterrània d'Estudis i Cooperació.

Mena García, María del Carmen. 1997. "La frontera del hambre: construyendo el espacio histórico en el Darién." In *Entre el hambre y el dorado: Mito y contacto alimentario en las huestes de conquista del XVI*, edited by Ricardo Piqueras Céspedes. Sevilla: Diputación, 215–56.

———. 1998. *Sevilla y las Flotas de Indias: La Gran Armada de Castilla Del Oro (1513–1514).* Sevilla: Universidad de Sevilla, Secretariado de Publicaciones.

Newson, Linda, and Susie Michin. 2007. *From Capture to Sale. The Portuguese Slave Trade to Spanish South America in the Early Seventeenth Century.* Leiden, The Netherlands: Koninklijke Brill NV.

Piperno, Dolores R. 2017. "Assessing Elements of an Extended Evolutionary Synthesis for Plant Domestication and Agricultural Origin Research." *Proceedings of the National Academy of Sciences of the United States of America* 114 (25). National Academy of Sciences: 6429–37. https://doi.org/10.1073/pnas.1703658114.

Piqueras, Ricardo, and Javier Laviña. 2015. "El Poder de la Marginalidad: Panamá y Cartagena de Indias en la colonia." In *Construcción Social y Cultural del Poder en Las Américas*, 61–74. Barcelona: Fundació Casa Amèrica Catalunya.

Portères, Roland. 1960. "Riz subspontanés et Riz sauvages en El Salvador (Amérique Centrale)." *Journal d'agriculture tropicale et de botanique appliquée* 7 (9): 441–46.

Requejo Salcedo, Juan. 1908 [1640]. "Relación Histórica y geográfica de la provincia de Panamá (1640)." In *Relaciones Históricas y Geográficas de América Central.* Madrid: Libería General de Victoriano Suárez.

Rojas-Sepúlveda, C. M., J. Rivera-Sandoval, and J. G. Martín-Rincón. 2011. "Paleoepidemiology of Pre-Columbian and Colonial Panamá Viejo: A Preliminary Study." *Bulletins et Mémoires de La Société D'anthropologie de Paris* 23 (1–2): 70–82.

Saldarriaga, Gregorio. 2011a. *Alimentación e Identidades en el Nuevo Reino de Granada, Siglos XVI Y XVII.* Bogotá: Ministerio de Cultura.

———. 2011b. "Alimentación, comunidad y poder en las fundaciones tempranas de Tierra Firme: claves para entender la mortandad de modorra en Santa María de la Antigua del Darién." In *Tierra Firme. El Darién en el Imaginario de los Conquistadores*, edited by Paolo Vignolo and Virgilio Becerra, 257–84. Bogotá: Universidad Nacional de Colombia.

Sinan, Rogelio. 1974. "Divagaciones sobre la fábula de La Cucarachita Mandinga y sobre una posible resurrección del Ratón Pérez." *Loteria*, 21–26.

Tardieu, Jean-Pierre. 2008. "Perlas y Piel de Azabache. El Negro en las Pesquerías de las Indias Occidentales." *Anuario de Estudios Americanos* 65 (2): 91–124.

———. 2009. *Cimarrones de Panamá. La Forja de Una Identidad Afroamericana en el Siglo XVI*. Madrid: Iberto.

Wang, Muhua, Yeisoo Yu, Georg Haberer, Pradeep Reddy Marri, Chuanzhu Fan, Jose Luis Goicoechea et al. 2014. "The Genome Sequence of African rice (Oryza glaberrima) and Evidence for Independent Domestication." *Nature Genetics* 49 (6): 982–88.

Wheat, David. 2016. *Atlantic Africa and the Spanish Caribbean, 1570–1640*. Chapel Hill, NC: University of North Carolina Press.

8 In the Kitchen

Slave Agency and African Cuisine in the West Indies[1]

Ilaria Berti

Introduction

This chapter presents an analysis of the Caribbean colonies, understood as a global space that was dominated by Europeans during the nineteenth century. More specifically, it examines the British and Spanish possessions in the West Indies as an area producing sugarcane, which according to the historian Frank Moya Pons determined "the historical unity of the region"; this agriculture was described by the Cuban anthropologist Fernando Ortiz as a one of the "essential bases" of his country's economy.[2] The sugarcane monoculture is thus a key element and a useful starting point for analyzing the British and Spanish possessions in the Caribbean together, given that both empires played an important part as sugar producers. The demand for sugar as a good for mass consumption was constantly increasing from the end of the eighteenth century onwards (Mintz 1996).

The form that agriculture took on the sugarcane plantations was based on the use of vast geographical areas and the concomitant labour of millions of slaves imported from Africa (Paget 2004, 157). A plantation was "a factory in the field", but it was much more than a productive space: plantations were a "sociospatial phenomenon that shaped the everyday lives of the people who lived and worked on them" (Hauser, Delle, and Armstrong 2011, 11).

While the British Empire abolished the slave trade and slavery as an institution in 1807 and 1833, respectively, the Spanish eliminated slavery from Cuba only in 1886; its sugarcane production, using workers with fewer rights and lower costs, therefore enjoyed a competitive advantage and could be maintained with greater profit despite the drop in sugar prices, due to the introduction of new technology that enabled the extraction of saccharose from the sugar beet grown in temperate climates. The emergence of Cuba as the leading island in sugar production was also aided by other developments; these included the slave revolt against French rule in Haiti (1791), which removed one of the most productive

DOI: 10.4324/9781003168058-9

competitors from the market. Moreover, the island's largely flat landscape made it easy to establish extensive planting fields, and sugar production thus became the island's main economic activity.

The British and Spanish Caribbean space, unified by the shared form of sugar-based agricultural production, thus provides an excellent case study in which we can assess the extent to which the introduction of practices from elsewhere influenced the development of colonial society and its incorporation in the global context. This chapter therefore focuses not on major events or processes, but on the seemingly ephemeral area of colonial cuisines, and especially on the role of cooks in influencing and transforming British, Spanish and US food models. The role of subaltern peoples in colonial cuisines is analyzed as an aspect of the social and spatial phenomenon of the plantation, where there were interactions between slaves and their owners, former slaves and other colonists who benefited from their cooking skills.

The space of the kitchens and the act of feeding others are therefore examined here as, respectively, an important environment and powerful cultural mechanism, which through the processes of acceptance, hybridization and rejection had a significant impact on colonial society. The Spanish and British dominated at the political, economic and formal levels, but this chapter will show that the slaves also performed an active role in transforming not only eating habits but also the colonies themselves. The practices of everyday life connected to preparing and serving dishes are understood as an area of mediation within which the slaves were able to negotiate a certain degree of autonomy, despite having to observe norms relating to the setting of the table, the best ways of presenting and serving food, the times at which meals had to be ready, and the preparation of some dishes: all these being imposed on them by the colonists.

Although some scholars have addressed the consumption habits and practices of the Creole elite in the Caribbean, for the most part historiographical analysis has ignored food and diet in the West Indian colonies as a focus of research.[3] As a result, while there have been some investigations into how Europeans adapted and modified the cuisine of the New World under their rule, the contribution of African slaves to Caribbean cooking is often underestimated or unacknowledged.[4] In studies of the food slaves ate in the colonies and their involvement in food production and distribution, reconstructions that feature slaves as agents affecting the cuisine of the colonists are also unfortunately limited.[5] This seems to be due to the scarcity or complete absence of sources regarding the slaves: documentation that is all but absent for the Caribbean, but also lacking for the analysis of slavery in the United States (Berti Forthcoming). It was only when this chapter was already being written that two new books appeared on this theme, probably due to the growing interest in food history.[6] In one of these, the historian Kelley Fanto Deetz examines the contribution of slaves to the invention of southern cooking in the United States, analyzing the activities of slaves in the kitchens of their owners.

While Deetz's principal aims are to reconstruct a less well-known aspect of slave life on the North American plantations and to analyze the impact of the slaves' work on the culinary traditions of the American South, this chapter goes further than just a reconstruction of the activity of slaves in the kitchens of the British and Spanish colonies. It draws attention to the ways that the slaves, their cooking and their food practices contributed, albeit indirectly and unconsciously, to the full integration of Latin America into the nineteenth-century global context. The slaves with African roots were using foodstuffs that were unknown or unfamiliar to the British, Spanish and North Americans, and were also using different cooking techniques. My hypothesis is that their habits contributed to the emergence of a new type of cuisine, in which elements of differing provenance were mixed together. While this cuisine has customarily been described as Creole, its nature was in fact global (Berti 2014).

This chapter thus has two related aims: to contribute to a widening of the historiography on consumption in the colonies and empires, and to assess the significance of food and food practices in the incorporation of the Spanish and British American colonies into the global context. In pursuit of these aims, a wide range of sources is analyzed and brought together for comparison. Leaving aside some of the archival documents and a Cuban cookbook, which is discussed in depth, many of the sources employed here can be called "ego documents": any source in which the author's presence, ideas, actions, feelings and emotions are apparent.[7] These sources have also been described as operating like a mirror: individual stories were written to reflect broader historical processes, and thus help us to reconstruct the everyday life and culture of the colonies (Procida 2002, 130).

It should be noted that one of the main problems about using the sources generated by the colonists of the West Indies to reconstruct the lives, work, kitchen practices and cuisine of the slaves results from the fact that the Creole and African slaves themselves, being essentially illiterate, left nothing in writing.[8] The methodological device used to address this issue has been described by the Jamaican historian Verene Shepherd as a sort of " 'ventriloquism", whereby the colonists speak for the colonized (Shepherd 2007, 268). This chapter thus uses the sources left by the colonists to explain the role that slaves played, through their cuisine, in the inclusion of Latin America in the global context during the nineteenth century. In a situation in which the slaves were in effect silent, colonist sources, although typically giving an incomplete picture, are crucial.[9] Although it was not their explicit intention, travel accounts, personal correspondence and novels provide incidental descriptions of phenomena outside the colonists' milieu, including the atmosphere, surroundings and other groups of people.

This chapter first discusses the slaves who worked in the kitchens of the British, Spanish and North American colonists and travellers: who were they? It goes on to examine whether and how these slaves were trained so that they could fulfil the role of cooks, and argues that, rather than remaining the passive recipients of their instructions, the slaves played an active part, despite the marked asymmetry of power in the colonial context, in the modification, invention and creation of a new type of cuisine that could in fact be described as global, being neither precisely that of the colonizers nor at all like the cooking that the slaves were used to. Finally, it shows how the recipes, which might be seen as an ephemeral topic when compared to the great events of political and economic history, also made their contribution to this volume's focus of analysis: the integration of Latin America in the global context.

Slave Cooks in the Colonists' Kitchens: Who Were They?

The first sources encountered that mention cooks were to be found in the archive of the Castle Wemyss Estate, a Jamaican sugarcane plantation of average dimensions, where in September 1823, according to the medical records, 109 men and 94 women were enslaved.[10] The presence of cooks can be discerned from the daily records of the number of workers used in the plantation's various activities: that month, alongside carpenters, coopers, masons, and ploughmen, on loading the carts, and with the livestock, there were five domestic servants and kitchen workers.[11] However, other than giving the number of those with cooking responsibilities, the archive provides no information about who the cooks were, nor as to whether they cooked only for the other slaves or also fed the plantation managers and other Europeans who worked there.

From a general understanding of the division of labour in the nineteenth century, we might suppose that cooks in the Caribbean kitchens of the period were women. Was this, however, actually the situation in the specific case of the British and Spanish colonies? Was it only enslaved women who worked in the kitchens, or were there also male cooks working as domestic slaves?

According to Mrs. Carmichael, an anti-abolitionist Scottish woman who lived on the islands of St. Vincent and Trinidad from 1820 to 1826, "The cook is frequently a male [. . .]; he has, if the family be large, either a boy or a woman to assist him".[12] While Mrs. Carmichael drew attention to the phenomenon of men in the kitchen, this emphasis was not common to all the sources, which include the correspondence of Fredrika Bremer (1801–1865), a Swedish feminist writer who visited Cuba in 1851.[13] Addressing her American friends, Bremer wrote that her objective had been to describe "that which I saw and found in the New World".[14] In regard to the sex of the slaves who looked after the food and kitchens, she referred to "the cook, always a negro woman, and if a man-cook, a negro also".[15] Thus although a woman cook may have been the norm in mid-nineteenth-century Cuba, it would not have been surprising to encounter a man in this role. The other source that provides indications as to the gender of cooks is the journal of Lady Maria Nugent, but this may represent only the kitchens of the political elite that ruled the Caribbean. Lady Nugent lived in Jamaica between 1801 and 1805, following her husband George's appointment as the island's governor by the British Crown. As can be seen from her diary, the Nugents' kitchen had to fulfil a primarily official function because they were constantly playing host to politicians, members of the planter class and aristocrats. Lady Nugent provided a little information about "Baptiste (our French cook)", describing him as "a St. Domingo *gentleman*".[16]

As well as mentioning the gender of cooks, the sources answer questions relating to the different ways in with they were supposed to be managed and trained so that their work best met the expectations of the slave owners and their guests.

How Owners Trained Their Cooks and Domestic Slaves

In 1823, at a point when the Jamaican sugar industry was entering a period of crisis due to the abolition of the slave trade, Thomas Roughley, who had owned a sugarcane plantation for nearly twenty years, published a manual regarding plantation management.[17] In his suggestions to other owners of the best ways of managing an estate, Roughley described the activities of slaves on plantations and included discussion of their role within the master's house. He noted that cooks and other domestic servants should never come from the group of workers that the plantation employed only on a seasonal basis:

> The house people should always be composed of the people of colour belonging to the property, or cleanly, well-affected slaves to white people, who understand the way of keeping a house clean in that country, the care of house-linen, needle-work in general, and cookery. They should be neat in their persons, without disease, not inclined to quarrelling or much talking, civil in their manners, not addicted to steal away to the negro-houses, neglect their work, to pilfering or drunkenness. Having such people as these in a dwelling house, the white people and themselves feel, that they are comparatively happy.[18]

Roughley suggested to the plantation owners and managers that the only way to achieve a happy and tranquil life at home was to avoid continually changing their domestic servants because of dissatisfaction with their work. If, instead, they replaced them "upon every frivolous occasion", their lives would remain unhappy: there would be frequent complaints, conspiracies and misdeeds, the house would always be dirty, the sheets always in tatters, there would be a needless waste of resources and, above all, they would feel constantly under threat.[19] Furthermore, Roughley suggested that great caution and sensitivity should be employed in order not to arouse any jealousy between domestic servants. His book was clear that if owners wanted a happy life they needed to pick their domestic slaves carefully and be sensible; owners should never, for example, put them to the test by entrusting them with the store keys.[20] Moreover, they should give the slaves some of the food that the owners themselves ate and allow them some free time, all within reason:

> Give them a small, but not a profuse part of what meals you partake of. Let them have due time, by relieving one another, in the course of the week, to work their provision grounds, and mind their little poultry and pigs, not suffering them to raise them about the dwelling or overseer's house.[21]

When owners therefore allowed their slaves some privileges and trained them according to principles of loyalty, including them in part of their lives and leaving them some marginal liberties as described above, according to the sources "good servants" would become one of the greatest advantages of life in the Caribbean.[22] However, Mrs. Williams, a member of Cuba's Creole elite, told the American traveller Mary Gardner Lowell that one could maintain a good servant only with "a steady hand and superintendance [sic] but when once you have established your authority but little discipline is necessary".[23] According to slave owners and other witnesses of the period, firmness in the management of cooks and domestic servants was thus necessary only in the initial phase of their training; subsequently, having learnt what their owners wanted, they could determine their own conduct.

Lady Nugent, introduced above, devoted time to training the household's cook Baptiste; as he was literate, her account explains that she did this in a specific way. On 10 November 1801, not long after her arrival in Jamaica, she wrote in her diary, "I employed my morning, translating all the family, but especially kitchen, regulations into French, for the benefit of Baptiste, who [. . .] scarcely understands a word of English; so now I hope the cuisine will go on more prosperously".[24] Thus it seems that a cook who could read had at his or her disposal a whole set of norms to observe; the "kitchen regulations" would almost certainly have covered instructions not only on the recipes to be used but also on what and how to serve at table and how to present a dish, information about mealtimes and so forth.

The sources consulted also indicate the violent methods that slave owners used in the attempt to establish their authority. An account of mistreatment as a form of education was given by Lieutenant Colonel

Thomas Staunton St. Clair, who in 1805 was transferred to the first battalion of the Queen's Royal Regiment and posted to what was then British Guiana.[25] As well as discussing the damp, the rain and the ravenous insects, the author recalled the group of British officers with whom he shared his life in the colony. Among these was Captain Yates, who had purchased two boys for use as domestic slaves. With amused detachment, St. Clair provided a detailed description of Yates's attempts to train the boys, who were to see to his food:

> The first, second, and third day we kept them during dinner standing behind our chairs. On the third day we made them begin to wait upon us, and such ridiculous scenes now took place as nearly killed us all at table with laughter. Yates began with Nero. "Nero, the mustard!" Poor Nero knew nothing more than the sound of his name, and stood, staring at his master, with his mouth open. "The mustard, Nero!" he again vociferated, pointing to the sideboard. Off flew Nero, and the mess-waiter, who was near, pointed to the mustard-pot; but, poor Nero, not giving himself time to observe the direction of his finger, seized a bottle of vinegar, and carried it to his master, who pretended to be in a great passion, and sent him back with it, calling out "Mustard! mustard!" This time the poor boy was more fortunate in catching the direction of the waiter's finger, and he succeeded in carrying back the article for which he was sent; when Yates, with the determination of impressing these ingredients more strongly on his memory, made him open his mouth, and put into it a spoonful of the contents, calling out, "Mustard, mustard," while the poor boy was spitting and sputtering, and dancing on the floor, from the effects of this hot substance. I practised the same discipline with Scipio, who had made a similar mistake with the cayenne pepper which I had called for. I, therefore, gave him a small portion of it for the same purpose of impressing it on his memory; which it did so completely that he never afterwards forgot its name.[26]

According to the unfeeling St. Clair, who was incapable of understanding the boys' suffering and amused by their discomfort in being forced to eat mustard and cayenne pepper, both irritant substances, this savage method of "educating" the young slaves had only positive outcomes: "These two boys, from being our constant companions in boating, fishing, and shooting, soon became strongly and faithfully attached to us; and it was wonderful to see their readiness in finding out our wishes and the rapidity with which they learned our language".[27] As in Mrs. Williams's reported observations on Cuban cooks, mentioned earlier, the severity of the initial phase of training could be relaxed when domestic slaves learnt what their owners wanted from them.

From Norm to Praxis: The Different Forms of Slave Agency

The documents available do not all concur in the depiction of an apparently idyllic world in which the colonists, with varying degrees of violence, imparted information that was then followed perfectly by their slaves. As emerges from Thomas Roughley's description, the owners of cooks and other domestic slaves constantly had to find compromises between what they wanted and the reality of established routines, different views, unexpected events and even attempts to erode or limit their authority.

Although the British, other Europeans and North Americans entrusted their nutrition to slaves, they often faced a range of difficulties in this regard, which, according to the sources, varied with the individuals involved. Matthew Lewis, a novelist and slave owner who adopted a humanitarian approach to the management of his two Jamaican sugarcane plantations, recorded the problems he encountered with his cook:

> [I]f the cook having succeeded in dressing a dish well is desired to dress just such another, she is certain of doing something which makes it quite different. One day I desired, that there might be always a piece of salt meat at dinner, in order that I might be certain of always having enough to send to the sick in the hospital. In consequence, there was nothing at dinner but salt meat. I complained that there was not a single fresh dish, and the next day, there was nothing but fresh. Sometimes there is scarcely anything served up, and the cook seems to have forgotten the dinner altogether: she is told of it; and the next day she slaughters without mercy pigs, sheep, fowls, ducks, turkeys, and everything that she can lay her murderous hands upon, till the table absolutely groans under the load of her labours.[28]

Lewis seemed not to recognize the possibility that misunderstandings might be part of a wider process of resistance towards both the owners and the very institution of slavery. His observations on these difficulties were instead part of a wider discourse on brain differences. In his opinion, mistakes in the kitchens resulted from a biological disparity whereby slaves misinterpreted their owners' instructions; he never related ostensible misunderstandings, such as those described above, to any process of artful insubordination or rebellion. The account of the anti-abolitionist Cynric Williams also raises the issue of whether apparent mistakes might in fact have been rebellious acts.[29] On 6 January 1823 he related an episode in which a seemingly banal instance of miscommunication, unquestioned, has disastrous consequences:

> We dined on tough mutton to-day, for our host, who does not keep a very grand table, [. . .] had dispatched a negro boy back to his house,

> to order a fat lamb to be killed. The negro carried the message right, with the exception of saying ram for lamb, and consequently a pet monster, which Mr. Klopstock intended to be the father of future flocks, fell a victim to Bacchus's blunder. The mistake was not discovered till we sat down to dinner, and the huge quarter of the veteran was uncovered, although the perfume intimated something not over fragrant.[30]

George Pinckard, a British physician attending to the health of British troops in the West Indies during the Napoleonic Wars, described a similar process. At a gala dinner he noted that the dining room was full of attendants, "black and yellow, male and female – perhaps too numerous to serve you well"; in his assessment, this surplus meant that specific duties were collective rather than individual and the slaves serving food all waited for one another to take responsibility, meanwhile remaining "idle and inactive".[31] Similar opinions were held by Richard Madden, who said that although the food served in local hotels was delicious, "The attendance, however, is not equal to the fare", because the waiters disappeared and failed to return even when called for repeatedly.[32]

Mrs. Carmichael, mentioned earlier, a shrewd observer of daily life in the Caribbean whose book could be seen as, in part, a manual for domestic management, described a situation not dissimilar to the one noted by Madden. The first evening meal to which she was invited after arriving on St. Vincent merited recording for its length alone. The interminable nature of this event related not just to the large number of courses served, but also to the fact that the domestic slaves serving at table were not performing their role in the manner she expected:

> Such a length of time elapsed before the second course made its appearance, that I began to conclude that among the many novelties I had seen, another might be, that the servants retired to consume the remains of the first course before they again made their appearance with the second.[33]

The long waits and poor service related to meals occurred in both private residences and, as seen in Madden's testimony, in hotels. John Bigelow, an anti-slavery journalist and political analyst who visited Jamaica in 1850 to document what changes had taken place sixteen years after the abolition of slavery, noted his impressions:

> There are no first-class hotels in Kingston. [. . .] It was [. . .] quite impossible to have anything done within any appointed period. If breakfast was ordered at eight o'clock, it was sure not to be ready till ten. If dinner were ordered at three, we congratulated ourselves if we got it by five. The waiters, of which there was an abundance, had no idea of saving steps. They would carry every article to the

> table separately, and would spend an hour running up and down stairs with things which, with a little forethought, they might have transported at a single trip.[34]

In the light of Bigelow's description of the table service, which has similarities to the accounts cited earlier, it is necessary to reflect on the probability that apparent misunderstandings and inefficiencies were aspects of a wider process of negotiation of power and liberty between the slaves and their colonial masters.

Despite the descriptions of shortcomings and misunderstandings in the kitchens and table service, slave owners were usually happy with the work of their own servants of African origin. Slaves were generally viewed as good cooks; only one clear exception emerged from the documents analyzed. This can be found in correspondence between Simon Halliday, the owner of the Castle Wemyss Estate's sugarcane plantation on Jamaica, and John Watson, one of the traders used by Halliday to send sugar and rum to Britain and to import consumer goods produced there.[35]

The letter from Watson, presumably indicating his wish to give Halliday a turtle, has not survived, but on 27 August 1825 the latter wrote that he was 'very obliged for your intended present of a turtle but we have neither consumers nor cooks sufficiently skilled'; having no confidence that it would be competently prepared, he turned it down.[36] Given that this is the only instance identified that relates to the inabilities of cooks in the British and Spanish colonies, some reflection on the particular nature of the ingredient on offer is merited. Turtle was in fact one of the essential ingredients in fine cuisine, and not easy to prepare; probably, therefore, not every cook would have had sufficient kitchen skills.

Halliday provides the only discordant note in the general picture that emerges from the sources, in which the abilities of cooks were often noted and celebrated. Fredrika Bremer, for example, writing about Cuba and its Creole population, stated that "[t]he ladies in this country have very light house-keeping cares", because they received such substantial help from their cooks.[37] She described the activity and talents of the slaves who looked after the food and kitchens:

> The cook, always a negro woman, and if a man-cook, a negro also, receives a certain sum of money weekly with which to provide the family dinners. She goes to market and makes purchases, and selects that which seems best to her, or what she likes. The lady of the house frequently does not know what the family will have for dinner until it is on the table; and I can only wonder that the mistress can, with such perfect security, leave these matters to her cooks, and that all should succeed so well; but the faculty for, and the pleasure in all that concerns serving the table, is said to be universal among the negroes, and they compromise their honor if they do not serve up a good dinner.[38]

As well as portraying ideal servants who are apparently always happy to oblige their owner, Bremer tells her readers about the degree of autonomy in decision-making and money management allowed to the cook both on her trips to the markets, which were also managed by slaves and offered goods and ingredients that they had usually cultivated, raised, gathered, fished or hunted, and in her production of food for the colonist family. It is interesting that Bremer's account gave not the slightest indication of any rejection, disapproval or criticism of the dishes that slaves prepared and served to European and North American families in Cuba. Mention is only made, by implication, of the good reputation that they wished to preserve. The genuine concern that slaves might have had about the food to be presented at their master's table is indicated by an anecdote published in *The Bermudian*, a Caribbean newspaper, in 1822, in which a slave's sly joke alludes to the fact that the seller's fish is scarcely fresh:

> A gentleman sent his black servant to purchase a fresh fish. He went to a stall, and taking up a fish began to smell it. The fishmonger observing him, and fearing the bystanders *might catch the scent*, exclaimed, "Hallo! You black rascal, what do you smell my fish for?" – The negro replied, "Me no smell your fish, Massa". – "What are you doing then, Sirrah?" "Why me talk to him, Massa." – "And what do you say to the fish, eh?" – "Why me ask what news at sea, dat's all, Massa." – "And what does he say to you?" ' – "He says he don't know; he no been dere dese three weeks."[39]

The Bostonian writer Maturin Ballou, writing, like Fredrika Bremer, about Cuba in the early 1850s, made very similar comments: when food was needed from the market, "The steward or stewardess of the house, always a negro man or woman, is freely entrusted with the required sum, and purchases according to his or her judgment and taste".[40] In this way, and possibly assessing the variable qualities of the goods on offer like the slave mentioned in *The Bermudian*, the cook could exercise personal choice and demonstrate her/his own creativity by perhaps choosing ingredients that were local or of African origin in order to cook a Spanish or British dish, or even one that was customarily eaten by the slaves themselves. Just like the women of Indian origin who lived on the Caribbean island of Trinidad, cooks seemingly without any power could "politicize the kitchen by converting it into a site of creativity" (Mehta 1999, 157). The slaves' creativity, skills and food culture are forces that have been seen as of secondary importance, and have therefore usually been ignored by historiography. However, these forces helped to ensure that the Caribbean colonies would play their part in a global cuisine, in which slave labour in the world's kitchens ensured that ingredients and cooking methods from different contexts were mixed together.

Mrs. Carmichael also provided evidence that the practices and ingredients that were part of the slaves' cultural heritage were also employed by the colonists. When moving house between two Caribbean islands, St. Vincent and Trinidad, she followed a recipe that her own slave had given her to cope with the journey by sea: she was able to go on deck "[w]ith the aid of my negro nurse, and his infallible recipe for sea sickness – a sprig of salt beef, broiled fire hot with capsicum, and sprinkled with lemon juice".[41]

Nuevo manual del cocinero cubano y español: *Ajiaco* as an Example of Global Cuisine

As well as imitating the slaves and learning from them different ways of improving their own health, the colonists fed on African and Caribbean dishes and ingredients. The sources analyzed provide helpful clues as to the role of slaves in introducing new dietary models that would modify the customs of the colonists and also contributed to the emergence of Creole and global cuisines, in which European methods and elements combined with indigenous and African ones.

The year 1857 saw the publication of *Nuevo manual del cocinero cubano y español* ("New handbook for the Cuban and Spanish cook"), a recipe book of Cuban cuisine.[42] Cookbooks have often been used in historiography to shed light on aspects of national or regional identity formation alongside the emergence of a cuisine; *Nuevo manual* also indicates the extent to which the ingredients and kitchen methods that were characteristic of slave cooking found their way into local tradition and the codification of Cuban cuisine, thus acquiring formal recognition.[43] In the case of *Nuevo manual*, this was the cuisine in which people who described themselves as Cuban could recognize themselves.[44] The well-known anthropologist and food scholar Sidney Mintz defines "cuisine" as "the ongoing foodways of a region, within which active discourse about food sustains both common understandings and reliable production of the foods in question" (Mintz 1996, 104). However, *Nuevo manual* also provides useful clues as to how the slaves introduced new dishes which then modified the customs of the colonists and also contributed to the emergence of a new dietary model that brought together recipes, methods and ingredients of diverse origin. Although this volume was first published in 1857, it should be emphasized that evolution towards a standardized cuisine codified in a cookbook is an aspect of medium- and long-term processes; this particular development would have started a long time before the recipes appeared in book form. In the case of national cuisines, or others that represent a specific identity, the recipes selected for a book ought normally to be well known and regularly eaten by those who feel that they have the identity that this describes.

The first point to highlight is that the intention of *Nuevo manual del cocinero cubano y español*, according to the title itself, was to assemble a range of recipes for both the Cuban and the Spanish cook, who were conceived of, in this heading, as two people who cooked in different ways. Second, although many cookbooks bring together recipes for special occasions, and therefore serve to indicate the status that their owners either have or aspire to, *Nuevo manual* was written for a mass public. It described itself as "needed by all social classes"; it had been written "for the people, whose language we speak", and its author had no doubt that it would be "welcomed by the general public'.[45] *Nuevo manual* presented a global cuisine that transformed indigenous, African and European ingredients into dishes whose many different descriptions included "a la turca", "a la oriental", "a la portuguesa", "a la inglesa", "a la escocesa" (Scottish), "a la italiana", "a la rusa" and "a la americana".[46] In addition, recipes were titled in terms of other countries, regions and islands in the Caribbean or on its shores: for example, "a la mejicana", "a la yucateca", "de Santo Domingo" and "puerto-riqueña".[47]

Furthermore, there was no culinary hierarchy in *Nuevo manual*; Spanish, French and other European recipes were not placed on a higher level, to be cooked on special occasions, above Cuban and other regional dishes for everyday use. Instead, the division was what we might expect in any cookbook and followed the order that is still accepted within a meal today.[48] In the opening section, soups were listed first, followed by "Cocidos, ollas y guisados" (cooked dishes, stews and casseroles) and then "Fritos" (fried dishes); the second assembled recipes for "Menestras, salsas, legumbres, frituras y menudencias" (vegetable stews, sauces, legumes, fried dishes and offal); and the book concluded with "Pastelería, dulcería y repostería" (pastries, confectionery and cakes), and also included alcoholic drinks.[49] Thus no distinction was made between the five recipes with the label "a la francesa", the nine described as "a la española", and other dishes that were classified in terms of their Spanish regional origins: "a la castellana", "a la catalana", "a la gallega", "a la valenciana", "a la manchega", "a la vizcaina", "a la andaluza", and "a la madrileña".[50] It is also significant that about sixty of the more than 560 recipes were specifically labelled "cubanas", "cubanos", "de Cuba", "a la cubana", "a la habanera", "a la camagueyana", "a la matancera", or with the names of other Cuban towns and cities.[51] However, nothing emerged from the search for a specific ingredient or particular method of preparation that might have resulted in a recipe being identified as "a la cubana"; some of these "Cuban" dishes were boiled, others stewed, and yet others fried. In some cases, beaten eggs were added to a dish that was apparently already cooked, but recipes "a la cubana" could be meat, fish or vegetables, and might be either savoury or sweet.

By the nineteenth century, corn, tomatoes and potatoes had already lost their American identity and had been absorbed into many cuisines across the world. Leaving them aside, *Nuevo manual* also informs us of the consumption of other indigenous and African items that had still not been included in the customary European diet. Among these were malanga, a tuber originating in the Caribbean; chayote and manioc (or cassava), a gourd and tuber, respectively, that were both native to the Americas; yam; the Caribbean fruits soursop and mamey; sapota, a Central American fruit; *quimbombò*, as the Cubans called okra, a vegetable much used in various African cuisines; sweet potato; guava; coconut; plantain, a type of banana suitable for cooking; and papaya.[52] All these ingredients, used by African cooks, would be transformed into dishes typical of Cuban cuisine.

According to the anthropologist Shannon Lee Dawdy, at least 46% of the vegetable food items mentioned in *Nuevo manual* or in other Cuban cookbooks of the period were not growing in Spain itself, nor present in the food and diet of the Iberian Peninsula, but were instead in common use by the cooks who fed their dishes to the colonists (Lee Dawdy 2002, 56).

As well as being in a large number of dishes in *Nuevo manual*, the varieties of fruit and vegetable that were either native to the Caribbean or of African origin were also the main ingredients in about forty different recipes, such as *platanos rellenos* (stuffed plantains), made with pork, capers and raisins: this recipe brought together a prime tropical ingredient with the intense flavours typical of many cuisines of the Mediterranean and Middle-Eastern area.[53] Thus the encounter between Spanish, indigenous and African food cultures was a constant presence in the cookbook and generated a cuisine in which their mixture together was the norm. *Nuevo manual* also contributed to the proper recognition of typically Cuban dishes, such as three variants of *ajiaco* with the names “olla cubana o ajiaco”, “ajiaco de tierra-dentro” and “ajiaco de Puerto Principe”.[54] *Ajiaco* is a stew made from several types of meat, including salted pork or beef, *tasajo* (a dried, salted meat), pancetta and poultry.[55] It also uses legumes such as chickpeas, still common today in the cuisine of the Iberian Peninsula; tubers and other starchy foodstuffs such as sweet potatoes, plantains, malanga and potatoes, which are termed *viandas* in Cuban Spanish; various vegetables like aubergines and marrows (a squash similar to courgette or zucchini); “todas clases de especias” (every kind of spice); salt and “ajì con ajos fritos con manteca, de donde viene derivado el nombre de *ajiaco*” (“*aji* [a type of chilli pepper] with garlic sautéed in butter, which gives it the name *ajiaco*”).[56] *Ajiaco*, in its older form *agiaco*, had been explained by Estéban Pichardo in his *Diccionario provincial de voces cubanas* as early as 1836:

> Comida compuesta de carne de vaca ó puerco, trozos de plátano, yuca, calabaza, & con abundancia de caldo cargado de sumo de limón y agì picante, de donde toma su nombre. Es el equivalente de la

olla española: pero acompañado del casabe y nunca del pan. Su uso es casi general [. . .], aunque se escusa en mesas de alguna etiqueta. [Dish consisting of beef or pork, small pieces of plantain, cassava and pumpkin, and plenty of broth seasoned with lemon juice and hot chilli pepper, from which it takes its name. It is the equivalent of *olla spagnola* (Spanish stew), but eaten with cassava, never bread. It is consumed regularly [. . .], although not on formal occasions.][57]

In ajiaco we thus see a blend of various ingredients: these include *tasajo*, a dried and salted meat whose mass production, in the European imperial context, was designed to deliver a high-protein food that kept well and could feed the slaves working on Cuban sugarcane plantations; starchy matter that could fill and satisfy hungry stomachs; and vegetables and spices (Sluyter 2010). Although it is fairly typical of cookbooks that they omitted quantities, at least until the late nineteenth century, it can be noted that in the case of *ajiaco*, the apparent randomness and haphazard choice, both of its ingredients and of their relative quantities, had the effect of recreating a dish typical of slave cuisine. *Ajiaco* is humble food, easily cooked and using whatever is at hand, but capable of meeting the essential needs of workers engaged in strenuous physical activity by providing high calorie intake at low cost. In his renowned *The Raw and the Cooked*, the French anthropologist Claude Lévi-Strauss recalled how boiling ingredients was a cultural advancement in comparison with roasting them. Boiling required a pot – a container in which the cook could place a liquid part and an ingredient – whereas roasting needed only food and an open fire. Meanwhile, boiling food is also part of an ethics of savings, because this form of cooking preserves the ingredients' juices while roasting looses them (Lévi-Strauss 1964). Also, as underlined by the French historian Madeleine Férrieres, various stews in which the ingredients are boiled in water or another liquid, such as the Italian *minestrone*, the French *pot-au-feu* and *potage*, the Spanish *olla podrida* and many others, use different terms to describe a similar dish that is part of a hunger cuisine (Ferrières 2003). This kind of cuisine has and had the main objective of filling the empty stomachs of hungry workers. The ingredients vary according to the geographical area in which they are cooked, the culture of the cook and of the people who eat those stews, and the ingredients available.

Prior to his introduction of the concept of "transculturation", Fernando Ortiz, discussing Cuban identity, used *ajiaco* as a metaphor:

Cuba is an ajiaco. [. . .] [T]herein go substances of the most diverse types and origins. The Indians gave us corn, the potato, malanga, the sweet potato, yuca, the chili pepper that serves as its condiment, and the white cassava *xao-xao* with which the good Creoles of Camagüey

> and Oriente decorate the ajiaco when they serve it. Such was the first ajiaco, the pre-Columbian ajiaco, with meat from hutias, from iguanas, from crocodiles, from majá snakes, from turtles, from sea snails, and from other hunted and fished creatures that are no longer appreciated for the palate. The Castilians cast aside these Indian meats and replaced them with their own. With their pumpkins and turnips they brought fresh beef, cured beef, smoked meats, and pork shoulder. And all of this went to give substance to the new ajiaco of Cuba. Alongside the Whites of Europe arrived the Blacks of Africa, and they brought us bananas, plantains, yams, and their cooking technique. And then the Asians with their mysterious spices from the East. And the French with their balancing of flavors, which softened the caustic quality of the savage chillies. And the Anglo-Americans with their domestic machines that simplified the kitchen. [. . .] Out of all this our national ajiaco has been made.[58]

Ajiaco, which was definitively identified as a national dish by Ortiz and is also frequently mentioned in other nineteenth-century sources, as well as in cookbooks and dictionaries, thus provides a good example of how slave cooking, as well as local ingredients and the activities of the colonists, played an essential role in the development of Caribbean cuisine.[59] Without being fully aware of all the dynamics in play regarding Cuban cuisine, including the active part played by African slaves in its emergence and codification, an anonymous woman author, travelling in Cuba at some point in or before 1870, commented in her memoirs that this was "a questionable amalgamation of American and Spanish cookery".[60]

Conclusions

David Bell and Gill Valentine's well-known work on food summarizes some of the themes covered in this chapter: "The foodstuffs we think of as definitionally part of a particular nation's sense of identity often hide complex histories of trade links, cultural exchange, and especially colonialism" (Bell and Valentine 1997, 169). Although diet and cuisine have often been seen as marginal themes in historical analysis, perhaps because of their constant presence in our lives, this chapter has shown that the analysis of relevant sources enables us to highlight aspects of the history of colonial societies that are actually of substantial interest. We have discussed how it was not only that Caribbean cuisine in the British and Spanish colonies made use of foods that came from various locations across the world but also that the colonists themselves depended on their slaves of African origin in regard to their food and diet. Who the cooks were in the colonists' kitchens; the use of various sorts of training methods to instruct them on the wishes and needs of their owners; the apparent difficulties and misunderstandings that were part of wider processes of negotiation of spaces of liberty; the opinions of those who ate slave cooking; and the case of the *ajiaco* that was described in cookbooks and dictionaries: all these elements show that people with neither power nor independence also played an active part in the entry of the Spanish and British colonial worlds into a society that by then had become global, in culinary terms as well as on other levels.

Notes

1. This research has received funding from the European Commission under the European Union's Horizon 2020 programme MSCA 2014, grant agreement 659541, as well as HAR2014–53797-P "Globalización Ibérica: Redes entre Asia y Europa y los cambios en las pautas de Consumo en Latinoamérica" [Iberian Globalization: Networks between Asia and Europe and Changes in Consumption Patterns in Latin America], financed by Ministerio de Economia y Competitividad, Spain. Also the PAI Group HUM-1000, "Historia de la Globalización: Violencia, negociación e interculturalidad" [History of Globalisation: Violence, Negotiation and Interculturality] and its principal investigator Igor Pérez Tostado which financed its publication in open access. The author is grateful to Routledge's anonymous reviewer for their suggestions and to her colleagues Bartolomé Yun-Casalilla and Omar Svriz for their cooperation and for sharing their expertise.
2. Moya Pons 2007, 309; Ortiz 1947, 5.
3. For one of the exceptions, see Petley 2012.
4. Some recent studies of European adaptation to and rejection of local cooking should be mentioned: Earle 2012; LaCombe 2012; Saldarriaga 2011; Leong Salobir 2011.
5. See the following chapters in *The Slavery Reader*, ed. Gad Heuman and James Walvin (London: Routledge, 2003): Hilary McD. Beckles, "An Economic Life of Their Own: Slaves as Commodity Producers and Distributors in Barbados," 507–20; Sidney W. Mintz, "The Origins of the Jamaican Market System," 521–44; Peter H. Wood, "Black Labor – White Rice," 224–43; Woodville K. Marshall, "Provision Ground and Plantation Labour in Four Windward Islands: Competition for Resources During Slavery," 470–85. See also Diana C. Crader, "Slave Diet at Monticello," *American Antiquity* 55, no. 4 (1990): 690–717.
6. Deetz 2017; Miller 2017. For earlier studies on the same theme, see, for example, Williams Forson 2006.
7. Jacques Presser, "Memoires als geschiedbrom," in *Winkler Prins Encyclopedie* (Amsterdam: Elsevier, 1958), vol. 8, 208–10; Rudolf Dekker, "Introduction," in *Egodocuments and History: Autobiographical Writing in Its Social Context Since the Middle Ages*, ed. Rudolf Dekker (Hilversum: Verloren, 2002), 7–20.
8. Or rather, when slaves did occasionally leave written documents, these provide no response to research questions about the slaves' role in the kitchens, their agency and their resistance to domination by the colonists. On the West Indies see, for example, Mary Prince, *The History of Mary Prince, a West Indian Slave. Related by Herself*, ed. T. Pringle (London: 1831). Prince's account says nothing that aids analysis of the role of slaves in inventing local Caribbean cuisine, nor analysis of food, kitchens and cuisine in the incorporation of Latin America into the globalized context.

9. See, for example, Katharine E. Harbury, *Colonial Virginia's Cooking Dynasty* (Columbia: University of South Carolina Press, 2004). Although one might think that the analysis of eighteenth-century Virginia's environment of slavery might include examination of slave kitchens, Harbury does not devote specific space to their work but just provides brief references to slave activity. This seems to have been due to the scarcity or complete absence of primary sources authored by slaves, as was the case for research for this chapter.
10. Institute of Commonwealth Studies, University of London (UK), archive of the Castle Wemyss Estate (hereinafter ICS 101), 3/2/1. Monthly medical records of the number of slaves and their health conditions, including notes with the headings "Increase of Negroes" and "Decrease of Negroes". September 1823 is mentioned here because of its representative nature. Documents in the archive relate especially to the period 1802–1842.
11. Ibid.
12. Mrs. [A. C.] Carmichael, *Domestic Manners and Social Condition of the White, Coloured, and Negro Population of the West Indies*, 2 vols. (London: Whittaker, Treacher, and Co., 1833), vol. 1, 114.
13. Fredrika Bremer, *The Homes of the New World: Impressions of America*, trans. Mary Howitt, 2 vols. (New York: Harper & Brothers, 1853).
14. Ibid., vol. 1, vii.
15. Ibid., vol. 2, 280. We return to this passage, in its fuller context, later in the chapter.
16. Lady [Maria] Nugent, *Lady Nugent's Journal of Her Residence in Jamaica from 1801 to 1805*, ed. Philip Wright (Kingston: University of the West Indies Press, 2002) (first pub. 1839), 36, 39; italics in the original. We should observe how these quotations raise as many questions as they answer. Did Lady Nugent meant that Baptiste was a French-style cook or that he was actually French or of French descent? What did Lady Nugent mean by the italicized word *gentleman*? And, why did she later refer to him as Monsieur Baptiste? To date I have found no solution to solve Lady Nugent's ambiguities in describing her cook.
17. Thomas Roughley, *The Jamaica Planter's Guide; Or, A System for Planting and Managing a Sugar Estate, or Other Plantation in that Island, and throughout the British West Indies in General* (London: Longman, Hurst, Rees, Orme, and Brown, 1823), v–vii.
18. Ibid., 97–98.
19. Ibid., 98.
20. Ibid.
21. Ibid., 98–99.
22. Mary Gardner Lowell, *New Year in Cuba: Mary Gardner Lowell's Travel Diary, 1831–1832*, ed. Karen Robert (Boston: Massachusetts Historical Society, 2003), 105.
23. Ibid.
24. Nugent, *Lady Nugent's Journal*, 39.
25. Thomas Staunton St. Clair, *A Residence in the West Indies and America, with a Narrative of the Expedition to the Island of Walcheren*, 2 vols. (London: Richard Bentley, 1834). This original edition is now available online; it was reissued as *A Soldier's Sojourn in British Guiana, 1806–1808*, ed. Vincent Roth (Georgetown: Daily Chronicle, 1947).
26. Ibid., vol. 1, 227–29.
27. Ibid., vol. 1, 229.
28. Matthew Gregory Lewis, *Journal of a West India Proprietor, Kept during a Residence in the Island of Jamaica*, ed. Judith Terry (London: John Murray,

1834, 393–94). For a more detailed analysis of the humanitarian policies of Matthew Lewis and various other slave owners, see Berti 2016.

29. Although Williams's account of his travels is written in the first person, it provides little information on the author himself. Williams states that his aim is to provide information on the state of Jamaica and the living conditions of the slaves, which in his opinion were better than those of workers in Britain. See Cynric R. Williams, *A Tour through the Island of Jamaica, from the Western to the Eastern End, in the Year 1823* (London: Hunt and Clarke, 1826), v–viii. Williams was also the author of a gothic novel published in 1827; see Janina Nordius, "Racism and Radicalism in Jamaican Gothic: Cynric R. Williams's 'Hamel, The Obeah Man'," *ELH* 73, no. 3 (2006): 673–93.
30. Williams, *A Tour through the Island of Jamaica*, 95–96.
31. George Pinckard, *Notes on the West Indies*, 2nd ed., 2 vols. (London: Baldwin, Cradock, and Joy, 1816) (first pub. in 1806), vol. 1, 111.
32. Richard R. Madden, *A Twelvemonth's Residence in the West Indies during the Transition from Slavery to Apprenticeship; with Incidental Notices of the State of Society, Prospects, and Natural Resources of Jamaica and Other Islands*, 2 vols. (London: James Cochrane; Philadelphia: Carey, Lea and Blanchard, 1835).
33. Carmichael, *Domestic Manners and Social Condition*, vol. 1, 36.
34. John Bigelow, *Jamaica in 1850: Or, The Effects of Sixteen Years of Freedom on a Slave Colony* (New York and London: Putnam, 1851), 12–13.
35. See the letter of 3 August 1828 in ICS 101, 2/5/36.
36. ICS 101, 2/2/40.
37. Bremer, *The Homes of the New World*, vol. 2, 280.
38. Ibid.
39. "Negro Reply," *The Bermudian* (St. George's, Bermuda), March 27, 1822, 4 (italics in the original). Digitized copies of *The Bermudian* can be consulted (on site only) at the British Library. This anecdote was reproduced numerous times in other nineteenth-century periodicals as an example of "Negro shrewdness".
40. Maturin M. Ballou, *History of Cuba: Or, Notes of a Traveller in the Tropics* (Boston: Phillips, Sampson, 1854), 103.
41. Carmichael, *Domestic Manners and Social Condition*, vol. 2, 43.
42. J. P. Legran, *Nuevo manual del cocinero cubano y español* (Havana: La Fortuna, 1864) (first pub. 1857). For an introduction to methodology for analyzing recipe books, see Gilly Lehmann, "Reading Recipe Books and Culinary History: Opening a New Field," in *Reading and Writing Recipe Books, 1550–1800*, ed. Michelle DiMeo and Sara Pennell (Manchester: Manchester University Press, 2013), 93–108.
43. On cuisine and identity formation, see Arjun Appadurai, "How to Make a National Cuisine: Cookbooks in Contemporary India," *Comparative Studies in Society and History* 30, no. 1 (1988): 3–24; B. W. Higman, "Cookbooks and Caribbean Cultural Identity: An English-Language Hors d'Oeuvre," *New West Indian Guide* 72, no. 1/2 (1998): 77–95; Susan J. Leonardi, "Recipes for Reading: Summer Pasta, Lobster à la Riseholme, and Key Lime Pie," *PMLA* 104, no. 3 (1989): 340–47; Anne Bower, "Bound Together: Recipes, Lives, Stories, and Readings," in *Recipes for Reading: Community Cookbooks, Stories, Histories*, ed. Anne L. Bower (Amherst: University of Massachusetts Press, 1997), 1–14.
44. For mention of how recipes function to demarcate social boundaries, see Palmié 2009, 54.
45. Legran, *Nuevo manual*, title page and unpaginated preface.

46. Ibid., 29, 47 ("a la turca"); 106 ("a la orientál"); 71, 104 ("a la portugesa"); 70, 78, 85, 95, 146 ("a la inglesa"); 113 ("a la escocesa"); 34, 45, 145, 154 ("a la italiana"); 39 ("a la rusa"); 26, 27, 32, 36, 99, 101, 104, 112 ("a la americana").
47. Ibid., 10, 42 ("a la mejicana"); 75, 114 ("a la yucateca"); 154 ("de Santo Domingo"); 88 ("puerto-riqueña").
48. The concept of the order of a meal is discussed by the structural anthropologist Mary Douglas, "Deciphering a Meal," *Daedalus* 101, no. 1 (1972): 61–81.
49. Legran, *Nuevo manual*, 5, 18, 48, 52, 117.
50. Ibid., 7, 31, 37, 59, 153 ("a la francesa"); 15, 23, 41, 52, 58, 69, 70, 106, 115 ("a la española"); 94 ("a la castellana"); 101, 106 ("a la catalana"); 113 ("a la gallega"); 58, 65 ("a la valenciana"); 24 ("a la manchega"); 33, 75, 108 ("a la vizcaina"); 63, 70, 96 ("a la andalusa"); 21, 57, 67, 81, 185 ("a la madrileña").
51. Ibid., 7, 10, 18, 20, 21, 26, 27, 29, 30, 35, 40, 48, 50, 54, 57, 58, 61, 66, 70, 72, 73, 77, 78, 81, 86, 87, 90, 91, 92, 95, 101, 103, 104, 110, 130, 184, 185, 186, 187.
52. Ibid., 61, 69 (malanga); 62, 82 (chayote); 63, 67, 122, 191, 195 (manioc or cassava); 60, 82, 127 (yam); 126 (soursop); 154, 191 (mamey); 184, 191 (sapota); 63, 81 (*quimbombò*); 18, 77 (sweet potato); 148, 189 (guava); 122, 154 (coconut); 10, 61, 69, 99, 130, 142 (plantain); and 129 (papaya). For a discussion of tropical ingredients in Cuba, see Shannon Lee Dawdy, "'La comida mambisa': Food, Farming, and Cuban Identity, 1839–1999," *New West Indian Guide/Nieuwe West-Indische Gids* 76, no. 1/2 (2002): 47–80, 47. The banana genus (*Musa*) was introduced to the Americas from Asia, but Lee Dawdy describes it as having been "nativized"; ibid.: 56. For a more detailed analysis of how the banana was considered an exotic item for much of the twentieth century, see Fabio Parasecoli, "Representations of Caribbean Food in U.S. Popular Culture," in *Caribbean Food Cultures: Practices and Consumption in the Caribbean and Its Diasporas*, ed. Wiebke Beushausen, Anne Brüske, Ana-Sofia Commichau, Patrick Helber, and Sinah Kloß (Bielefeld: Transcript, 2014), 133–50.
53. Legran, *Nuevo manual*, 45.
54. Ibid., 14, 17, 18.
55. According to Andrew Sluyter, *tasajo*, or "jerked beef" in English, was "the salt-cured beef produced along the Rio de la Plata, shipped to Cuba, and consumed by African slaves", above all in the nineteenth century. Feeding the slaves who were growing sugarcane, *tasajo* was "a low-value commodity" that "became essential to the production of a high-value commodity". See Andrew Sluyter, "The Hispanic Atlantic's Tasajo Trail," *Latin American Research Review* 45, no. 1 (2010): 99–101. According to John Wurdemann, who in 1844, writing anonymously as "a physician", published an account of his stay in Cuba, the "putrid-like odors" of tasajo tainted the air of Havana. See [John G. Wurdemann], *Notes on Cuba* (Boston: James Munroe, 1844), 45–46.
56. Legran, *Nuevo manual*, 17, 18. For a definition of *ajì*, see Estéban Pichardo, *Diccionario provincial casi-razonado de vozes y frases cubanas*, 4th ed. (Havana: El Trabajo, 1875), 42.
57. Estéban Pichardo, *Diccionario de voces cubanas* (Matanzas: Imprenta de la Real Marina, 1836), 8. Translation into English by Stuart Oglethorpe.
58. Fernando Ortiz, "The Human Factors of 'Cubanidad'," trans. João Felipe Gonçalves and Gregory Duff Morton, *HAU: Journal of Ethnographic Theory* 4, no. 3 (2014): 460–62 (first pub. in Spanish in 1940; italics

in the original). For the concept of transculturation, see Ortiz, *Cuban Counterpoint*.

59. John Wurdemann, for example, wrote about seeing "a large pot of very white boiled rice, and another full of vegetables and meats, the favorite *olla podrida* of the creole". Wurdemann, *Notes on Cuba*, 34.
60. Anon, *Rambles in Cuba* (New York: Carleton, 1870), 108. The anonymous woman author headed her opening journal entry "Havana, March 1, 18" –. Ibid., 7.

Bibliography

Anon. 1870. *Rambles in Cuba*. New York: Carleton.

Appadurai, Arjun. 1988. "How to Make a National Cuisine: Cookbooks in Contemporary India." *Comparative Studies in Society and History* 30 (1): 3–24.

Ballou, Maturin M. 1854. *History of Cuba: Or, Notes of a Traveller in the Tropics*. Boston: Phillips, Sampson.

Beckles, Hilary. 2003. "An Economic Life of Their Own: Slaves as Commodity Producers and Distributors in Barbados." In *The Slavery Reader*, edited by Gad Heuman and James Walvin, 507–20. London: Routledge.

Bell, David, and Gill Valentine. 1997. *Consuming Geographies: We are Where we Eat*. London: Routledge.

Berti, Ilaria. 2014. "Curiosity, Appreciation, and Old Habits. Creolization of Colonizers' Food Patterns of Consumption in Three English Travelogues on the Caribbean." In *Caribbean Food Cultures: Practices and Consumption in the Caribbean and Its Diasporas*, edited by Wiebke Beushausen, Anne Brüske, Ana-Sofia Commichau, Patrick Helber and Sinah Kloß, 115–32. Bielefeld: Transcript.

———. 2016. "Feeding the Sick upon Stewed Fish and Pork": Slave Health and Food in West Indian Sugar Plantation Hospitals." *Food & History* 14 (1): 81–105.

———. Forthcoming. *Colonial Recipes in the Nineteenth-Century British and Spanish Caribbean: Food Perceptions and Practice*. Amsterdam: Amsterdam University Press.

Bigelow, John. 2006 [1851]. *Jamaica in 1850: Or, The Effects of Sixteen Years of Freedom on a Slave Colony*. Chicago: University of Illinois Press (first pub. New York and London: Putnam, 1851).

Bower, Anne. 1997. "Bound Together: Recipes, Lives, Stories, and Readings." In *Recipes for Reading: Community Cookbooks, Stories, Histories*, edited by Anne L. Bower, 1–14. Amherst: University of Massachusetts Press.

Bremer, Fredrika. 1853. *The Homes of the New World: Impressions of America*. Translated by Mary Howitt. 2 vols. New York: Harper & Brothers.

Carmichael, Mrs. [A. C.]. 1833. *Domestic Manners and Social Condition of the White, Coloured, and Negro Population of the West Indies*. 2 vols. London: Whittaker, Treacher, and Co.

Crader, Diana C. 1990. "Slave Diet at Monticello." *American Antiquity* 55 (4): 690–717.

Deetz, Kelley Fanto. 2017. *Bound to the Fire: How Virginia's Enslaved Cooks Helped Invent American Cuisine*. Lexington: University Press of Kentucky.

Dekker, Rudolf. 2002. "Introduction." In *Egodocuments and History: Autobiographical Writing in Its Social Context since the Middle Ages*, edited by Rudolf Dekker, 7–20. Hilversum: Verloren.

Douglas, Mary. 1972. "Deciphering a Meal." *Daedalus* 101 (1): 61–81.

Earle, Rebecca. 2012. *The Body of the Conquistador: Food, Race and the Colonial Experience in Spanish America, 1492–1700*. Cambridge: Cambridge University Press.

Ferrières, Madeleine. 2006 [2003]. *Sacred Cow, Mad Cow: A History of Food Fears*. New York: Columbia University Press.

Gardner Lowell, Mary. 2003. *New Year in Cuba: Mary Gardner Lowell's Travel Diary, 1831–1832*. Edited by Karen Robert. Boston: Massachusetts Historical Society.

Harbury, Katharine E. 2004. *Colonial Virginia's Cooking Dynasty*. Columbia: University of South Carolina Press.

Hauser, Mark W., James A. Delle, and Douglas V. Armstrong. 2011. "Introduction: Historical Archaeology in Jamaica." In *Out of Many, One People: The Historical Archaeology of Colonial Jamaica*, edited by James A. Delle, Mark W. Hauser, and Douglas V. Armstrong, 1–20. Tuscaloosa: University of Alabama Press.

Higman, B. W. 1998. "Cookbooks and Caribbean Cultural Identity: An English-Language Hors D'Oeuvre." *New West Indian Guide* 72 (1/2): 77–95.

LaCombe, Michael. 2012. *Political Gastronomy: Food and Authority in the English Atlantic World*. Philadelphia: University of Pennsylvania Press.

Lee Dawdy, Shannon. 2002. " 'La comida mambisa': Food, Farming, and Cuban Identity, 1839–1999." *New West Indian Guide/Nieuwe West-Indische Gids* 76 (1/2): 47–80.

Legran, J. P. 1864. *Nuevo manual del cocinero cubano y español*. Havana: La Fortuna (first pub. 1857).

Lehmann, Gilly. 2013. "Reading Recipe Books and Culinary History: Opening a New Field." In *Reading and Writing Recipe Books, 1550–1800*, edited by Michelle Di Meo and Sara Pennell, 93–108. Manchester: Manchester University Press.

Leonardi, Susan J. 1989. "Recipes for Reading: Summer Pasta, Lobster à la Riseholme, and Key Lime Pie." *PMLA* 104 (3): 340–47.

Leong Salobir, Cecilia. 2011. *Food Culture in Colonial Asia: A Taste of Empire*. Abingdon: Routledge.

Lévi-Strauss, Claude. 1983. *The Raw and the Cooked: Introduction to a Science of Mithology*. Chicago: University of Chicago Press (first pub. 1964).

Lewis, Matthew Gregory. 1999 [1834]. *Journal of a West India Proprietor, Kept during a Residence in the Island of Jamaica*. Edited by Judith Terry. Oxford: Oxford University Press.

Madden, Richard R. 1835. *A Twelvemonth's Residence in the West Indies during the Transition from Slavery to Apprenticeship; with Incidental Notices of the State of Society, Prospects, and Natural Resources of Jamaica and Other Islands*. 2 vols. London: James Cochrane.

Marshall, Woodville K. 2003. "Provision Ground and Plantation Labour in Four Windward Islands: Competition for Resources During Slavery." In *The Slavery Reader*, edited by Gad Heuman and James Walvin, 470–85. London: Routledge.

Mehta, Brinda J. 1999. "Indo-Trinidadian Fiction: Female Identity and Creative Cooking." *Alif: Journal of Comparative Poetics* 19 ('Gender and Knowledge', special issue): 151–84.

Miller, Adrian. 2017. *The President's Kitchen Cabinet: The Story of the African Americans Who Have Fed Our First Families, from the Washingtons to the Obamas*. Chapel Hill: University of North Carolina Press.

Mintz, Sidney W. 1996. *Tasting Food, Tasting Freedom: Excursions into Eating, Culture, and the Past*. Boston: Beacon Press.

———. 2003. "The Origins of the Jamaican Market System." In *The Slavery Reader*, edited by Gad Heuman and James Walvin, 521–44. London: Routledge.

Moya Pons, Frank. 2007. *History of the Caribbean: Plantations, Trade, and War in the Atlantic World*. Princeton, NJ: Markus Wiener.

Nordius, Janina. 2006. "Racism and Radicalism in Jamaican Gothic: Cynric R. Williams's 'Hamel, The Obeah Man'." *ELH* 73 (3): 673–93.

Nugent, Lady [Maria]. 2002 [1839]. *Lady Nugent's Journal of Her Residence in Jamaica from 1801 to 1805*. Edited by Philip Wright. Kingston: University of the West Indies Press.

Ortiz, Fernando. 1947. *Cuban Counterpoint: Tobacco and Sugar*. New York: Alfred A. Knopf (first pub. in Spanish in 1940).

———. 2014. 'The Human Factors of 'Cubanidad' ", trans. João Felipe Gonçalves and Gregory Duff Morton. *HAU: Journal of Ethnographic Theory* 4 (3): 445–80 (first pub. in Spanish in 1940).

Paget, Henry. 2004. "The Caribbean Plantation: Its Contemporary Significance." In *Sugar, Slavery, and Society: Perspectives on the Caribbean, India, the Mascarenes, and the United States*, edited by Bernard Moitt, 157–87. Gainesville: University Press of Florida.

Palmié, Stephan. 2009. "Intangible Cultural Property, Semiotic Ideology, and the Vagaries of Ethnoculinary Recognition." *African Arts* 42 (4) ('Art and Heritage', special issue): 54–61.

Parasecoli, Fabio. 2014. "Representations of Caribbean Food in U.S. Popular Culture." In *Caribbean Food Cultures: Practices and Consumption in the Caribbean and Its Diasporas*, edited by Wiebke Beushausen, Anne Brüske, Ana-Sofia Commichau, Patrick Helber, and Sinah Kloß, 133–50. Bielefeld: Transcript.

Petley, Christer. 2012. "Gluttony, Excess, and the Fall of the Planter Class in the British Caribbean." *Atlantic Studies* 9 (1): 85–106.

Pichardo, Estéban. 1836. *Diccionario de voces cubanas*. Matanzas: Imprenta de la Real Marina.

———. 1875. *Diccionario provincial casi-razonado de vozes y frases cubanas*. 4th ed. Havana: El Trabajo.

Pinckard, George. 1816. *Notes on the West Indies*. 2nd ed. 2 vols. London: Baldwin, Cradock, and Joy (first pub. in 1806).

Presser, Jacques. 1958. "Memoires als geschiedbrom." In *Winkler Prins Encyclopedie*, Vol. 8, 208–10. Amsterdam: Elsevier.

Prince, Mary. 1831. *The History of Mary Prince, a West Indian Slave. Related by Herself*. Edited by T. Pringle. London.

Procida, Mary A. 2002. " 'The Greater Part of My Life has been Spent in India': Autobiography and the Crisis of Empire in the Twentieth Century." *Biography* 25 (1): 130–50.

Roughley, Thomas. 1823. *The Jamaica Planter's Guide; Or, A System for Planting and Managing a Sugar Estate, or Other Plantation in that Island, and throughout the British West Indies in General*. London: Longman, Hurst, Rees, Orme, and Brown.

Saldarriaga, Gregorio. 2011. *Alimentación e identidades en el Nuevo Reino de Granada, siglos XVI y XVII*. Bogotá: Editorial Universidad del Rosario.
Shepherd, Verene A. 2007. "Resisting Representation: Locating Enslaved and Indentured Women's Voice in the Colonial Caribbean." In *Caribbean Culture: Soundings on Kamau Brathwaite*, edited by Annie Paul, 265–86. Kingston: University of the West Indies Press.
Sluyter, Andrew. 2010. "The Hispanic Atlantic's Tasajo Trail." *Latin American Research Review* 45 (1): 98–120.
St. Clair, Thomas Staunton. 1834. *A Residence in the West Indies and America, with a Narrative of the Expedition to the Island of Walcheren*. 2 vols. London: Richard Bentley.
Williams, Cynric R. 1826. *A Tour through the Island of Jamaica, from the Western to the Eastern End, in the Year 1823*. London: Hunt and Clarke.
Williams Forson, Psyche A. 2006. *Building Houses out of Chicken Legs: Black Women, Food, and Power*. Chapel Hill: University of North Carolina Press.
Wood, Peter H. 2003. "Black Labor – White Rice." In *The Slavery Reader*, edited by Gad Heuman and James Walvin, 224–43. London: Routledge.
Wurdemann, John G. 1844. *Notes on Cuba*. Boston: James Munroe.

9 Food, Colonialism and the Quantum of Happiness[1]

Rebecca Earle

> Among all the labours of life, if there is one pursuit more replete than any other with benevolence, more likely to add comforts to existing people, and even to augment their numbers by augmenting their means of subsistence, it is certainly that of spreading abroad the bounties of creation, by transplanting from one part of the globe to another such natural productions are likely to prove beneficial to the interests of humanity.[2]

In 1799 a group of wealthy women in Madrid began a decade-long experiment aimed at discovering the best substitute for breast milk. The ladies, members of the Junta de Damas affiliated with Madrid's Royal Economic Society, had taken over the management of the city's foundling hospital, which provided motivation for their investigation and a ready supply of infants on whom to test their experimental formulas. Unable to find enough wet-nurses for the hundreds of babies now in its charge, the Junta explored substitutes, including goat's milk, goat's milk mixed with fennel, and donkey's milk drunk directly from the animal's teat. Members kept notes on the outcome of their tests and discussed the results with doctors from the Royal Academy of Medicine. Disappointingly, almost all the babies died. The Junta was therefore eager to try a new substance that came highly recommended as an infant feed. *Maranta arundinacea*, or arrowroot, originated in Cuba, where it was reportedly used to great effect. The powder was tested on twenty-two babies. After twenty deaths the trial was halted. The surviving infants were handed over to a wet-nurse and the Junta's medical team concluded that despite the fanfare this Caribbean root was not a suitable baby food.[3]

The Junta's arrowroot experiment was one example of the hundreds of investigations undertaken across eighteenth-century Europe to assess the nutritive qualities of extra-European plants. Many substances – sweet potatoes, quinoa, peanuts, wild rice – were evaluated as possible supplements or staples.[4] Although schemes to popularize these foods stressed their "universal" appeal, the ambition was usually to increase

DOI: 10.4324/9781003168058-10

consumption by – as one promoter put it – "a poor man with a large family", or by foundlings.[5]

The transformative impact of new-world foods on old-world diets is of course well known. Alfred Crosby's pioneering works, together with more recent studies, have deftly charted the ways in which global eating practices were revolutionized by the "Columbian exchange" – the transfer of plants, animals and human populations between the Americas and the Old World in the fifteenth and sixteenth centuries. The eighteenth-century quest for new foods to feed Europe forms part of this larger history, while at the same time reflecting central aspects of enlightened science, as the Junta's careful experiments suggest. A growing corpus of research indeed points to the importance of food in framing eighteenth-century debates about knowledge and health.[6] This promotion of novel staples in Europe ran parallel to eighteenth-century efforts to identify new commercial crops, edible or otherwise, that might profitably be exploited in European colonies. A rich scholarship has documented the sustained efforts by European states to discover such commodities, and where possible to relocate production to their own colonial orbits. Research has amply demonstrated the close links between natural history, colonialism and commerce.[7]

These better-known efforts at commercial botany, and at discovering new foods for the peoples of Europe, were accompanied by a third enterprise that formed part of this larger assemblage of eighteenth-century food transfers. This was the search for new staples to feed labouring populations not in Europe but in its colonies. This chapter explores two foods that were persistently advocated as ideal staples for "workers and black people" from Cuba to Calcutta: breadfruit and potatoes.[8]

These endeavours rarely succeeded in their ostensible aim of transforming subaltern eating practices, but they reveal much about the role of food in the eighteenth-century imagination. Ample supplies of nutritious foods were viewed as crucial to building the healthy and energetic populations that formed the basis for agricultural, commercial and industrial wealth. The close associations between strong populations, nourishing foods and enlightened governance meant that interventions in colonial diets were rarely concerned solely with practical matters of supply. Ultimately, for botanists, colonial officials and settlers, the appeal of schemes to disseminate breadfruit in Guatemala or potatoes in Bengal lay in their ability to encapsulate a complex of enlightened desiderata about benevolence, improvement and public happiness. These links between the provision of food and the pursuit of happiness fuelled and legitimated enlightened promotion of new foods in the eyes of their advocates, and explain why colonial elites were so enthusiastic about such plant transfers, despite their limited success in modifying popular diets.

These stories reflect the global nature of the Enlightenment. While scholars once viewed the Enlightenment as a fundamentally European phenomenon that either naturalized or withered in other parts of the world, more recent research has focused less on the origin of ideas and practices, and more on their interconnections.[9] The global circulation of breadfruit plants or recipes for potato bread illustrates precisely these connected histories. It was the breadfruit's movement, across empires and islands, that made it a powerful symbol of enlightenment. Potatoes resonated differently in Lima, Paris and Calcutta, but in all three locations discussion of their merits formed part of a body of ideas whose central themes were the relationships between nutritious food, good governance and happiness. Examining these histories helps concretize our understanding of the simultaneously mobile and localized nature of enlightened projects and imaginaries.

Let us begin by taking a closer look at the Junta de Damas' infant formula.

"How Many Labourers! How Many Honest Grenadiers!"

As the Junta's sourcing of the root from Havana indicates, arrowroot grew in Meso-America and the Caribbean. Its significance in precolonial culture is unclear, but from the seventeenth century Europeans reported that Caribbean islanders employed it to treat wounds, especially those caused by poisoned arrows. French and English settlers, attracted by the root's medicinal qualities, endorsed its utility and widened the range of conditions for which it was considered effective. Once converted into flour, moreover, it made a smooth jelly recommended for those with delicate digestions. By the mid-eighteenth century it was cultivated in the West Indies for local use and as a commodity exported (on a very small scale) to Europe.[10] At the time of the Junta's experiments, arrowroot was represented in a number of European botanical gardens, and was considered a suitable food for infants and the infirm.[11] The Junta's interest in the root, therefore, was not prompted by its recent appearance on the European scene.

Rather, it reflected the quest for foodstuffs which would facilitate the social, political and economic transformations desired by enlightened thinkers across Europe. A central concern, embraced by the Junta, was the creation of a substantial population of healthy and active workers. As Spanish ministers affirmed, echoing a widely shared conviction, "a large population that is usefully employed is the greatest treasure a state can possess, the foundation of its true power".[12] Were sickly foundlings transformed into healthy adults, rhapsodized one writer, "how many individuals – which we now lack – would we have for public works! How many labourers! How many honest grenadiers!"[13] The conversion of Madrid's orphans into productive members of society was thus a patriotic act. Similar efforts were underway in other European cities, where the shocking mortality rates at foundling hospitals attracted increasing attention for reasons both philanthropic and economic (Morel 1976; Sherwood 1988; Andrews 1989; Guimarães Sá 2000). Writers across Europe insisted that a flourishing economy depended on a well-nourished and vigorous population. While philosophers disputed whether large populations were invariably preferable to smaller ones, all agreed that to be productive the existing population needed to be well fed. For this reason, a nation's strength was closely correlated with its possessing "the greatest possible quantity of foodstuffs", as the economic theorist Jean-François Melon noted. An adequate supply of affordable and nourishing food was thus essential for the "security, wealth and glory of a state".[14]

Since a nation's wealth depended on the vigour of its population, public-minded individuals diligently examined ways not simply to prevent famine but to provide the healthy and agreeable food necessary to create this energetic workforce. Identifying more nourishing sources of food therefore constituted a topic "worthy of the meditations of philosophers and the protection of government", in the view of Antoine-Augustin Parmentier, one of the century's great potato promoters[15] (Parmentier 1781, 3–4). The search for nourishing new foodstuffs, and the promotion of efficient ways to prepare them, were not simply responses to shortages, but rather reflected new ways of thinking about governance, and new debates about the sources of wealth and economic prosperity.

What, however, constituted a nourishing food? Was arrowroot such a substance, for instance? Although some British enthusiasts insisted that it could form the basis of an improved diet for "natives" in India and "our new African settlements", the root's status as a food for babies and invalids militated against its promotion as a staple.[16] Before the nineteenth-century invention of the calorie, which provided a numerical scale for ranking putative energy value, assessment of a food's nourishing qualities did not rely on a single indicator.[17] Claims that a food was nutritive were usually linked to a perception that it was sustaining, in that it enabled a lengthy period of work. Working people often evaluated a food's ability to nourish in this way. In 1790s England, for instance, labourers in the southern counties considered barley and potato soup "washy stuff, that affords no nourishment" and thus would not allow them to undertake a day's work. Peasants in the Vaud made the same complaints about potato bread. Labourers in various regions seem to have viewed meat as particularly nourishing.[18]

For many scientists, nourishing foods were those that contained a greater quantity of starch. The physician James Clark made this clear in a 1797 report on the starchy qualities of various West Indian roots. Clark, who practiced for many years in Dominica, conducted experiments on manioc, eddoes, arrowroot and a number of other common foodstuffs, with a view to determining how much starch each yielded, and thereby how nutritious each was. Sweet manioc, for instance, proved to be more nutritious than the bitter variety because it contained more starchy matter. Guinea yam and sweet potato contained equal quantities of starch, and so were equally nourishing. Other plants such as plantain proved more difficult to reduce to a starch through chemical experimentation, but Clark was certain that their reputation as a "hearty food for hard working people" meant that they must contain a great deal of starch. Indeed, he declared that all these commonly consumed foods "contain starch, and are looked upon to be very nutritious".[19] Starchy foods were highly nourishing, and therefore suitable for labourers. It was fortunate for the enslaved population of the West Indies that this was so, since, as Clark happily noted, starchy substances formed their principal food. He therefore felt confident in concluding that their diet was wholesome and nourishing.[20] As Emma Spary has observed, "It was over the question of nourishing the poor that administrators and savants first began to collaborate in generating new definitions of dietary requirements and experimenting with new nutritional resources" (Spary 2014, 23; Simmons 2015).

This equation of nutritive value with starchiness explains why the many efforts to identify new foods for colonized populations focused almost exclusively on starchy substances. While arrowroot was being recommended as a food for colonized Africans, colonial official Robert Kyd, founder of the Calcutta Botanical Garden, was encouraging the introduction of sago palms from the Malay Peninsula to India – sago being another supremely starchy substance, to which arrowroot was often compared.[21] Writing a decade after the devastating Bengal famine (exacerbated, if not indeed caused, by British policies), Joseph Banks, president of the Royal Society, imagined the multiple benefits which would accrue from Kyd's proposals. The introduction of sago, Banks believed, would not only provide an immensely wholesome food for "natives" but would also lead these natives to "revere the name of their British Conquerors", whom they would thank for delivering them from "famine, the most severe scourge with which Providence had afflicted them". Banks thereby endorsed the dissemination of sago while simultaneously disavowing British responsibility for the circumstances that prompted its introduction.[22] These eighteenth-century dreams of beneficent starchy foods for natives were thus inherently connected to European ideals of good governance, which justified such interventions in the eating practices of ordinary people, and obscured, at least to the dreamers, the structures of power and coercion that made them appear necessary.

The Celebrated Breadfruit

Advocates of sago and arrowroot often alluded to the century's most sensational act of nutritional botany: the transfer of breadfruits from the South Pacific to the Caribbean. The story of the breadfruit's journey from Tahiti to the West Indies is as well known now as it was at the time, as is the spectacular fate of the *Bounty*, the ship which transported the original cache of seedlings. Fletcher Christian's 1789 mutiny against Captain Bligh was provoked in part by the demands imposed on the crew by the delicate cargo, which monopolized much of the ship's space and water supply. On seizing the vessel, the mutineers promptly tossed the saplings overboard. This setback did not deter the British government from funding a second expedition, again under Bligh, which in 1792 succeeded in bringing the trees to the Caribbean (Bligh 2013 [1792]; Dening 1992; Spary and White 2004).

Breadfruit promoters stressed two features: that the fruit was nutritious, and that it offered a highly suitable food for enslaved people. John Ellis, a colonial agent for Dominica, stated pithily in a 1775 pamphlet why the plant merited attention. Breadfruit, he explained, "affords a great deal of nourishment, and is very satisfying, therefore proper for hard-working people". For this reason, it "might be easily cultivated in our West India islands, and made to supply an important article of food to all ranks of their inhabitants, especially to the Negroes".[23] The breadfruit, insisted another planter, "would be of infinite importance to the West India Islands" because it would afford "a wholesome & pleasant food to our Negroes".[24]

The conviction that the West Indies needed breadfruit seems to have originated with Joseph Banks. During his voyage to the South Pacific with James Cook, Banks identified the plant as an almost limitless source of nutrition. Because the Tahitians subsisted apparently effortlessly on the bountiful breadfruit, the young Banks recorded, they "may almost be said to be exempt from the curse of our forefather; scarcely can it be said that they earn their bread with the sweat of their brow".[25] As David Mackay observed, for Banks the breadfruit represented not so much a foodstuff as "a symbol of a simple and idyllic life free from worries about work or property" (Mackay 1974, 63; Spary and White 2004). Banks therefore lobbied vigorously for their transfer to the Caribbean. For Banks's Caribbean interlocutors, too, the prospect of a food source that required no labour whatsoever was tantalizing. The West Indian plantation system depended on the enslaved to grow most of their own food in kitchen gardens and provision grounds. This necessarily diverted labour from commercial to subsistence agriculture. The breadfruit tree offered the possibility of converting enslaved bodies yet more efficiently into sugar. The time required to cultivate food, for planters a tiresome distraction from the business of profit, could perhaps be redirected wholly into sugarcane. The breadfruit thus lay at the potent convergence of the capitalist logic of the plantation system and an enlightened fantasy of a life without labour.[26]

As various scholars have remarked, there is a deep irony in the expectation that breadfruits, representatives of a paradisiacal world without toil, should serve as food for the enslaved. That enslaved people displayed little enthusiasm for them further illustrates the marginal place of the subaltern eater within these schemes of nutritional generosity; colonial writers complained that through "some unaccountable indifference" these "valuable acquisitions obtained by the munificence of our King" were shunned by their intended beneficiaries.[27] At the same time, new-world plantations were a natural location for such experiments, given the associations of productive labour and nourishing foods with the kindly governance that eighteenth-century planters insisted, loudly, was characteristic of the plantation system.[28]

Imperial interest in the breadfruit derived from these associations far more than from practical concerns about food supply in the Caribbean. During the same years that it underwrote the breadfruit voyages, the British state explicitly rejected claims that the West Indies was suffering a food shortage such as might necessitate the introduction of a new staple. When the West India lobby urged Parliament to lift an embargo on trade with the United States, alleging that without food imports the enslaved population faced starvation, Pitt's government stated repeatedly that food provisions were adequate (Sheridan 1976, 4). The British state did not fund the transportation of thousands of breadfruits from Tahiti to solve a subsistence crisis whose very existence it denied. Rather, the enterprise was framed as a demonstration of altruism and commitment to the public good. As Bligh insisted, "If a man plants ten [breadfruit trees] in his life-time, which he may do in about an hour", he would instantly fulfil "his duty to his own and future generations" (Bligh 2013 [1792], 12). Breadfruits signalled beneficence, regardless of whether anyone ate them.

The British were not alone in viewing breadfruit as an almost talismanic agent of enlightenment. The celebrated German anatomist Johann Friedrich Blumenbach reported excitedly on the arrival in Göttingen of a single specimen of this "inestimable benefit" to mankind, and colonial officials and naturalists elsewhere laboured to disseminate the tree in their own empires.[29] Bligh's efforts were in fact preceded by a French mission to naturalize breadfruits, which successfully transported the plant from the South Pacific to Martinique. Agronomists later advocated its cultivation in France's North African colonies.[30] Like Banks, French naturalists viewed the plant as a highly symbolic food that encapsulated nature's bounty. French celebration of the breadfruit resonated with British writings to help establish the fruit as a transformative foodstuff whose mere possession would not simply banish hunger but also increase human happiness. The man who succeeded in bringing the plant to France's colonies, stated the head gardener of the Jardin du Roi, will "have done more for the happiness of mankind than all the savants of the world" (Letouzey 1989, 234; Spary 2000, 128–30). By the 1790s breadfruits were growing in British and French botanical gardens in the East and West Indies, where they demonstrated commitment to benevolent governance, without serving as a significant source of food.[31] Indeed, within a few years of the tree's arrival in the Caribbean, planters had lost interest in its dietary potential. "The fact is", stated the superintendent of the St. Vincent botanical garden in 1806, "planters hate giving it a place on their estates, as they regard it as an intruder on their cane land, and they dislike any other object but canes." "For to say he had such a thing", he noted, a planter might "make a nigro plant it", but after that he would accord it no more attention.[32] In this context the tree was less a solution to a provisioning dilemma than a sign of Europe's commitment to its colonies and an emblem of enlightenment.

Spanish officials and botanists watched these developments with interest. Peninsular newspapers reported the efforts by rival colonial powers to disseminate the tree, and in 1779, after reading English and consular reports, the director of Madrid's botanical garden concluded that the introduction of breadfruit to Spanish America would be "extremely useful . . . because it is highly nourishing for workers and black people".[33] As with the proposal to introduce arrowroot to "our new African settlements" or breadfruit to Martinique, this assertion was not motivated by a particular moment of dearth. Neither was it a response to a recent encounter with breadfruit. Spanish explorers and missionaries in the Pacific had long been familiar with the plant, which they had not hitherto regarded as a particularly promising food source. Indeed, a few years before the botanical garden's director advocated their dissemination, a group of Spanish Franciscans stationed in Tahiti clashed repeatedly with locals when the missionaries began felling breadfruit trees for use as timber.[34] The new-found enthusiasm rather reflected the breadfruit's recent elevation to a "wonder food" within the republic of letters.

The fruit's status as an agent of enlightenment may be glimpsed in a satirical essay published in a Spanish literary journal in 1788.[35] After reporting British plans to transport the fruit to the Caribbean, the journal observed that its readers would doubtless welcome the discovery of "a healthy and plentiful foodstuff, which the earth spontaneously offers to mankind, and which multiplies so rapidly that effort is required not to encourage but rather to contain it". The breadfruit, in short, seemed the very fruit of paradise. Doubtless, the journal continued, readers would admire "the activities of an enlightened nation" in disseminating this bountiful food. But, the journal warned, readers must not be seduced by the breadfruit's apparent attractions. All too often enterprises guided by "charitable and humane instincts" had led to disaster. Warming to its theme, the journal insisted that popularizing the breadfruit would deal a fatal blow to monopoly trade, unjust privilege and inequality, because its immense nutritive qualities would enable colonies to be self-sufficient. What a threat to tyranny the innocent breadfruit posed! It might spell the end of colonialism itself. Perhaps, the journal concluded, it would be wise to start a war to prevent its reaching the Americas. The author of this sardonic essay captured neatly the near-miraculous qualities ascribed to the exotic fruit.

As in Britain and France, in Spain the state encouraged its dissemination, ordering botanists in the Philippines to experiment with growing breadfruit, and arranging for samples to be sent to Mexico.[36] These imperial directives were accompanied by more local efforts, which demonstrate both the global relevance of the language of enlightened governance, and the ways in which this language was inflected through local contexts. One such effort was championed by the Royal Economic Society of Guatemala, one of the many patriotic organizations in Europe and the Americas devoted to disseminating useful knowledge.[37] Improved agricultural practices featured largely in their concerns, as (in the words of a Chilean merchant) no nation "that encourages agriculture has not enjoyed a large population, or improved industry, or failed to establish an advantageous commerce".[38] The Guatemalan society accordingly stressed that its remit was "the perfecting of agriculture and the mechanical arts". Most of its attention was focused on commercial agriculture; the "decay" of cacao cultivation was a topic of persistent concern, as were efforts to develop the linen industry.[39] The society moreover experimented with new fodder crops such as guinea grass, for which it sought out seeds and published guides to cultivation.[40]

The society was also concerned with the kingdom's food supply. Its newspaper, the *Gazeta de Guatemala*, echoed the views of Spanish economic theorists that it was impossible for arts and industry to flourish when food was expensive or scarce. It monitored the availability and cost of basic foodstuffs such as corn, and was indignant when critics suggested it was not doing enough to address particular moments of shortage. In its publications the society insisted that it had a long history of promoting new varieties of food plants.[41] Its practical activities in this direction were in fact limited, but this did not deter it from celebrating its efforts to disseminate an iconic foodstuff: the breadfruit.

In 1801 Alejandro Ramírez, the *Gazeta*'s editor, announced that he was in possession of a supply of exotic seeds and plants – "many of them unusual, all useful, and most unknown in this kingdom" – which he and a Guatemalan merchant had obtained on a visit to Jamaica.[42] Among the seedlings were several varieties of breadfruit. This was not the first time that visitors to Jamaica from the Spanish Circum-Caribbean had returned home with horticultural treasures. In 1795 officials in Cuba reported that they had acquired specimens of various modish plants, including breadfruit, from Jamaica. After reviewing the miserable fate of the *Bounty*, they observed with satisfaction that Cuba had freely acquired these Jamaican plants, "which constitute part of that island's wealth", and for which Britain had paid such a high price.[43] Botany and science were never disconnected from competition over imperial power. At the same time, local networks of exchange made possible collaborations that worked across such jealousies of trade. Cuban botanists and the Guatemalan society obtained their breadfruits from a neighbouring British colony. Officials in Madrid, in contrast, were obliged to design a complex transoceanic programme to import the plants from the Philippines, which ultimately failed to deliver a single live specimen.[44] If breadfruits represented enlightenment, then the New World was no less enlightened than the old.

The Guatemalan Society had established a small acclimatization garden in Truxillo, on the Caribbean coast, and it was there that the plants were raised. The agents of the transfer, Alejandro Ramírez and Francisco Sosa, congratulated themselves that through their efforts the kingdom's families would in the future subsist on breadfruit, a hyperbolic statement that did not reflect any serious ambition to promote breadfruit consumption, but which captured well the era's breadfruit discourse.[45] The experiment, however, went poorly. By 1802 the reportedly superior Tahitian variety had died, and other plants were attacked by disease, insects and cattle. Labels became detached from the specimens, which meant that the gardener was no longer certain of the identity of some of the plants in his care. He subsequently left Truxillo under a cloud; by the time a new gardener took over, many of the plants had perished. The society, however, considered the experiment a success because the "celebrated" breadfruit remained alive, its reputation untainted by its failure to produce a single fruit.[46]

For the society the breadfruit was less a plausible replacement for corn, the kingdom's staple, than an emblem of Guatemala's participation in a global conversation about botany, acclimatization and enlightenment. As scholars have repeatedly observed, colonial botany embraced far more than the practical quest for useful or exotic plants. It also constituted a symbolic display of legitimate governance.[47] In this spirit the presence of even a single breadfruit tree was heralded in Guatemala, the West Indies, Nueva Granada, Brazil, Tenerife and other corners of the Atlantic world, not because it provided a significant source of food but because it represented a commitment to enlightenment, political economy and the public good.[48] This is why in 1825 the newly formed Republic of Bolivia incorporated a breadfruit tree into its official shield. Its designers explained that the "prodigious" breadfruit symbolized Bolivia's natural wealth, just as the liberty tree they included on the coinage clearly proclaimed the new state's enlightened, republican ambitions.[49] For such statesmen, as for Joseph Banks and the Guatemalan society, the breadfruit's appeal lay less in its practical utility as a source of food than in its powerful ability to encapsulate, underneath its wrinkled skin, enlightenment, and, in the words of the Jardin du Roi's head gardener, "the happiness of mankind".

The Valuable Potato

Discussions of breadfruits often compared them to the plant that in Europe was the object of the most intense promotion during the eighteenth century: the potato. John Ellis's 1775 pro-breadfruit pamphlet likened the fruit to "the potatoe-bread made in the West of England". In his assessment of the quantity of starch yielded by West Indian tubers, the physician James Clark carefully compared each to potatoes, which he treated as a bench-mark for nutritition.[50] Breadfruit, its advocates hoped, might come to play a role in Africa or the Caribbean comparable to that of the potato in Europe. But might not the potato itself fulfil this role? Why make recourse to distant, unfamiliar plants when a suitable food was already close to hand?

The potato's journey from the Andean highlands around the globe mostly predated its intense promotion in Europe in the late eighteenth century, when it was widely touted as an ideal food.[51] By the early seventeenth century, potatoes were cultivated and eaten in many parts of Europe; British, Iberian and French navigators moreover left a trail of potatoes as they voyaged across the globe.[52] By the eighteenth century, potatoes were completely naturalized in many parts of the extra-European world; both the Iroquois in upstate New York and ladies in New England consumed potatoes, while visitors to Botany Bay were astonished by the settlement's flourishing potato plots.[53] To a significant degree, the potato established itself as an important global staple independently of the vigorous eighteenth-century pro-potato propaganda. This propaganda nonetheless suited enlightened savants in Spanish America and British India who were eager to demonstrate their commitment to the pursuit of useful knowledge and the public good. Their own potato schemes helped articulate a colonial vision of paternalist improvement, even if they had little effect on local diets.

The potato was the object of a sustained propaganda campaign in eighteenth-century Spain. Local economic societies investigated the potato's qualities, experimented with new varieties, offered premiums for the largest harvest, and edited treatises on approved horticultural techniques. Newspapers printed recipes for potato bread.[54] Charles III issued orders encouraging potato cultivation, and sponsored the publication of an entire book extolling the tuber, which was into its fourth edition by 1804.[55] All this was accompanied by a patriotic insistence that the rest of Europe was indebted to Spain; newspapers recorded with pride that it was "our conquistadors" who had brought this "precious fruit" to Europe.[56]

Organizations such as the Guatemalan society were familiar with the potato's lofty reputation in Spain. The society subscribed to Spain's principal agricultural journal, which reported regularly on the potato's merits and its promotion by states and economic societies across Europe.[57] The society's own publications translated extracts from the essays of the celebrated Count Rumford, famous for his low-cost potato soup. Likewise the *Gazeta de Guatemala* reprinted Spanish recipes for economical potato bread, although in Guatemala potatoes were in short supply and hardly provided a useful substitute for wheat flour.[58] At no stage, however, did the society make any effort to increase potato consumption, a major aim of analogous European organizations. As with its celebration of the breadfruit, the society's enthusiasm for the potato reflected its commitment to an Atlantic conversation about enlightenment. It did not form part of a practical project of dietary reform, but rather demonstrated the society's fluency in the language of improvement, public happiness and good governance.

The separation of the potato's importance as an emblem of enlightenment from its local relevance as a foodstuff is particularly clear in the case of Peru, where Spaniards had first encountered the potato in the sixteenth century. The Peruvian analogue of the Guatemalan society was the Academic Society of the Friends of Lima, whose members enthusiastically embraced the rhetoric of utility, reason and enlightenment. Their journal, the *Mercurio peruano*, returned repeatedly to the need to promote agriculture, commerce and industry, and displayed a keen awareness of the importance of natural history, in particular, to wealth and improvement. As the botanizing bishop of Trujillo observed in a letter reprinted in the *Mercurio*, knowledge of natural history and geography was vitally important to governance.[59] The journal likewise detailed the useful and unusual plants cultivated in Lima's botanical garden and drew pointed comparisons between Britain's ill-fated efforts to transport "the prodigious breadfruit" to Jamaica and Spain's numerous state-funded botanical expeditions around the world. Like its counterparts in the Iberian Peninsula, the Peruvian society lauded Spain's role in introducing the potato to Europe, which in its view helped to disprove hostile assertions that Spain's colonization of the Americas had contributed nothing the advancement of humanity. Viewed from this perspective, the potato was evidence of Peru's, and Spain's, contribution to knowledge and its participation in the community of enlightened states.[60]

At the same time, enlightened Peruvians could not have been less enthusiastic about potatoes when it came to eating them. In the Andes the potato had long been regarded by Europeans as a distinctly indigenous foodstuff. In one of the earliest descriptions it was called "a certain food eaten by Indians".[61] Potatoes were moreover important in Inca religion; the Jesuit naturalist and theologian José de Acosta, for instance, noted in his 1590 chronicle that Amerindians venerated certain oddly shaped potatoes, "which they call *llallahuas* and kiss and worship". Seventeenth-century writers such as the Jesuit chronicler Bernabé Cobo likewise stressed the potato's dietary and cosmological importance.[62] Potatoes were thus strongly linked to the indigenous world, and therefore, in the eyes of colonial elites, to poverty and incivility. The *Mercurio*'s discussion of the tuber largely reproduced this set of associations. "Paltry" and "miserable" were the words most closely linked to potatoes in its pages.[63]

Worse, some Peruvian writers suspected that potatoes were actually unhealthy. In the thesis that earned him a medical degree from the University of Montpellier, the Limeño José Manuel Davalos attributed the ailments typically afflicting Lima's residents to their overuse of local foodstuffs, most notably heavily seasoned pork, manioc and potatoes. Citing Linnaeus, Davalos noted that the potato "is a true species of *Solanum*, and hence it is easy to judge it to be suspect. If used frequently it produces a harmful effect even in small quantities".[64] The *Mercurio* likewise published warnings about the lethal effects of excessive potato consumption by travellers, especially when it was accompanied by spicy foods and alcohol. At best travellers could hope for indigestion, but a fatal dysentery was more likely.[65] Far from promoting potato consumption, Peru's community of patriotic savants discouraged its use, because of its links to poverty and indigeneity.

In fact, potatoes were a significant commercial crop in eighteenth-century Peru. As the *Mercurio* itself documented, they were an important item of commerce within the viceroyalty and between neighbouring colonies. Grown by indigenous and non-indigenous farmers alike, potatoes were traded up and down the Andes and along the Pacific coast, providing a handsome profit for those able to develop large-scale trade. They were not a miserable substance associated solely with deprivation.[66] Within the pages of the *Mercurio*, then, "potato" was at once a commodity, a despised food, and an example of Hispanic enlightenment.

The promotion of the potato in British India provides a final example of the potato's ability to index good governance, independent of its uptake as a dietary staple. As in Spanish America, colonists in India established local societies intended to promote good agricultural practice and general improvement. The Agricultural and Horticultural Society of India, for instance, was formed in 1820 to effect the "general amelioration of the agricultural condition of India". The society made a sustained effort to encourage potato cultivation, alongside its commitment to developing new commercial crops.[67] Its founding prospectus stated clearly that one "object to be pursued by an Agricultural Society is, *the introduction of new and useful Plants*". Already, its first president insisted, the promotion of the potato by a few colonists demonstrated the merits of this ambition. "How much more then", he continued, "might be accomplished by the joint efforts of a number of persons arduously engaged in the same pursuit!"[68] To this end the society established an acclimatization garden in which members grew potatoes alongside tobacco, apples, Seville oranges, nectarines, cherimoyas and avocados. They also imported seed potatoes from Europe and distributed them to members, who experimented with the effect of different manures and soils on the productivity of "this valuable vegetable".[69]

The society's ambitions were not satisfied by gentlemanly pottering. It wanted Indians too to grow European vegetables. Using a long-established technique, the society sponsored prizes for the cultivation of potatoes, peas, cauliflowers and other plants by "native farmers". While such incentives were aimed in part at remedying the "deplorable lack of good produce" in the markets that provisioned their own kitchens, their goal was to induce Indians not simply to grow but also to eat potatoes and cauliflowers. The society therefore conducted questionnaires on the tuber's reception among India's different religious communities, and was pleased when particular villages embraced the potato.[70] It regarded these enterprises as an uphill struggle against the "ignorance or mistaken ideas of the natives relative to those things which concern their own interests", but was confident overall that it was working to increase happiness and improve the well-being of India's rural population. For the Indian society, efforts to encourage potato consumption provided vivid evidence of the beneficent intentions of colonists, and also of the obstinate refusal of "native farmers" to embrace enterprises so clearly in their own interest.[71]

As David Arnold has shown, the society could count some modest successes in their agricultural programme, but the dissemination of the potato was not one of them. Well before it embarked on its promotional scheme, "this salutary and useful root" had already attained the status of a commercial crop in Calcutta, the western Deccan and elsewhere, spread in part by the tastes of the British troops garrisoned there. The society's activities did little to alter this situation.[72] Far more lasting was its local articulation and development of the discourse of improvement, and the perception of India as a derelict region in need of agricultural renewal. Its promotion of the potato, and conviction that through such actions Indian peasants would experience a "happiness till now unknown in India", in turn, reflect both the global reach of the fascination with the potato, and also the strong conviction that the dissemination of such staples was a privileged means of promoting public happiness.[73]

Conclusion: "What Comfort for Them! What Happiness for the Nation!"

Promoters of new foods often observed that their schemes would result in an increase in public happiness. If poor people were to eat more potatoes, commented a French advocate, their healthier bodies could better contribute to the glory and prosperity of the state: "What comfort for them! What happiness for the Nation!".[74] Since root vegetables were a superior foodstuff, their greater consumption within Spain would bring every possible benefit, insisted the country's leading agricultural journal. "What a simple means of promoting national happiness!", it concluded.[75] Discussing George III's support for the breadfruit venture, the superintendent of the St. Vincent botanical garden waxed lyrical: no undertaking, he proclaimed, was "more pregnant with benevolence" than that which, "while it increased the comforts and means of subsistence, multiplied, at the same time, the happiness and numbers of mankind".[76] Happiness both individual and public was thus enhanced by the introduction of these foods.

That it was everyone's duty to promote happiness – the "great goal of the century" – was universally accepted.[77] Indeed, the promotion of public happiness was not only an obligation incumbent on all individuals but also constituted the highest aim of government. "It is undeniable, or at least I have reason to believe that in this enlightened century it is a universally recognised truth, that the first object of any government is to make its people happy", stated the Marquis de Chastellux in a treatise on happiness.[78] In short, to disseminate better foods was to spread happiness, the fundamental aim and purpose of existence, in the view of many philosophers of all political stripes.

The power of this assemblage linking nutritious food, good governance and happiness is reflected in the persistent eighteenth-century efforts to quantify it. Quantification, that "quintessential form of modern thought", which spread rapidly across many areas of eighteenth-century life from cookbooks to forestry, offered an authoritative new language for analyzing the world.[79] Presenting the components of happiness mathematically underscored the importance of their interconnections, as well as adding precision. The Irish philosopher Francis Hutcheson, for instance, produced a complicated arithmetical formula for measuring the relationship between virtue, evil and happiness, expressed as a series of equations. Jeremy Bentham's "felicific calculus" likewise sought to provide a mathematical basis for evaluating pleasure and woe. The quantifying spirit enabled the Marquis de Chastellux to construct an "index of happiness", which demonstrated that the inhabitants of regions with an abundant supply of wholesome food were the happiest.[80] Plentiful food led, mathematically and philosophically, to happiness.

Just as the new discipline of political economy oscillated between the individual and the nation as its points of reference, so happiness was theorized as an individual condition that occurred within a nation-state. The Scottish agronomist John Sinclair's "quantum of happiness", for instance, measured the happiness of a state by adding up the happiness of its inhabitants.[81] In their small way, even the Junta's foundlings formed part of the population; their individual happiness therefore contributed to their country's overall happiness, because happiness was both a personal and a national good. This did not mean that philosophers disdained the well-being of foreigners, or that public-spirited individuals did not dream of increasing the happiness of all humankind. The natural unit of measure for public happiness, however, was rarely the entire globe. Rather, whether an action increased happiness was generally determined by considering its impact on the population of an individual country. The New England Congregationalist minister Timothy Dwight indeed treated the terms "public happiness" and "national happiness" as synonymous in his own attempts to calculate levels of felicity.[82] The public of *félicité publique* was the population of the nation-state, not the whole world.

What place did colonies occupy in this felicific framework? Were they part of the public whose well-being statesmen and philosophers championed? In the cold logic of colonialism the answer was probably no. Modern colonies, explained the *Encyclopédie ou Dictionnaire raisonné des sciences, des arts et des métiers*, "are established solely to benefit the metropole".[83] From this perspective, metropolitan happiness contributed to – indeed, constituted – the nation's quantum of happiness, but colonial happiness did not. Colonies could perhaps be seen as happiness "ghost acres" – extra-territorial regions that supplied essential commodities to the metropolis, whose own needs were not taken into account. Critics of mercantilism such as James Mill made precisely this point when they argued against the colonial system. Because it failed to account for the well-being of colonists, colonialism in reality diminished the net "quantity of happiness", in his estimation. Advocates of colonial reform in turn reminded ministers that because colonies were in fact "art of the metropolis", the state was responsible for ensuring happiness in both zones. The geography of happiness, and the happiness entitlement of colonists, thus formed part of the larger debate about the benefits of colonialism.[84]

The communities of enlightened colonial writers considered here did not doubt that they, and their homelands, were entitled to happiness. Writers from across the colonial world composed treatises, drafted proposals and discussed among themselves the ways in which they might promote *félicité publique*. The Guatemalan society insisted that its principal aim, underpinning all its activities, was "the happiness of the nation", by which it meant the kingdom of Guatemala.[85] Such organizations were less certain about the happiness entitlement of the "workers and black people" who attracted the attention of breadfruit and potato promoters. Did their well-being contribute to the aggregate happiness of Guatemala or India? Colonial writers equivocated, sometimes insisting, in the words of the Indian society, that their efforts were directed at augmenting the "general happiness" of native peoples, while at the same time displaying scant interest in matters far more likely to improve well-being than the distribution of seed potatoes. Indeed, the experimental potato plots of the Calcutta botanic garden were constructed on lands confiscated from locals.[86] Ultimately, it was the society's well-being that mattered to India's overall index of happiness, not that of "natives". For these colonial writers, the enthusiastic celebration of nutritious foods was a way to affirm their own place within the geography of happiness, regardless of the practical impact of their gestures of nutritional largesse.

In his writings on population Thomas Malthus insisted that food was closely linked to "human happiness". Colonial spaces, Alison Bashford and Joyce Chaplin have shown, were central to his analysis, because neither Malthus nor his critics believed it was possible to assess the relationship between food, population growth and public happiness without addressing colonial spaces and colonial peoples (Bashford and Chaplin 2016). Breadfruit, potatoes, political economy and happiness were indeed entangled in the enlightened imagination in ways that both reflected and transcended food's actual ability to nourish. It was perhaps for this reason that posterity's most famous proponent of the pursuit of happiness, Thomas Jefferson, was so enthusiastic about his own role in disseminating new foodstuffs. Looking back on his contributions to the nation he helped to found, he concluded with satisfaction that his efforts had not been negligible. In his list of achievements he recorded his promotion of new foods, and concluded: "The greatest service which can be rendered any country is to add an useful plant to its culture; especially a bread grain".[87] Jefferson's comments reflect the wider faith in the transformative effects of new foods on the body politic. These effects were best measured not through actual changes in eating practices, but rather in the nation's quantum of happiness, which was destined to rise even if, through "some unaccountable indifference", these new foods did not enjoy the reception to which their immense nutritional qualities entitled them. The British government's 2010 embrace of gross national happiness should remind us of the enduring power of these eighteenth-century shell games.[88]

Notes

1. This research has been carried out within the framework of the project HAR2014–53797-P "Globalización Ibérica: Redes entre Asia y Europa y los cambios en las pautas de Consumo en Latinoamérica" [Iberian Globalization: Networks between Asia and Europe and Changes in Consumption Patterns in Latin America] financed by Ministerio de Economía y Competitividad, Spain, of which the principal investigator is Bartolomé Yun-Casalilla.
   It is a pleasure to thank Kenneth Banks, Betsy Cazden, Elizabeth Earle, Gretchen Henderson, Dennis Landis, Cinthia Otto, Ana Maria Proserpio, Elena Serrano, Cristobal Silva and Carmen Soares for advice and assistance in tracking down documents. I am also immensely grateful to the John Carter Brown Library for providing the fellowship, and stimulating ambiance, that led me to breadfruits. This chapter first appeared in the *History Workshop Journal* 84 (2017), 170–93. I am grateful to the editors at *HWJ* for allowing it to be reprinted here.
2. Bryan Edwards, *The History, Civil and Commercial, of the British Colonies in the West Indies* (London, 1793), vol. 1, 13.
3. Pascual Mora to Junta de Damas, [Madrid], 20 September 1817, Archivo Regional de la Comunidad de Madrid, Madrid, box 8342/7, Pascual Mora, *El hombre en la primera época de su vida* (Madrid, 1827), vol. 1, 239–44; Sherwood 1988, 197–210; Serrano 2012, 49–63.
4. For peanuts, etc., see Tabares de Ulloa [1800] 1997; Antonio Targioni Tozzetti, *Cenni storici sulla introduzione di varie piante nell'agricoltura ed orticoltura Toscana* (Florence, 1853), 46; Hamy 1905, 42; Koerner 1999; Zilberstein 2015.

5. William Buchan, *Observations Concerning the Diet of the Common People* (London, 1797), 32.
6. Crosby 1972; Sucheta Mazumdar 1999; Carney 2001; McCann 2005; Carney and Rosomoff 2009; Spary 2012, 2014.
7. Galloway 1979; Miller and Reill 1996; McClellan III and Regourd 2000; Drayton 2002; Spary 2000; Touchet 2004; Castro Gómez 2005; Schiebinger and Swan 2005; De Vos 2007; Schiebinger 2009.
8. Casimiro Gómez Ortega, *Instrucción sobre el modo más seguro y económico de transportar plantas vivas por mar y tierra a los paises mas distantes* (Madrid, 1779), 41–42.
9. McClellan III and Regourd, "The Colonial Machine: French Science and Colonization in the Ancien Regime," *Osiris* 15 (2000); Kapil Raj, "Colonial Encounters and the Forging of New Knowledges and National Identities: Great Britain and India, 1760–1850," *Osiris* 15 (2000); Jorge Cañizares Esguerra 2006; McClellan III 2010; Roberts 2009; Sebastian Conrad 2012, 2016, 76.
10. Jean Baptiste du Tertre, *Histoire générale des isles de Christophe, de la Guadeloupe, de la Martinique, et autres dans l'Amérique* (Paris, 1654), 151–52; Hans Sloan, *A Voyage to the Islands Madera, Barbados, Nieves, S. Christophers and Jamaica* (London, 1707), vol. 1, 253–54; William Wright, "An Account of the Medicinal Plants Growing in Jamaica," *London Medical Journal* 8, no. 3 (1787): 269–70; Martín de Sessé y Lacasta and José Mariano Mociño y Losada, *Plantae Novae Hispaniae, c.1804* (Mexico City, 1893 [c. 1804]), 1; Robert Richardson, *Some Account of the Indian Arrow-Root, Produced and Manufactured on the Islands of Bermuda* (London, 1809) and Handler 1971.
11. For arrowroot in invalid and infant feeding, see, for instance, Michael Underwood, *A Treatise on the Disorders of Childhood and Management of Infants from the Birth* (London, 1797), vol. 1, 153. For botanical description, see Charles Plumier, *Nova Plantarum Americanarum Genera* (Paris, 1703), 16; Philip Miller, *The Gardener's Kalendar* (London, 1739), 296; Carl Linnaeus, *Species Plantarum* (Stockholm, 1762), vol. 1, 203; Sessé y Lacasta and Mociño y Losada, *Plantae Novae Hispaniae*, 1; and for its presence in botanical gardens, Isaac Rand, *Horti Medici Chelseiani* (London, 1739), 125; Johan Nowodworsky, *Elenchus Plantarum* (Prague, 1804), 39; Augustin Pyrame de Candolle, *Catalogus Plantarum Horti Botanici Monspelliensis* (Montpellier, 1813), 41.
12. Pedro Rodríguez de Campomanes, *Discurso sobre el fomento de la industria popular* (Madrid, 1774), 136; Bernardo Ward, *Proyecto económico, en que se proponen varias providencias, dirigidas á promover los intereses de España* (Madrid, 1779), 70, 196; José del Campillo y Cosío, *Nuevo sistema de gobierno económico para la América* (Madrid, 1789), 17. On populationist discourse, see Foucault 2009; Riley 1985; Charbit 2011; Bashford and Chaplin 2016.
13. Joaquín Xavier de Uriz, *Causas prácticas de la muerte de los niños expósitos en sus primeros años* (Pamplona, 1801), vol. 1, 85.
14. Jean-François Melon, *Essai politique sur le commerce* (n.p., 1736), 12; Claude-Marc-Antoine Varenne de Béost, *La cuisine des pauvres* (Dijon, 1772), 50.
15. Antoine Augustin Parmentier, *Les pommes de terre, considérées relativement à la santé & à l'économie* (Paris, 1781), 3–4.
16. West-India Planter, *Remarks on the Evidence Delivered on the Petition presented by the West-India Planters and Merchants* (London, 1777), 35;

Thomas Ryder, *Some Account of the Maranta, or Indian Arrow-Root* (London, 1796), 18–19.

17. On nineteenth-century evaluations of food energy, see Rabinbach 1992 and Carpenter 1994.
18. Antoine Augustin Parmentier, *Traité sur la culture et les usages des pommes de terre, de la patate, et du topinambour* (Paris, 1789), 257; Frederick Morton Eden 2011 [1797], vol. 1, p. 533; Mandelblatt 2007; Muldrew 2011.
19. James Clark, "An Account of Some Experiments Made with a View to Ascertain the Comparative Qualities of Amylaceous Matter, Yielded by the Different Vegetables Most Commonly in Use in the West Indian Islands," in *Medical Facts and Observations* (London, 1797), 304–7. Carpenter 1994, *Protein and Energy*, reviews scientific debates over nutritiveness.
20. Clark, "An Account of Some Experiments Made with a View to Ascertain the Comparative Qualities of Amylaceous Matter, Yielded by the Different Vegetables Most Commonly in Use in the West Indian Islands," 305–7.
21. Proceedings of the governor-general . . . relative to the establishment of a botanical garden in Calcutta, 1786, British Library, London (henceforth BL) IOR H/Misc/799; Robert Kyd to the Court of Directors, 1786, in Chambers, vol. 2, 2008, 113–16; Mackay 1985, 177; Drayton 2002, 118–20.
22. Joseph Banks to Henry Dundas, 1787, *IPCJB*, vol. 2, 205. On the Bengal famine, see Arnold 1999.
23. John Ellis, 1775, *A Description of the Mangostan and the Bread-Fruit*, London, pp. 11 and 13. "From the health & strength of whole nations whose principal food it is, I don't scruple to call it one of the most useful vegetables in the world", noted the botanist Daniel Solander: Solander to John Ellis, 1776, in Duyker and Tingbrand 1995, 363–64.
24. Hinton East to Joseph Banks, 1784, *IPCJB*, vol. 2, 62–63. The Kingston *Royal Gazette*, 9 February 1793, likewise predicted that the plants would come to provide "the chief article of sustenance for our negroes".
25. Banks 1962, vol. 1, 341. See also George Vancouver to Joseph Banks, 1787, *IPCJB*, vol. 2, 218–20.
26. Marshall 1993; Tobin 2004, for provision grounds; Beckert and Rothman 2016, for capitalist logics.
27. Alexander Anderson to Joseph Banks, 1793; James Wiles to Joseph Banks, 1793; Alexander Anderson to Joseph Banks, 1796; all in *IPCJB*, vol. 4, 132, 181, 371–72; David Collins, *Practical Rules for the Management and Medical Treatment of the Negro Slaves in the Sugar Colonies* (London, 1803), 111–12; John Stewart, *An Account of Jamaica and Its Inhabitants* (London, 1808), 99–101; Landsdown Guilding, *An Account of the Botanic Garden in the Island of St. Vincent from Its Establishment to the Present Time* (Glasgow, 1825), 13, 32; Dening 1992, 77.
28. Spary and White 2004; De Loughrey 2007, for irony; Lambert 2005, for the "planter ideal".
29. Johann Friedrich Blumenbach to Joseph Banks, 1794, *IPCJB*, vol. 4, p. 214.
30. *Affiches américaines*, Port-au-Prince, March 1, 1788, 107, October 18, 1788, 522, December 18, 1788, 628; *Supplément aux Affiches américaines, Feuille du Cap-François*, November 22, 1788, 1,006; Médéric Louis Elie Moreau de Saint Méry, *Description topographique, physique, civile, politique et historique de la partie française de l'isle Saint-Domingue*, 2 vols. (Philadelphia, 1797), vol. 1, 653; McClellan III 2010, 158; Spary and White 2004, 79–80. For North Africa, see *Annales de la colonisation algérienne* (Paris, 1854), vol. 5, 173.

31. List of trees and shrubs in garden of East India Company, 1789; William Ramsay to Joseph Banks, 1792; William Urban Buée to Joseph Banks, 1796; James Wiles, 1799; and William Urban Buée to Joseph Banks, 1799; all in *IPCJB*, vol. 3, 82–84, 386, vol. 4, 425, vol. 5, 57, 92–93; Thomas Dancer to Samuel More, Bath, Jamaica, 20 July 1794, Royal Society of Arts, London, PR/MC/104/10/240; Dancer to More, 1 February 1796; Guilding, *An Account of the Botanic Garden in the Island of St. Vincent from Its Establishment to the Present Time*, 34; Mackay 1985, 177; Touchet 2004, 63–64, 160, 188–90, 200.
32. Guilding, *An Account of the Botanic Garden in the Island of St. Vincent from Its Establishment to the Present Time*, 32 (first quote); Alexander Anderson to Joseph Banks, 1793, *IPCJB*, vol. 4, 132 (second quote). See also James Wiles to Joseph Banks, 1793; Alexander Anderson to Joseph Banks, 1796; both in *IPCJB*, vol. 4, 181, 371–72. Whether from "ignorance or incredulity", planters in Jamaica likewise viewed the plant as useless, complained the curator of the Bath Botanic Garden: Dancer to More, 20 July 1794.
33. Casimiro Gómez Ortega to Marqués de Sonora, Madrid, 17 April 1787, Archivo General de Indias, Seville (henceforth AGI), Indiferente, 1546; Casimiro Gómez Ortega, *Instrucción sobre el modo más seguro y económico de transportar plantas vivas por mar y tierra a los paises mas distantes* (Madrid, 1779), 41–42; Bañas Llanos 2000, 338–48. Spanish papers reported extensively on the breadfruit's progress; see, for instance, *Mercurio de España*, Madrid, April 1790, 304–6.
34. Fernández de Quiros, Pedro, *Historia del descubrimiento de las regiones australes, c. 1607*, ed. Justo Zaragoza (Madrid, 1876), 2 vols., vol. 1, 50–51; Corney 1913–18. The free-felling conflicts are in "Daily Narrative Kept by the Interpreter Máximo Rodríguez at the Island of Amat, otherwise Otahiti, in the Year 1774", in *The Quest and Occupation of Tahiti by Emissaries of Spain in 1772–76*, trans. and ed., Bolton Glanville Corney, 3 vols., vol. 3, 23–29.
35. *Espíritu de los mejores diarios*, Madrid, September 8, 1788, 349–51.
36. Real Compañía de Filipinas to Conde de Revillagigedo, Manila, 10 July 1789; Conde de Revillagigedo to Antonio Valdes, Mexico City, 10 January 1790; Marqués de Branciforte to Diego de Gardoqui, Mexico City, 12 January 1795; all in AGI, Indiferente, 1546; Juan de Cuellar to Antonio Porlier, Manila, 27 June 1791; Juan de Cuellar to Pedro de Acuña, Manila, 22 July 1794; both in AGI, Filipinas, 723; and Bañas Llanos 2000, 338–48.
37. On the society, see Brockmann 2013.
38. Gabriel Paquette 2007, 280. For patriotic societies in the Hispanic world, see Paquette 2008; more generally, Stapelbroek and Marjanen 2012.
39. *Periódico de la Sociedad Económica de Guatemala* (henceforth *PSEG*), Nueva Guatemala, 1 May 1815. See also *Noticia de la pública distribución de los premios aplicados a las mejores hilanderas al torno*, 1796, Nueva Guatemala; *Gazeta de Guatemala* (henceforth *GG*), Nueva Guatemala, 2 April 1798, 56; 21 April 1798, 88; Antonio García Redondo, 1799, *Memoria sobre el fomento de las cosechas de cacaos y de otros ramos de agricultura*, Nueva Guatemala; and the annual reports on the Society's *Juntas Públicas* published from 1796 to 1811.
40. *GG*, supplement no. 57, 1798, 28 February 1803, 39–40; 7 March 1803, 45; *PSEG*, 15 November 1815, 219; 1 February 1816, 298–99.
41. Nicolás de Arriquibar, *Recreación política: reflexiones sobre el amigo de los hombres en su tratado de población* (Vitoria, 1779), 150–61; *GG*, 28 February 1803, 33; 18 July 1803, 286–87.

42. *Correo mercantil de España y sus Indias*, Madrid, 10 August 1801, 506; *GG*, 28 February 1803, 39–40; 7 March 1803, 47; Brockmann 2015, 96.
43. *Correo mercantil de España y sus Indias*, Madrid, 2 November 1795, 698.
44. Conde de Revillagigedo to Antonio Valdes; Luis de la Concha to Marqués de Branciforte, Mexico City, 10 January 1795, AGI, Indiferente, 1546; Marqués de Branciforte to Diego de Gardoqui; Bañas Llanos 2000, 338–48. Spain had rejected an earlier offer from the British to co-operate in transporting the breadfruit: Samuel More to [Juan de Virio], London, 4 November 1786, Royal Society of Arts, London, PR/MC/104/10/72; Gómez Ortega to Marqués de Sonora.
45. *Correo mercantil de España y sus Indias*, Madrid, 10 August 1801, 506–8, 13 August 1801, 514–15.
46. *Octava junta pública de la Real Sociedad . . . de Guatemala*, 1811, Nueva Guatemala, 17–18; *PSEG*, 1 February 1816, 299–300.
47. Mackay 1985; Osborne 1994, *Nature, the Exotic, and the Science of French Colonialism*, Bloomington: Indiana University Press; Miller and Reill 1996; Spary 2000; Drayton 2002; Nieto 2001; Touchet 2004; Schiebinger and Swan 2005; McClellan III 2010; Cowie 2011; Bleichmar 2012.
48. *Semanario del Nuevo Reyno de Granada*, 1809, Bogotá, 1942, vol. 3, 15–20; Alexander von Humboldt and Aimé Bonpland, *Personal Narrative of Travels to the Equinoctial Regions of the New Continent during the Years 1799–1804* (London, 1814), vol. 1, 128–30; Henry Koster, *Travels in Brazil* (London, 1816), 36; Robert Southey, *History of Brazil*, 3 vols. (London, 1810–1819), vol. 3, 742; Guilding, *An Account of the Botanic Garden in the Island of St. Vincent from Its Establishment to the Present Time*, 13.
49. *Colección oficial de leyes, decretos, ordenes, & de la República Boliviana*, [1834], La Paz, vol. 1, p. 24.
50. John Ellis, *A Description of the Mangostan and the Bread-Fruit* (London, 1775), 14; Clark, "An Account of Some Experiments Made with a View to Ascertain the Comparative Qualities of Amylaceous Matter, Yielded by the Different Vegetables Most Commonly in Use in the West Indian Islands", 308.
51. For potato promotion, see Salaman 2000 [1949]; Talve 1981; Piqueras Haba 1992; Kisbán 1994; Gentilcore 2012; Spary 2014.
52. Carolus Clusius, *Rariorum Plantarum Historia* (Antwerp, 1601), 80; Olivier de Serres, *Le théâtre d'agriculture et mesnage des champs* (Paris, 1603), 513–14; Gaspar Bauhin, *Prodromos theatri botanici* (Frankfurt, 1620), 89; John Parkinson, *Paradisi in Sole Paradisus Terrestris* (London, 1629), 516–18; Johann Royer, *Eine gute Anleitung wie man . . . Garten-Gewächse . . . nützen solle* (Braunschweig, 1651), 104–5; Philip Gidley King to Joseph Banks, Norfolk Island, 24 May 1793, *IPCJB*, vol. 4, 129; Vandenbroeke 1971; Letouzey 1989, 177–78, 213–14, 228–29; Hawkes and Ortega 1993; Frost 1996; Mazumdar 1999; Salaman 2000 [1949]; Bravo 2005, 50; Gentilcore 2012.
53. *Agreeable to an Act of Assembly of the State of Connecticut, for Regulating the Prices of Labour* (New London, 1778); Anonymous manuscript cookbook, c. 1780, Schlesinger Library, Radcliffe, Harvard University (henceforth SL); Belinda Clarkson, manuscript receipt book, c. 1793, SL; Frost 1996; and Mt. Pleasant 2011, 473.
54. On the potato's promotion by Spanish economic societies, see Riera Climent and Riera Palmero 2007; Palanca Cañon 2011, 42–43, 64; Piqueras Haba 1992.
55. Henrique Doyle, *Instrucción formada de orden del Consejo por D. Enrique Doyle, para el cultivo y uso de las patatas* (Madrid, 1785); Henrique Doyle,

Tratado sobre el cultivo, uso y utilidades de las patatas ó papas, é instrucción para su mejor propagación (Madrid, 1797).

56. Guillermo Bowles, *Introducción a la historia natural y de la geografía física de España* (Madrid, 1775), 231; *Memorial literario, instructivo y curioso de la corte de Madrid* 121, (Madrid, 1790), 362–65; *Semanario de agricultura y artes* 17 (Madrid, 1805), 199. Writers elsewhere often attributed its introduction to Walter Raleigh.
57. On the *Semanario de agricultura y artes dirigido a los párracos*, launched with state support in 1797, see Larriba 1999. The Guatemalan society subscribed the following year: *Quarta junta pública de la Real Sociedad Económica de Amantes de la Patria de de Guatemala,* 1798, Nueva Guatemala.
58. *GG*, 14 June 1802, 145 (Rumford soup), 7 February 1803, 10 (potato bread); *Octava junta pública de la Real Sociedad . . . de Guatemala,* 1811, Nueva Guatemala, 23. On Rumford soup, see also Benjamin Thompson, "Of Food, and Particularly of Feeding the Poor," in *Essays, Political, Economical and Philosophical*, 3 vols. (London, 1797–1803), vol. 1, 189–299; Redlich 1971.
59. Baltasar Jaime Martínez Compañón to Charles IV, *Mercurio peruano de historia, literatura, y noticias públicas* (henceforth *MP*) 11 (Lima, 1794), 3; Soule 2014.
60. Francisco González Laguna, "Memoria de las plantas extrañas que se cultivan en Lima", in *MP* 11 (Lima, 1794), 165, 168–70, 171–77.
61. Domingo de Santo Tomás, *Grammatica, o Arte, que ha compuesto de la lengua general de los indios, del Peru* (Valladolid, 1560), 159v. See also Andagoya 1986 [1545], 138–39; Pedro de Cieza de León, 1553, *Parte primera de la chrónica del Perú*, Seville, book 1, chap. 40; Jiménez de la Espada 1965, vol. 1, 156, 234, 586; Acosta 2002 [1590], 148, 201–2.
62. Molina 2010, 62–63; Acosta 2002 [1590], 262; García 1981 [1607]; and Bernabé Cobo, *Historia del Nuevo Mundo* [c. 1653], ed. Marcos Jiménez de la Espada, 3 vols., Editorial Atlas (Sevilla, 1892).
63. "Idea general del Perú", *MP*; "La Province of Caxatambo"; and "Descripción de la Provincia de Chachapoyas"; both in *MP* 5 (Lima, 1792), 6, 190, 194, 225; Alonso Carrió de la Vandera, *El lazarillo de ciegos caminantes desde Buenos Aires, hasta Lima* (Cervantes Virtual, 1773), 301, 335; Joseph Ignacio Lequanda, "Descripción de Caxamarca," in *MP* 10, (Lima, 1794), 202; Francisco López, "Descripción de Porco," in *MP* 11 (Lima, 1794), 19, 29–30, 37–38, 63, 68–72, 77, 87–89, 92.
64. José Manuel Davalos, *De morbis nonnullis Limae, grassantibus ipsorumque therapeia* (Montpellier, 1787), 11–12. Davalos was obliged to matriculate in France because Peruvian universities would not accept those who, like Davalos, were classified as people of mixed race.
65. Panacio Montano, "Medicina práctica," in *MP* 1 (Lima, 1791), 45–47; Hipólito Unanue, *Observaciones sobre el clima del Lima y sus influencias en los seres organizados* (Lima, 1806), 153.
66. López, "Descripción de Porco," 101–2; Manuel Espinavete López, "Descripción de la Provincia de Abancay," in *MP* 12 (Lima, 1795), 131, 137, 145–46, 156–57.
67. Richard Temple, "The Agri-Horticultural Society of India," *The Calcutta Review* 22 (1854): 341, 342–50.
68. William Carey, "Prospectus of an Agricultural and Horticultural Society in India, 1820," in *Transactions of the Agricultural and Horticultural Society of India* (henceforth *TAHSI*), (Calcutta, 1838), vol. 1, 211–21 (quotations on pp. 216, 219).
69. *TAHSI*, vol. 2, pp. 23, 27, 36, 81, 175 (quotation), 253, 264, 265.

70. *TAHSI*, vol. 1, pp. 21, 235 (quotation), 237–38, vol. 2, pp. 30ff, 81, 253, 264, 265; Temple, "The Agri-Horticultural Society of India"" 356–58.
71. *TAHSI*, vol. 1, p. 8; Temple, "The Agri-Horticultural Society of India", 354–58. On the discourse of improvement, see Drayton 2002, and David Arnold 2005, 505–6.
72. Joseph Banks to the Court of Directors, 1789; George Sinclair, 1798; both in *IPCJB*, vol. 2, p. 396, vol. 5, p. 24; " 'Bazaar prices in Calcutta", June 1791, Robert Kyd papers, BL MSS EUR/F95/2, 193b; Minute of William Bentinck, 12 November 1803, BL IOR F/4/179, 5r – 6r; Benjamin Heyne to William Bentinck, Bangalore 21 January 1805, BL IOR P/242/73, 684–88; Whitelaw Ainslie, *Treatise on the edible vegetables of India*, 12 September 1810, BL IOR/F/4/379/9495 and Arnold 2005, 519.
73. *TAHSI*, vol. 1, 8.
74. Claude-Marc-Antoine Varenne de Béost, *La cuisine des pauvres* (Dijon, 1772), 11; Spary 2014, 181.
75. "Carta de un médico de Paris sobre la sopa económica del Conde de Rumford", in *Semanario de agricultura y artes* 8 (Madrid, 1800), 120, 141. Or see Henrique Doyle, *Tratado sobre el cultivo, uso y utilidades de las patatas ó papas, é instrucción para su mejor propagación* (Madrid, 1797), 5.
76. Guilding, *An Account of the Botanic Garden in the Island of St. Vincent from Its Establishment to the Present Time*, 12.
77. On the eighteenth-century pursuit of happiness, see Bruni and Porta 2003; Wahnbaeck 2004; McMahon 2006, 200; Paquette 2008, 56–92.
78. Marquis de Chastellux, *De la félicité publique, ou Considérations sur le sort des hommes* (Amsterdam, 1772), vol. 1, 15.
79. On the quantifying spirit, see Michel Foucault 1991; Frangsmyr, Heilbron, and Rider, 1990, 2.
80. Francis Hutcheson, *Inquiry into the Original of Our Ideas of Beauty and Virtue* (London, 1725), 163–78; Marquis de Chastellux, *De la félicité publique, ou Considérations sur le sort des hommes* (Amsterdam, 1772), vol. 2, 97–144; Jeremy Bentham, *An Introduction to the Principles of Morals and Legislation* (London, 1789), 26–27; McMahon 2006, 205–22.
81. John Sinclair, *The Statistical Account of Scotland* 20 (Edinburgh, 1798), xiii–iv.
82. Timothy Dwight, *The True Means of Establishing Public Happiness* (New Haven, 1795).
83. François Véron de Forbonnais, '*Colonie*', *Encyclopédie ou Dictionnaire raisonné des sciences, des arts et des métiers* (Paris, 1753), vol. 3, 650. "The purpose of the colony is to benefit the patria, to whom it owes its being". José del Campillo y Cosío, *Nuevo sistema de gobierno económico para la América* (Madrid, 1789), 24.
84. James Mill, "Colony", in *Supplement to the Encyclopaedia Britannica* (London, 1825), 22 (first quote); Cabarrús 1778 [1992], 109–10 (second quote). On the debate over colonies, see Winch 1965; Pincus 2012.
85. *Quinta Junta pública de la Real Sociedad Económica de Amantes de la Patria de Guatemala* (Nueva Guatemala, 1799), 1, 19, 26. Alcaide 1962, studies the society's embrace of happiness, "that magic word" (p. 134).
86. Proceedings of the governor-general and council, pp. 59–169; *TAHSI*, esp. vol. 1, 8, 31, 130, 220, 225.
87. Thomas Jefferson 1800, Summary of Public Service, In *The Papers of Thomas Jefferson Digital Edition*, ed. Barbara Oberg and J. Jefferson Looney (Charlottesville, 2008–16), vol. 32, 124. On Jefferson's concept of happiness: Wills 1978, 149–64, 229–55.
88. David Cameron, 25 November 2010, www.gov.uk/government/speeches/pm-speech-on-wellbeing.

Bibliography

Acosta, José de. 2002 [1590]. *Natural and Moral History of the Indies*. Translated by Frances López Morillas. Durham: Duke University Press.

Alcaide, Elisa. 1962. *La Sociedad Económica de Amigos del País de Guatemala*. Seville: Escuela de Estudios Hispano-Americanos.

Andagoya, Pascual de. 1986 [1545]. "Relación." In *Relación y documentos*. Edited by Adrian Blázquez. Madrid.

Andrews, Donna. 1989. *Philanthropy and Police: London Charity in the Eighteenth Century*. Princeton, NJ: Princeton University Press.

Arnold, David. 1999. "Hunger in the Garden of Plenty: The Bengal Famine of 1770." In *Dreadful Visitations: Confronting Natural Catastrophe in the Age of Enlightenment*, edited by Alessa Johns, 81–111. London: Routledge.

———. 2005. "Agriculture and 'Improvement' in Early Colonial India: A Pre-History." *Journal of Agrarian Change* 5 (4): 505–25.

Bañas Llanos, María Belén. 2000. *Una historia natural de Filipinas: Juan de Cuéllar*. Barcelona: Ediciones del Serbal.

Banks, Joseph. 1962. *The Endeavour Journal, 1769–1770*. 2 vols. Edited by J. C. Beaglehole. Sydney: Public Library of New South Wales.

Bashford, Alison, and Joyce Chaplin. 2016. *The New Worlds of Thomas Robert Malthus: Rereading the Principle of Population*. Princeton, NJ: Princeton University Press.

Beckert, Sven, and Seth Rothman, eds. 2016. *Slavery's Capitalism: A New History of American Economic Development*. Philadelphia: University of Pennsylvania Press.

Bleichmar, Daniela. 2012. *Visible Empire: Botanical Expeditions and Visual Culture in the Hispanic Enlightenment*. Chicago: University of Chicago Press.

Bligh, William. 2013 [1792]. *A Voyage to the South Sea for the Purpose of Conveying the Bread-fruit Tree to the West Indies*. Cambridge: Cambridge University Press.

Bravo, Michael. 2005. "Mission Gardens: Natural History and Global Expansion." In *Colonial Botany: Science, Commerce and Politics in the Early Modern World*, edited by Schiebinger, Londa, and Claudia Swan, 49–65. Philadelphia: University of Pennsylvania Press.

Brockmann, Sophie. 2013. "Surveying Nature: The Creation and Communication of Natural-Historical Knowledge in Enlightenment Central America." PhD diss., University of Cambridge.

———. 2015. "Sumatran Rice and "Miracle" Herbs: Local and International Natural Knowledge in Late-Colonial Guatemala." *Colonial Latin American Review* 24 (1): 84–106.

Bruni, Luigino, and Pier Luigi Porta. 2003. "*Economia civile* and *pubblica felicità* in the Italian Enlightenment." In *Oeconomies in the Age of Newton*, edited by Margaret Schabas and Neil de Marchi, 361–85. Durham: Duke University Press.

Cabarrús, Francisco. 1778 [1992]. "Discurso sobre la libertad de comercio." In Santos Manuel Coronas González. 1992. "Espíritu ilustrado y liberación del tráfico comercial con Indias." *Anuario de historia del derecho español* 62: 102–111.

Cameron, David. November 25, 2010. Accessed April 9, 2018. www.gov.uk/government/speeches/pm-speech-on-wellbeing.

Cañizares Esguerra, Jorge. 2006. *Nature, Empire and Nation: Explorations of the History of Science in the Iberian World*. Stanford, CA: Stanford University Press.

Carney, Judith. 2001. *Black Rice: The African Origins of Rice Cultivation in the Americas*. Cambridge: Harvard University Press.

Carney, Judith, and Richard Rosomoff. 2009. *In the Shadow of Slavery: Africa's Botanical Legacy in the Atlantic World*. Berkeley: University of California Press.

Carpenter, Kenneth. 1994. *Protein and Energy: A Study of Changing Ideas in Nutrition*. Cambridge: Cambridge University Press.

Carrió de la Vandera, Alonso. 1773. *El lazarillo de ciegos caminantes desde Buenos Aires, hasta Lima*. Biblioteca Virtual Miguel de Cervantes. www.cervantesvirtual.com

Castro Gómez, Santiago. 2005. *La hybris del punto cero: ciencia, raza e ilustración en la Nueva Granada (1750–1816)*. Bogotá: Editorial Pontificia Universidad Javeriana.

Chambers, Neil, ed. 2008. *The Indian and Pacific Correspondence of Sir Joseph Banks, 1768–1820*. 5 vols. London: Pickering & Chatto.

Charbit, Yves. 2011. *The Classical Foundations of Population Thought from Plato to Quesnay*. London: Springer.

Conrad, Sebastian. 2012. "The Enlightenment in Global History: A Historiographical Critique." *American Historical Review* 117 (4): 999–1027.

———. 2016. *What is Global History?* Princeton, NJ: Princeton University Press.

Corney, Bolton Glanville, trans. and ed., 1913–18. *The Quest and Occupation of Tahiti by Emissaries of Spain in 1772–76, told in . . . Contemporary Documents*. 3 vols. London: Hakluyt Society.

Cowie, Helen. 2011. *Conquering Nature in Spain and its Empire, 1750–1850*. Manchester: Manchester University Press.

Crosby, Alfred. 1972. *The Columbian Exchange: Biological and Cultural Consequences of 1492*. Westport: Greenwood Press.

De Loughrey, Elizabeth. 2007. "Globalizing the Routes of Breadfruit and Other Bounties." *Journal of Colonialism and Colonial History* 8 (3). http://0-muse.jhu.edu.pugwash.lib.warwick.ac.uk/article/230160

Dening, Greg. 1992. *Mr Bligh's Bad Language: Passion, Power and Theatre on the Bounty*. Cambridge: Cambridge University Press.

De Vos, Paula. 2007. "Natural History and the Pursuit of Empire in Eighteenth-century Spain." *Eighteenth-Century Studies* 40 (2): 209–39.

Drayton, Richard. 2002. *Nature's Government: Science, Imperial Britain, and the 'Improvement' of the World*. New Haven: Yale University Press.

Duyker, Edward, and Per Tingbrand, eds. 1995. *Daniel Solander: Selected Correspondence, 1753–1782*. Melbourne: Miegunyah Press.

Dwight, Timothy. 1795. *The True Means of Establishing Public Happiness*. New Haven.

Eden, Frederick Morton. 2011 [1797]. *The State of the Poor, or a History of the Labouring Classes in England, from the Conquest to the Present Period*. 3 vols. Cambridge: Cambridge University Press.

Foucault, Michel. 1991. *Discipline and Punish: The Birth of the Prison*. Translated by Alan Sheridan. London: Vintage.

———. 2009. *Security, Territory, Population: Lectures at the Collège de France, 1977–1978*. Edited by Michel Senellart. Translated by Graham Burchell. New York: Palgrave.

Frangsmyr, J. L., Heilbron Tore, and Robin Rider, eds. 1990. *The Quantifying Spirit in the Eighteenth Century*. Berkeley: University of California Press.

Frost, Alan. 1996. "The Antipodean Exchange: European Horticulture and Imperial Designs." In *Visions of Empire: Voyages, Botany, and Representations of Nature*, edited by David Philip Miller and Peter Hanns Reill, 58–79. Cambridge: Cambridge University Press.

Galloway, J. H. 1979. "Agricultural Reform and the Enlightenment in Late Colonial Brazil." *Agricultural History* 53 (4): 763–79.

García, Gregorio. 1981 [1607]. *Orígen de los indios del Nuevo Mundo*. Edited by Franklin Pease. Mexico City: Fondo de Cultura Económica.

Gentilcore, David. 2012. *Italy and the Potato: A History, 1550–2000*. London: Bloomsbury.

Guimarães Sá, Isabel dos. 2000. "Circulation of Children in Eighteenth-Century Portugal." In *Abandoned Children*, edited by Catherine Panter Brick and Malcolm Smith, 27–40. Cambridge: Cambridge University Press.

Hamy, Ernest Théodore, ed. 1905. *Joseph Dombey: Médécin, naturaliste, archéologue, explorateur du Pérou, du Chili et du Brésil*. Paris: Librerie Orientale et Amércaine.

Handler, J. S., 1971. "The History of Arrowroot and the Origin of Peasantries in the British West Indies." *Journal of Caribbean History* 2: 46–93.

Hawkes, J. G., and J. Francisco Ortega. 1993. "The Early History of the Potato in Europe." *Euphytica* 70: 1–7.

Jefferson, Thomas. 1800. "Summary of Public Service." In *The Papers of Thomas Jefferson Digital Edition*, Vol. 32, edited by Barbara Oberg and J. Jefferson Looney. Charlottesville, 2008–16. http://rotunda.upress.virginia.edu/founders/TSJN.html

Jiménez de la Espada, Marcos, ed. 1965. *Relaciones geográficas de las Indias: Perú*. 3 vols. Madrid: Editorial Atlas.

Kisbán, Eszter. 1994. "The Beginnings of Potato Cultivation in Transylvania and Hungary: Government Policy and Spontaneous Process." In *The Origins and Development of Food Policies in Europe*, edited by John Burnett and Derek Oddy, 178–91. London: Leicester University Press.

Koerner, Lisbet. 1999. *Linnaeus: Nature and Nation*. Cambridge: Harvard University Press.

Lambert, David. 2005. *White Creole Culture, Politics and Identity During the Age of Abolition*. Cambridge: Cambridge University Press.

Larriba, Elisabel. 1999. "Un intento de reforma agraria por y para las clases productoras: el *Semanario de agricultura y artes dirigido a los párracos*." *Brocar* 23: 87–117.

Letouzey, Yvonne, ed. 1989. *Le Jardin des Plantes á la croisée des chemins avec André Thouin*. Paris: Éditions du Muséum.

Mackay, David. 1974. "Banks, Bligh and Breadfruit." *New Zealand Journal of History* 8 (1): 61–77.

———. 1985. *In the Wake of Cook: Exploration, Science and Empire, 1780–1801*. New York: Crook Helm.

Mandelblatt, Bertie. 2007. "A Transatlantic Commodity: Irish Salt Beef in the French Atlantic World." *History Workshop Journal* 63: 18–47.

Marshall, Woodville. 1993. "Provision Ground and Plantation Labor in Four Windward Islands." In *Cultivation and Culture: Labor and the Shaping of Slave Life in the Americas*, edited by Ira Berlin and Philip Morgan, 203–20. Charlottesville: University of Virginia Press.

Mazumdar, Sucheta. 1999. "The Impact of New World Food Crops on the Diet and Economy of China and India." In *Food in Global History*, edited by Raymond Grew, 58–78. Boulder: Westview Press.

McCann, James. 2005. *Maize and Grace: Africa's Encounter with a New World Crop, 1500–2000*. Cambridge: Harvard University Press.

McClellan III, James. 2010. *Colonialism and Science: Saint Domingue in the Old Regime*. Chicago: University of Chicago Press.

McClellan III, James, and François Regourd. 2000. "The Colonial Machine: French Science and Colonization in the Ancient Regime." *Osiris* 15: 31–50.

McMahon, Darrin. 2006. *Happiness: A History*. New York: Grove Press.

Miller, David Philip, and Peter Hanns Reill, eds. 1996. *Visions of Empire: Voyages, Botany, and Representations of Nature*. Cambridge: Cambridge University Press.

Molina, Cristóbal de. 2010. *Relación de las fábulas y ritos de los incas*, c.1573. Edited by Paloma Jiménez del Campo. Madrid: Iberoamericana.

Morel, Marie France. 1976. "Théories et pratiques de l'allaitement en France au XVIIIe siècle." *Annales de démographie historique* 1: 393–427.

Mt. Pleasant, Jane. 2011. "The Paradoxes of Plows and Productivity." *Agricultural History* 85 (4): 460–92.

Muldrew, Craig. 2011. *Food, Energy and the Creation of Industriousness: Work and Material Culture in Agrarian England*. Cambridge: Cambridge University Press.

Nieto, Mauricio. 2001. *Remedios para el imperio: historia natural y la apropiación del nuevo mundo*. Bogotá: Instituto Colombiano de Antropología e Historia.

Osborne, Michael. 1994. *Nature, the Exotic, and the Science of French Colonialism*. Bloomington, IN: Indiana University Press.

Palanca Cañon, J. David. 2011. "Introducción y Generalización del Cultivo y Consumo Alimentario y Médico de la Patata en el País Vasco." PhD diss., Universidad del País Vasco.

Parmentier, Antoine-Augustin. 1781. *Les pommes de terre, considérées relativement à la santé & à l'économie*. Paris: Chez Nyon l'aîné, libraire.

Paquette, Gabriel. 2007. "State-Civil Society Cooperation and Conflict in the Spanish Empire: The Intellectual and Political Activities of the Ultramarine *Consulados* and Economic Societies." *Journal of Latin American Studies* 39: 263–98.

———. 2008. *Enlightenment, Governance, and Reform in Spain and its Empire, 1759–1808*. Houndsmill: Palgrave Macmillan.

Pincus, Steve. 2012. "Rethinking Mercantilism: Political Economy, the British Empire, and the Atlantic World in the Seventeenth and Eighteenth Centuries." *William and Mary Quarterly* 69 (1): 3–34.

Piqueras Haba, Juan. 1992. "La difusión de la patata en España (1750–1850): El papel de las Sociedades Económicas y del clero rural." *Ería: revista cuatrimestral de geografía* 27: 80–89.
Rabinbach, Anson. 1992. *The Human Motor: Energy, Fatigue and the Origins of Modernity*. Berkeley: University of California Press.
Raj, Kapil. 2000. "Colonial Encounters and the Forging of New Knowledges and National Identities: Great Britain and India, 1760–1850." *Osiris* 15: 119–34.
Redlich, Fritz. 1971. "Science and Charity: Count Rumford and his Followers." *International Review of Social History* 16 (2): 184–216.
Riera Climent, Luis, and Juan Riera Palmero. 2007. "Los alimentos americanos en los *Extractos de la Bascongada* (1768–1793): el maíz y la patata." *Llull* 30: 525–40.
Riley, James. 1985. *Population Thought in the Age of the Demographic Revolution*. Durham: Duke University Press.
Roberts, Lissa. 2009. "Situating Science in Global History: Local Exchanges and Networks of Circulation." *Itinerario* 33 (1): 9–30.
Salaman, Redcliffe. 2000 [1949]. *History and Social Influence of the Potato*. Edited by J. G. Hawkes. Cambridge: Cambridge University Press.
Schiebinger, Londa. 2009. *Plants and Empire: Colonial Bio-prospecting in the Atlantic World*. Cambridge: Harvard University Press.
Schiebinger, Londa, and Claudia Swan, eds. 2005. *Colonial Botany: Science, Commerce and Politics in the Early Modern World*. Philadelphia: University of Pennsylvania Press.
Serrano, Elena. 2012. "Science for Women in the Spanish Enlightenment 1753–1808." PhD diss., Universitat Autònoma de Barcelona.
Sheridan, Richard. 1976. "The Crisis of Slave Subsistence in the British West Indies During and After the American Revolution." *William and Mary Quarterly* 33 (4): 615–41.
Sherwood, Joan. 1988. *Poverty in Eighteenth-Century Spain: The Women and Children of the Inclusa*. Toronto: University of Toronto Press.
Simmons, Dana. 2015. *Vital Minimum: Need, Science and Politics in Modern France*. Chicago: University of Chicago Press.
Soule, Emily Berquist. 2014. *The Bishop's Utopia: Envisioning Improvement in Colonial Peru*. Philadelphia: University of Pennsylvania Press.
Spary, Emma. 2000. *Utopia's Garden: French Natural History from Old Regime to Revolution*. Chicago: University of Chicago Press.
———. 2012. *Eating the Enlightenment: Food and the Sciences in Paris, 1670–1760*. Chicago: University of Chicago Press.
———. 2014. *Feeding France: New Sciences of Food, 1760–1815*. Cambridge: Cambridge University Press.
Spary, Emma, and Paul White. 2004. "Food of Paradise: Tahitian Breadfruit and the Autocritique of European Consumption." *Endeavour* 28 (2): 75–80.
Stapelbroek, Koen, and Jani Marjanen, eds. 2012. *The Rise of Economic Societies in the Eighteenth Century*. Basingstoke: Palgrave Macmillan.
Tabares de Ulloa, Francisco. 1997 [1800]. *Observaciones prácticas sobre el cacahuete, o maní de América*. Valencia: Universitat de Valencia.
Talve, Ilmar. 1981. "The Potato in Finnish Food Economy." In *Food in Perspective: Proceedings of the Third International Conference on Ethnological Food*

Research, edited by Alexander Fenton and Trefor Owen, 277–82. Edinburgh: J. Donald.

Tobin, Beth. 2004. *Colonizing Nature: The Tropics in British Arts and Letters, 1760–1820*. Philadelphia: University of Pennsylvania Press.

Touchet, Julien. 2004. *Botanique & Colonisation en Guyane française (1720–1848)*. Cahors: Ibis Rouge.

Vandenbroeke, Christian.1971. "Cultivation and Consumption of the Potato in the 17th and 18th Century." *Acta Historiae Neerlandica* 5: 15–39.

Wahnbaeck, Till. 2004. *Luxury and Public Happiness: Political Economy in the Italian Enlightenment*. Oxford: Oxford University Press.

Wills, Gary. 1978. *Inventing America: Jefferson's Declaration of Independence*. Boston: Houghton Mifflin.

Winch, Donald. 1965. *Classical Political Economy and Colonies*. London: G. Bell.

Zilberstein, Anya. 2015. "Inured to Empire: Wild Rice and Climate Change." *William and Mary Quarterly* 72 (1): 127–58.

Part III

America and the Eurasian Products in a Global Perspective

10 Elites, Women and Chinese Porcelain in New Spain and in Andalusia, Circa 1600

A Global History[1]

José L. Gasch-Tomás

Introduction

At the end of the sixteenth century, the establishment of a pioneering trading route across the Pacific Ocean opened up a sea of possibilities to merchants in East Asia and Spanish America as well as to consumers in the Atlantic world, who began to receive Asian manufactured goods, especially silks and Chinese porcelain, in hitherto unknown quantities. This was the Manila galleon trade route, which was inaugurated shortly after 1565. Coinciding with the Spanish conquest of the Philippine Islands, and regulated from the 1580s onwards, two galleons made annual round-trip voyages between Manila and Acapulco, on the west coast of the Viceroyalty of New Spain. These two galleons transported silver and an annual maintenance grant to subsidize Spanish political structures and soldiers in Manila on their westward journey, as well as Asian products on the eastbound journey (Yuste López 1984).

A great deal of new studies have emerged in recent years into the production and distribution of Chinese porcelain worldwide in the modern era, as well as the history of the Manila galleons and material culture from a global perspective, although communication between historians has not always lived up to the demands that the development of such knowledge requires. The most important Chinese export center for porcelain was the city of Jingdezhen, located on the banks of the Chang River in the east of China. Jingdezhen was also the center of porcelain production for the imperial court. Accordingly, the city's craftsmen were experts not only in the production of ceramics, but especially in the production of high-fired glazed ceramics. The discovery of kaolin allowed ceramics to be fired at higher temperatures than the Europeans were able to achieve until the eighteenth century, giving the Chinese porcelain that characteristic intense white color resulting from the fusion of clay with kaolin, which was mixed with cobalt oxide from the fourteenth century onward. The use of cobalt resulted in porcelain with blue and white tones (Gerritsen 2012). From then on, blue and white Chinese porcelain became an item of interest to elite consumers worldwide, both geographically

DOI: 10.4324/9781003168058-11

and cross-culturally, setting fashion trends that brokered and connected trading and consumption patterns between far-distant places around the planet (Batchelor 2006).

One of those places was Spanish America, especially the Viceroyalty of New Spain, as within the realm of the Spanish monarchy it had a monopoly of trade with the Philippines through the port of Acapulco. This furthered the expansion of Chinese porcelain in this part of the world in the late sixteenth century, a development that had not yet taken place in Europe. The study of Chinese porcelain in New Spain has a long tradition with a predominant focus on its artistic aspects, its material culture and the uses of Chinese porcelain among the viceroyalty elite (Kuwayama 1997; Curiel 2007, 299–317; Bonta de la Pezuela 2008), or viewed from a historical perspective highlighting the trading relations between New Spain and the Philippines, especially in the eighteenth century (Yuste López 2007; Bonialian 2012). Other studies have endeavored to combine both dimensions (Gasch Tomás 2014a). Among these is the recent work of Meha Priyadarshini, who has done the remarkable job of tracking Chinese porcelain from its production centers in China to its consumption in New Spain (Priyadarshini 2018).

In this historiographical context, a number of key questions arise. Why did the Mexican elite want Chinese porcelain? To what extent did this occur in the Iberian Peninsula? Which social groups in the Spanish empire were interested in Chinese porcelain? What role did women play in New Spain and the Iberian Peninsula in creating a taste for Chinese porcelain and establishing consumption patterns in the empire? In an attempt to answer these questions, this chapter proposes a comparative methodology focused on the possession of Chinese porcelain by elite groups in two of the most important cities of the Spanish empire: Mexico, capital of the Viceroyalty of New Spain, and Seville, which enjoyed a monopoly of trade with America in Spain until the eighteenth century. The document base for our study consists of 104 probate inventories from Mexico City and 146 from Seville, in which the possession of Chinese porcelain in relation to other objects will be analyzed from a gender perspective (in other words, a perspective that takes into consideration the role of material culture in defining the femininity of the Spanish elite) and at the same time takes account of the social structure of both cities. The chosen chronological frame is the forty-year span from 1590 to 1630, an early period in the distribution of Chinese porcelain in the Atlantic world and the early years of the Manila galleons' commercial expansion.

Chinese Porcelain in the Spanish Empire

The aim of this chapter is to further our knowledge of the circulation of Chinese porcelain in the Spanish empire and, above all, to discover which socio-economic groups were the main acquirers, owners and users of Chinese porcelain in Mexico, one of the main places in the world outside China where this product was purchased and used. The comparison between the possession and use of Chinese porcelain in the city of Mexico and another Spanish city, Seville, located in Europe rather than America, will help to clarify by whom and for what purpose Chinese porcelain was purchased in Mexico around the year 1600. As previously mentioned, our primary source, although not the only one, used in discovering who owned Chinese porcelain in Mexico City (and in Seville) between 1590 and 1630 has been probate inventories. Their use in the study of material culture and consumption in the modern era represents nothing new. Probate inventories are the official documents drawn up by a notary with the assistance of an appraiser and clerk who recorded the assets and property of individuals after their death to organize the distribution of their estate. First used by modern researchers in the 1980s, and particularly in the 1990s, today they are recognized as solid sources for the study of material culture and consumption in the past. Nevertheless, as various researchers have underlined, a degree of caution is required in the use of these inventories as historical records. A first and well-known methodological caveat is the socioeconomic bias of the source. In European and American societies of the modern era, in which life for the majority of the population was fragile and their purchasing power was very low, only a minority either needed or could afford to go to a notary. The second caveat relates to the fact that inventories do not represent direct proof of the acquisition and consumption of goods, as exhibited by their sale and the deterioration of the product itself; the evidence they provide is indirect. Inventories reflect the possession of goods at a very specific moment (after their death), and from which point alone can we infer their use and consumption. A third methodological caveat arises from the previous proviso. Despite the fact that in those days life expectancy was lower and the mortality rate for all ages substantially higher than at present, it can nevertheless be assumed that many of the inventories belonged to people who were elderly or had at least attained a stage in life when they had acquired a certain quantity of goods.[2]

Mindful of these constraints, we can pursue the question of the scale of Chinese porcelain acquired by the Mexican and Sevilian elite classes, the socio-economic profile of those who acquired Chinese porcelain and whether these changed substantially over time. Existing bibliography comprehensively points to the social elite in New Spain as pioneers in the acquisition of Asian products and a much more receptive market for Asian goods than were European markets in the late sixteenth and early seventeenth centuries, largely due to its direct connection to Southeast Asia provided by the Manila galleons.[3] However, this conclusion proves insufficient when we take a closer look at the content of the Chinese porcelain stock in the Mexican inventories. A detailed analysis of the Mexican probate inventories that include Chinese porcelain in comparison with similar records from Seville may provide us with more far-reaching conclusions. In particular, an analysis that relates the number of inventories including Chinese porcelain to the total number of inventories and to the number of inventories listing other Asian products (not only porcelain but also Chinese silks, Japanese furniture, etc.) can offer a wealth of information on the role of Chinese porcelain in the material culture of the New Spanish elite, as well as trends in its acquisition and use.

The data in Tables 10.1 and 10.2 shows that the percentage of inventories with Chinese porcelain in relation to total inventories (both those that contain Asian products and those that do not), is much higher in the case of Mexico (26%) than in the case of Seville (8.2%). This can be very clearly seen in both of the chronological sets analyzed which, in addition, indicate a much greater liking for Chinese porcelain in Mexico than in Seville. While in the case of Mexico about one in four inventories contains porcelain from China, this proportion is reduced to less than one in ten in the case of Seville. If we look at information on the number of inventories that include Chinese porcelain with respect to the total inventories containing any Asian product, we see that the percentage is similarly higher in the case of Mexico (36.6%) compared to Seville (19.3%). Moreover, if we look at time periods (1591 to 1610 and 1611 to 1630), in both cases the figures are higher for Mexico. These figures, unlike the previous ones, would not necessarily have to be greater for Mexico than Seville. In other words, it is not simply a question of more products arriving in Mexico from Asia, as in this case the percentages shown relate to inventories containing other Asian products. The Mexican elite not only

Table 10.1 Inventories with Chinese Porcelain in Mexico (1591–1630)

	1591–1610	*1611–1630*	*TOTAL*
Inventories with Chinese porcelain	18 (31) (39,1)*	9 (19,6) (28,1)*	27 (26) (34,6)*
Inventories with Asian goods	46 (79,3)**	32 (69,6)**	78 (75)**
Inventories without Asian goods	12	14	26
Total inventories	58	46	104

Sources: Archivo General de Indias (Seville), Contratación; Archivo General de la Nación (México), Intestados; Archivo General de Notarías de Ciudad de (México).

Notes:

* The number in the first parenthesis of the row headed "Inventories with Chinese porcelain" indicates the percentage of inventories with Chinese porcelain in relation to the total number of inventories. The number in the second parenthesis of the row "Inventories with Chinese porcelain" indicates the percentage of inventories with Chinese porcelain over total of them with Asian products.

** The number in the parenthesis in the row "Inventories with Asian products" indicates the percentage of inventories with Asian products in relation to all the inventories.

Table 10.2 Inventories with Chinese Porcelain in Seville (1591–1630)

	1591–1610	*1611–1630*	*TOTAL*
Inventories with Chinese porcelain	8 (10,5) (34,8)*	4 (5,7) (10,2)*	12 (8,2) (19,3)*
Inventories with Asian goods	23 (30,3)**	39 (55,7)**	62 (42,5)**
Inventories without Asian goods	53	31	84
Total inventories	76	70	146

Sources: Archivo Histórico Provincial de Sevilla, Protocolos.

Notes:

* The number in the first parenthesis of the row "Inventories with Chinese porcelain" indicates the percentage of inventories with Chinese porcelain in relation to the total of inventories. The number in the second parenthesis of the row "Inventories with Chinese porcelain" indicates the percentage of inventories with Chinese porcelain over total of them with Asian products.

** The number in the parenthesis of the row "Inventories with Asian products" indicates the percentage of inventories with Asian products in relation to all the inventories.

purchased and used more Chinese porcelain than their Sevilian counterparts, but they bought and used more Chinese porcelain compared to other Asian goods than their contemporaries in Seville. As I will explain, the reasons for this are linked to the Mexican elite's liking for and use of Chinese porcelain, and not merely to factors relating to its availability within the largest distribution center of porcelain in the Viceroyalty of New Spain; in both Mexico and Seville Chinese porcelain was supplied and distributed by the same trading and family networks as other Asian products (Gasch Tomás 2014b, 2018, 153–202).

Nonetheless, a comparison of data in both tables by time period clearly demonstrates that both in the case of Mexico and Seville, the percentage of inventories with Chinese porcelain in relation to the total number of inventories with Asian products declines over time. This does not indicate that the elite in both cities buy less porcelain in global terms, but they buy less *compared to* other Asian products, including Chinese silk, Japanese furniture, screens and religious objects such as ivory manufactures, which had an increasing presence in Mexican and Sevillian inventories as time went on. In other words, the Mexican elite and their Seville counterparts began diversifying their tastes within the framework of material culture from Asia. Chinese porcelain, with a higher presence in percentage terms over the decades from 1591–1610 to those of 1611–1630, thus played an epistemological role in the opening of the market to Asian products in both societies to the extent that these were pioneering products, along with Chinese silk and other Asian goods, in American and European markets. This is especially true in the case of porcelain, which was a finished product with its typically Chinese decoration (despite the fact that over the years many of the designs that decorated the porcelain were commissioned and represented typically European decorative elements such as heraldic shields). Some of the most notable Chinese decorative elements are flowers typical of the east coast of China and Southeast Asia: lotus flowers and chrysanthemums, as well as gardens, pagodas, birds and even scenes with human figures (Carswell 1985; Kuwayama 1997; Priyadarshini 2018). Unlike porcelain, much of the Chinese silk that reached the American and European markets was raw silk or thread – in other words, undecorated. There were, of course, damask and decorated taffetas, but most of the Chinese silk merchandise was composed of raw silk or spools of thread (Gasch Tomás 2018, 131–39). In short, Chinese porcelain, along with silk, spearheaded the entry of Asian products into the Viceroyalty of New Spain and into Castile. They were the first products to be known by consumers who gradually developed a taste for Asia, and accordingly played an important role in the configuration of an Asian goods market in New Spain and later in Castile.

As previously indicated, one of the methodological caveats for historians to consider when analyzing probate inventories is that these inventories, by their very nature, are a reflection not of the consumption patterns of society as a whole but of the elite. It is therefore worth making an effort to gain further insight into the social groups most likely to acquire and own Chinese porcelain in New Spain and Castile.

In the case of Mexico, possession of Chinese porcelain was relatively diversified across the various social strata of the elite. Of course, the most powerful groups of the viceroyalty, including those holding office in the main viceregal institutions (Court of the Viceroy, Archbishopric, City Hall, Audiencia Real, etc.), had Chinese porcelain in their palaces. However, they were not the only ones. In Mexico many undoubtedly privileged social groups (Spaniards or Creoles), whose purchasing power was far below that of the most powerful elite of the viceroyalty, also bought Chinese porcelain, and sometimes quite extensively. These were individuals, men and women, whose social and career profiles could be classified as belonging to the "liberal professions" or the middle-class elite, including, for example, groups of people involved in the retail trade, merchants rather than large traders, as well as craftsmen and sailors.

Examples from the rich and powerful upper classes in Mexico whose Chinese porcelain identified in inventories decorated the rooms of their houses and palaces include the lawyer Pedro de Rojas, mayor of the Court of Mexico, who died in 1598; the doctor and *corregidor* Francisco Muñoz de Monforte, who died in 1607, and Dr. Salvador Cerón Baena, presbyter and canon of the Metropolitan Cathedral of Mexico, who died in 1621. Pedro de Rojas, who had a strong taste for Asian goods (15% of the value of his personal assets were products from Asia), possessed tableware consisting of about a hundred pieces of Chinese porcelain, among which were dishes of all sizes, bowls and saucers.[4] The presbyter had twenty-eight small Chinese porcelain plates and three *limetas* (bottles) from China.[5] Also among his possessions were three small plates from China, one of which was broken, and three more Chinese *borçelanas* (porcelain items). The small number of pieces owned by the presbyter, as well as the fact that one of them was broken, clearly indicates that they were his property and not the property of the Metropolitan Cathedral.[6]

Turning our attention to social groups in Mexico which, despite being privileged in the context of colonial society, did not have the same purchasing or political power as the upper-class elite, we find one in particular that stands out in terms of its significant acquisition of Chinese porcelain: the small traders. Within this group, shopkeepers and peddlers merit our attention, for not only among their properties were pieces of porcelain for sale, which appeared together with merchandise from their stores or in boxes marked for sale, but also items for their own use, as can be deduced from the fact that on the inventory listing they appear along with other household objects, such as furniture and cutlery, sometimes indicated by the notary as "used" goods. For example, among the goods that were valued on the death in 1592 of the shopkeeper Alexandre Mallón – according to the contents of his inventory, most probably a specialist in fabrics, including Chinese silks – there was a knife from China.[7] According to his inventory, Antonio de la Fuente, also a shopkeeper, who died in 1602, owned goods itemized as two golden plates, thirteen small plates, one large and one medium-sized dish, fifteen bowls (which, according to the document, were known as Chinese *cubos*) and a basin, among other Chinese porcelain objects, some of which were broken.[8] There are many other similar cases of storekeepers and small traders who owned Chinese porcelain.[9] Mexican inventories also include numerous tradesmen who, in some cases without exceptional means, made considerable efforts to buy Chinese porcelain.[10]

Within this group of relatively privileged individuals, we find a certain number of lower socio-economic standing, such as Claudio de Pontanaris, a surgeon with an extraordinary taste for Asian products, as evidenced by the fact that no less than 30% of the value of his personal property was composed of products from Asia, especially China. There was probably not a single room in his house that did not contain some object from China. On his death in 1607 he owned many *limetas*, cups, bowls and plates of Chinese porcelain.[11] Another such case was that of the innkeeper Domingo Álvarez (dead in 1610), whose possessions included a Chinese plate which the notary specified as antique.[12]

Finally, another group merits our attention on account of the commonality encountered, despite the disparity in the purchasing power of its members. This is the group of seafarers, sailors and people involved in the rigging, maintenance and navigation of ships and galleons. There were some sailors who were so wealthy that they owned boats with the royal privilege of forming part of the fleet of the Manila galleons. Others, however, were sailors whose circumstances were closer to poverty than a life of comfort. In any case, their common denominator was that they all owned a substantial stock of Chinese porcelain. This was the case of Antonio de Casamonte, chief pantryman on a Manila galleon, the *San Antonio*, who died in Mexico in 1598; he had two Chinese cups of exceptional quality, qualified by the appraiser and inventory notary as fine;[13] Domingo de Elguíbar, owner and purser of the galleon *Nuestra Señora de los Remedios*, who left behind a sizeable estate when he died in 1610 – the ship he owned was valued at more than 9,600 pesos – and according to his probate inventory had "ten porcelain items from China", but without any specific reference to the type of pieces;[14] Cristóbal del Huerto, a pilot from Seville who died in the Philippines in 1605, was the owner of ninety-six pieces of *lossa* (crockery) from China which were similarly unspecified[15]; and Sebastián Guillén (dead in 1616), a sailor, whose most prized possessions included twelve small plates from China.[16] The presence of so many individuals who owned a remarkable number of items of Chinese porcelain and whose way of life was closely linked to the sea is historically relevant. In the context of the sixteenth and seventeenth centuries, when limited transport determined strong price differences between markets (with significant increases in the price of products when transported from one market to another), sailors had easy access to imported products, such as Chinese porcelain.[17]

At the end of the sixteenth century and the beginning of the seventeenth century there were certain similarities but also major differences in the socio-economic profile of individuals in Seville with Chinese porcelain among their possessions. One of the similarities was that, as in Mexico, thanks to their mobility, seafarers (sailors, captains, etc.) possessed more Chinese porcelain than their peers in the same city, which tells us about the structure, limits and organization of international markets in the early modern era as well as consumption patterns in the Andalusian city. One such seafarer was Captain Gaspar de Guadalche, who died in 1600 and in whose house in the parish of Triana two Chinese bowls were found.[18] Another case is that of Juana Rodríguez de Oliva, who died in the same year and whose possessions included a plate from China.[19] She was married to Petty Officer Lorenzo Pérez, who was abroad when she died, as were her sons, who were in the Indies. Another case is that of Captain-General Juan Gutiérrez Garabai (dead in 1617), a Knight of the Order of Santiago and also captain-general of the fleets that annually crossed the Atlantic Ocean between Seville and New Spain. His ties with the viceroyalty must have been very close, because in his will he asked for one of his carriages to be sent to New Spain. This would also explain his ownership of several pieces of "clay and crockery from China", in other words, porcelain pieces not specified by the notary.[20]

Another relevant similarity with Mexico is the importance of the religious elite of Seville as owners of Chinese porcelain. These included notable members of the ecclesiastical hierarchy such as Juan Gutiérrez (dead in 1600), presbyter and administrator of one of the most important monasteries of the city, the Dulcísimo Nombre de Jesús, who had two cruets, nine bowls and five Chinese dishes on his desk located on the ground floor of his home.[21] Another group was the elite of the Inquisition, people like Antonio de Sarauz, secretary of the Holy Office in the city, who in 1611 left to his heirs many kitchen utensils and fine silverware, including a *caxon de lossa de China* (a casket of Chinese ware) whose specific contents were not identified by the appraiser and notary.[22]

As to the differences in social milieu in the two cities, the owners of porcelain made in China were much higher up the social and economic scale in Seville. Unlike what we have seen in Mexico, no tailors, hosiers, carpenters, manufacturers and artisans in general, innkeepers or individuals involved in medicine or surgery are recorded as having Chinese porcelain among their possessions. In Seville, owning Chinese porcelain was fundamentally linked to the most exclusive and powerful political and religious elite groups. Members of the Sevilian upper classes who owned porcelain were nobles who also engaged in trade, representatives of a process of social hybridization between the local landed gentry and traders, with the nobility contributing titles and the merchant classes providing capital in an era of commercial expansion (Vila Vilar 1991). One such person was Don Lope de Tapia (dead in 1600) who, in addition to belonging to the nobility, had an extraordinary estate, representing commercial dealings with New Spain, houses and inheritances and various levies and government bonds on sales and taxes in places like Seville and Carmona, among others. Among his movable assets were clay and earthenware from China valued at 8,500 *maravedís*.[23] Another outstanding case is that of the noblewoman Doña Beatriz de la Cueva (dead in 1611), who belonged to one of the richest families in Seville – she was the wife of the accountant Don Francisco de Torres Machuca – and had a collection of Chinese porcelain worthy of the richest families in New Spain, in which there were thirty-seven medium-sized Chinese earthenware plates, four large Chinese earthenware dishes and one large Chinese earthenware platter.[24]

Also belonging to this group were the bureaucrats and royal officials who had bought their positions in city administration, royal affairs or trade with the Indies. Among these was Dr. Arias de Borja, *oidor* (judge) of the Casa de la Contratación (1600), whose possessions included four dozen plates and bowls and a large porcelain dish from China.[25] Also in this group was Don Francisco Tello (1608), treasurer of the same institution and an influential figure in the city – he was the son-in-law of Diego de Portugal, an alderman known as Gentleman Veinticuatro in Seville – who had two bowls (*jícaras*) from China, one of which was broken.[26]

In short, the inventories indicate the extent to which there was more Chinese porcelain in Mexico than in Seville and how this was quite usual in the homes of members of social groups whose counterparts in Seville were neither familiar with nor acquired such products. By focusing our attention more closely on this particular aspect, other historical facts can be concluded. Bonta de la Pezuela states that Chinese porcelain provides us with two-fold information on the society in which it was used: firstly, through its decoration, to which we have referred above, and secondly, through its form (Bonta de la Pezuela 2008, 140). Our interpretation of the significance of Chinese porcelain in the colonial society of New Spain depends to a large extent on its use and the place it occupied within the home.

As to the pieces listed in the inventories analyzed, Chinese porcelain has consistently appeared in the form of plates, cups, bowls, *limetas*, sauce jugs, basins, cruets and even bowls (*jícaras*). Plates are the most frequently recurring pieces in the inventories because they are the principal items of any dinner service. Although historiography has repeatedly insisted that Chinese porcelain belonging to the same collection with the same decoration constituted an innovation in eighteenth-century Mexico, because in the seventeenth century such collections existed only in the case of silverware,[27] the information from the inventories analyzed seems to contradict this statement. The large number of dishes that appear together in the inventories of the Mexican elite, sometimes in the same box or located in the same place (for example, in a desk) seems to indicate that they were part of the same package or collection. Bowls were also a basic piece of any collection of kitchen and tableware and came in all forms, sizes and materials. These were hemispherical vessels without handles and not always very different from pots or deep pans, but in any event they were used to contain liquids (water, wine, liquors, chocolate) and solid foods. Somewhat less common, although equally important, were the *limetas*, as containers for all kinds of liquids. The presence of *limetas* – a typically Spanish bottle used since the Middle Ages – made of Chinese porcelain indicates the extent to which Chinese production was adapting to the taste of the Spanish elite. The same can be said of sauceboats and basins. The former, commonly in the shape of a boat and used as containers for sauces of all kinds – as time went on sauces used more and more Asian spices, such as cinnamon and pepper – were essential in the dining ware of the Hispanic elite. Basins, whose concave shape made them an essential item for barbering, were more common in the homes of the majority of the population, although made of poor materials, such as pewter. The fact that both of these items had been imported into New Spain from Castile since the beginning of the Conquest denotes the extent to which Chinese porcelain was making inroads in the markets of New Spain ahead of Iberian earthenware (Sánchez 1998); so much so that the mention in inventories of objects such as Chinese porcelain *castañas*, which are very likely sauceboats in the form of chestnuts, denotes yet another type of porcelain produced on an ad hoc basis for the Spanish American markets. Deserving of special mention are the *vinajeras* (cruets) which, even more than the *limetas*, denote an early adaptation of Chinese porcelain to demand in New Spain. These cruets were a typically Catholic product: they were small jugs used for carrying water and wine at mass, out of which the priest poured the liquids into the chalice (Heredia Moreno and López Yarto 2001). The use of Chinese cruets in Catholic ceremonies represented an innovation in the Spanish empire as early as the beginning of the seventeenth century.

We have reserved for last the question of the Chinese porcelain cups found in Mexican probate inventories, in some cases in substantial numbers, because their use was linked to a purely Creole practice that later spread to the Iberian Peninsula. This was the practice of chocolate drinking, adopted socially by the viceregal elites, who, as we have seen, were not necessarily the richest and most powerful members of society. Especially noteworthy is that this practice of pre-Spanish origin was adopted by the elite of the new colonial society using receptacles made in China. The inventories, in spite of their relatively early dates, clearly demonstrate that the practice of drinking chocolate and the use of cups and other china goods was firmly integrated among the elite. Thus, for example, the hosier Elvira del Rincón (dead in 1599) not only had four Chinese porcelain pieces including a saucer and a china bowl, but alongside them, a stick called a *molinillo* (or chocolate grinder).[28] The same is true for the Mexican tailor Alonso del Riego (dead in 1603), who, along with his eight plates and his china bowl, had several chocolate cloths and *molinillos* for making chocolate.[29] Del Riego not only ground the cocoa in his own house to make chocolate, but in all likelihood he and his family drank it out of china crockery. Another case – and there could be many more – is that of the pilot Cristobal del Huerto, who not only had a large dinner service comprising ninety-six pieces of china but also no less than eight barrels of chocolate.[30] The fact that pieces like Chinese gourds appeared not only in Mexican inventories but also in those listed in Seville,[31] and this despite the fact that the *jícara* was a type of American bowl that was used specifically to drink chocolate, only confirms that New Spain was the point of departure from which consumer practices that intermingled Asian and native American practices spread to the homeland. The absence in the inventories of other containers also used for the consumption of chocolate, such as *tibores* (jars), *mancerinas* (saucers with a ring in the center to hold a cup) or *chocolateros* (chocolate pots) (Priyadarshini 2018, 121–23), denotes that such containers came later or that around 1600 drinking chocolate was still associated with pieces such as *limetas* and *jícaras*.

Finally, in concluding this section, the term *loza* warrants special comment. The term is frequently associated with Chinese porcelain containers. There are, however, good reasons to believe that Chinese *loza* is porcelain. One of these is the fact that the term in Spanish refers to a trousseau of household objects, but it is not the only reason. There is no entry under the term *loza* in the *Tesoro de la lengua castellana o española* (1611) by Sebastian de Covarrubias. However, there is an entry on porcelain, which is defined as "a transparent mud from which vessels are made with many labors. It is brought from China, and it is said that the material from which they are made lasts in seasoning and for a long time" (Covarrubias 1611). A century later, the *Diccionario de Autoridades* includes the word *loza*, which it defines as "all that is manufactured from fine, lustrous mud, such as plates, serving dishes and bowls",[32] and the word *porcelain*, which it says is "a certain type of fine, transparent, clear, lustrous earthenware, regularly manufactured in China and Japan".[33] Lastly, the fact that clerks, notaries and appraisers came to use formulas such as *porçelanilla de lossa de China* (porcelain crockery from China), as we have seen in the case of the inventory of Doña Beatriz de la Cueva (dead in 1611), denotes the extent to which the term *loza* was employed in reference to Chinese porcelain goods and tableware.

The Role of the Women of New Spain in the Receipt of Chinese Porcelain

Spanish society in the Iberian Peninsula and colonial America was patriarchal. This meant, among many other things, that there were differences in male and female roles in relation to the home and domestic activities of the elite, besides the fact that men and women belonging to these elite groups socialized differently. Material culture has clearly demonstrated this. Many works underline how studies on domesticity and material culture can throw light on everyday life in the modern era from a gender perspective. The works of Marta Ajmar and Flora Dennis and Elizabeth Currie were pioneering in their field, as they were among the first to systematically present the domestic world of the wealthy urban elite of the Italian Renaissance, their decor and the role of women in that decoration (Ajmar and Dennis 2006; Currie 2006). In fact, authors such as Amanda Vickery have outlined how recent economic historiography has underscored the existence of a division of labor in relation to the household responsibilities of the Western elite during the early years of the modern era. Thus, while refurbishments, the provision of the main household fittings, the consumption of wine and other alcoholic beverages and everything related to carriages, horses and the rigging of horse carts were eminently masculine activities, everything to do with child care, the provision of tableware and utensils made of glass, silver and porcelain, food in general, bedding and interior decoration belonged fundamentally to the female domain (Vickery 2009, 10–20). The question arises as to what extent these categories and this general historical framework constitute a useful resource when interpreting the possession and use of Chinese porcelain in the Spanish empire around 1600.

First of all, we must consider whether the probate inventories identify a gender component in the acquisition, possession and use of Chinese porcelain in the cities of Mexico and Seville: did women from the urban elite have more Chinese porcelain than men did in the decades immediately before and after 1600? One way to address this question is to conduct an inventory analysis similar to the previous one, but with the introduction of a gender variable; that is, comparing the percentages of inventories of women and men with Chinese porcelain in relation to the total inventories and to those with one or more products from Asia. The conclusions we can draw from gender differences are certainly risky, given the source limitations and the fact that the vast majority of inventories relate to men. Nonetheless, attempting an analysis of this kind is worthwhile, because the methodological risks can be reduced thanks to the use of secondary sources.

Despite their limitations as a source, the data we can glean from probate inventories are evident. In Mexico, the possession of Asian products and Chinese porcelain in particular was strongly feminized at the close of the sixteenth century and the beginning of the seventeenth century. Ownership of Chinese porcelain with respect to the total of inventories and inventories with Asian products is extraordinarily high in the case of the women from the Mexico elite (40.9% and 42.8%, respectively, in the case of inventories for women, compared to 21.9% and 31.5% in the case of inventories for men; see Table 10.3). This is highly relevant, since this is the period in which Asian products began to become available in the New World. In Seville, however, the feminization of Chinese porcelain ownership is not as evident as in Mexico, at least in the chronological period under analysis (7% of total inventories and 21.4% of total inventories that included products from Asia in the case of women and 8.7% and 18.7%, respectively, in the case of men; see Table 10.4). This is most likely due to the fact that Chinese porcelain was still very scarce in the homes of the Sevillian elite at the beginning of the seventeenth century. The conclusion, therefore, is very clear: it is the women of the Mexican upper classes who are setting the standard in terms of the acquisition and consumption of Asian porcelain.

The socio-economic profile of Mexican upper-class women who owned Chinese porcelain was similar to that of men, ranging from women of exceptional wealth from the most influential families of the viceroyalty to women who were hosiers, shopkeepers or engaged in small businesses. Unlike Seville, where it is impossible to find inventories of women tailors or shopkeepers who owned Chinese porcelain, the notable presence of porcelain among women who were privileged but who are not among the most exclusive groups of the viceroyalty indicates to what extent the acquisition and management of porcelain from China was strongly

Table 10.3 Women's Inventories with Chinese Porcelain in Mexico (1591–1630)

	Women	*Men*	*TOTAL*
Inventories with Chinese porcelain	9 (40,9) (42,8)*	18 (21,9) (31,5)*	27
Inventories with Asian goods	21 (95,4)**	57 (69,5)**	78
Inventories without Asian goods	1	25	26
Total inventories	22 (21,1)***	82 (78,9)***	104

Sources: Archivo General de Indias (Seville), Contratación; Archivo General de la Nación (México), Intestados; Archivo General de Notarías de la Ciudad de (México).

Notes:

* The number in the first parenthesis of the row "Inventories with Chinese porcelain" indicates the percentage of inventories with Chinese porcelain in relation to the total number of inventories. The number in the second parenthesis of the row "Inventories with Chinese porcelain" indicates the percentage of inventories with Chinese porcelain over the total of them with Asian products.

** The number in the parenthesis of the row "Inventories with Asian products" indicates the percentage of inventories with Asian products in relation to all inventories.

*** The number in the parentheses of the row "Total Inventories" indicates the percentage of men's and women's inventories regarding all of them.

feminized in the viceroyalty. This is logical, given that in the Spanish world (both in the Iberian Peninsula and in America) the domestic arena was strongly regulated by gender. Whereas in households of the poorest classes the division of space between male and female was not so obvious, given the smallness of their dwellings, among the elite the division of domestic space by gender was patently evident. Thus, for example, if it was economically feasible, the home had to have specifically female rooms or areas, such as a dais or dressing table, which was located as far as possible from the entrance, generally in the inner rooms and close to the area designated for the servants and children. This contrasted with the space designated for the men, located in the more external parts of the house (Blasco Esquivias 2017, 69–70). Gender divisions of domestic space were linked to uses and consumption patterns in the home, which was clearly reflected in material culture. Thus, according to the morals of the time, it was not only appropriate that the woman should remain in the home, but, consequently, her socializing and consumption patterns were also linked to the home. In this connection, the role of women in the preparation and consumption of chocolate was essential, as was the role of other food-related products in the Spanish monarchy.[34] This being said, the women of the Mexican elite were pioneers in the Atlantic world in the consumption of chocolate and also in the use of Chinese porcelain containers for drinking it. Furthermore, for that very reason, they played a fundamental role in the exportation of Asian manufactured goods from the Philippines to Mexico (Gasch Tomás 2014b, 210–11). The case of Elvira del Rincón, the Mexican hosier who had

Table 10.4 Women's Inventories with Chinese Porcelain in Seville (1591–1630)

	Women	*Men*	*TOTAL*
Inventories with Chinese porcelain	3 (7) (21,4)*	9 (8,7) (18,7)	12
Inventories with Asian goods	14 (32,6)**	48 (46,6)**	62
Inventories without Asian goods	29	55	84
Total inventories	43 (29,5)	103 (70,5)***	146

Sources: Archivo Histórico Provincial de Sevilla, Protocolos.

Notes:
* The number in the first parenthesis of the row "Inventories with Chinese porcelain" indicates the percentage of inventories with Chinese porcelain in relation to the total of inventories. The number in the second parenthesis of the row "Inventories with Chinese porcelain" indicates the percentage of inventories with Chinese porcelain over total inventories with Asian products.
** The number in the parenthesis in the row "Inventories with Asian products" indicates the percentage of inventories with Asian products in relation to total inventories.
*** The number in the parentheses in the row "Total inventories" indicates the percentage of men and women's inventories regarding all of them.

several Chinese porcelain pieces as well as a *molinillo* for grinding cocoa and making chocolate, is not unique.[35] Other women from the Mexican elite, like María de Mosquera (dead in 1601), the shopkeeper María de Morales (dead in 1608) and Isabel Mexía (dead in 1614) had, in addition to Chinese porcelain containers, several chocolate cloths and napkins, which were used to wrap and store the cocoa beans.[36]

In short, the role of women in the New Spain elite was a fundamental factor in linking the Chinese porcelain market to new consumption patterns in the Spanish-speaking world on both sides of the Atlantic, and ended up becoming the norm across the entire Western world. Thus, for example, in eighteenth-century Britain, the women from the wealthiest families played a fundamental role in the ritual of tea drinking. In fact, the association between women and femininity, on the one hand, and the use of Chinese porcelain or Chinese imitation teacups, on the other, was such that it became satirized by misogynist caricaturists, who regarded it an example of female superficiality (Berg 2005, 234–45). As we have seen, the women of the New Spain elite were precursors in the definition and dissemination of consumption patterns for beverages regarded as exotic – at least for a time – in containers made of Chinese porcelain.

Conclusion

Despite the acknowledged importance of the transpacific trade and the Manila galleon commercial route between East Asia and Spanish America, even today the process of dissemination of Asian products in the

Atlantic world is still viewed as strongly linked to the trading companies of northern European countries and the trading that took place along the Cape of Good Hope route. This chapter has turned the spotlight on the reception and dissemination of Chinese porcelain among the urban elite of the Latin American city Mexico and their counterparts in the Iberian city of Seville, when Chinese porcelain was making its entry into the markets of the Atlantic world (around 1600).[37] The introduction of variables such as geographical location (Mexico or Seville), the social milieu of the owners of Chinese porcelain, their gender and the use of porcelain in the context of the social activities of these elite groups and their material culture, has provided an insight into some of the social and cultural mechanisms that facilitated the acquisition and dissemination of Chinese porcelain in the Spanish empire. The fact that the Mexican elite acquired Chinese porcelain prior to their Iberian peers represents nothing new in our knowledge of the subject. However, what is new is the fact that privileged social groups in Mexico who were not part of the most powerful viceregal elite – artisans, tailors, tavern keepers, shopkeepers and peddlers – acquired Chinese porcelain at a time when artisans and shopkeepers in an Iberian city as cosmopolitan as Seville had neither come across, nor had access to or had even rejected such products. Looking at the similarities, we see that those who acquired porcelain were the wealthiest members of both societies and included members of the Catholic Church hierarchy, as well as sailors and seafarers, who had acquired cosmopolitan tastes from living and socializing in several worlds and had easier access to imported products precisely because they were engaged in international markets. The answer to why Chinese porcelain was more widely extended across the social strata in Mexico than in Seville is not merely that it arrived in large quantities aboard the galleons from Manila and consequently was a cheaper product in America, however essential such factors may be. After all, these privileged classes could have rejected the product, as had happened in other instances with other products. In an attempt to further our knowledge of the dissemination of Chinese porcelain in the empire, we have seen how the differences rather than the similarities in the reception and porcelain consumption patterns of the Mexican and Sevlilian elite have clarified and provided explanations for the demand for Chinese porcelain. In fact, the taste, the identity of the American elite groups, their social make-up and the role of women in home decoration are all categories that shed light on the success of Chinese porcelain in America and its subsequent dissemination to Spain.

In Mexico, many more individuals from Creole social groups (artisans, small merchants, etc.) had Chinese porcelain, which is indicative of the role that the product played in defining the identity of emerging Spanish-American social groups. Chinese porcelain became part of the material culture of these Mexican groups, not only because it was a decorative object that conveyed the idea of access to distant markets through its distinctive decoration, but also because it was integrated into activities of pre-Spanish origin, such as the drinking of chocolate, which contextualized the social behaviour of the elite. The shapes of the Chinese porcelain containers in the Mexican probate inventories, which reflected their various uses, as well as their association with cocoa, the production of chocolate and objects related to chocolate consumption, indicate that Chinese porcelain became an object that influenced new patterns of consumption. In this process the role of women from the Mexican elite was essential. Once again, the comparison with Seville here is very significant. While in Seville there is no clear pattern linking women to the possession of Chinese porcelain, because women's inventories do not contain a higher percentage of porcelain containers than those relating to men, this is not the case in Mexico. In Mexico the pattern is very clear, as is its connection with home decoration and the possession of objects related to the consumption of chocolate.

Notes

1. This research has been carried out within the framework of the project HAR2014–53797-P "Globalización Ibérica: Redes entre Asia y Europa y los cambios en las pautas de Consumo en Latinoamérica" [Iberian Globalization: Networks between Asia and Europe and Changes in Consumption Patterns in Latin America] financed by Ministerio de Economía y Competitividad, Spain, of which the principal investigator is Bartolomé Yun-Casalilla. Also the PAI Group HUM-1000, "Historia de la Globalización: Violencia, negociación e interculturalidad" [History of Globalisation: Violence, Negotiation and Interculturality] which is financed by the Regional Government of Andalusia and its principal investigator Igor Pérez Tostado have cooperated.
2. Gasch Tomás 2014b, 196–97; De Vries 1993, 102–3; Yun-Casalilla 1999; Shammas 1990, 169–81; Ramos Palencia 2001, 21–52.
3. Schurz 1992; Yuste López 1984. For a summary of the bibliography on the subject, see also Gasch Tomás 2014a, 153–72.
4. Archivo General de Indias (henceforth AGI), Contratación, 259B, N.2, R.3
5. AGI, Contratación, 375A, N.4.
6. Archivo General de Notarías de Ciudad de México (henceforth AGNCM), Notario Andrés Moreno (374), Vol. 2474, fs. 308r-313r.
7. AGNCM, Notary Juan Bautista Moreno (375), Vol. 2483, fol. 199r-205r.
8. AGNCM, Notary: Andrés Moreno (374), Vol. 2467, fs. 465–486.
9. Catalina Villegas, who lived in a prominent district of the city of Mexico (the Amor de Dios hospital district) and was the wife of a small trader, Francisco Pérez, owned several Chinese porcelain goods, including eight small plates, another medium-sized plate and four bowls (AGNCM, Notary Juan de Porras Farfán (498), Vol. 3363, fs. 672r-678r.). María de Morales, who also ran a store in the capital, died in1608 and had 23 Chinese plates (AGI, Contratación, 298, N.1, R.5).
10. These included many tailors and hosiers. Notable examples were Isabel de Villalobos, who owned twenty-one pieces of Chinese porcelain, including plates and bowls, and Alonso del Riego. Apart from precious stones and silverware, he had a collection composed of eight plates and a bowl from

China. The former died in 1591 and the second in 1603. The group of craftsmen also included arms manufacturers like Cristóbal Gudiel and carpenters like Bartolomé Rodríguez, both of whom died in 1612. Included among the possessions of the former was a *castaña de China*, that is, a vessel or jar in the form of a chestnut tree, while the latter had nine Chinese plates. AGI, Contratación, 487, N.1, R.25; AGI, Contratación, 274A, N.1, R.11, 27r; AGNCM, Notary Juan Pérez de Rivera (497), *Libro Protocolos* 11, fs. 13r-20v; AGI, Contratación, 515, N.1, R.1.

11. AGI, Contratación, 503B, N.13.
12. AGI, Contratación, 509, N.9.
13. AGI, Contratación, 495, N.1, R.2.
14. AGI, Contratación, 510, N.1, R.4.
15. AGNCM, Notario José de la Cruz (106), vol. 718, fs. 34–53.
16. AGI, Contratación, 326B, N.3, R.7.
17. I have been able to demonstrate this with the use of refined statistical techniques (multiple regression) after creating a forecast model of consumption of Asian products that introduces several variables (Gasch Tomás 2014b, 189–221).
18. Archivo Histórico Provincial de Sevilla (hereafter AHPS), Protocolos, Leg. 16138, fol. 295r-297r.
19. AHPS, Protocolos, Leg. 3565. fol. 7r-10v.
20. AHPS, Protocolos, Leg. 12728, fol. 97–160.
21. AHPS, Protocolos, Leg. 14426, fol. 1098r-1105v.
22. AHPS, Protocolos, Leg. 8504, fol. 480–529v.
23. AHPS, Protocolos, Leg. 14437, fol. 895r-1035r.
24. AHPS, Protocolos, Leg. 12678, fs. 835–49.
25. AHPS, Protocolos, Leg. 13733. fol. 223r-225v
26. AHPS, Protocolos, Leg. 1147, fol. 269 ff.
27. Stated by Bonta de la Pezuela citing Howard and Ayers (Bonta de la Pezuela 2008, 144–45).
28. AGI, Contratación, 493B, N.19.
29. AGI, Contratación, 274A, N.1, R.11.
30. AGNCM, Notario José de la Cruz (106), vol. 718, fs. 34–53.
31. AHPS, Protocolos, Leg. 1147, fol. 269 y siguientes.
32. *Diccionario de Autoridades – Tomo IV* (Madrid: Francisco del Hierro, 1734).
33. *Diccionario de Autoridades – Tomo V* (Madrid: Francisco del Hierro, 1737).
34. Zamora Rodríguez 2014, 182–83. Indeed, the link between femininity (and servitude) and food processing in the modern era was not confined to the Spanish-speaking world but applied to the Western world in general (Ogilvie, Küpker, and Maegraith 2008).
35. AGI, Contratación, 493B, N.19.
36. AGI, Contratación, 298, N.1, R.5; AGNCM, Notario: Andrés Moreno (374), Vol. 2467, fs. 405–8; AGNCM, Notario: José Rodriguez (555), Vol. 3839, without a folio number.
37. See more details about this process in Gasch Tomás 2018.

Bibliography

Ajmar, Marta, and Flora Dennis, eds. 2006. *At Home in Renaissance Italy*. London: Victoria & Albert Museum.

Batchelor, Robert. 2006. "On the Movement of Porcelains. Rethinking the Birth of Consumer Society as Interactions of Exchange Networks." In

Consuming Cultures, Global Perspectives. Historical Trajectories, Transnational Exchanges, edited by John Brewer Frank Trentmann, 95–121. New York: Berg Publishing.

Berg, Maxine. 2005. *Luxury and Pleasure in Eighteenth-century Britain*. Oxford: Oxford University Press.

Blasco Esquivias, Beatriz. 2017. "Vivir y convivir. Familia y espacio doméstico en la Edad Moderna." In *La(s) casa(s) en la Edad Moderna*, edited by Margaria María Birriel Salcedo, 65–92. Zaragoza: Instituto Fernando el Católico.

Bonialian, Mariano Ardash. 2012. *El Pacífico Hispanoamericano. Política y Comercio Asiático en el Imperio Español (1680–1784). La Centralidad de lo Marginal*. México, D.F.: El Colegio de México.

Bonta de la Pezuela, María. 2008. *Porcelana china de exportación para el mercado novohispano*. México, D. F.: UNAM.

Brewer, John, and Roy Porter, eds. 1993. *Consumption and the World of Goods*, ed. John Brewer and Roy Porter. London: Routledge.

Carswell, John. 1985. *Blue and White. Chinese Porcelain and Its Impact on the Western World*. Chicago: University of Chicago Press.

Covarrubias, Sebastián de. 1611. *Tesoro de la lengua castellana o española*. Madrid: Luis Sánchez.

Curiel, Gustavo, ed. 2007. *Orientes-Occidentes. El Arte y la Mirada del Otro*. México, D.F.: UNAM.

Currie, Elizabeth. 2006. *Inside the Renaissance house*. London: Victoria & Albert Museum.

De Vries, Jan. 1993 "Between Purchasing Power and the World of Goods: Understanding the Household Economy in early Modern Europe." In *Consumption and the World of Goods*, edited by John Brewer and Roy Porter, 85–132. London: Routledge.

Diccionario de Autoridades – Tomo IV. 1734. Madrid: Francisco del Hierro.

Diccionario de Autoridades – Tomo V. 1737. Madrid: Francisco del Hierro.

Gasch Tomás, José L. 2014a. "Asian Silk, Porcelain and Material Culture in the Definition of Mexican and Andalusian Elites, c. 1565–1630." In *Global Goods and the Spanish Empire, 1492–1824. Circulation, Resistance and Diversity*, edited by Bethany Aram and Bartolomé Yun-Casalilla, 153–72. London: Palgrave Macmillan.

———. 2014b. "Globalisation, Market Formation and Commoditisation in the Spanish Empire. Consumer Demand for Asian Goods in Mexico City and Seville, c. 1571–1630." *Revista de Historia Económica – Journal of Iberian and Latin American Economic History* 32 (2): 189–221.

———. 2018. *The Atlantic World and the Manila Galleons. Circulation, Market, and Consumption of Asian Goods in the Spanish Empire, 1565–1650*. Leiden: Brill.

Gerritsen, Anne. 2012. "Ceramics for Global and Local Markets: Jingdezhen's Agora of Technologies." In *Cultures of Knowledge. Technology in Chinese History*, edited by Dagmar Schäfer, 161–84. Leiden: Brill.

Heredia Moreno, Maria del Carmen, and Amelia López Yarto Elizalde. 2001. *La edad de oro de la platería complutense (1500–1560)*. Madrid: CSIC.

Kuwayama, George. 1997. *Chinese Ceramics in Colonial Mexico*. Honolulu, HA: University of Hawai'i Press.

Ogilvie, Sheilagh, Küpker, Markus, and Janine Maegraith. 2008. "Women and the Material Culture of Food in Early Modern Germany." *Early Modern Women: An Interdisciplinary Journal* 4: 149–59.

Priyadarshini, Meha. 2018. *Chinese Porcelain in Colonial Mexico. The Material Worlds of an Early Modern Trade*. London: Palgrave Macmillan.

Ramos Palencia, Fernando. 2011. "Notas metodológicas sobre la utilización de los inventarios post-mortem: Clasificación de bienes de consumo, bases de datos e impacto de créditos y deudas." In *Comprar, vender y consumir. Nuevas aportaciones a la historia del consumo en la España moderna*, edited by Daniel Muñoz Navarro, 21–52. Valencia: PUV.

Sánchez, José María. 1998. "La cerámica exportada a América en el sigo XVI a través de la documentación del Archivo de Indias (II). Ajuares domésticos y cerámica cultual y laboral." *Laboratorio de arte* 11: 121–33.

Schurz, William L. 1992. *El galeón de Manila*. Madrid: Cultura Hispánica.

Shammas, Carole. 1990. *The Pre-Industrial Consumer in England and America*. Oxford: Oxford University Press.

Vickery, Amanda. 2009. *Behind the Closed Doors. At Home in Georgian England*. New Haven and London: Yale University Press.

Vila Vilar, Enriqueta. 1991. *Los Corzo y los Mañara. Tipos y arquetipos del mercader con Indias*. Sevilla: Escuela de Estudios Hispano-Americanos.

Yun-Casalilla, Bartolomé. 1999. "Inventarios post-mortem, consumo y niveles de vida del campesinado del Antiguo Régimen. Problemas metodológicos a la luz de la investigación internacional." In *Consumo, condiciones de vida y comercialización. Cataluña y Castilla, siglos XVII-XIX*, edited by Bartolomé Yun-Casalilla and Jaume Torras Elias, 27–40. Valladolid: Junta de Castilla y León.

Yuste López, Carmen. 1984. *El Comercio de la Nueva España con Filipinas, 1590–1785*. México, D.F.: Instituto Nacional de Antropología e Historia.

———. 2007. *Emporios transpacíficos. Comerciantes mexicanos en Manila, 1710–1815*. México, D. F.: UNAM.

Zamora Rodríguez, Francisco. 2014. "Interest and Curiosity: American Products, Information and Exotica in Tuscany." In *Global Goods and the Spanish Empire, 1492–1824. Circulation, Resistance and Diversity*, edited by Bethany Aram and Bartolomé Yun-Casalilla, 174–93. London: Palgrave Macmillan.

11 "That in the *Reducciones* Had Been Noise of Weapons . . ."

The Introduction of Firearms in the Seventeenth-Century Jesuit Missions of Paraguay[1]

Omar Svriz-Wucherer

Introduction

The phrase "That in the *reducciones* had been noise of weapons . . ." is the order given by the Provincial Superior, Father Nicolás Durán, that appears in the Annual Letters of 1628. In it Father Durán authorized the use of arms in the towns the Jesuits set up for indigenous peoples in Paraguay known as *reducciones* (reductions) or *misiones* (missions). The wording "noise of weapons" prompts us to agree with Jaime Cortesão in considering this to be an *early* reference to the detonation of firearms among these Guaraní peoples, although other authors have expressed their doubts about this interpretation.[2] Leaving aside the question of the precise date of the first use of firearms in the Paraguay missions, two arguments substantiate the belief that the Jesuits armed the Guaraní to protect their villages: first, the constant attacks by the Portuguese from Brazil (called *bandeirantes*) on the area of the Jesuit reductions in the first decades of the seventeenth century and, second, the lack of material and/or human assistance from the authorities and inhabitants of nearby cities (Asunción, Villa Rica and Corrientes) to protect the missions from *bandeira* raids.

It is interesting to observe this process from an imperial perspective. The provision of firearms to the Guaraní Indians illustrates the kind of arrangements developed by the empires of the modern era to introduce European products to native Americans, which afforded them the possibility of better protecting their frontiers against internal and external threats.[3] Furthermore, this case study provides us with clues concerning a larger phenomenon that we might call "the globalization of war technology", which occurred between the fifteenth and eighteenth centuries in various parts of the globe: a complex process that even today historians need to redefine, establishing its scope and limitations.[4]

DOI: 10.4324/9781003168058-12

Thus, the task in hand is to gain a better understanding of how this war equipment was incorporated and/or rejected by peoples across different continents and the ensuing socio-cultural mutations that it produced. This demands a broad-ranging analysis of the incorporation and development of this type of weaponry in local populations, from Asian territories, such as China and Japan (Brown 1948; Andrade 2016), to the Ottoman Empire (Ágoston 2005) as well as various American regions.[5] The contributions of Kenneth Chase (2003) and Jeremy Black (2013), who outline the development of firearms and war technology in different parts of the globe, are significant, both works being based on a broad time-frame, from the fourteenth century to the present day. In the case of Latin America, and specifically during the Spanish Conquest, the studies by Alberto M. Salas (1986) and Pablo M. Gómez (2001) have indicated the characteristics of the weapons used by natives and Spaniards, and their influence on the development of their subsequent relations. However, in all these works the socio-cultural mutations that this type of weaponry generated in local populations are not dealt with explicitly.

Daniel Headrick contends that in order to understand the development of empires in the New World, we must focus on the available resources and the context in which Europeans and native Americans met, with due regard for European successes, but without overlooking their failures (Headrick 2011, 95–96). Therefore, an analysis of case studies that covers a longer period of time, focused especially on frontier areas linked to this "failure of the conquest", allows us to observe the numerous processes of adaptation and technological exchange. These processes are clear and evident at the particular frontier under analysis. For example, the incorporation of the horse into the daily lives of the Guaraní and Chaco Indians modified not only diverse socio-cultural aspects of these groups but also the way in which war developed. Similarly, traditional Guaraní weapons acquire new meanings and social roles in relation to weapons of European origin, with both playing an important role in the military organization of the Jesuit missions in Paraguay. We believe that there is still a need for a greater understanding of the sociocultural influence of the firearms and hostilities exchanged between native American populations and the Europeans who "conquered" them, which we aim to pursue further in this chapter.

Jane Burbank and Frederick Cooper define empires as large, political units that were expansionist or with a memory of territorial expansion, entities that maintained distinctions and hierarchy as they incorporated new peoples. Burbank and Cooper also emphasize that methods of violence and coercion are employed as fundamental parts of the building process of empires and their *modus operandi* (Burbank and Cooper 2010, 1–2, 8). In this sense, it is important to bear in mind that maintaining an empire over time depends on a variety of factors, but especially on money and weapons[6] (Marichal and Von Grafenstein 2012, 9). However, the implementation of violence and coercion on the part of empires should not lead us to think of a one-way system, in which violence is monopolized by the imperial authorities and indigenous groups play a passive role. On the contrary, the empires of the modern era developed mechanisms of negotiation with the native groups to achieve their objectives, one of the most important of which was to protect their possessions from attacks from other empires and/or other indigenous factions (Daniels and Kennedy 2002). Negotiations with the natives took on their own set of characteristics peculiar to each imperial area. Nonetheless, to a greater or lesser extent, in practically all of them we find commodity exchanges that promoted or facilitated such agreements. However, a very different situation presents itself when we analyze the introduction of firearms in the various imperial regions. The European empires resorted to furnishing such weaponry to the indigenous peoples who inhabited their overseas possessions in only a few instances, but in cases where this occurred, significant sociocultural changes were experienced.[7]

Against this background, an analysis of the introduction of firearms into the Jesuit reductions in Paraguay inevitably poses the question of what happened in other similar overseas territories and compels us to find common answers that explain this type of imperial arrangement.

Firearms and Cultural Changes in the Guaraní Indians' Living

Arjun Appadurai and then Bruno Latour developed the assignation of agency to objects within a society and the changes they generate in it (Appadurai 1988; Latour 2008). Latour says, "[A]part from 'determining' and serving as 'a backdrop for human action', things might authorize, allow, afford, encourage, permit, suggest, influence, block, render possible, forbid, and so on" (Latour 2008, 107). In this sense, the firearms incorporated in the reductions can be regarded as a key element enabling our understanding of a whole series of alterations in relations between the actors on this frontier.

The Guaraní Indians were part of the Tupi-Guaraní linguistic family that occupied an extensive territory from the Amazon River to the Río de la Plata. Current archaeological studies prevent us from knowing the precise nature of the differences that existed between the groups making up this linguistic family.[8] However, from a territorial viewpoint we know that the Tupi occupied the middle and lower section of the Amazon Basin and a large part of the Atlantic seaboard, that is, from the Amazon to the Cananea. For their part, the Guaraní inhabited lands stretching from that Tupi territory to the current Brazilian state of Rio Grande do Sul, including the great waterways that penetrate the plateau. Their ability as canoeists allowed the Guaraní to travel along the great waterways of the region, especially the Paraná–Río de la Plata basin and its numerous tributaries, and in this way expand their occupied territories.[9] This mobility was aided by the slash-and-burn agriculture they developed and their prophetic belief in the existence and search for a "Land without Evil", which especially influenced Guaraní migrations following the arrival of Europeans in the region (Mineiro Scatamacchia 2014). Fundamentally, however, it was their combative disposition that induced these periodic forays, impelling them to conquer other indigenous groups and annex new territories. Having identified their warlike character soon after they arrived in the region, the Jesuits endeavored to curb these traits, especially their practice of cannibalism, and redirect them towards protecting the reductions.[10]

The change was not simple or swift: for the Guaraní, abandoning their semi-nomadic life to settle in a fixed reduction took a considerable length of time. To facilitate the transition, the Jesuits developed arrangements that allowed for the coexistence of different Guaraní leaders in a much smaller space. This approach sought to "balance" power within a reduction, for which they established the practice of *cacicazgos de papel* in place of the older and traditional *cacicazgos*.[11] In addition, the priests distributed posts related to the organization of the town (stewards, magistrates, council members, etc.) to the new leaders, and created confraternities that consolidated their evangelizing work and strengthened social positions within the reduction.

However, war continued to occupy a key role within the reduced Guaraní society. The annexation of territories and resources, the subjugation of other groups and/or the ritual anthropophagy of their defeated enemies were no longer allowed. In exchange, their warring temperament was channeled towards the protection not only of their own reductions but also of nearby territories and cities which they defended in the name of the Spanish monarchy.

This entire series of changes influenced not only the "objective" of the war being waged on the border but also the weapons employed in it. Traditional Guaraní weapons such as bows, arrows, spears and clubs were rendered obsolete in the face of the Portuguese enemy.[12] Thus, the need arose to train the Guaraní in European weaponry, techniques and tactics in order to challenge their opponents. In spite of the great difficulties of the early years, firearms were rapidly adopted by the Guaraní Indians, who saw them as key (in conjunction with the military training they received from the Jesuits) to consolidating their power ahead of the other indigenous groups.

In addition, the incorporation of these weapons in the first decades of the seventeenth century reinforced the strategic alliance between the Jesuits and certain Guaraní chiefdoms. This process served to deepen the differences between the confederate *caciques* under Jesuit tutelage. The most important Guaraní leaders in the reductions carried blunderbusses, muskets and/or swords, showing off their power at every call to service, while lower-ranked *caciques* were equipped with traditional weapons (Avellaneda 2005, 23). This allowed the Jesuits to bolster certain roles within the reduction and achieve a greater balance of power. Furthermore, the Spanish organization model of militias was introduced in the villages, whereby the Guaraní were divided into companies, usually comprising fifty soldiers, according to the arms they were carrying.[13] Just like the Spanish infantry organization known as the *tercios*, the Guaraní natives were separated into arquebusiers, pikemen and/or swordsmen. Rather than carrying three types of weapons to the battlefield, which would be expensive and impractical, instead the Guaraní militiamen began to specialize, like their European counterparts.

With the passage of time, it was not only the weapons they carried that marked the difference in the power yielded by the various *caciques* within the reduction; the title of "war captain" was awarded to Guaraní who excelled in services to the crown. Kazuhisa Takeda recounts that fourteen Guaraní leaders were awarded military positions by the governors in the years 1629, 1639, 1640 and 1656, thirteen of whom already had the honorific title of *Don*. During the second half of the seventeenth century, however, natives who attained these military positions did not necessarily come from the traditional *cacicazgos* in each reduction.[14] This demonstrates the process of "balancing" power within a reduction, whereby the Jesuits distributed these positions among a greater number of individuals from different clans.

The Arrival of Firearms During the First Half of the Seventeenth Century

References to firearms in the Jesuit reductions of Paraguay date back to a very early period, but present us with considerable inaccuracies regarding their number and distribution. One of the earliest reports is from the Asunción Cabildo records of 21 March 1618, in which the members report to the governor of the province that the Jesuit Superior General, Joseph Pablo de Castañeda, had insinuated in a letter that he had a hundred guns in his possession. The same report indicates that the arms had been intercepted by the Jesuits in the city of Santa Fe and, despite being originally bound for the city of Asunción, they were sent to the natives in the reductions to defend themselves against the Portuguese.[15] Although we may entertain doubts as to whether or not the Jesuits actually had such a number of guns at that time and whether the senior members of the Society of Jesus acted in the manner described by the Cabildo members, what is striking is that in those early years the members of the order were already linked to the acquisition of arms of this type to defend their missions.

Moreover, in their report the Asunción town councilors underscored the ongoing problems experienced along the border at that time and in the years thereafter, namely the lack of weapons and the attacks from the Chaco Indians. The councilors claimed to have more than 2,000 men employed "incessantly" in the defense of the province, but without the weapons necessary to defend themselves or to undertake retaliatory raids on the Payaguá Indians.[16]

Between 1620 and 1640, attacks from the Brazilian *bandeirantes* accounted for the unquestionable increase in the number of firearms within the Jesuit reductions.[17] But the key question is how they managed to get hold of these armaments. The Jesuit Antonio Ruiz de Montoya produced a report in 1633 in which he tried to silence the rumors that the Indians in the reductions had 103 shotguns and ammunition, all given to them by the Jesuits, with which "they could injure or could have injured the Spaniards".[18] In support of his argument, Ruiz de Montoya cited as witnesses the Jesuits Joseph Cataldino, Simón Maceta and Juan Agustín de Contreras. But, although the main purpose of that document was to deny the presence of firearms in the villages, these records provide us with clues about trading in firearms in the region. Two Jesuits attached to the San Ignacio mission, Cataldino and Maceta, refer to exchanges whereby the natives in the missions obtained arms and ammunition. They mention that a local *cacique* named Lycuquaratí obtained a shotgun from a neighbor from Ciudad Real (Alonso de Morinigo) in exchange for a canoe and two pigs, adding that no other Indian possessed a shotgun and that exchanges of gunpowder occurred routinely between Spaniards in the city and the natives.[19] In the Nuestra Señora de Loreto mission, Father Contreras not only identified weapons in his reduction, but he also mentioned that they were obtained from a neighbor of Villa Rica, in violation of the prevailing laws:

> [I]n this mission there is no Indian with a shotgun given to him by any of our clergy and those who have one in this town are but three: one who was given his by a *cacique* Carlos de Vera, neighbor of Villa Rica, and it was after Luis de Cespedes ordered that that no person should give them shotguns, that the said Carlos de Vera gave him the said shotgun.[20]

These clues point to a possible commercial network between the Jesuit reductions of Guairá and the inhabitants of the cities of Villa Rica del Espíritu Santo and Ciudad Real. However, these cities were small and marginalized from the Atlantic commercial market, and would have difficulty in supplying weapons and related equipment to these missions.

Consequently, it would seem that these references allude to wider commercial routes which to date have been the subject of virtually no historical analysis. José Carlos Vilardaga (2017) states that the Spanish cities and the Guairá Indians reductions had used the waterways to establish trade connections with the Brazilian Atlantic coast and especially with the town of São Paulo, at least during the period 1600–1630.[21] Concerning the role of the Guairá missions, we do not have exact information on the volume of trade involved and it is unclear whether the frequency of the *bandeira* incursions put a stop to it.[22] Undoubtedly, this trading relationship must be studied in greater detail, but we cannot underestimate its usefulness in providing firearms and supplies to the reductions.

Father Antonio Ruíz de Montoya affirms that in 1636 the first firearms (only seven in total) were handed out among the Guaraní by the governor of Paraguay, Pedro de Lugo y Navarra.[23] According to the Jesuit, these arms were handed out in the face of Portuguese advances and were returned at the end of that successful battle. We cannot rule out the possibility that this assistance was provided by the governor of Paraguay. Nonetheless, it would appear to be a very paltry number of weapons in order to overcome "five hundred well-armed Portuguese" and "to strip them of two thousand captive Indians under their control" (Artigas 2016, 290). Aside from this report, we believe that at the time, this type of weaponry had already been introduced in the reductions; otherwise the Guaraní could hardly have defeated the Portuguese *bandeirantes*.

In short, the references to the number of firearms in the Jesuit villages during this period are scarce and in our view this is attributable to two factors.

The first of these is that the Jesuits had not defined whether it was advisable for the members of the order and the Guaraní to use this type of weapon in the reductions, and consequently they were suspicious and/or hesitant about detailing their firearms numerically in letters, briefs or other documents. The question of the use of firearms was the main topic of discussion at the Sixth Provincial Congregation, 18 July to 8 August 1637, which spoke of the Jesuits wounded in the battlefield defending their missions. However, the congregation did not adopt a definitive view on the issue.[24] In a subsequent letter, Father General Vitelleschi, in reply to questions from his Provincial Superior, is unambiguous about the difficulty of the issue and mentions that he did not like nor could he approve of recent actions in defense of the Indians.[25]

It is remarkable how historiographers later developed the notion that the temporary coadjutors (mainly former soldiers in Europe) were responsible for introducing and using firearms in the reductions, and for training the Guaraní. Initiation of the process was attributed to the tardy arrival of Brother Domingo de Torres to the Paraguay reductions in 1637.[26] This historiographical perspective released the Jesuit priests from such a charge, an idea that undoubtedly suited the interests of the Society of Jesus in these territories, and thereby managed to separate temporal from spiritual matters.

The second factor giving rise to this lack of clarity concerning the number of firearms in the reductions was that for most of those years the Jesuits were awaiting final approval for the use of these weapons. Therefore, the members of the society did not want the authorities to know that they already had access to this type of armament. Superior General Mutio Vitelleschi was clear about this, stating in a letter addressed to the Provincial of Paraguay, Diego de Boroa, that it was lawful to defend the Indians "in the best way they could, giving them firearms and making them strong so that they could impede the passage of their enemies." Vitelleschi, however, also clarified aspects that were not permissible:

> [W]hat I cannot approve is that our priests be like captains guiding them in the struggle, both on account of the indecency of it and because I do not recognize the need, and that there is such a lack of Ladino Indians, and of Spaniards for this task [. . .] and I was confirmed in this resolve after they told me that Father Christoval de Mendoza died not *in odium fidei*, and for that cause but in armed combat along with Father Mola, and it remains to be seen if this is something permissible.

Finally, the Superior General ordered the Provincial of Paraguay not to consent to this type of action.[27] He considered the possibility of favoring the natural defense of the Indians, but that did not mean the Jesuits would be the first line of defense of the reductions, let alone armed.

From the 1640s onwards, the situation changed with regard to firearms in the Paraguayan missions. In 1637 Ruiz de Montoya was elected procurator of the Jesuit province of Paraguay before the Spanish Court, but he did not arrive there until 22 September 1639, and finished his work on 7 August 1640. His dealings with the Crown were slow, but Ruiz de Montoya finally obtained a Royal decree from King Philip IV (21 May 1640), which is of considerable significance in this connection. The charter ordered the Viceroy of Peru to grant license and deliver firearms to the Guaraní in the Jesuit reductions of Paraguay.[28] This meant that the monarchy recognized the need to allow the Guaraní natives access to this type of weaponry to protect those lands. Later, the successes of the indigenous troops against the Portuguese, especially in the battle of Mbororé of 1641, demonstrated the foresight of this provision. Success in these military activities led to the monarchy's approval and recognition of the Guaraní in the reductions as militias of the king, assigning them the protection of the border against the Portuguese enemy (1647). Thus, the armed Indians in the missions became the militiamen of the Spanish king and accordingly Guaraní and Jesuits had to develop suitable military training, in which firearms would play a leading role.

From then on, weapons for the Jesuit reductions were obtained in three ways. The first was through legal or illegal trade in the region, but no longer using the connections between São Paulo, the Guairá region and the cities of Villa Rica and Asunción, as had been the case in the first decades of the seventeenth century (Viladaga 2017); this was mainly concentrated on the Paraguay–Paraná–Río de la Plata waterways linking the capital with Corrientes, Santa Fe and the port of Buenos Aires, and in all these cities the procurators of the Jesuit colleges played a key role in commercial transactions. The second way was via the seizure of weapons abandoned by the Portuguese enemy on the battlefields; while the third, less documented by historians, was via the manufacture of this type of weaponry by the Guaraní in their villages.[29] In this regard, Brother Simón Méndes mentioned in 1641 that 600 firearms had been made in the reductions under the tutorship of a priest, an endeavor initiated by Brother Domingo de Torres.[30] Later reports highlighted the learning capacity of the Guaraní and their ability to produce this type of weaponry.[31]

Sources from subsequent years provide us with more precise details regarding the organization of the armed defense of the reductions. The Jesuits decreed that each village should have the necessary weapons to fight the enemy in the case of invasion and determined that it was unworkable for firearms to be concentrated in just one or two reductions.[32] Such an arrangement would have posed a serious risk, because if their enemies were to attack the particular locations where arms were stored, they could easily capture all available weapons. Furthermore, from a practical point of view, it would make for a very slow system because the weapons could not be relocated quickly to protect a settlement under attack.

For his part, the Franciscan friar Gabriel de Valencia, who was a Jesuit for some fifteen years, decided to inform the governor of Tucumán about the firearms in the Jesuit reductions in Paraguay. His report gives us a different perspective and a more critical view of the presence of these weapons in these towns. Valencia affirms that during the confrontation with the Portuguese, the Jesuits had some 4,000 firearms in their possession and that there were four forges in the reductions constantly producing muskets. According to the Franciscan friar, this was a task initiated twenty years previously by Brother Domingo de Torres and therefore, by 1657 the number of firearms in the reductions amounted to 14,000, with fourteen medium-sized pieces of artillery.[33] These numbers are quite possibly exaggerated, especially if we compare them with the figures recorded at the time of the governor's visits to the reductions in 1647 and 1657. Nevertheless, this report provides us with interesting clues as to the possible strategies used by the Jesuits to increase armaments in their villages. Valencia affirms that the reductions managed to capture firearms through trade or illegal methods, and he cites the case of the reduction of San Ignacio Guazú. This town was located in a commercial enclave near the *camino real de las vacas*, which connected the cities of Corrientes and Asunción. According to him, the inhabitants of the reduction took advantage of their geographical location to steal the merchants' boats. Natives of the Jesuit settlements captured merchandise, including firearms, and then blamed the Guaicurú Indians for these activities.[34]

Friar Valencia raised an interesting question in his report: the inhabitants of the reductions, with or without the consent of the Jesuit fathers, stole firearms from merchants travelling along that road and accused the native Chaco of these crimes. This demonstrates how the natives (or the Jesuits themselves) took advantage of the prevailing border relations, or the categories of "friendly Indians" and "enemy Indians," for their own benefit.

The Importance of *Pertrechos* (Military equipment) and the Fears of an Indian Rebellion

Jesuit writings indicate two fundamental questions that arose once firearms were allowed in the reductions: the need for trade in munitions that would guarantee the reliable functioning of these weapons, and a growing fear among the inhabitants and authorities of the region of a possible armed Guaraní rebellion. However, the Jesuits themselves were not slow in linking these two aspects in order to protect themselves from criticism leveled against them. They argued that "there are no materials to make gunpowder or bullets, so it is necessary that these be brought from Peru or Buenos Aires; there is never any danger as it is easy to remove what they have, either by throwing them in the river or onto the fire, so the blunderbusses would be of no use to them".[35]

In other words, the shortage of munitions in the reductions and the need to acquire them through commercial channels provided a guarantee against armed uprisings on the part of the natives.

However, aside from the Jesuit arguments in defense of providing arms to the Guaraní, the supply of ammunition was an essential consideration for the operation of this weaponry. Understanding how bullets, gunpowder and other equipment came to the reductions gives us a more complete picture of how the defense of that border was developed.

One of the scarcest and most difficult-to-produce elements in the region was gunpowder. In 1639 the Jesuits stated that the Indians "do not know how to make gunpowder and even if they did, they lack the [requisite] materials, because they do not have salt or sulphur or lead."[36] For this reason, references to requests from the reductions and purchases of the product in other territories are constant. In 1644 the dispatch of twenty *botijas* (jars) of gunpowder to the reductions was approved in Chuquisaca, which the Jesuits would pay over eight months, at three pesos per pound plus the value of the jugs.[37] Later, Father Diego de Boroa reaffirmed that the Indians in the reductions had no materials with which they could manufacture the product.[38]

The most complete records of firearms in the reductions date from around the mid-seventeenth century and refer not only to their number but also to their distribution. These records lead us to surmise, therefore, that the Jesuits and Guaraní in the missions had managed by then to guarantee the provision of the requisite supplies of ammunition, enabling them to use their weaponry. For instance, a wooden box with a lock and key containing ammunition consisting of gunpowder, match-rope and bullets is mentioned in most of the reductions visited during Governor Blásquez de Valverde's tour in 1657.[39] Figure 11.1 includes the information drawn from two visits to the reductions recording the number, growth and distribution of the armaments encountered.

The greatest number of arms was concentrated in the reductions close to the border with Portuguese territory; meaning that there were still fears within the reductions of further attacks from the Portuguese. However, according to these visits, there was a striking absence of weapons in the reduction of San Ignacio Guazú, which was visited on both occasions, yet its inhabitants were actively involved in border defense.[41]

Changes in Crown policy on the matter led to the disappearance of weapons counts in the reductions in the second half of the seventeenth century. A Royal decree in 1661 prohibited the use of these weapons in the missions. According to the ruling, these had to be stored in Asunción and could be used by the Indians in the reductions only in the case of attack.[42] This type of defense was clearly unfeasible because of the considerable distance between the city of Asunción and the Jesuit reductions, preventing any rapid distribution of these arms. Despite this, the members of the Society of Jesus maintained the semblance of compliance with this royal norm and handed over the weapons they possessed.

Nevertheless, we note that Vice-Provincial Andrés de Rada visited the reductions and sanctioned an order (13 April 1664) to continue with the defensive organization of the reductions, which would appear to

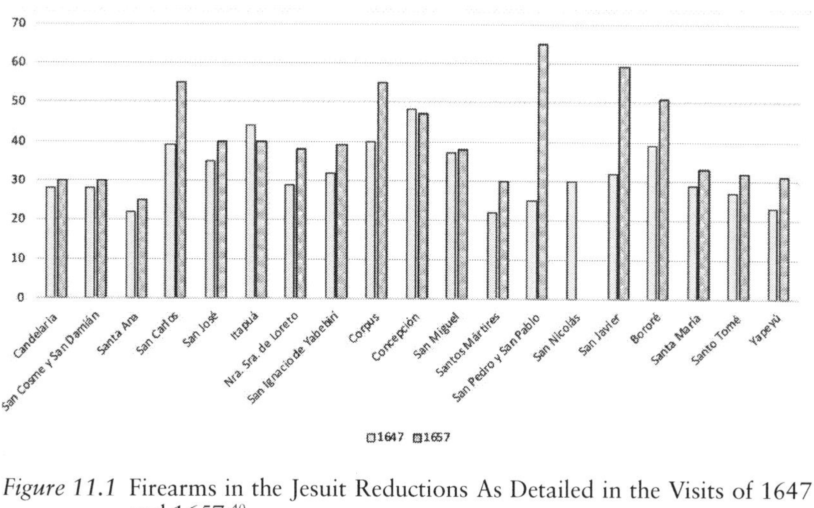

Figure 11.1 Firearms in the Jesuit Reductions As Detailed in the Visits of 1647 and 1657.[40]

demonstrate that at least part of the weapons remained in the hands of the natives in the reductions.[43] This regulation also advocated the handling, composition and cleaning of weapons, and established that each mission be supplied with gunpowder.[44]

Later, Rada was appointed Provincial Superior, and he issued the first ruling dealing entirely with the organization and training of the militias in the reductions (17 November 1666). This provision was consistent with the royal ruling and focused on the handling of "traditional" Guaraní weapons such as spears, stones, bows and arrows.[45] This regulation may well have been only a front, given that the Guaraní militias continued to use this type of weaponry during their activities, which demonstrates that not all the firearms had been sent to Asunción.[46]

Later in the seventeenth century, the crown once again permitted the use of firearms. A Royal decree of 25 July 1679 forced the authorities in Asunción to return the arms and ammunition that had been brought from the villages. The governor of Paraguay, Alonso Fernández Montiel, wrote to the king on 29 October 1685 indicating the quantities involved: 836 muskets were brought, forty-three *arrobas* of lead and 229 *arrobas* of gunpowder.[47]

On the basis of the above, we cannot state with any degree of accuracy whether the Jesuits had delivered all the firearms available after the 1661 provision, or only a part of them. We do know, however, that during that decade the reductions had at least 836 guns, which gives us an indication of the armaments that they came to possess in the reductions.

Subsequent regulations decreed by the Jesuit authorities continued to adapt to the reality of the prevailing border war, some of which even contradicted the Constitutions of the Society of Jesus. On 19 November 1693 the Provincial Superior Lauro Nuñez ordered that firearms could be held in the schools of Tucumán, Santiago del Estero, Asunción and Corrientes, that is, in all those schools located on lands near the Chaco border.[48] In this way, the rules of the society were adapted to suit local needs and their schools no longer served solely as training centers for future missionaries, but also became product redistribution centers, where firearms were very much in evidence.

However, the incorporation of firearms also gave rise to major difficulties within the reductions. On several occasions, there were fears of indigenous uprisings using such weapons, especially in adverse situations (attacks by the Portuguese or other Indians, plagues, droughts and/or food shortages), circumstances that frequently affected the missions and that could spark an uprising or cause part of the population to take flight. This is illustrated by events in 1661, with the return of six unit captains after serving the Crown in Buenos Aires. One of them, Pedro Mbayuguá, attempted to assume civil, political and economic power in the settlements, leaving only ecclesiastic rule in the hands of the Jesuits. The conflict dragged on for two months and five reductions joined the movement.

Eventually, an alliance formed between the Jesuits and the former *cacicazgos* in each reduction prevailed over the young militiamen, who became isolated and finally laid down their arms (Susnik 1983, 19–21). However, the incident served as a warning to the Jesuits of the dangers of leaving this type of weaponry in the hands of the Guaraní. It is possible that the previously described arrangements put in place by Father Rada were devised to ensure a greater control of such weaponry, and by doing so to prevent the recurrence of confrontations similar to the uprising of Pedro Mbayuguá and his allies.

Conclusion

What has been said thus far allows us to reflect on the complex process by which European products such as firearms prompted significant mutations in Native American societies, in this case among the Guaraní natives of the Jesuit reductions in Paraguay during the seventeenth century. Meanwhile, ongoing complex negotiations between the monarchy, the regional authorities and the inhabitants of the border area were conducted concurrently, leading to their defense within the framework of the Spanish empire. The peculiarities of those territories with different population groups participating in the trade and exchange of products made it difficult to establish a route for these weapons to the reductions. Most probably these armaments reached the settlements through (legal or illegal) trade established by the Jesuits with various cities and towns in the region. In the first three decades of the seventeenth century, it is likely that, as Vilardaga (2017) states, this type of armament reached the reductions via the inland waterways linked to the Brazilian Atlantic coast, with the cities of the Guairá region acting as the necessary intermediaries in such exchanges. However, establishing exact figures for the trade and number of weapons that reached the reductions is challenging, not least on account of the Jesuits' indecisive response during those years.

Bandeira raids and the resulting loss of Indian towns and reductions across the region caused the Guaraní to relocate in safer and protected places. Consequently, the main exchanges to and from the Jesuit reductions took place thereafter through the Paraguay–Paraná–Río de la Plata waterways. For this reason, the Jesuits set up schools in the nearby cities (Asunción, Corrientes, Santa Fe and Buenos Aires) and inaugurated the figure of the procurator in charge of trade in commodities, which included the firearms destined for the reductions of Paraguay. Victory on the battlefields against the Portuguese provided a sizeable number of captured firearms and the support of the Spanish monarchy for the training of the Guaraní in European military techniques and tactics. Thus, the so-called Guaraní militias came into being. In addition, we have references to the effect that, after 1637 at least, the temporary coadjutors managed to manufacture firearms in the reductions, an activity that substantially increased the number of these weapons in subsequent years, as indicated in some reports.

From the second half of the seventeenth century we have more precise references to the firearms in the reductions, with reports from visiting governors in 1647 and 1657 providing details regarding their number and distribution. Primarily, however, the incorporation of firearms brought about a whole series of changes to the cultural norms of the Guaraní in the reductions. A system of military organization along Castilian lines was introduced, whereby natives were distinguished with military ranks. The Guaraní became specialized in certain types of weapons, which had their corresponding military units. Thus, leaderships were consolidated according to the type of weapons carried by the natives in their military activities. As a result, the use of firearms strengthened certain *cacicazgos* against others. This process is very significant because during the second half of the seventeenth century, the Jesuits chose to "create" new *cacicazgos* in order to "balance" power within the reductions. The honorary title of *Don*, primarily based on performance in certain military mobilizations, was granted to natives who did not come from the traditional lineages of the town.

On the basis of the above, it is clear that the arrival of this type of armament to the Jesuit reductions of Paraguay not only brought about mutations in the Guaraní practice of warfare and performance on the battlefields of the New World, but also implied a whole series of sociocultural changes that influenced (and at the same time explain) the way in which the Spanish monarchy was defended in these border areas throughout the seventeenth century.

This type of sociocultural transformation also can be found on other frontiers of the Hispanic empire. For example, Boccara's studies of the Kingdom of Chile have revealed important changes within the Mapuches' society due to their interaction with the Spanish. However, the complexity of their border relations often led these "auxiliary or friendly Indians" to await the outcome of the battle and intervene toward its end on behalf of the winner (Salas 1986, 240). Similar relationships occurred on the Chichimeca border of New Spain, as Philip Powell (1977) has demonstrated.

Although this phenomenon was not exclusive to the Spanish empire, as demonstrated by, Chase (2003), Headrick (2011) and Black (2013), among others, we consider that it achieved its own specific characteristics among the Guaraní natives and promoted a "process of globalization of war technology" that we must continue to analyze to understand how it occurred in American border lands throughout the sixteenth and seventeenth centuries.

Notes

1. This research has been carried out within the framework of the project HAR2014–53797-P "Globalización Ibérica: Redes entre Asia y Europa y

los cambios en las pautas de Consumo en Latinoamérica" [Iberian Globalization: Networks between Asia and Europe and Changes in Consumption Patterns in Latin America] financed by Ministerio de Economía y Competitividad, Spain, of which the principal investigator is Bartolomé Yun-Casalilla, and the ERC Starting Grant GECEM (Global Encounters between China and Europe: Trade Networks, Consumption and Cultural Exchanges in Macau and Marseille, 1680–1840), whose principal investigator is Professor Manuel Perez-Garcia. Also the PAI Group HUM-1000, "Historia de la Globalización: Violencia, negociación e interculturalidad" [History of Globalisation: Violence, Negotiation and Interculturality], financed by the Regional Government of Andalusia, and its principal investigator, Igor Pérez Tostado, have cooperated. This last project has also paid for the open access of this chapter.

2. Cortesao 1951, 272–73, note no. 1. Magnus Mörner considers the interpretation of this sound as the noise of firearms to be exaggerated (Mörner 2008, 48–49, note no. 32, 229–30).
3. Throughout the seventeenth century, the Society of Jesus produced a collection of writings whereby its members justified the use of violence to these ends. For example, the work *Imago primi saeculi* (1640) by the Jesuit Jan Bolland formulated the notion of *amica violentia*, or "benign violence". Girolamo Imbruglia refers to this notion as advancing the type of empire adopted by the Jesuits, for whom, according to Imbruglia, the goal of civilizing and converting these peoples justified the use of coercion and violence (Imbruglia 2014, 24).
4. Authors like Roberts 1967, Cipolla 1967 and Parker 1988, illustrated how the expansion of the European empires was triggered by a whole range of technological developments in the military field ("Military Revolution")
5. Some of the American cases of technology transfer analyzed were those of the native Americans and their negotiations with the English and French (Lee 2011, 49–79); exchanges between Miskitos, Zambos and English colonists (Ibarra Rojas 2011); and the case of the Tupis and their alliances with the Dutch on the coast of present-day Brazil (Meuwese 2009, 2012).
6. We will confine ourselves here to the circulation of weapons within the Spanish empire, but we should not lose sight of the importance of understanding how this empire was financed in order to ensure, among other aspects, the defense of its borders. Yun-Casalilla 2004; Ramos Palencia and Yun-Casalilla 2012; Sánchez Santiró 2015.
7. Bibliography cited in Note no. 4.
8. In recent years, archaeological studies of different groups of natives that integrated this linguistic family have made considerable progress from the ceramics they made, especially with regard to their distribution and expansion during the pre-Spanish period. Noelli 2004; Bonomo et al. 2015.
9. Garavalia and Marchena, vol. 1, 2005, 87. Indigenous navigation was one of the main disseminators of Guaraní culture, creating a Guaraní cultural ambience or pan-Guaraní culture.
10. The Guaraní, like other native American groups, practiced ritual cannibalism, whereby they believed the warrior strength of the vanquished was absorbed if consumed in this way.
11. Wilde 2009, 137–44. The indigenous *cacicazgo* (chieftaincy) in the reductions can be qualified in two ways: first, as a control device entrusting the *cacique* with the management of space and the mission records; but, secondly, the *cacicazgo* could generate (and did on several occasions) certain autonomous forms of governance in defiance of Jesuit political rule that led to demonstrations and constant acts of indigenous resistance. Wilde 2009, 131.

12. Spears were introduced to the Guaraní following the incorporation of the horse as a result of contact with the Spanish in the first stages of colonization.
13. According to the Jesuits Francisco Jarque and Diego Altamirano, "[I]n every hamlet there are companies of infantry and cavalry, made up of all the men capable of taking up arms each with its own captain, lieutenant, sergeant, corporal and other officers, as is customary in the military, with their insignias, drums, bugles and flags . . . in the same way as at home in Spain, better cared for in the campaigns and frontiers". Jarque and Altamirano 2008 [1687], 59. An analysis of the implementation of European military ideas within the reductions is in Takeda 2016b.
14. Cf. Takeda 2012, 67, 2016a, 93. The transcription of these documents is in Salinas 2006.
15. Cortesao 1951, 160–62 Commercial transactions in the region of Paraguay at the time were made with the so-called currency of the land (Romano 1998, 175 and note 96). Therefore, a purely monetary system, imposed by the Crown, and a purely natural system of self-sufficiency and barter coexisted in the Río de la Plata during the colonial period. However, the divide was unclear and there were infiltrations between the two systems (Romano 1998, 202).
16. Cortesao 1951, 160.
17. The affected reductions developed certain defence systems to protect themselves against attacks, such as trenches, outer walls and fences. Given the rustic nature of these defences, they were singularly ineffective in preventing the destruction of these villages (Gutiérrez 1977, 29–30).
18. Cortesao 1951, 425.
19. Cortesao 1951, 426 y 428.
20. Cortesao 1951, 429–30.
21. This period coincides with the union of the Iberian monarchies under the same king. Furthermore, Vilardaga describes the trading route and its considerable commercial activity (Vilardaga 2017, 132–33). The governor of Paraguay, Luis Céspedes de Jería, who travelled from São Paulo to take office, drew up a map (dated 8 November1628) in which he indicates the route between the two jurisdictions, which was probably the one undertaken during this enterprise. Archivo General de Indias (henceforth AGI), *Mapas y Planos*, Buenos Aires, 17.
22. The majority of these reductions were destroyed by the *bandeirantes*, which forced the Jesuits to move the remaining reductions to new territories. However, Vilardaga indicates the complex and diverse nature of the incursions carried out by the *bandeirantes*. They were not solely targeted at capturing natives and looking for gold; the expeditionaries also engaged in commercial exchanges using various products (Viladarga 2017, 135–36).
23. This military aid from the governor of Paraguay came in the wake of a refusal from the governor of Buenos Aires to provide assistance. Lugo issued seven muskets and mobilized seventy Spaniards to protect the reductions. Artigas 2016, 277–77.
24. We know that in the defense of the Jesus Maria reduction, Fathers Pedro Romero, Pedro de Mola, as well as brothers Antonio Bernal and Juan de Cárdenas had fired muskets at the *bandeirantes*, according to the report written by the Provincial Superior P. Diego of Boroa (4 March 1637), with all four suffering gunshot wounds in the clash. Cortesao 1969, 143–44.
25. Morales 2005, 581–82; note "g".
26. This coadjutor brother is mentioned as the first to have introduced firearms into the reductions on his arrival in Paraguay in 1636. His biography is in Storni 1980, 286–87.

27. Morales 2005, 556.
28. Hernández, Vol. 1, 1913, 73; Pastells 1915, 49–51. Ruiz de Montoya had already prepared the 1633 report, and at the age of nineteen, before becoming a member of the Society of Jesus, he had participated as a soldier in the campaigns against the Mapuche Indians of Chile. Thus, he had experience in this type of border area and understood the importance of the use of firearms in these regions. Ganson 2016, 199.
29. For example, following the battle of Mbororé in 1641, the Portuguese "were stripped of more than 400 muskets and 300 canoes" (Avellaneda 2005, 23).
30. Pastells 1915, 59–61, note no. 1.
31. The testimony of Brother Gabriel de Valencia, an ex-Jesuit, recounts that Brother Torres had begun the work of building firearms in the reductions twenty years previously and taught this to Father Francisco de Molina. Friar Valencia affirms that, at the time of writing his report, there would have been Indian officials in the reductions who had made the grade of teachers in this activity. Cortesao 1952, 259–60.
32. Cortesao 1952, 71.
33. Ibid., 259.
34. Ibid., 256. According to Valencia, the inhabitants of the reductions in Itatin employed similar strategies to capture firearms and blamed the Payaguá Indians. Cortesao 1952, 257.
35. Cortesao 1952, 72.
36. Cortesao 1969, 310. The Jesuits followed this stance in subsequent years, and this is the very same line of argument that was presented to the King by Antonio Ruiz de Montoya in 1643. (Artigas 2016, 289)
37. Cortesao 1970, 400.
38. Cortesao 1952, 111.
39. AGI, *Audiencia de Charcas*, leg. 120. f.374v; f.410v; f.446v; f.479v; f.508v; f.550v; f.599v; f.633v; f.678v; f.755v; f.818; f.866; f.898v; f.939v; f.990v; f.1025; and f.1104.
40. Prepared by the author. Source: Cortesao 1970, 437–39; y AGI, *Audiencia de Charcas*, leg. 120. f.374v; f.410v; f.446v; f.479v; f.508v; f.550v; f.599v; f.633v; f.678v; f.755v; f.818; f.866; f.898v; f.939v; f.990v; f.1025; f.1104. During the visit in 1657, the weapons held in the reductions of Apóstoles and San Nicolás were counted together. The first visit recorded a total of 609 firearms and the second about 738; however, the number of weapons recorded on the first visit was increased soon after, with the shipment of 150 weapons sent by the Viceroy of Peru (Álvarez Kern 1982, 172–73; Note 78.)
41. A series of orders from the governors of Paraguay state that at least 1,873 natives were mobilized for essentially military purposes (to defend Asunción, to escort a governor or build/repair forts) from San Ignacio Guazú to Asunción between 1662 and 1680. AGN, Room IX, Society of Jesus (1595–1675) 06 09 03 Society of Jesus (1676–1702) 06 09 04; ANA, History Section, Vol. 2, No.27–30; 32–36; 39–40; 44; and Vol. 45. No.4. AGI, Charcas, 92, No 9.
42. This provision was based on the aforementioned visit of Governor Juan Blázquez de Valverde, see Royal decree in Hernández, vol. 2 1913, 533–35.
43. Vice-Provincial Rada appointed as war superintendents Diego Suárez (Uruguay River upstream), Juan de Porras (Uruguay River downstream) and Luis Ernote (Paraná River); as war consultants Diego Suárez and Alejandro Valaguer (Uruguay River) and Francisco Clavijo and Antonio Palermo (Paraná River). *Cartas Provinciales Jesuitas*, BNM. Manuscripts. No. 6.976. Madrid. f.32.
44. *Cartas Provinciales Jesuitas*, BNM. Manuscripts. No 6976. Madrid. f.32. On the subject of gunpowder, Father Rada mentions in this provision that

the old explosives should be used up and the fresh powder from the port be reserved for *las veras*, which not only points to a different quality of gunpowder but also indicates that the purchase of gunpowder in the port of Buenos Aires continued despite the prohibitions.

45. *Cartas Provinciales Jesuitas*. BNM. Manuscripts. No. 6976. Madrid: 36–39.
46. In 1660, 220 armed Indians were mobilized from the Jesuit reductions to stifle the rebellion in Arecayá, where the governor of Paraguay, Alonso Sarmiento de Figueroa, was in danger. The following year an unspecified number of these troops carried out a raid on the Gran Chaco in reprisal for the attacks on Itatine and Spanish towns. In 1662 about one hundred armed San Ignacio Indians participated in a fresh assault on the Chaco that lasted four months. "Información del padre Jaime de Aguilar" [1735] AGN. Colección Andrés Lamas. Sección Documentos Varios. f.41–43vta.
47. AGI. Charcas, 15. f.1. One *arroba* equals twenty-five pounds or 11.3398 kilograms. Thus, 1,075 pounds or 487.6 kilograms of lead and 5,725 pounds or 2,596.81 kilograms of gunpowder had been taken from the reductions. This gives us an idea of the approximate volume of lead and gunpowder stored in the reductions in those years.
48. *Cartas Provinciales Jesuitas*, BNM. Manuscripts No. 6.976. f.163-f.164. This contradicts the constitutions of the order, which stated, "Arms should not be kept in the house nor instruments for vain purposes", *Constituciones de la Compañía de Jesús*, Part 3:266, 14. In: www.documentacatholicaomnia.eu/03d/1491-1556,_Ignatius_Loyola,_Constituciones_de_la_Compania_de_Jesus,_ES.pdf (20/02/18).

Bibliography

Ágoston, Gábor. 2005. *Guns for the Sultan. Military Power and the Weapons Industry in the Ottoman Empire*. Cambridge: Cambridge University Press.

Álvarez Kern, Arno. 1982. *Missões: uma utopia política*. Porto Alegre: Mercado aberto.

Andrade, Tonio. 2016. *Gunpowder Age. China, Military Innovation, and the Rise of the West in World History*. Princeton, NJ: Princeton University Press.

Appadurai, Arjun, ed. 1988. *The Social Life of Things. Commodities in Cultural Perspective*. Cambridge: Cambridge University Press.

Artigas, María Isabel. 2016. "Montoya testigo de su tiempo. Memoriales." *IHS. Antiguos Jesuitas en Iberoamérica* 4 (2): 255–300.

Avellaneda, Mercedes. 2005. "El ejército guaraní en las reducciones jesuitas del Paraguay." *Historia Unisinos* 9 (1): 19–34.

Black, Jeremy. 2013. *War and Technology*. Bloomington, IN: Indiana University Press.

Bonomo, Mariano et al. 2015. "A Model for the Guarani Expansión in the Plata Basin and Littoral Zone of Southern Brazil." *Quaternary International* 356: 54–73.

Brown, Delmer. 1948. "The Impact of Firearms on Japanese Warfare, 1543–98." *The Far Eastern Quarterly* 7 (3): 236–53.

Burbank, Jane and Cooper, Frederick. 2010. *Empires in World History. Power and the Politics of Difference*. Princeton, NJ and Oxford: Princeton University Press.

Chase, Kenneth. 2003. *Firearms: A Global History to 1700*. Cambridge: Cambridge University Press.

Cipolla, Carlo. 1967. *Cañones y velas en la primera fase de la expansión europea 1400–1700*. Trad. castellana de Gonzalo Pontón. Barcelona: Ariel.

Constituciones de la Compañía de Jesús. c. 1556. www.documentacatholicaomnia.eu/03d/1491-1556,_Ignatius_Loyola,_Constituciones_de_la_Compania_de_Jesus,_ES.pdf

Cortesao, Jaime, ed. 1951. *Manuscritos da Coleçao de Angelis. Tomo I. Jesuitas e bandeirantes no Guairá (1549–1640)*. Río de Janeiro: Biblioteca Nacional.

———. 1952. *Manuscritos da Coleçao de Angelis. Tomo II. Jesuitas e bandeirantes no Itatim (1596–1760)*. Río de Janeiro: Biblioteca Nacional.

———. 1969. *Manuscritos da Coleçao de Angelis. Tomo III. Jesuitas e bandeirantes no Tape (1615–1641)*. Río de Janeiro: Biblioteca Nacional.

———. 1970. *Manuscritos da Coleção de Angelis. Tomo IV. Jesuitas e bandeirantes no Uruguai (1611–1758)*. Río de Janeiro: Biblioteca Nacional.

Daniels, Christine, and Michael V. Kennedy. 2002. *Negotiated Empires. Center and Peripheries in the Americas, 1500–1820*. New York and London: Routledge.

Ganson, Bárbara. 2016. "Antonio Ruiz de Montoya, Apostle of the Guaraní." *Journal of Jesuit Studies* 3: 197–210.

Gómez, Pablo Martín. 2001. *Hombres y armas en la conquista de México*. Madrid: Almena.

Gutiérrez, Ramón. 1977. *Evolución urbanística y arquitectónica del Paraguay. 1537–1911*. Resistencia: Universidad Nacional del Nordeste.

Headrick, Daniel R. 2011. *El poder y el imperio. La tecnología y el imperialismo de 1400 a la actualidad*. Trad. Castellana de Juanmari Madariaga. Barcelona: Crítica.

Hernández, Pablo. 1913. *Organización social de las Doctrinas Guaraníes de la Compañía de Jesús*. Vols. 1 y 2. Barcelona: Gustavo Gili.

Ibarra Rojas, Eugenia. 2011. *Del arco y la flecha a las armas de fuego: los indios mosquitos y la historia centroamericana, 1633–1786*. Costa Rica: Editorial Universidad de Costa Rica.

Imbruglia, Girolamo. 2014. "A Peculiar Idea of Empire: Missions and Missionaries of the Society of Jesus in Early Modern History." In *Jesuit Accounts of the Colonial Americas. Intercultural transfers, Intellectual Disputes, and Textualities. Theorising the Ibero-American Atlantic*, edited by Marc André Bernier; Clorinda Donato and Hans-Jurgen Lusenbrink, 21–49. Ontario: University of Toronto Press, UCLA Center for Seventeenth and Eighteenth Century Studies and The William Andrews Clark Memorial Library.

Jarque, Francisco, and Diego Francisco Altamirano. 2008 [1687]. *Las misiones jesuíticas en 1687. El estado que al presente gozan las Misiones de la Compañía de Jesús en la Provincia del Paraguay, Tucumán y Río de la Plata*. Buenos Aires: Academia Nacional de la Historia, Union Académique Internationale.

Latour, Bruno. 2008. *Reensamblar lo social. Una introducción a la teoría del actor-red*. Buenos Aires: Manantial.

Lee, Wayne E., ed. 2011. *Empires and Indigenes. Intercultural Alliance, Imperial Expansion, and Warfare in the Early Modern World*. New York and London: New York University Press.

Marichal, Carlos Marichal, and Johanna Von Grafenstein, coords. 2012. *El secreto del imperio español: los situados coloniales en el siglo XVIII*. México: El Colegio de México, Centro de Estudios Históricos, Instituto Mora.

Meuwese, Mark. 2009. "Subjects or Allies. The Contentious Status of the Tupi Indians in Dutch Brazil, 1625–1654." In *Bridging the Early Modern Atlantic World. People, Products, and Practice on the Move*, edited by Caroline A. Williams, 113–30. Farnham, Burlington: Ashgate.

———. 2012. *Brothers in Arms, Partners in Trade. Dutch-Indigenous Alliances in the Atlantic World, 1595–1674*. Leiden and Boston; Brill.

Mineiro Scatamacchia, Maria Cristina. 2014. "Las migraciones Tupí-guaraní en América del sur oriental." In *Historia comparada de las migraciones en las Américas*, coord. by Patricia Galeana. México: Universidad Nacional Autónoma de México, Instituto de Investigaciones Jurídicas, instituto Panamericano de Geografía e Historia.

Morales, Martín, ed. 2005. *A mis manos han llegado. Cartas de los PP. Generales a la Antigua Provincia del Paraguay (1608–1639)*. Madrid, Roma: Universidad Pontificia Comillas.

Mörner, Magnus. 2008. *Actividades políticas y económicas de los jesuitas en el Río de la Plata*. Buenos Aires: Centro Editor de Cultura.

Noelli, Francisco Silva. 2004. "La distribución geográfica de las evidencias arqueológicas guaraní." *Revista de Indias* XIV (230): 17–34.

Parker, Geoffrey. 1988. *The Military Revolution. Military Innovation and the Rise of the West, 1500–1800*. Cambridge: Cambridge University Press.

Pastells, Pablo. 1915. *Historia de la Compañía de Jesús en la Provincia del Paraguay. (Argentina, Paraguay, Uruguay, Perú, Bolivia y Brasil, según los documentos originales del Archivo General de Indias). Tomo II (1638–1668)*. Madrid: Librería General de Victoriano Suárez.

Powell, Philip Wayne. 1977. *La guerra chichimeca (1550–1600)*. México: Fondo de Cultura Económica.

Ramos Palencia, Fernando, and Bartolomé Yun-Casalilla, eds. 2012. *Desde Estambul a Potosí. Ciudades estado, imperios y mercados en el Mediterráneo y en el Atlántico ibérico, C.1200–1800*. Valencia: Universitat de València.

Roberts, Michale. 1967. "The Military Revolution, 1560–1660." *Essays in Swedish History*, 195–225.

Romano, Ruggiero. 1998. *Moneda, seudomonedas y circulación monetaria en las economías de México*. México: El Colegio de México, Fideicomiso Historia de las Américas, Fondo de Cultura Económica.

Salas, Alberto M. 1986. *Las armas de la conquista de América*. 2nd ed. Buenos Aires: Plus Ultra.

Salinas, María Laura. 2006. "Liderazgos indígenas en las misiones jesuíticas. Títulos de capitanes concedidos a los caciques guaraníes en el siglo XVII." *Folia Histórica del Nordeste* (16): 267–76.

Sánchez Santiró, Ernest, coord. 2015. *El gasto público en los imperios Ibéricos, siglo XVIII*. México: Instituto Mora.

Storni, Hugo. 1980. *Catálogo de los jesuitas de la provincia del Paraguay (Cuenca del Plata): 1585–1768*. Roma: Institutum Historicum S.I.

Susnik, Branislava. 1983. *El rol de los indígenas en la formación y vivencia del Paraguay*. Vol. 2. Asunción: Instituto Paraguayo de Estudios Nacionales.

Takeda, Kazuhisa. 2012. "Cambio y continuidad del liderazgo indígena en el cacicazgo y en la milicia de las misiones jesuíticas: análisis cualitativo de las listas de indios guaraníes." *Tellus* (23): 59–79.

———. 2016a. "Los padrones de indios guaraníes de las misiones jesuíticas (1656–1801): análisis dinámico y comparativo desde la óptica de los cacicazgos." *Surandino Monográfico* (1): 66–105.

———. 2016b. "Las milicias guaraníes en las misiones jesuíticas del Río de la Plata: un ejemplo de la transferencia organizativa y tácticas militares de España a su territorio de ultramar en la primera época moderna." *Revista de Historia Social y de las Mentalidades* 20 (2): 33–72.

Vilardaga, José Carlos. 2017. "Na bagagem dos peruleros: mercadoria de *contrabando* e o caminho proibido de São Paulo ao Paraguai na primeira metade do século XVII." *Anais do Museu Paulista* 25 (1): 127–47.

Wilde, Guillermo. 2009. *Religión y poder en las misiones guaraníes*. Buenos Aires: Editorial SB.

Yun-Casalilla, Bartolomé. 2004. *Marte contra Minerva. El precio del imperio español, c.1450–1600*. Barcelona: Crítica.

12 Transatlantic Markets and the Consumption of Sevillian Art in the Viceroyalty of Peru

The Portobelo Fairs in Tierra Firme (Seventeenth Century)[1]

Fernando Quiles

There are stories that are not told, because they are only for their own protagonists. And even if they were only supporting actors, their presence would have enabled us to better comprehend the events recalled in the chronicles. In relation to the encounter between Europe and America, this intra-history would have provided us with long and detailed stories of great interest. Fortunately, the selective process of the recovery of documentary sources is allowing these secondary characters to return to the scene. On this subject José Luis Comellas would say:

> If we were to limit ourselves to the repercussions of trade and commerce on the social and economic reality of Seville in the sixteenth and seventeenth centuries, not only would we be left with only part of the truth, but we would also be falsifying the truth, apart from exposing ourselves to not understanding anything at all. Seville's contact with America was total, from the human element, to the transfer of ideas, devotions, art, the way of building houses, the celebration of festivals, to the transfer of plants and animals, elements of the landscape transplanted from one shore to the other.
>
> (Comellas 1992, 137)

In this instance, the incidental may have been the main component and therefore must be recovered. The Portobelo fairs provided the scenario for fruitful artistic exchange between Spain and the Viceroyalty of Peru. This has been revealed through research, despite the paucity of sources.

Nombre de Dios, one of the first Spanish settlements on the Isthmus of Panama, did not live up to expectations in terms of serving the interests of the Crown.[2] Too many risks and problems of all kinds emerged. Also on the Atlantic shore of the Isthmus, Portobelo seemed to be the better alternative. It was the gateway to Tierra Firme, that is to say, to continental South America, and met with government expectations, but above all

DOI: 10.4324/9781003168058-13

Portobelo matched the requirements of the business community. Linked to the city of Panama, it is located to the west, on the road of Las Cruces and the Chagres River, a route drawn up at the behest of Emperor Charles V in 1527. It was here that the fleet from Seville docked, mainly to load a variety of goods as well as gold and silver from the mines of Peru destined for Europe, and to unload commodities arriving from the port of Seville. But not even the better geographical and defensive conditions of Portobelo prevented normal business transactions from being affected by certain unforeseeable circumstances, such as the effects of the inclement tropics, the rampant pirate activities in the Caribbean, the threatening presence of the English and the Dutch and, worse still, the clash of interests between Sevillian merchants and those settled in the viceroyalty, the so-called *peruleros*.[3]

Nevertheless, Portobelo was a cultural melting pot at the confluence of two worlds: the European world, bringing with it a new creative seed, and the American, which encouraged that seed to germinate, giving rise to a new artistic universe. Unfortunately, there are many shadows that blur the outlines of this chapter in the history of Ibero-American baroque art. Dates have been established, names have been linked and figures have been provided for the volume of sales and the nature of these transactions. But nothing conclusive has been said, nor indeed does the present work claim to do so, to highlight the huge significance of this mercantile enclave in the exchange of art between the mainland and the viceroyalties.

Portobelo: A Place in the Caribbean

Portobelo's beginnings were marked with difficulty and were tolerated only "begrudgingly"[4] by the inhabitants of Nombre de Dios, mostly merchants, who were forced to move to the new enclave. The bishop of Panama (from 1534), known for his work in opening the Chagres road, did not have the best opinion of the place and its inhabitants, saying that it was a "cave of thieves and a burial place of pilgrims".[5] It was in the year 1595 when the engineer Bautista Antonelli was ordered from Havana to undertake the construction of the port and the city of Portobelo with its fortification.[6] Thankfully he gave us a description of the place.[7]

Some years later the city would be described as "crescent-shaped, with the tips pointing to the East and West, and the main part between the sea and the foothills of a mountain range", with two main streets and others intersecting, as well as two squares, the main one being the "square of the sea". From 1630 onwards this became the Customs Office, which is why the square ended up being called "the Royal Accounting Office Square".[8] With its customs building, the square became the center of royal power, although there is every indication that it failed to deliver in terms of fiscal efficiency, since the authorities never managed to fully control shipping cargoes. Smuggling was the order of the day, despite the fact that attempts were made to provide the customs authorities with greater resources. The truth is that conflict between the state and private economic power was inevitable. It was impossible to unravel the web created by the myriad of financial operations carried out by private individuals. It has been said that there was nothing more confusing than the dealings between shipping agents, known as *flotistas* or *galeonistas*, and the merchants of the Indies, while the viceroy's agents did their best to guarantee the Crown's share of profit. Complaints about the way in which public and private interests were intermingled in the profits obtained in Portobelo are countless (Walker 1979, 58–73).

This lack of control over the cargoes being loaded and unloaded in the port heavily affected the Portobelo fairs. The supervisory capacity of the customs authorities was called into question on multiple occasions. Not even the imposing stone Custom House achieved the desired result. In January 1611, while the Consejo de Indias was recommending the construction of a new building, it justified its existence so that "royal rights are not denied".[9] Officials of the Crown complained about bales that were unloaded before they ever reached port.[10]

One can only imagine the expectation aroused by the arrival of the fleets. Even the merchants of the viceroyalty were called upon to attend the event. Edicts were published all over the territory by emissaries or "messengers of the fairs". And over the period of a month and a half, or even two months, transactions were always conducted under the alleged supervision of the official authorities.[11] However, the marketing of large quantities of goods in a short period of time led to a decline in the control of prices, which fell sharply in response to the spasmodic increase in supply. Occasionally even certain sales operations were thwarted, as happened to the buyer of gold and silver Juan de Ochoa, according to his brother, living in Guayaquil.[12]

The Portobelo Fairs as an Artistic Distribution Center in America

Any attempt to pinpoint the role played by the Portobelo fairs in the two-way traffic of works of art would lead to over-simplification. It was a distribution center for goods, including artistic goods, where paintings were sold in stock canvases sent from Seville, whose transmission was entrusted to the mediators. It was also a pivotal meeting point of artistic exchange routes between the mainland and the viceroyalties. Huge quantities of artistic objects passed through the kingdoms of Tierra Firme with a fixed destination, in one direction or another. This was the privilege enjoyed by Portobelo that derived from the Crown's efforts to control the movement of goods.

Bernardo de Ulloa describes the importance of this annual meeting with a degree of hyperbole: "No monarch had in his domains such a powerful fair as the one held in Portobello [sic] annually and the envy of nations. It witnessed how twenty, thirty and sometimes up to forty million pesos in silver and gold, cocoa and other estimable fruits of those kingdoms passed from the power of the merchants of Lima and Peru to the merchants of Spain instead of the ten or twelve million worth brought from Spain".[13]

Obviously, in the context of the total volume of trade, the sale and purchase of artistic goods is little more than insignificant. There are no – nor will there ever be – figures recording the number of items that changed hands. We will never know the final destination of many of the works put on sale. The retail market does not furnish us with the means of tracing them. Many ended up in religious venues, but the majority remained in the hands of private individuals.

The figures provided by those who have first-hand access to the documentary sources are rather limited, and do not clarify the final destination of the items. Kinkead calculated the shipment to America to have been 1,309 paintings between 1645 and 1665, while for his part García Fuentes calculated this to be 240 rolls of 30–100 canvases each from 1660 onwards.[14] According to him, 80% of the shipments were distributed between Portobelo and Lima.

As for the suppliers, there are references in contracts to artists who made repeat deliveries. This was the case of Francisco de Zurbarán – and his studio – and Bartolomé Esteban Murillo, two of the most famous seventeenth-century Spanish artists, as well as Miguel Güelles, Juan de Luzón and even some of their disciples. In this respect, it can be said that Zurbarán acted "collegially", supplying the market with works from his studio, and that it was not even strange that the names of some of his disciples appeared in contracts for the delivery of canvases signed by the master. On the other hand, in the case of Murillo, for example, the studio operated autonomously even though his own contribution is barely recognized in the few documentary references. Thus, his followers and disciples also painted for the Americas, but managed the deliveries at their own risk. So it was with Juan López Carrasco, who did official work for the Casa de la Contratación and sent some consignments of paintings to the Indies. Perhaps it was no coincidence that he rented a warehouse on Vizcaínos street and half a house on Genoa Street.[15]

There are reports indicating the transactions of another disciple of Murillo, Esteban Márquez de Velasco, author of a Franciscan series consisting of a dozen large canvases, which is preserved in the Regional Museum of Guadalajara. Although contracted on 13 February 1694, with a year to execute the paintings, it does not seem to be part of the lot of 120 canvases that had been prepared for dispatch in July 1695, as the dimensions did not match.[16] Equally interesting is the fact that he had also prepared another 150 canvases for the province of Tierra Firme, "which according to Spanish prices are worth six thousand seven hundred and fifty *reales de vellon*" (debased copper coinage). Or the "sixteen canvases with half-length portraits for dispatch on the two galleons, which according to [Spanish] prices are worth seven hundred and eighty *reales de vellon*."[17] And a further illustration of the painter's talent for negotiation is that he had also prepared twenty-six pairs of silk stockings for delivery to the same destination. This demonstrates an attitude commonly found among artists and craftsmen at the turn of the seventeenth century and even more so in the following century: the search for security in American trade by amassing other commodities in addition to artistic goods, with a view to guaranteeing reasonable profits.[18]

Freight agents, forwarders and fleet captains were largely responsible for brokering the transport and sale at the fair of the commissioned works of art. The transactions were calculated in dozens, indicating the name of the middleman. One such broker was Diego Velasco, who had married his daughters to two painters, Lorenzo Vela and Francisco López Caro. In 1655, in his will, he recorded the delivery of "a chest of paintings", for the sale of which he was still owed some money.[19]

Painters also acted as intermediaries, picking up works from their studio colleagues and handing them over to the corresponding broker. This was the case of Alonso Pérez, who collected canvases for dispatch to Tierra Firme, doubtless to Portobelo. Documentation exists relating to the delivery by Juan Fajardo of 200 unframed canvases, each measuring two and a quarter rods, valued at forty-eight *reales* each.[20] A document also records how the Flemish painter Sebastián Faix entrusted his son Francisco Miguel Faix with the sale of "various goods" in the isthmus.[21]

A lawsuit filed by Francisco de Zurbarán against Captain Diego de Mirafuentes relating to paintings he had given him in April 1636, but which he did not sell because they had suffered serious damage en route, provides us with information on the aforementioned navigator, who apparently exhibited the paintings as if on a stage. It seems that the canvases were mounted. This was an unusual practice, as illustrated by the outbound records of the Casa de la Contratación, which indicates only "rolls" or "drawers" of paintings. What we do know, as evidenced by the details of the lawsuit filed by the painter, is that the cost of the damaged merchandise was significant and implied a substantial loss of earnings for the artist. The mounting of canvases may have constituted a differential element between works of greater and lesser quality and value. A witness in the case, José Durán, from Zurbarán's studio, argued that "most of them [the paintings] were original, done at the home of the said Francisco de Zurbarán, by his hand and others of the best painters of this city" (Palomero Páramo 1990, 313–30). His comment is interesting for several reasons. First of all, the reference to the "original" character of the works, as they were created by the master and other outstanding local craftsmen. It also highlights the fact that copies were a viable option when it came to filling the ship's hold. Accordingly, copies were likely to have been quite commonplace. Unsurprisingly, therefore, in the list of goods on board, paintings are always referred to as "scrolls" and nothing else.[22]

Returning to the conflict generated by the foiled delivery of Zurbarán's canvases, the financial implications are worth consideration. In the contract signed by Zurbarán and Captain Mirafuentes, a price was set for the sale of the consignment: two thousand pesos, which was precisely the amount for which the paintings could have been sold in Spain. Under no circumstance could the price be lowered. And if the deal was unsuccessful in Portobelo, the works were to be transferred to another agent, who would sell them in Lima.[23],[24] These details provide us not only with an insight into pricing, but similarly they allow us to deduce information about the market hierarchy. Portobelo was definitely a good location for sales, on account of the low costs involved. Similarly, Lima appeared to be a better alternative for the sale of quality paintings from Panama. This is confirmed by our sources, with plenty of reports on the prices of the works dispatched to the fairs. Interestingly, seven years prior to Fajardo making his delivery, Juan Luzón valued each of the 181 canvases sent to Tierra Firme at the exact same amount (forty-eight *reales*) (Kinkead 1984, 281–82. Other archive references indicate similar prices for canvases measuring no more than two rods on their longest side.

However, business in America was not always profitable. Apart from price fluctuations often determined by excessive supply, deals were regularly affected by misadventures en route, sometimes due to the sinking of a ship or the loss of cargo and damages to the canvases. This brings us back to the Zurbarán-Mirafuentes case. Four years after the delivery of the paintings, the painter had to abandon his lawsuit because the damage incurred on "fair day" prevented their sale. One of the master's disciples testified in the lawsuit:

> If any damage was caused, it was due to the bad payment made by the people who commissioned it, having heard the witness tell many people who went with Don Diego de Mirafuentes, that during a party he organized while under sail, he hung many of the paintings in the galleon and they could have been damaged as a result.
>
> (Palomero Páramo 1990, 324; Delenda 2009, 61, 64 and 65)

This was not the only incident encountered by Zurbarán in his eventful business dealings. There was talk of a foiled sale in Buenos Aires, a setback that may well have been the final straw that exhausted the patience of the artist, who from then on may have changed tack in relation to the sale of his paintings.[25]

As can be seen, there was no shortage of risks involved in these sales that took place in a fluctuating environment. The obligatory contract signed between artist and agent did not necessarily guarantee a successful outcome to the transaction, as we have already seen. There was additional uncertainty associated with going to court to enforce the terms of the agreement. And on this particular point one should also mention the possibility afforded to the purchasing party to make proposals in relation to the contents of the canvases. It would be interesting to analyze to what extent the broker could predetermine the form and content of the work.[26] Unlike paintings sold on the free market and offered in stock, which is always conditioned by prevailing tastes,[27] those sold under a contract system were subject to the criteria of the client or at least of the intermediary who signed an agreement with the painter. Documents abound providing us with specific details relating to this system of selling. The promissory notes subscribed before a notary public itemized the number of paintings, their dimensions and contents.[28]

Seville, Repository of the Fleet and Workshop of the Americas

Traffic to America was to leave a profound impression on artistic production in Seville. With the Casa de la Contratación, a new period in the artistic history of Seville came into being, characterized, over and above any aesthetic twists and turns, by the establishment of a system designed to meet the needs of a diverse clientele, with a complex mercantile structure and the complicity of an artistic community that had to transform its artisanal production methods to others closer to manufacturing processes.[29] This in turn brought about changes in the relationship between the guilds and the administration. The Crown responded to the growth in shipments of works of art, especially paintings, by levying fees, which the painters themselves tried to reduce or eliminate. In this context we must also acknowledge the *Art of Painting* lawsuit filed by its overseers, Matías de Arteaga and the unknown Juan Joseph, against the lessor of the *almojarifazgo* (customs tariff), for charging "exit duties on religious paintings produced in this city by the masters of this art in their houses and studios" being sent to the ports of the Indies.[30]

Aside from the possible restructuring of the local artistic environment, it is evident that there were changes in the size of the studios, with a noticeable increase in the number of apprentices and officials. And the studios moved to better locations in the city area, concentrated around the district of San Juan de la Palma and in particular the areas adjacent to the Calle de la Feria, in its two sections. The weekly market was organized along this route and the streets crisscrossing it and the local painters made full use of the proximity of their studios to engage with this street trade.

Ceán Bermúdez, who was familiar with the fair in its final stages at the beginning of the nineteenth century, had the following to say:

> Many artists and craftsmen live in this neighborhood and supply almost all of Andalusia with their works, especially paintings. . . . Formerly there was much more traffic and dispatch of these paintings than now, because they were constantly being shipped to America, which provided another new stimulus for the progress of art, because then they were not as bad as the ones painted in the day, and many teachers of merit, when they did not have work to do, went to the shippers to the Indies, who never gave up using them, paying them in proportion to their ability.
>
> (Ceán Bermúdez 1968, 35–37)

These craftsmen, who were called *pintores de feria*, as described by Ceán, "executed [their paintings] with such haste, that on more than one occasion they painted the image or saint that the devout buyer was asking for while the price was still being negotiated" Ceán Bermúdez 1968, 35–37). And it is likely that under these conditions Murillo would have embarked on his American career. For, as related by Palomino, "having learned what was required for this *pintura de feria* he made a consignment of paintings for shipment to the Indies" (Palomino 1947, 1.031). The news, by virtue of the fact that it was recounted by Palomino, appears credible. And it could well have had an impact on the artistic production of the young painter (Quiles 2009, 30).

In any case, let us not lose sight of what we said earlier about the mass production of the Seville studios serving the large market generated via the Casa de la Contratación. This enormous production forced them to work with immovable iconographic patterns, not in the form of prints, but canvases crafted from fully accepted models, formal codes defined by the *maestro* of the studio, but also guided by foreign references (Caturla 1953, 40–41; Navarrete Prieto 1999, 23). The case of Zurbarán is a classic example. His were the series of holy martyrs, with human archetypes well defined by the painter.[31] The same is true for his series *The Twelve Tribes of Israel*. With these repertoires Zurbarán displays his mastery of creating patterns, or "his capacity", as Navarrete would say, "to create models and stereotypes that would be responsible for later versions, copies, derivations and imitations".[32]

Consumption Patterns and Trans-Atlantic Demand

This traffic of works between Seville and Portobelo, as well as its impact on the city of Panama, cannot be explained, however, without a fundamental distinguishing factor differentiating it from other cultural transfers studied by historians: American demand derived from the fact that the type of consumer and the consumption patterns which, in principle, they sought to serve were the same; that is, Spaniards from various social classes and above all from the elite settled in the New World. Key to this was the remarkable popularity of the commodity among the elites, which included affluent American merchants. The wealthy nobility based in Seville and overseas stimulated production and contributed to the popularization and dissemination of themes that were refined in Seville. The new American lines involved the inclusion of "peninsular environments and experiences", as Juan Miguel Serrera said (Serrera 1988, 68). In some cases, artists catered for public interests. Hence, for example, the interest in the list of paintings that were leaving Seville for the Indies in 1586, mainly destined for New Spain and comprising battle paintings, images of the Emperor Charlemagne, the victories of Charles V and the Histories of the Emperors, which were very common themes.[33]

As an illustration of this sense of artistic community between Seville and Tierra Firme, the gateway to the viceroyalty, with Panama and Portobelo as meeting points, one cannot omit the extraordinary crossover of artistic religious production that was already taking place in the sixteenth century. The carving of the Virgin of Copacabana housed in the Sevillian convent of Madre de Díos dates from 1617 and has been attributed to the Indian sculptor Sebastián Acostopa Inca. In contrast, there is the growing presence of the Sevillian *Virgen de la Antigua* in the Americas. This is reflected in the place-name: after Nuñez de Balboa founded the city of Santa María de la Antigua del Darién in 1510, many other American enclaves adopted the name. At the same time, reproductions of the sculpture appeared in numerous places throughout the viceroyalty, including the statue in the Chapel of the Kings, in the cathedral of Lima (1545), and the one that Angelino de Medoro painted in Santo Domingo de Tunja, Colombia (1587). The Virgin of Guadalupe, of New Spanish origin, was very popular in the peninsula, while Saint Ferdinand had considerable influence in the new territories, which implied an exchange of iconographies and artistic models in both directions. All this was possible with the assistance of religious institutions and secular and regular clergy, as has been documented either through commissions or accounting records. This is how the scale of this artistic flow can be measured and, while many works have been lost, it is at least possible to evaluate authors and origins, dates and prices. Another contributing factor to the process of creating hybrid and mixed patterns on an Atlantic scale is the movement of artists, as reflected in the Archivo General de Indias' records.[34] In addition, the religious orders not only favored changes to the artist studios on the mainland, but they also stimulated the work of artists of American origin. Some of these became well known, such as Tito Yupanqui or Acostopa Inca, who spread native techniques and materials, such as corn cane paste or maguey.[35] Even several decades after the creation of this common area, we still find other successful sculptors in this terrain. One of these is Alfonso Martínez, an artist from the glory days of the baroque era, in the circle of José de Arce in Seville. We have various reports of his relations with Portobelo, such as the debts owed to him without any particular explanation as to the reasons, but which are doubtless connected to his artistic production. In relation to another painter, Juan de Uceda Castroverde, we have confirmation of his American itinerary. His administrative records allude to his trip to Lima to "settle certain deals that I have negotiated with and communicated by letters that I have sent and that certain people in this city have responded to regarding altarpieces and paintings which is my art at the service of the parish churches and the monasteries and convents of friars and nuns of that city" (Navarrete Prieto 1997, 231–32; Stastny 1998, 23–28).

Of course, all of the above does not rule out the fact that colonial art maintained a certain independence from that of the mainland. Some studies on the use of furniture and artistic objects in Panamanian homes, although not conclusive, present us with a cultural mosaic of such diversity that it is hard to believe that artistic uses and customs were entirely conditioned by the mainland. The presence in homes of glazed earthenware or majolica from places as distant as Xalapa or Callao illustrates a geographical reality that prevailed over dependence on the mainland. As with other types of goods, such as silks or porcelain, as seen in the study by José Luis Gasch-Tomás, it was common to mix styles so that these hybrid products would end up articulating their own style – Creole – which was neither Spanish nor American, but a mixture of both, with the inclusion of Asian elements in some cases (Gasch Tomás 2018). The development of genuinely American schools, such as the one in Cuzco in the eighteenth century, demonstrates this autochthonous ability to create their own unique styles.[36] This is not inconsistent with the fact that, for a long time, Seville was an important supplier of works of art, assuming a certain responsibility in the development of the artistic sensitivities of viceregal society,[37] thus echoing the words of Michèle Moret, that Seville was, first and foremost, America.

Notes

1. I would like to thank Bartolomé Yun-Casalilla for his generosity in accepting this work. Not only has he shown great patience with the slow process of its preparation, but he has also read it numerous times, introducing countless improvements. In a way, it is as much his as mine.
2. In the haphazard life of the Atlantic terminals of the isthmus, Nombre de Dios had not even a century of existence, 1510 to 1597 (Mena García 2000, 77–96).
3. Perhaps the best-known work on the issue is by García Fuentes 1997.
4. The expression is from Mena García 2007, 386. This subject has been addressed on several occasions by the same author, among others Mena García 2000, 77–96.

5. The complete commentary, made in a letter written in February 1535 and addressed to Charles I, is: "It is fitting that Your Majesty command the people of Nombre de Dios, which is a cave of thieves and a burial place of pilgrims, for which I certify to Your Majesty that it is disheartening to see the injustices being committed there, and those who ought to remedy them are mainly responsible, because they are the owners of the pack animals but who do not want to give them, until the owners of the shops sell to them [goods or agricultural products they have to transport]" (Figueras Vallés 2013, 7).
6. Archivo General de Indias (henceforth AGI.). Sec. Patronato, 26, R. 35, 1595.
7. This is what he said: "The two places, one where the city has to be made and the other where the fortress has to be made; where the city is to be made is a plain where a large population can settle and the ground is all gravel, and a freshwater stream runs through it and it seems to be healthier land than Nombre de Dios [. . .] I believe that the second fleet will come to this port to unload and when the loading of the first fleet to Panama is finished, the inhabitants of Nombre de Dios will be able to come here to build their houses, so that people will arrive and the food will be cheaper, and everything will help boost the defenses of the port and thus some salaries could be spared." AGI, Patronato, 26, R. 35, fols. 1 r/v.
8. Transcription of the *Descripción de Portobelo de 1610*, in Mena Garcia 2000, 77–78.
9. AGI, Panama, 1, N. 255, fol. 1r. The letter, apart from suggesting the expenditure of 6,000 ducats from the Royal Treasury, in addition to expenditure on materials, refers to making available slave labor from the fortifications: "the slaves of the fortifications that Your Majesty has there are mainly officials. . . ".
10. "They do not pass through customs, because everyone takes them from the beach to their homes, having lost all fear of doing so, confident that there is no justice, no royal officer, no guard who dares to inquire whether the bundles and trunks are registered or have been charged duties" (Álvarez Nogal 2011, 20).
11. The president of the Panama Court, the general of the galleons and two trade representatives (Gutiérrez Álvarez 1993, 30–32).
12. In a letter dated 16 November 1672 he said, "[Y]ou know the sadness that was caused in this place by the bad fair that has taken place in Portobelo and more so in Cartagena, because the clothes that arrived in the Armada have been sold at a lower price than they would have been worth in Spain. . . . From Portobelo I came to Cartagena to sell your wines and oils, but I couldn't do it on account of the large amount of clothes and merchandise already there" (Lobato Franco 2005, 213).
13. *Noticias sobre el Reino de la Nueva España*, doc. IV de 1745, pág. 32. Quoted for the reference by Abel Juárez Martínez 1977, 25.
14. However, these consignments did not only go to Portobelo (Kinkead 1984, 303–4; García Fuentes 1982, 324.
15. The landlord was José Belero. Contract signed on 8 June 1676 (Kinkead 1984, 294).
16. Contract published by Roda Peña 1988, 16 and 17. See Cruz Lara 2014.
17. Document transcribed in Quiles and Cano 2006, 258–59.
18. It was not uncommon to try to sell other products, with which a minimum profit was ensured (Méndez Rodríguez 2005, 166–68).
19. "I declare that in Portobelo and in December 1651 Diego de Yuste, resident, was given a drawer with my paintings and as a result I have received from

Antonio de Juste, his brother, 300 pesos of 8 reales each in silver reales, with the remainder of the value of the paint drawer being due, which was delivered by Diego de Juste to Don Pedro de Peñarrieta, a resident of the Indies, despite having exceeded the order I gave for collection, I have authorized Antonio de Juste to collect the rest" (Quiles 2009, 61).

20. In 1664 (Kinkead 2006, 135–36).
21. As recorded in his will. Archivo Histórico Provincial de Sevilla [AHPS], lib. 3701, pp. 260–61; 25-X-1660.
22. In spite of the fact that Caturla, a great connoisseur of Zurbarán's art, was of the opinion that "the master hardly put his brush on them" (Cartula 1953, 41).
23. Palomero Páramo 1990, 313–30; Caturla and Delenda 1994, 305. The bibliography relating to the Portobelo fairs is well known, with some classic texts such as Allyn Loosley's being of particular note (Loosley 1933, 314–35; Vila Vilar 1982, 275–340; Álvarez Nogal 2006.
24. According to the expert, Muñoz Naranjo, the paintings were sold in Portobelo "for the highest prices possible, with attention to the prices referred to in the report which were cost prices in Spain. And if he had wished to sell them in this city they were paid very favorably on account of them being very good and the reason for giving them to the said Diego de Mirafuentes was because he said that in the Indies he would get treble the money that was being paid for them here" Palomero Páramo 1990, 323–24.
25. It is possible that Zurbarán may have given up his American business affairs after the unsuccessful deal in Buenos Aires, in 1661 (Caturla 1951, 27–30).
26. How artists became conditioned by the personal taste of their clients is a matter I have previously dealt with (Quiles 2009, 117).
27. Morán recognizes the modern nature of sales of stock. Morán Turina 1997, 115.
28. For example, Luis Carlos Muñoz, who had promised Don Juan Antonio de la Torre to give him several series of canvases after four months, namely twenty-four angels with *ceras de flores*, two sets of virgins, twelve canvases of famous men, six images of Nuestra Señora de la Soledad, six images of Nuestra Señora de la Concepción, six images of Nuestra Señora del Rosario, and six images of Nuestra Señora del Pópulo, 2.33 x 1.33 v. Kinkead 1983, 98, doc. no.20.
29. Gállego and Gudiol explained it as follows: "Zurbarán's workshops of the time in Seville were authentic factories of wholesale paintings". Gállego and Gudiol 1975, 39; Sánchez 2013, 177–96.
30. Published by Gestoso y Pérez, Vol. III, 1899–1909, 271, and related by Kinkead 1984, 307, and weighed up by Navarrete 1990, 23). The *almojarifazgo* was a medieval tax, which Alfonso X set at one-eighth of the price of goods passing through customs, whether in a port or at the entrance to a city. It was used especially on the American route, on goods unloaded in port and those loaded on ships. More information in Gil Blanco 1986.
31. I have greatly simplified the masterful way in which Zurbarán operated. For further information, see Navarrete Prieto 2015, 62–63, 67–68.
32. Navarrete Prieto 2015, 63. Also Navarrete Prieto 1995, 45–99. See also Fraile Martín 2017, 32–44.
33. Andrés Franco was given the six painted canvases of battles and Diego de Guerra an altarpiece of the Emperor Charlemagne; and, finally, also in New Spain, he received eleven painted canvases of Charles' victories. Twenty-four canvases of *The History of the Emperors* "were sent to Tierra Firme, in the name of Baltasar de Navarrete". Cited by Iván A. Quintana Echevarría,

"Notas sobre el comercio artístico entre Sevilla y América en 1586," *Anales del Museo de América* (8), 103–10.

34. For instance, the sculptor from Seville, Cristóbal de Ojeda, travelled to Peru in the mid-seventeenth century (Romero Sánchez 2013, 863–76). From this article I have extracted a very explicit documentary reference on the reason why the sculptor from Seville travelled to Peru: "In this province there are no teachers of this craft . . . and it is fitting that there should be teachers of all the arts and especially of this one which is a liberal art, very necessary for divine worship and the adornment of churches, especially now that the king has commanded that churches be built in all the Indian villages and other settlements, and it is also necessary that there should be altarpieces and images for the use and devotion of the people and Indians of that land" (Romero Sánchez 2013, 866).
35. Much has been written on the subject and although they refer to an Andalusian context, I think it is worth considering the comments of Rodriguez Becerra and Rodriguez Hernandez, in relation to the influence of religious orders on baroque composition in the region (Rodriguez Becerra and Rodriguez Hernandez 2008, 171–95). See the chapter on "La series de Fundadores de Órdenes" in Navarrete Prieto 1999, 43–47.
36. From the extensive bibliography on this subject, I should like to highlight two brief but insightful works, both with regard to the evolution of the school and the symbolic repertoire of its production (Campbell 2009, 101–13; Valenzuela 2015, 153–69).
37. In 1964 Michèle Moret began the second part of his study on "Aspects de la société marchande de Séville du début du XVIIe siècle" in these terms: "Séville au début du XVIIe siècle, c'est, d'abord, l'Amérique. Sur ce point capital, aussi notre documentation enrichit de quelques touches un tableau devenu classique". Moret 1964, 546–90, quotation from p. 546.

Bibliography

Álvarez Nogal, Carlos. 2006. "Mercados o redes de mercaderes: el funcionamiento de la feria de Portobelo." In *XIV Internacional Economica History Congress*. Helsinki, 21–25 August 2006, sesión 18. www.helsinki.fi/iehc2006/papers1/Alvarez.pdf

———. 2011. "Mercados o redes de mercaderes: el funcionamiento de la feria de Portobelo." In *Redes y negocios globales en el mundo ibérico, siglos XVI-XVIII*, edited by Nikolaus Böttcher, Bernd Hausberger and Antonio Ibarra, 53–86. Madrid, Frankfurt and Main: Iberoamericana, Vervuert.

Campbell, Aida Balta. 2009. "El sincretismo en la pintura de la Escuela Cuzqueña." *Cultura* (23): 101–13.

Caturla, Maria Luisa. 1951. "Zurbarán exporta a Buenos Aires." *Anales del Instituto de Arte Americano e Investigaciones Estéticas* (4): 39–43.

———. 1953. *Zurbarán*. Exhibition catalogue. Madrid: Dir. General de Bellas Artes.

Caturla, Maria Luisa, and Odile Delenda. 1994. *Francisco de Zurbarán*. Paris: Wildenstein Institute.

Ceán Bermúdez, Juan Agustín. 1968. *Carta de D. Juan Agustín Ceán Bermúdez a un amigo suyo, sobre el estilo y gusto en la pintura de la escuela sevillana*. Sevilla: Ayuntamiento.

Comellas, José Luis. 1992. *Sevilla, Cádiz y América: El trasiego y el tráfico*. Málaga: Arguval.

Cruz Lara, Adriana. 2014. "De Sevilla al Museo Regional de Guadalajara. Atribución, valoración y restauración de una serie pictórica franciscana." PhD diss., Universidad Nacional Autónoma de México.

Figueras Vallés, Estrella. 2013. "El cruce del Istmo centroamericano. Un proyecto renacentista." In *América. Poder, conflicto y política*, coord. by Gabriela Dalla Corte Caballero, Ricardo Piqueras Céspedes and Meritxell Tous, 401–14. Murcia: Universidad de Murcia.

Fraile Martín, Isabel. 2017. "El *Zurbaranismo novohispano*. Revisión a los modelos iconográficos más influyentes en Puebla." *Quiroga* (12): 32–44.

Gállego, Julián and José Gudiol. 1975. *Zurbarán. 1598–1664*. Barcelona: Polígrafa.

García Fuentes, Lutgardo. 1997. *Los peruleros y el comercio de Sevilla con las Indias, 1580–1630*. Seville: Universidad de Sevilla.

———. 1982. *El comercio español con América 1650–1700*. Seville: Diputación Provincial.

Gasch Tomás, José Luis. 2018. *The Atlantic World and the Manila Galleons. Circulation, Market, and Consumption of Asian Goods in the Spanish Empire, 1565–1650*. Leiden: Brill.

Gestoso y Pérez, José. 1899–1909. *Ensayo de un diccionario de los artífices que florecieron en Sevilla: Desde el siglo XIII al XVIII inclusive*. 3 vols. Seville: Oficina de la Andalucía Moderna.

Gil Blanco, Emiliano. 1986. "El almojarifazgo como índice de interpretación del comercio del puerto de Veracruz, 1600–1622." *Estudios de historia social y económica de América* (2): 89–119.

Gutiérrez Álvarez, Secundino José. 1993. *Las comunicaciones en América: De la senda primitiva al ferrocarril*. Madrid: Mapfre.

Juárez Martínez, Abel. 1977. "Las ferias de Xalapa 1720–1778." *Primer Anuario*, 17–44.

Kinkead, Duncan T. 1983. "Artistic Trade between Seville and the New World in the Mid-seventeenth Century." *Boletín del Centro de Investigaciones Históricas y Estéticas* (25): 73–101.

———. 1984. "Juan de Luzón and the Sevillian Painting Trade with the New World in the Second Half of the Seventeenth Century." *The Art Bulletin* 66 (2): 303–10.

———. 2006. *Pintores y doradores en Sevilla 1650–1699: documentos*. Bloomington, IN: Authorhouse.

Lobato Franco, Isabel. 2005. "El negocio de Indias y la quiebra mercantil en el siglo XVII: la quiebra de Juan Ochoa de Iurretauría, comprador de oro y plata." In *El sistema atlántico español (siglos XVII-XIX)*, edited by Carlos Martínez Shaw and José María Oliva Melgar, 203–22. Madrid: Marcial Pons.

Loosley, Allyn. 1933. "The Puerto Bello Fairs." *Hispanic American Historical Review* 13: 314–35.

Mena García, Carmen. 2000. "Portobelo y sus interminables proyectos de traslado." *Tiempos de América* (5–6): 77–96.

———. 2007. "Traslado y reconstrucción de la nueva ciudad de Panamá (1673)." In *Orbis Incognitvs. Avisos y legajos del Nuevo Mundo: homenaje al profesor*

Luis Navarro García, coord. by Fernando Navarro Antolin, 385–96. Huelva: Universidad de la Hueva.
Méndez Rodríguez, Luis. 2005. *Velázquez y la cultura sevillana*. Seville: Universidad de Sevilla.
Morán Turina, Miguel. 1997. "Público, públicos e imágenes." In *El arte de mirar. La pintura y su público en la España de Velázquez*, edited by Miguel Morán and Javier Portús, 83–92. Madrid: Istmo.
Moret, Michèle. 1964. "Aspects de la société marchande de Séville du début du XVIIe siècle." *Revue d'histoire économique et sociale* 42 (4): 546–90.
Navarrete Prieto, Benito. 1995. "Génesis y descendencia de Las doce tribus de Israel y otras series zurbaranescas." In *Zurbarán. Las doce tribus de Israel. Jacob y sus hijos*, edited by Gabriele Finaldi, 45–99. Madrid: Museo del Prado.
———. 1997. "El viaje del pintor Juan de Uceda a Lima." *Archivo Español de Arte (AEA)* (279): 331–32.
———. 1999. *Zurbarán y su Obrador. Pinturas para el Nuevo Mundo*. Cat. Exp. México: Museo Nacional de San Carlos.
———. 2015. "Las santas de Zurbarán y el concepto de persuasión en el siglo XVII." In *XV Jornada de Historia de Fuente de Cantos: Zurbarán, 1598–1664.350 aniversario de su muerte*, coord. by Felipe Lorenzana and Rogelio Segovia, 57–68. Fuente de Cantos: Lucerna Asociación Cultural.
Palomero Páramo, Jesús M. 1990. "Notas sobre el taller de Zurbarán. Un envío de lienzos a Portobelo y Lima." In *Extremadura en la evangelización del Nuevo Mundo*, edited by Sebastián García, 313–30. Madrid: Sociedad Estatal Quinto Centenario.
Palomino, Antonio. 1947. *El museo pictórico y escala óptica*. Madrid: Aguilar.
Quiles, Fernando. 2009. *Sevilla y América en el Barroco. Comercio, ciudad y arte*. Seville: Bosque de Palabras.
Quiles, Fernando, and Ignacio Cano. 2006. *Bernardo Lorente Germán y la pintura sevillana de su tiempo (1680–1759)*. Madrid: Simois.
Quintana Echevarría, Iván A. 2000. "Notas sobre el comercio artístico entre Sevilla y América en 1586." *Anales del Museo de América* (8): 103–10.
Roda Peña, José. 1988. "Una serie desconocida sobre la vida de San Francisco, embarcada para Nueva España, obra del pintor Esteban Márquez." *Topo'92. La Revista del 92* (2): 16–17.
Rodriguez Becerra, Salvador, and Salvador Hernández González. 2008. "Las órdenes religiosas y la religiosidad en Andalucía durante el barroco." In *Congreso Internacional Andalucía Barroca*, coord. by Alfredo J. Morales, 171–96. Seville: Junta de Andalucía.
Romero Sánchez, Guadalupe. 2013. "El escultor sevillano Cristóbal de Ojeda y su partida al Perú." *Laboratorio de Arte* (25): 863–76.
Sánchez, José María. 2013. "Los obradores artísticos sevillanos del siglo XVI: Adaptaciones y cambios para satisfacer los encargos del mercado americano." *Anales del Instituto de Investigaciones Estéticas* (103): 177–96.
Serrera, Juan Miguel. 1988. "Zurbarán y América." In *Zurbarán*. Catalogo Exposición, 63–83. Madrid: Museo del Prado, Ministerio de Cultura.
Stastny, Francisco. 1998. *Redescubramos Lima: Conjunto Monumental de Santo Domingo*. Lima: Banco de Crédito.

Valenzuela, Fernando Z. 2015. "Pintura colonial andina: Estructura simbólica y sincretismo." *Atenea* (512): 153–69.

Vila Vilar, Enriqueta. 1982. "Las ferias de Portobelo: Apariencia y realidad del Comercio con Indias." *Anuario de Estudios Americanos* (39): 275–340.

Walker, Geoffrey. J. 1979. *Política española y comercio colonial. 1700–1789*. Barcelona: Ariel.

Afterthoughts

13 From Goods to Commodities in Spanish America

Structural Changes and Ecological Globalization From the Perspective of the European History of Consumption[1]

Bartolomé Yun-Casalilla

One of the most accepted ideas by contemporary historians is that America's contact with Eurasia and Africa in 1492 produced an unprecedented upheaval in human history. Authors such as McNeill (1977), Crosby (1986), and Diamond (1997), to name but a few of the most influential, have made it clear how the "encounter" between European and American ecosystems – microbial complexes, animals, plants, etc. – produced the destruction of the latter, and with it a hecatomb of a far-reaching demographic nature that would dramatically and irreversibly change the lives of the original Americans and their societies. This is, without a doubt, the most important turning point of what we can call American globalization, which is the focus of our attention here.

As stated in the introduction, the globalization of America entailed more than this process. We must also consider as part of it the inverse development by which America flooded the world with products, goods, plants, animals, and commodities, which contributed to deep changes not only in European societies but also in their political economies and economic thought (Carmagnani 2012). But our focus here is to examine the many transformations that American forms of consumption and material culture underwent since the arrival of the Europeans in 1492. It is also in this context that I would like to reflect in general terms on two different but complementary avenues. On the one hand, I want to underline the complexity and the obstacles involved in the process of introducing European and Asian goods into Spanish America. In doing so, I will also share some observations on how studying the case of America sheds light and serves to criticize many of the existing – and by degrees revised – clichés in relation to the history of consumption. In this connection, we must understand what happened from a dual perspective: its significance in the long-term process of globalization of material cultures that humanity has witnessed since its origins; and what this signified in terms of trade. These are two perspectives which, while they refer to the same

DOI: 10.4324/9781003168058-14

phenomenon, have not been linked by historiography. Secondly, I would like to draw attention to the need to compensate for the emphasis that some studies, such as Crosby's, place on what he called the "ecological imperialism" of Europeans and "neo-Europes" and, above all, his insistence on its most destructive aspects. These questions will hopefully serve to tie up some of the more or less loose ends of this book and, above all, to create some questions and approach a definition of the concept of American globalization as stated in the title.

* * *

Studies on the history of consumption and changes in material culture in Spanish America represent nothing new. They may even precede those undertaken in Europe, where since the 1980s scholars like McKendrick (1982), Roche (1989), and others dealt with a subject on which Braudel (2000) had produced some very interesting reflections. In effect, the history of consumption and of material culture have been continuously present in the many works of anthropologists and historians who have focused on social and economic change, as well as the processes of "acculturation", dominance and intercultural resistance or dialogue in general occurring in American societies since 1492.[2]

Arnold Bauer's pioneering book (2001), which articulates and systematizes a good deal of that knowledge, would scarcely have been possible without those precedents. Much of the secondary information he uses does not come from specific studies on consumption and material culture, but from works that adopt the above-mentioned perspectives. This precocity of Americanist historiography – sometimes not perceived by scholars from other areas of the world, and from Europe in particular – is in part due to the importance of the works of anthropologists, which is much greater in the case of Spanish America than in studies on early modern Europe. And perhaps it should also be related to the fact that the phenomenon of conquest and intercultural encounters forced everyone – historians and anthropologists alike – to include aspects relating to material culture and consumption in works dealing with a more extensive range of issues.

What is evident in these studies, as well as in those that have come since, is a series of increasingly pronounced characteristics that have also been gradually noticeable in the European past and that necessitate a rethinking of the history of consumption, material cultures, and even globalization. The original works of McKendrick, Roche, and even in certain aspects – although to a lesser extent – those of Braudel underlined the importance of the market and marketing, of social emulation, of fashion trends, of the processes of social levelling and of the convergences between the diverse regimes of consumption. What the history of America and of Latin America in particular shows us, however, is a panorama with different accents. Of course, mercantile persuasion, emulation and even trickle-down processes also came into play in the New World. But compared to what we historians of early modern Europe have been thinking, the differences have been quite significant. It has been demonstrated, for example, that there could have been reasons behind the concept of emulation that had nothing to do with conspicuous consumption or with the desire to imitate that Veblen spoke of (Veblen 2009). To cite just one example, what Indian chiefs or even slaves who imitated Spanish consumption patterns were often seeking – and certainly not only that – was a way to avoid being classified socially as Indians, to avoid paying taxes, and to avoid social degradation.[3] The use of coercion and even violence could coexist with marketing, vicarious consumption, or persuasion. Persuasion could be exercised through intimidation and was based on fear rather than market trends. This is demonstrated by a multitude of cases from all over the continent.[4] The agents of the process were often traders, but more frequently than not they were civil servants or members of the clergy eager to get taxes in return or to "civilize". Among the civil servants, the *repartimiento de mercancías* system was very common. This institution implied that the native American population – often represented by *caciques* and local authorities – received from an agent, who could be a merchant but was often a mayor or an authority of the king, a series of goods in exchange for other commodities that were normally oriented to extra-regional marketing.[5] Regarding priests, contrary to the image we might have of them, their promotion of certain forms of consumption and merchandise also could have had financial motivations, as has been demonstrated in the case of the Jesuits in many American regions (Svriz-Wucherer 2019). In Europe, the adoption (or not) of certain consumption patterns or elements of material culture has been associated with hierarchical divisions and deep-rooted forms of consumption norms that, only in the eighteenth century and in England especially, would have given way to forms of consumerism in which only economic availability, and not the fact of belonging to a closed social order, would limit the spread of fashion trends (McKendrick 1982).[6] What Latin American colonial societies show is that purchasing power was an important factor in the demand of some goods, and that its importance was accentuated in certain regions and consumer segments. But, on many occasions purchasing power may have been less influential than social divisions in determining the dissemination of new products.[7] Added to this was the fact that access to particular commodities – in a much higher proportion than in Europe for many years – was not via the markets and that the price differential was very dissimilar from that of Europe, with the result that the popularization or otherwise of some goods could also vary, as in case of beef in a number of regions. This situation was not about to go away, but would very possibly increase over time in some consumer segments, partly due to the introduction of the caste imaginary, as a reaction to the opposite process.

There are also several aspects worth considering that have not been dealt with so systematically by historiography until relatively recently, and which provide an even greater contribution to our understanding of the globalization of consumer regimes.

The first of these refers to the relations between consumption, material culture and social change. Classical studies on Europe have already placed some emphasis on this aspect. In fact, studies have underlined from the outset how a change in appearances could constitute a change of attitude in social relations (Roche 1989). There has even been talk of how changes in consumption patterns have triggered revolutionary processes. And, of course, it has been emphasized how social change has been accompanied by transformations in material culture and consumption.[8] Nevertheless, the Latin American case goes much further and constitutes a laboratory for something that was the rule in early globalization: the encounter of societies at very different stages and models of development. It is precisely this fact that forces us to consider the relationship between changes in consumer patterns and material culture and in social structures as something that does not operate in a two-way direction. This was in fact a single process in which the market played a less central role, especially in the early stages of the process. As Crosby pointed out in his famous book, the encounter between European and American societies meant, in many cases – according to the social structures of those societies – the coming together of cultures that had long since surpassed the Neolithic revolution and developed forms of political, social and economic organization, as well as technological advancement, with others that were barely in the Iron Age, and only approaching the Neolithic revolution (Crosby 1986 *passim*). In these circumstances it is unthinkable – not to say impossible – that European products, technology, and material culture would meet with rapid acceptance in America, at least in many areas, social segments and consumer sectors. Or, in other words, contact with the settlers who came to America would simultaneously and in a parallel but selective manner activate social change, as well as the same forms of consumption and material culture. This reasoning, which undoubtedly may be viewed as tautology, nevertheless helps us – or so I hope – to understand that we need a very different approach to the one we use when we talk about this type of phenomena in Europe.

Given the diversity of pre-Columbian societies, this also implies the existence of a very wide variety of cases. The case of the Maya, studied by Nancy Farriss, among others, is that of a group in which the superposition of a system of *encomenderos* and an ecclesiastical administrative structure seem to have led to a series of transformations sparked by existing interregional family relations. The result is a superposition of societies that perhaps, with the exception of Campeche, were able to maintain their original structures for quite some time, which did not prevent the diffusion of products such as hens, nor the strong resistance of corn and potatoes, which were not to be supplanted by wheat on their land. All this was favored by the fact that the Maya seem to already belong to an advanced phase of the Neolithic revolution in which extensive slash-and-burn cultivation lasted for quite some time (Farriss 1992, 205–21).

In the absence of a more detailed comparison, it is possible to assume that the Guaraní of Paraguay followed a model which, although not necessarily the opposite, was in a sense different. Here signs of agrarian development were beginning to appear; but at least on the surface, it was even more in its infancy than in the case of the Maya. Among these peoples, activities such as hunting and gathering, typical of groups in constant movement, were vital and even determined their social structure and the associated consumer regimes and material culture. The arrival of the Jesuits was thus a hugely significant element. The *reducciones* were set up in this frontier zone for the purpose of evangelization, as they explicitly acknowledged, but also with the aim of providing the region with a defense force to protect the nearby villages and the growing production and trade of the beverage known as *mate*, of which the Society of Jesus was an important beneficiary.[9] In that framework, assigning land to a people like the Guaraní was vital for the Jesuits. But this implied a transformation of their social structures and material culture. In fact, the Jesuits encouraged a kind of induced Neolithic revolution that took place in very different conditions to those in other parts of the planet and even in other parts of America. In effect, it was not demographic pressure on resources that led to a system of settled agriculture, in accordance with the general model (at least in appearance) of Neolithic revolution in human history.[10] In this case, it was rather a case of induced settlement at a time when war was being reinforced as an essential activity, which affected the social structure. This implied the introduction of crops such as wheat – which encountered difficulties when competing with corn – and, above all, the adoption of property systems introduced by the Spaniards into the very core of Guaraní society, important changes in gender relations (with women increasingly involved in cultivation and men in war), and, above all, the growing appreciation of objects such as weapons that in the same process and in tandem transformed social structures, and the patterns of consumer behavior. This is an example of how, rather than a two-way process – from consumption to social transformations and from the latter to consumption – what took place in these societies were inseparable transformations within the social structure in its twofold dimension as producer and consumer.[11]

The second aspect relates to the importance of ecological factors in these mutations, something that has hardly concerned historians dealing with the subject in Europe. In fact, given that these were to a large extent transformations that operated through the productive system and given the variety of American ecosystems, natural conditions had to be decisive for the alteration in consumption trends. This was true above all until solid interregional markets were developed that allowed access to certain products, not due to changes in societies but due to their import from areas of different productive specialization, which was frequent in Europe but did not become reality in many American areas until well into the seventeenth century. The work presented in this volume by Manuel Díaz-Ordóñez is a good example of the limits to the massive production of a crop like hemp that had become widespread in the Old World, and particularly in Russia. For a long time, not even the active policy of the Crown managed to turn it into a plantation product that could potentially modify the history of Chile, as happened with so many other products, among them tobacco, sugar, cotton and others around which the plantation economy developed. Other products, such as wheat, wine and olives – the Mediterranean trilogy – also encountered difficulties or expanded more or less easily depending on the circumstances of the ecosystems. Their dissemination also rely on a combination of food culture, natural conditions, the possibilities of foreign trade and supply, the strength of the European presence and the regulations of the Crown, apparently important in relation to oil and other products.[12] The adoption of European consumption patterns was thus severely limited by a set of factors, including what Horden and Purcell (2000) called the "microregions", which were to play an important role.

All of this has implications far beyond American history, which also refers us to the history of globalization in its trade-related aspect. I refer here to the enormous complexity and slow pace of change in consumption patterns, and the introduction of European habits. The writings of Americanists from Bauer to the present day have spoken of rejection and resistance to these products, although it is recognized that the receptivity of the Amerindian populations varied depending on circumstance. On the other hand, it is evident that cultural distance and the physical distance of the ecosystems to which we refer imposed a relatively long lapse of time before these transformations could take place. In any case, many products took a long time to adapt, often because of their inferiority to the original products, which, as we have said, was the case with some goods such as wheat, which competed poorly in many areas with corn, cassava and potatoes. Fabrics that were fashionable in Europe, although at times overly heavy and hot until the arrival of new draperies from northern Europe, nevertheless spread across many areas. But often they could only do so with strong competition from local products and by placing lifestyle ahead of comfort and convenience (Bauer 2001). The introduction of European techniques in textile workshops and the development of local industries may also have limited the adoption of Old World fabrics (Miño 1991). It is evident, too, that the development of what some Americanists have called a monetary economy and, with it, the establishment of markets, was not an automatic process. Although it was highly developed in some areas and for some products, this form of economy, and again hens are a good example, was not established until products of this type transformed family economies and even the gender relations within them, and brought them ever closer to the marketplace. Without these transformations, there could be no longer an "industrious revolution" as described by Jan de Vries (2008), but not even a process that would make the original peoples sell more products and labor in the market and, at the same time, consume more goods – even if not of an industrial nature – in those markets.[13] We often forget that the conquest of America triggered the circulation of American products on their own continent, which in turn limited the entry of European goods. A well-known case is that of cassava, which Spanish soldiers introduced to regions where it was previously unknown (Saldarriaga 2012 chapter V). Another is that of *mate*, whose consumption and trade extended from the current Argentina to Peru thanks to the integration of regional markets derived from European colonization (Assadourian 1982). And these are just two examples that make us think about the process of American globalization in a more complex way than that of a solely bipolar relationship between the Old and the New World. Returning to the issue of the potential of the emerging American market, we must also consider the effects of demographic change. Even if we were to believe – although it is inconceivable – that there were no rejections, adaptations or hybridizations that limited the use of European goods, we must bear in mind that the demographic catastrophe drastically limited the possibilities of this potential market, making the growth of the number of possible consumers very slow. As is well known, historians have not agreed on the dimensions of the demographic disaster in America, but the figures, in any case, show a very clear decline (Romano 2004, chapter 1). On the other hand, the growth of the "white" population, the one previously best adapted to European consumption patterns, was very slow, which, together with the slow incorporation of the Indian population to the consumption of European and African products, made the market for these goods grow more slowly than had been expected (Yun-Casalilla 2019, 289). In many areas, the arrival of African populations was accompanied by the introduction of their own consumption patterns, which also hampered the development of those from Europe, as can be deduced from some known cases in the Caribbean (see, for example, Eltis, Morgan, and Richardson 2007). Although very difficult to measure, similar effects derived from sumptuary laws which the Crown aimed at maintaining the social differentiation between the indigenous and slave populations or even the most dispossessed classes of the colonizers, on the one side, and the elites of cities like Mexico or Lima, on the other.[14]

The fact that the introduction and dissemination of European products was not as automatic as had been often assumed helps to explain why the emergence of an American market for these products was not as rapid as economic historians tried to present it a few decades ago. For a long time, historians have considered the development of American markets to be a key episode in the development of European capitalism. It was even believed that Spain and Portugal missed a unique opportunity by becoming semi-peripheries in that process (Wallerstein 1979). If we pause to consider the above, however, we realize that this is a difficult assumption to sustain. Furthermore, some very rough calculations from a commercial perspective prove quite revealing. If we take into account the consignments of silver sent to Seville by Spanish emigrants to America around 1590, we can conclude that the official export trade to the New World could have been about twenty-five million *reales* a year. Naturally, this is a smaller amount than the total trade figure, given the importance of smuggling and the possible reinvestments of profits from that trade in America. But this difference is partly compensated by the fact that these figures also included the repatriation to Spain of many kinds of benefits, not all of them commercial. Moreover, given that the profits from smuggling, while significant, were far from what might have been expected, these figures can be thought of as an acceptable minimum and approximate to the volume of goods shipped from Spain. Be that as it may, the amount was equivalent to the internal trade of a city like Cordoba, which did not reach more than 2% of the gross domestic product of Castile (Yun-Casalilla 1998, 128 and 131). In these circumstances it is difficult to consider the colonial market as a potential driver of the expansion neither of European economies, nor even of the Castilian or Spanish economies, at least well into the seventeenth century. We would have to wait, most probably until the eighteenth century, for this to be attained, a fact that is underpinned by the processes described in this book.

* * *

As has previously been stated, it is very difficult to separate the study of changes in consumption and material culture in Latin America from their ecological aspects.

America has rightly been presented as one of the main victims of ecological imperialism that has dominated globalization since the fifteenth century. But that approach – rightly, of course – may have downplayed other aspects of the phenomenon that, although well known, do not always play the role they deserve in general discussions on the subject.

The first thing to consider is that the ecological globalization of the Americas was a quantum leap. At present there is a debate regarding what could be understood in some way as a previous step in the process of ecological globalization on a worldwide scale, and in the long term. I am referring to the concept of the "green revolution", which, according to some authors, had been taking place in Europe since the Muslim era. Its alleged gateway was via the Iberian Peninsula and it consisted of the reception and dissemination throughout the Mediterranean of products – many of them from distant origins in Asia – in particular citrus fruits, many types of vegetables, almonds, honey and others.[15] Horden and Purcell (2000) drew attention to the fact that it is difficult to speak of a revolution, since most of these products – and especially the most important for the Mediterranean economy, such as wheat, olive trees and vineyards – already existed. In any case, the transfer to America of many of these products is a fundamental milestone in ecological globalization. As we mentioned previously, America was inundated – albeit at a very slow pace – with the result of centuries and centuries of plant and animal development.[16] The products brought there were often the result of centuries and in some cases thousands of years of crossbreeding and migrations within Eurasia of species which were further strengthened by cross-breeding and the struggle between the various strains. In some cases, this transfer implied the existence of complementary ecological chains. Wheat was directly associated with livestock breeding and in particular with fertilization systems based on animals such as sheep, or with rotation systems and agro-pastoral cycles typical of the Mediterranean. The expansion of mules, a Eurasian "invention" of huge importance in America, was equally relevant and linked to the cultivation of barley and the use of natural grasslands.[17] Often forgotten is the fact that this animal – perhaps because it does not correspond to the image of a wild animal, in the style of those which in Crosby's vision would sweep the Americas – became a key element in Latin American economies and especially in the creation of interregional markets (Assadourian 1982 and Glave Testino 1989). Also crucial would be the use of other draft and farm animals, nonexistent – at least with the necessary level of efficiency – in the New World.

When we introduce the technology that mediates relations between human beings and the environment into the concept of the ecosystem, what was happening acquires even more significant proportions. First of all, Mediterranean technology and inventions such as the Muslim waterwheel, and then a wider technological spectrum derived from European processes of propagation and interaction, also contributed to changing the American ecological systems. Such technologies also facilitated – or were the result of – the expansion of European crops and products with which they had been associated for centuries in an exceptional laboratory created in medieval Europe, but which in many respects cannot be separated from Asia (White 1963). This process, often forgotten when historians refer solely to the enormous impact of American products on the rest of the world, not only on Europe but also on Asia and Africa, enables a better understanding of decisive steps in global history within a more complete perspective.

The second consideration is closely linked to the first. What is striking on rereading the works of Crosby and McNeill following the long time lapse since they first appeared is that although they account for a two-pronged process, they focus mainly on the destructive impact of the clash of ecosystems in the New World, leaving very much in the background the processes of environmental reconstruction arising from that clash. To give an example, a term like "weeds", used by Crosby and criticized by him, is very relative. A plant can be a weed in one ecosystem but also a fundamental and positive factor in another ecosystem's biotic chain. Clover, whose destructive character Crosby highlights, is in itself a plant that has contributed to high-productivity crop rotation systems in Europe. The pig, which by reproducing in omnivorous herds capable of destroying indigenous crops contributed to weakening the ecological balance in America, has been and remains one of the most important sources of calories for European peoples for centuries. This also became the case in America only a few decades after its introduction. And we could continue with further examples.[18]

It is also important to emphasize that the demographic and human disaster that occurred in the Americas represented a fundamental element in the ecological balance, and a decisive factor in achieving new and undoubtedly more positive balances between resources and population. The fact is all the more important because, although we know that in many areas of Latin America the relationship between resources and population was comfortable, some calculations estimate that a "full world" situation had been reached by 1492 (McNeill 1977, 179). And if one considers that the population was very possibly reduced by more than 60–70%, it is obvious that despite the initial destruction of resources, the relationship between the number of people and the environment was changing. What would happen from the second half of the seventeenth century onwards represented a new situation: a much smaller population would enjoy the available resources – some in clear relative abundance – created by ecological changes.

Also in this regard, technological transfers to America played a very important role, which, as we have said, must also enter into the equation, and be included under the concept of the ecosystem.[19] This technology was not limited to the use of animals, such as the mules mentioned above. The grinders and mills for the production of sugar perfected during centuries in Europe became a key element in the intensive use of hitherto untapped natural resources. Their usage was also associated with animals such as oxen and others that for decades had been domesticated for this type of activity. The Mediterranean plow, the thresher, the mills – also associated with the use of horses and cattle and used in all kinds of work, from the milling of cereals to sugar grinding or mining – shears, the pedal loom, the carding board, the spinning wheel, or simply the wheel applied in all types of activities in trolleys, wheelbarrows, carriages and rudimentary transport systems, all of which were new to many American regions, had the same effect when Mediterranean crops were introduced, despite the slow rate at which some of these innovations were launched. It has even been said that the machete increased productivity by four in

Brazilian *palo* farms. And there is little more that remains to be said about the introduction of Eurasian technology in mining and its effects on productivity and production or textile technology, which made it possible to increase efficiency in the processing of fibers in the workshops where it was introduced.

Although not exactly what we are stating here, Ruggiero Romano synthesized some of these ideas into an excellent book. The demographic collapse was accompanied by an increase in forced migrations, but also by an improvement in available technology and the ability to use animal labor. And, according to the author, this would lead to a different but positive combination between what he calls endosomatic working instruments (human muscular force) and exosomatic instruments (tools and machines, and animals as a source of mechanical energy applied to production) (Romano 2004, 35 et seq.). This combination proved positive insofar as it generated more wealth and available resources per inhabitant and, therefore, greater possibilities of growth that would become effective during the eighteenth century.[20] Added to this is another equally important equation. The increase in the amount of available suplies per person involved in these new production systems facilitated access to food and goods with scarcely any investment in terms of time or work in certain areas. This is the case of zones such as the Argentine pampa or some areas of Nueva Granada, where the capture of animals – cattle and horses, above all – was so easy that it made cattle rearing, as traditionally conceived, almost unnecessary. It is not surprising that both population and production increased during the eighteenth century. Moreover, it has rarely been stressed that the combination of American animals or plants with European technology or vice versa could have very positive multiplier effects. This is the case of cassava and pigs in areas where the abundance of the former facilitated more efficient feeding of these animals in captivity (Saldarriaga 2012). Another example is the use of meat, especially abundant thanks to the development of bovine production, which was used to feed the indigenous population exposed to strenuous work and whose traditional diet, based mainly on carbohydrates, was hardly sufficient for the enormous expenditure of energy required by their new work regime.[21]

All this should not make us forget that this reconstruction of the ecosystems encouraged the importation of enslaved people from Africa, and the marketing of human beings to supply the factor in scarcest supply in these new ecosystems: the labor force. Nor should we forget that these new schemes were by no means self-sustainable from the point of view of ecological balance and that they would encourage unsuspected social imbalances among pre-Columbian communities. This is particularly true since they have become an integral part of capitalist development to this day and have associated forms of production that are damaging to the environment with the large-scale production of “frontier commodities”, with devastating effects, for more than two centuries in many areas of Latin America.[22] This is another facet of American globalization from the perspective of this book. Indeed, in order to comprehend the transformations described above, one must take into account that ecological processes, changes in consumption patterns and the transformations of native communities cannot be understood without the process of mercantile globalization that was taking place at the same time. In reality, this is what was driving the development of mining – especially silver mining – and the spread of the plantation economy that was changing that world and encouraging the production and consumption of new products.

* * *

All of the above calls for reflections of a more general nature. Firstly, when changes in consumption patterns are considered in this global perspective – or American, if you like – many of the conventions in use become very relative. It ratifies the idea that alterations in consumption can no longer be understood as something located geographically. Theories such as those of McKendrick and others thus become less and less functional. Changes in consumption patterns have derived in human history from the interrelationship between geographically separated societies. The mutual influences between them have had as much or more importance than the changes in the social structures of each of them. But it is also evident – and this is not so apparent in these writings – that these changes have not always derived from marketing techniques or strategies, but frequently from intercultural relations often tinged with rejections, violence, coercion and adaptations, if not from unintended cultural transfers derived from simple contacts between societies. These are relationships which, moreover, take place in local intercultural and ethnic encounters which oblige us to study the great changes on a global scale by means of very local case studies. It is also very difficult to draw a general chronology of these changes for the whole American continent. Their rhythm depended on a multitude of factors that affected the different phases of Europeanization and globalization or the changes – also very unequal – in the border character of many regions. In addition, what is less frequent in historiography, changes in consumption patterns and in the material culture of the different peoples have been linked to profound transformations in the social system: in the passage, for example, from economies based on hunting and gathering to settled agro-pastoral communities through procedures whose complex mechanisms have remained outside the dominant currents in the history of consumption. This should be said without forgetting, as mentioned in the introduction, that coercion and more or less forced persuasion could also derive from ways of creating trust between social agents that permitted cultural and technological transfers. These are changes that cannot be dissociated: consumption does not modify with social transformation and the latter does not change the former. They are in many ways the same thing. One of the institutions that best reflects this fact is the *repartimiento de mercancías* (see a description above), which was a way of incorporating the Indians into the market while changing their consumption patterns and productive structures. Alterations in local society and its forms of consumption were thus inextricably linked.[23]

The magnitude of the processes described here also requires a review of the ideas of some economists on globalization. This cannot be understood solely from a mercantile perspective and less still from the perspective of the evolution of convergence or not between prices and wages on a planetary scale. To define it as classical economics of a narrow perspective usually does is to forget about the very large-scale transformations that have had equally important or more important effects than price convergence on millions of people.[24]

Furthermore, by looking at the problem in this way and situating it in areas that have undergone radical ecological transformation, the study of ecosystem changes becomes essential in the history of consumption. This is exactly what happened in colonial America. And this is not only in terms of the history of food, usually linked to changes in production processes, but also to other spheres of consumption. The history of consumption and material culture renovates its tone completely when we look at it from this more global perspective, in which some of the mechanisms that have been considered normal in European transitions are presented to us as exceptions, or at least as specific journeys very different from those that other peoples have lived through. Was Europe the exception? This is the question we must ask ourselves, but it would do no harm to look at Europe from an American point of view in a comparative heuristic exercise in order to look for many of the phenomena found in America, an exercise that we cannot enter into here. In view of some reflections on the globalization of consumption in recent years, America, and the way in which social habits changed there, is *also* part of the global history of consumption. While this may be regarded as a commonplace, it is nonetheless important because any history at this level that does not take into account the mechanisms that Latin American historians have been referring to for years is not a global history of consumption. It is only an approximation that does not take into account a specific case of the utmost importance that affected and continues to affect millions of human beings.

Notes

1. This research has been carried out within the framework of the project HAR2014–53797-P "Globalización Ibérica: Redes entre Asia y Europa y los cambios en las pautas de Consumo en Latinoamérica" [Iberian Globalization: Networks between Asia and Europe and Changes in Consumption Patterns in Latin America] financed by Ministerio de Economía y Competitividad,

Spain, of which I am the principal investigator, and the ERC Starting Grant GECEM (Global Encounters Between China and Europe: Trade Networks, Consumption and Cultural Exchanges in Macau and Marseille, 1680–1840), whose principal investigator is Professor Manuel Perez-Garcia. This last project has also paid for the open access of this chapter. Also the PAI Group HUM-1000, "Historia de la Globalización: Violencia, negociación e interculturalidad" [History of Globalisation: Violence, Negotiation and Interculturality], which is financed by the Regional Government of Andalusia, and its principal investigator Igor Pérez Tostado have cooperated.

2. See Farriss 1992; Boccara 1998; Wilde 2009, and others.
3. See Saldarriaga on the difficulties of the development of emulation in such different societies. Saldarriaga 2012, 142–43.
4. The most common case of mixed strategies was the creation of tax obligations on certain products. The case of hens has been studied here, but tax levies on cotton, cocoa, eggs and textiles were frequent (De la Puente Brunke 1992; Bauer 2001, 53, 67). This, while logical in low-monetized economies with a strong domestic consumer sector, also represented a way of disseminating these goods.
5. The very broad literature on this subject has provoked more than a few debates among specialists. A good synthesis also concerned with the system's rationality can be found in Rodolfo Pastor 2002.
6. The idea is developed by Yun-Casalilla 2007. On consumer norms, see Appadurai 1988.
7. On occasion the most important factor could be the need to create group or ethnic identities (Bauer 2001, 76–77), which could have a notable force in such a multiracial society.
8. This is actually a recurring theme in bibliographical terms since the early works of McKendrick, Brewer, and Plumb 1982. Brewer and Porter represent a cornerstone on this issue (1993).
9. See Garavaglia 1983 on the consumption and trade of *mate* in this region.
10. See Cohen in particular (1977).
11. This development on the Guaraní emanates above all from Omar Svriz-Wucherer (2019).
12. On the influence of the Spanish mental universe on Latin American food systems, see Earle (2012). Even the expansion of products and consumption patterns typical of the peninsula was affected by diverse opinions. Some of them opted for the prohibition of developing certain crops in America under the pretext that this was damaging to export possibilities and promoted the independence of the colonies from the metropolis. See, for example, Archivo General de Indias, Gobierno, Indiferente General, 2690 (07/09/1633). I appreciate the reference to Sergio Serrano.
13. See the chapter in this volume written by Gregorio Saldarriaga.
14. See, for example, certain passages in Ricardo Cappa, SJ (1892). Regarding slaves' depositions, see Manuel Lucena Salmoral 2000.
15. See, among others, Watson 1981. On the evolution of the concept, see Squatriti 2014.
16. On the introduction of certain products and technologies toward the end of the sixteenth century, see Bernardo De Vargas Machuca 1892, especially books II and III.
17. On the importance of this animal in Asia before its arrival into America, see various works by this author (Clarence-Smith 2015).
18. Works on dietary changes and above all the increase in the consumption of meat, at least until the last decades of the eighteenth century, have increased

for a substantial number of zones in Spanish America. See, for example, Saldarriaga 2012.

19. In another work we reflected on the importance of Iberia as the intersection of technologies and knowledge, which meant that it was an exceptional platform for the dissemination of technology in America (Yun-Casalilla 2017).
20. This is the argument adopted in Yun-Casalilla 2019, 414–17, from the reasoning put forward by Romano 2004, and Arroyo Abad and Van Zanden 2016.
21. On meat consumption in these conditions, see Saldarriaga 2012, 274–75. On the effects of the work imposed by Spanish settlers on account of the type of diet in some American regions, see Bennassar 1980.
22. Beckert 2014, among others.
23. A well-studied case is that of the *repartimientos* associated with the production and export of grana or cochineal in Oaxaca; see Basket 2000. For a series of critical comments, see Carmagnani 2004 and Menegus 2000. However, the *repartimiento de mercancías* did not always result in profound changes in indigenous consumption regimes, because, frequently, the Indians received goods that were part of their usual consumption patterns prior to the conquest.
24. Obviously I am referring to the view expressed in various works by O'Rourke and Williamson 2002, among others.

Bibliography

Appadurai, Arjun. 1988. "Introduction: Commodities and Politics of Value." In *The Social Life of Things: Commodities in Cultural Perspective*, edited by Arjun Appadurai, 3–63. Cambridge: Cambridge University Press.

Arroyo Abad, Leticia, and Jan L. Van Zanden. 2016. "Growth under Extractive Institutions? Latin American Per Capita GDP in Colonial Times." *The Journal of Economic History* 76: 1182–215.

Assadourian, Carlos S. 1982. *El sistema de la economía colonial. Mercado interno, regiones y espacio económico*. Lima: Instituto de Estudios Peruanos.

Basket, Jeremy. 2000. *Indians, Merchants and Markets. A Reinterpretation of the Repartimiento and the Spanish-Indian Economic Relations in Colonial Oaxaca, 1750–1821*. Stanford, CA: Stanford University Press.

Bauer, Arnold J. 2001. *Goods, Power, History: Latin America's material culture*. Cambridge and New York: Cambridge University Press.

Beckert, Sven. 2014. *Empire of Cotton: A Global History*. New York: Alfred A. Knopf.

Bennassar, Bartolomé. 1980. *La América española y la América portuguesa. Siglos XVI–XVIII*, Madrid: Akal.

Boccara, Guillaume. 1998. *Guerre et ethnogenèse mapuche dans le Chili colonial. L'invention du soi*. Paris: L'Harmattan.

Braudel, Fernand. 2000. *Civilisation matérielle, économie et capitalisme: XVe-XVIIIe siècle*. Paris: Armand Colin.

Brewer, John, and Roy Porter, eds. 1993. *Consumption and the World of Goods*. London: Routledge.

Cappa, Ricardo S. J. 1892. *Estudios críticos acerca de la dominación española en América*. Madrid: Librería Católica de Gregorio del Amo.

Carmagnani, Marcello. 2004, "Una institución económica colonial: repartimiento de mercancías y libertad de comercio." *Historia Mexicana* 54 (1): 249–62.

———. 2012. *Las islas del lujo. Productos exóticos, nuevos consumos y cultura económica europea, 1650–1800*. Madrid: Colegio de México/Marcial Pons.
Clarence-Smith, William G. 2015. "Breeding and Power in Southeast Asia: Horses, Mules and Donkeys in the Longue Durée." In *Environment, Trade and Society in Southeast Asia. A Longue Durée Perspective*, edited by David Henley and Henk Schulte Nordholt, 32–45. Leiden: Brill.
Cohen, Mark N. 1977. *The Food Crisis in Prehistory: Overpopulation and the Origins of Agriculture*. New Haven: Yale University Press.
Crosby, Alfred W. 1986. *Ecological Imperialism: The Biological Expansion of Europe, 900–1900*. Cambridge and New York: Cambridge University Press.
De la Puente Brunke, José. 1992. *Encomienda y encomenderos en el Perú (estudio social y político de una institución colonial)*. Sevilla: Diputación de Sevilla.
De Vargas Machuca, Bernardo. 1892. *Milicia y descripción de las Indias*. Madrid: Librería de Victoriano Suárez [first edition 1599].
De Vries, Jan. 2008. *The Industrious Revolution: Consumer Behavior and the Household Economy, 1650 to the Present*. Cambridge and New York: Cambridge University Press.
Diamond, Jared. 1997. *Guns, Germs, and Steel: The Fates of Human Societies*. New York: W. W. Norton & Company.
Earle, Rebecca. 2012. *The Body of the Conquistador: Food, Race, and the Colonial Experience in Spanish America, 1492–1700*. Cambridge: Cambridge University Press.
Eltis, David, Philip Morgan, and David Richardson. 2007. "Agency and Diasporas in Atlantic History. Reassessing the African Contribution to Rice Cultivation in the Americas." *The American Historical Review* 112 (5): 1329–58.
Farriss, Nancy M. 1992. *Maya Society under Colonial Rule: The Collective Enterprise of Survival*. Princeton, NJ: Princeton University Press.
Garavaglia, Juan C. 1983. *Mercado interno y economía colonial. Tres siglos de historia de la yerba mate*. México: Grijalbo.
Glave Testino, Luis Miguel. 1989. *Trajinantes: caminos indígenas en la sociedad colonial, siglos XVI-XVII*. Lima: Instituto de Apoyo Agrario.
Horden, Peregrine, and Nicholas Purcell. 2000. *The Corrupting Sea: A Study of Mediterranean History*. Oxford and Malden, MA: Blackwell.
Lucena Salmoral, Manuel. 2000. *Leyes para esclavos. El ordenamiento jurídico sobre la condición, tratamiento, defensa y represión de los esclavos en las colonias de la América Española*. Consulted on June 29, 2020. www.europeana.eu/en/item/2022705/lod_oai_larramendi_es_1151_ent1.
Menegus, Margarita, comp. 2000. *El repartimiento forzoso de mercaderías en México, Perú y Filipinas*. México: Instituto de Investigaciones Dr. José María Luis Mora, Universidad Nacional Autónoma de México.
McKendrick, Neil. 1982. "Introduction." In *The Birth of a Consumer Society: The Commercialization of Eighteenth-century England*, edited by Neil McKendrick, John Brewer, and J. H. Plumb. London: Europa.
McKendrick, Neil, John Brewer, and J. H. Plumb. 1982. *The Birth of a Consumer Society. The Commercialization of Eighteenth-Century England*. Bloomington, IN: Indiana University Press.
McNeill, William Hardy. 1977. *Plagues and Peoples*. Oxford: Blackwell.
Miño, Manuel. 1991. "La manufactura colonial: aspectos comparativos entre el obraje indiano y el novohispano." In *El sistema colonial en la América española*, edited by Heraclio Bonilla, 102–53. Barcelona: Crítica.

O'Rourke Kevin H., and Jeffrey G. Williamson. 2002. "When did Globalisation Begin?" *European Review of Economic History* 6: 23–50.

Pastor, Rodolfo. 2002. "El repartimiento de mercancías y los alcaldes mayores novohispanos: un sistema de explotación, de sus orígenes a la crisis de 1810." In *El gobierno provincial en la Nueva España, 1570–1787*, edited by Woodrow Borah, 219–58. México: Universidad Nacional Autónoma de México, Instituto de Investigaciones Históricas.

Roche, Daniel. 1989. *La culture des apparences: une histoire du vêtement (XVIIe-XVIIIe siècle)*. Paris: Fayard.

Romano, Ruggiero. 2004. *Mecanismo y elementos del sistema económico colonial americano. Siglos XVI – XVIII*. Mexico: Colegio de México/Fondo de Cultura Económica.

Saldarriaga, Gregorio. 2012. *Alimentación e identidades en el Nuevo Reino de Granada, siglos XVI y XVII*. Bogotá: Ministerio de Cultura de Colombia.

Squatriti, Paolo. 2014. "Of Seeds, Seasons, and Seas: Andrew Watson's Medieval Agrarian Revolution Forty Years Later." *The Journal of Economic History* 74 (4): 1205–20.

Svriz-Wucherer, Pedro Miguel Omar. 2019. *Resistencia y negociación. Milicias guaraníes, jesuitas y cambios socioeconómicos en la frontera del imperio global hispánico (ss. XVII-XVIII)*. Rosario: Prohistoria.

Veblen, Thorstein. 2009. *The Theory of the Leisure Class*. Oxford: Oxford University Press.

Wallerstein, Immanuel. 1979. *The Modern World-system*. Berkeley: University of California Press.

Watson, Andrew M. 1981. "A Medieval Green Revolution: New Crops and Farming Techniques in the Early Islamic World." In *The Islamic Middle East, 700–1900: Studies in Economic and Social History*, edited by Abraham L. Udovitch. Princeton, NJ: The Darwin Press.

White, Lynn. 1963. *Medieval Technology and Social Change*. Oxford: Oxford University Press.

Wilde, Guillermo. 2009. *Religión y poder en las misiones guaraníes*. Buenos Aires: Editorial SB.

Yun-Casalilla, Bartolomé. 1998. "The American Empire and the Spanish Economy: An Institutional and Regional Perspective." *Revista de Historia Económica* 16 (1): 123–55.

2007. "Consumi, società e mercati: verso uno spazio economico europeo?" In *Le radici storiche dell'Europa. L'età moderna*, edited by Maria Antonietta Visceglia, 87–105. Rome: Viella.

———. 2017 "Social Networks and the Circulation of Technology and Knowledge in the Global Spanish Empire" in *Global History and New polycentric Approaches. Europe, Asia and Americas in the World Network System* edited by Manuel Pérez and Lucio de Sousa, 275–301. Singapore: Palgrave Macmillan.

———. 2019. *Iberian World Empires and the Globalization of Europe, 1415–1668*. Singapore: Palgrave Macmillan.

Contributors

Amelia Almorza Hidalgo is a Lecturer in Economic History at the Universidad Pablo de Olavide (Seville, Spain). Her research focuses on the analysis of the emigration of women and families to the Viceroyalty of Peru during the colonial period, considering also its impact on social mobility. She is currently working on the material culture and the circulation of goods in relation to gender in the Spanish Empire.

Bethany Aram is Principal Investigator, European Research Council Consolidator Grant 648535, "An ARTery of EMPIRE. Conquest, Commerce, Crisis, Culture and the Panamanian Junction (1513–1671)", and Professor of Early Modern History at the Universidad Pablo de Olavide (Seville, Spain). Her research has focused on the Spanish monarchy and sixteenth-century globalization.

Ilaria Berti teaches history of the Americas at the Università degli Studi di Firenze (Italy). She has been an MSCA fellow at the Universidad Pablo de Olavide and a visiting fellow at the European University Institute and at the Munich Centre for Global History. Her monograph *Colonial Recipes in the Nineteenth-Century British and Spanish Caribbean: Food Perceptions and Practice* (Amsterdam University Press, forthcoming) reflects her interest in food history.

Luis Miguel Córdoba Ochoa is Associate Lecturer in History at the Universidad Nacional de Colombia, sede Medellin. His research focuses on the problems related to the different cycles of wars between Spaniards and indigenous Americans in the sixteenth and seventeenth centuries.

José Manuel Díaz Blanco is Lecturer in Early Modern History at the Universidad de Sevilla (Seville, Spain). He studies the relations between Spain and Latin America during the early modern period. His research interests focus on political and institutional aspects of the Carrera de Indias. He is the author, among other monographs, of *Así trocaste tu gloria: Guerra y comercio colonial en la España del siglo XVII* (IUHS–Marcial Pons, 2012).

Manuel Díaz-Ordóñez is Lecturer in Economic History at the Universidad de Sevilla, Co-Director of the Master's Program in History and Digital Humanities at the Universidad Pablo de Olavide (Seville, Spain) and Research Fellow in the GECEM Project (ERC-St.G.-679371). His research focuses on the study of the naval rigging of the Spanish Royal Armada in the eighteenth century, with special attention to hemp's global expansion from a comparative perspective.

Rebecca Earle is Full Professor in the Department of History at the University of Warwick (United Kingdom). Her research has concentrated primarily on the relationship between everyday life and broader categories of identity such as those associated with race or nation. She has examined the relationship between everyday eating practices and the evolution of, first, racial categories, and, more recently, notions of governance and the idea of the free market. Her latest publication is *Feeding the People: The Politics of the Potato* (Cambridge University Press, 2020).

Manuel Enrique García-Falcón, a nutritionist, obtained a Master of Arts in History and Digital Humanities from the Universidad Pablo de Olavide (Seville, Spain).

Alejandro García-Montón is a Juan de la Cierva–Incorporación Fellow at the Universidad Pablo de Olavide (Seville, Spain). His research focuses on Genoese merchant networks, the trans-imperial slave trade in the wider Atlantic world, and the role of second-hand markets in the early modern period. He is the author of *Genoese Entrepreneurship and the Asiento Slave Trade* (Routledge, forthcoming).

José Luis Gasch-Tomás is an Honorary Collaborator of the Area of Early Modern History at the Universidad Pablo de Olavide (Seville, Spain). His book *The Atlantic World and the Manila Galleons: Circulation, Market, and Consumption of Asian Goods in the Spanish Empire, 1565–1650* (Brill, 2019) offers an account of the trade, distribution and consumption of Asian goods in colonial Spanish America and East Asia.

Fernando Quiles is Professor of Art History at the Universidad Pablo de Olavide (Seville, Spain). His studies of the Sevillian baroque examine the artistic environment, artists, and their patrons. Among other monographs, he is the author of *Sevilla y América en el Barroco: Comercio, ciudad y arte* (Bosque de Palabras, 2009).

Gregorio Saldarriaga is Senior Lecturer in History at the Universidad de Antioquia (Colombia). His work has focused on the history of food during the sixteenth and seventeenth centuries in Colombia and Latin America, emphasizing the relationship between production, symbols and identities. He is the author of *Alimentación e identidades en el*

Nuevo Reino de Granada, siglos XVI y XVII (Ministerio de Cultura de Colombia, 2012).

Omar Svriz-Wucherer is a postdoctoral researcher in the Project GECEM (ERC-StG.- 679371) and teaches Early Modern History at the Universidad Pablo de Olavide (Seville, Spain). He has carried out research stays at a number of institutions in Argentina, Spain, Italy, Germany and Asia. His most recent monograph is *Resistencia y negociación. Milicias guaraníes, jesuitas y cambios socioeconómicos en la frontera del imperio global hispánico* (ss. XVII–XVIII) (Prohistoria, 2019). (Available in open access).

Bartolomé Yun-Casalilla is Full Professor of Early Modern History at the Universidad Pablo de Olavide (Seville, Spain), and has been Full Professor at the European University Institute of Florence (2003–2013). He specializes in the study of political economies, the Spanish empire, the history of consumption and the history of European aristocracies. His most recent book is *Iberian Empires and the Globalization of Europe 1415–1668* (Palgrave, 2019). (Available in open access).

Index

Made in the USA
Monee, IL
13 September 2026

62977688R00179